ESTHER SHALEV-GERZ

Musée cantonal des Beaux-Arts/Lausanne

TABLE OF CONTENTS
SOMMAIRE

FOREWORD
ESTHER SHALEV-GERZ. BETWEEN TELLING AND LISTENING

"That which lies between listening and telling is the image. But the image is not simply the visible. It is the device within which the visible is caught."[1]
– Jacques Rancière

Exhibitions often come about as a result of encounters—with works, an emotion, an image, an idea. Works too sometimes come into being as a result of encounters—with a set of questions, a story, a memory, a place, people. The works of Esther Shalev-Gerz fall into that category. They open up time-spaces in order to apprehend what was the first impulse behind their realization—be it in the time taken up by the projection of slides or a video, or in the space taken up by the image and the installation. Image and sound enter into dialogue, or suspend their concordance to make it possible to see better, or hear better. *Between Telling and Listening*: before making this the title of her exhibition, Esther Shalev-Gerz used it in the titles of two of her works. One in 2002, a magnificent two-phase portrait of a woman between two cultures, two places, two timeframes (*White Out—Between Telling and Listening*); the other in 2005, an impressive installation commemorating the 60th anniversary of the liberation of Auschwitz-Birkenau concentration camp (*Between Listening and Telling: Last Witnesses, Auschwitz 1945–2005*). Between what is articulated and what is heard, there is the image, Jacques Rancière tells us, that is the place where the meeting with the viewer becomes possible: "One is not in front of, nor in the place of—one is always *between*. The thing has to be understood in two senses: *to be between* is to belong to a certain type of community, a constructed and precarious community that does not define itself in terms of shared identity but in terms of possible sharing. But that which is to be shared is itself caught within a sharing, traveling between two beings, two places, two acts. What can be termed the image is actually the movement of this translation."[2]

"To be between" likewise presupposes the discomfort of never being wholly in our place; it is being both here and there, both in- and outside what is seen, or done, or said. "To be between" necessarily implies movement, displacement. And consequently the question of place; of the linking of places with one another; of our relationship to them. In *Inseparable Angels: An Imaginary House for Walter Benjamin* (2000) and in *Still/Film* (2009), Esther Shalev-Gerz films and photographs the gap between places, travels from one to the other to try and capture the possible link between Weimar on the one hand and Buchenwald on the other, between Alytus where her mother lived and Vilnius where she herself was born. As if the time taken in traveling from one place to the other also made it possible to capture what those places were at another time,

1
Jacques Rancière, "The Work of the Image," *Esther Shalev-Gerz*, Fage Éditions & Éditions du Jeu de Paume, Lyon & Paris 2010, p. 139.

2
Ibid., p. 138.

for people other than us. Like portraits of landscapes that might echo portraits of people. In her very first photographic works, Esther Shalev-Gerz already worked on these return journeys between two places, but at that time within one and the same image, at the folding point between two realities. Thus in *Just One Sky* (1987–1989), the artist photographed the city of Jerusalem—which she left in 1984—from different angles, then superimposed those images, so juxtaposing areas that were not next to one another in reality. Or later, in *Daedal(us)* (2003), a project carried out with the help and cooperation of the residents of a district in Dublin, photographs of facades were projected onto other buildings, so that there was collusion between two places and two times—that of the taking of the view, and that of its projection. "Being between" is also being between two or several languages, all present to a greater or lesser extent, all associated with specific contexts, but which travel for that very reason. Lithuanian, Russian, Hebrew, Yiddish, German, English, French in the case of the artist; Arabic, Persian, Hebrew, Yiddish, French, and English in the case of Rola Younes, the young woman whose portrait is in dialogue with that of Jacques Rancière in the video *On Two* (2009), and whose songs give body to the different languages and the affects they convey in the space occupied by the installation.

The Portraits of Stories (1998–2008), *White Out—Between Telling and Listening* (2002), *Does Your Image Reflect Me?* (2002), *First Generation* (2004), *Between Listening and Telling: Last Witnesses, Auschwitz 1945–2005* (2005), *On Two* (2009), *The Last Click* (2010): Esther Shalev-Gerz's entire oeuvre can be assimilated to incessant work on the question of the portrait. As often as not filmed in still shots, the people she talks to answer questions, tell stories, are suspended in the instant that precedes speech, or in the instant of listening—listening to the words of others or their own pronouncements, which have also become "other" through the distance introduced by the device of filming. One of the most striking forms of "portrait" is in the installation *MenschenDinge—The Human Aspect of Objects* (2004–2006). Commissioned to create a project for the Buchenwald Concentration Camp Memorial, Esther Shalev-Gerz chose to invite museum professionals to talk—the director, a historian, an archaeologist, a female restorer, and a female photographer: people who are in daily contact with the objects found in the grounds of the camp. They talk about their encounters—professional, personal, and imaginary—with these objects created or diverted by the detainees. Thus it is through portraits of individuals located in the present that portraits of those who fashioned these objects are recreated, tokens of humanity within a totalitarian system intended to divest them totally of that quality. As Georges Didi-Huberman puts it in *Écorces*, "Therefore we can never say: there is nothing to see, there is no longer anything to see. To know how to doubt what we see, we have still to know how to see, to see in spite of everything. In spite of the destruction, the obliteration of all things. We have to know how to look as an archaeologist looks. And it is through such a way of looking at what we see—such a way of questioning it—that things start to matter to us from their buried spaces and long-gone times."[3] Through the means she deploys, it is precisely these return journeys between past and present that Esther Shalev-Gerz makes possible—the past is "updated" to the present of her protagonists, rather than relegated into the comfortable distance of what no longer exists and therefore no longer "matters" to us.

In the exhibition Esther Shalev-Gerz has devised for the Musée cantonal des Beaux-Arts in Lausanne, the artist has designed an itinerary reflecting the different periods of her creative output. Major works are displayed non-chronologically, to match the rooms and the questions they explore. Questions of place and landscape, questions of commemorative traces contained in objects or stories, questions of portraits structured by speech and silence. Thus *Just One Sky* (1987–1989) opens the exhibition alongside *Still/Film* (2009), *Books Inhaled by the Sky* (1998) echoes *Inseparable Angels* (2000) and *MenschenDinge* (2004–2006), while *Does Your Image Reflect Me?* (2002) responds to *Between Listening and Telling: Last Witnesses, Auschwitz 1945–2005* (2005). Elsewhere, *White Out* (2002) and *On Two* (2009) both evolve in their own space, but at the same time act as a transition between the other works. Finally, works devised for and in public space are presented in the form of photographic or filmed documentary records.

We would like to extend our special thanks to Esther Shalev-Gerz for her enthusiasm and her involvement in this project. It would not have been possible without the collaboration of the collectors and institutions that support her work, or the authors of this monograph, Nora M. Alter, Georges Didi-Huberman, Annika Wik, and James E. Young, whose essays open up new paths to follow in thinking about her work. We would like to take this opportunity to express our very sincere gratitude to all of them.

Nicole Schweizer
Musée cantonal des Beaux-Arts/Lausanne

3
Georges Didi-Huberman, *Écorces*, Éditions de Minuit, Paris 2011, p. 61.

AVANT-PROPOS
ESTHER SHALEV-GERZ. ENTRE L'ÉCOUTE ET LA PAROLE

« Ce qu'il y a entre l'écoute et la parole, c'est l'image. Mais l'image n'est pas simplement le visible. C'est le dispositif dans lequel ce visible est pris. »[1]
– Jacques Rancière

Les expositions naissent souvent de rencontres. Avec des œuvres, avec une émotion, une image, une idée. Les œuvres elles aussi naissent, parfois, de rencontres. Avec un questionnement, une histoire, un souvenir, un lieu, des gens. Les œuvres d'Esther Shalev-Gerz sont de cet ordre-là. Elles ouvrent des espaces-temps pour appréhender ce qui a été l'impulsion première de leur réalisation – que ce soit dans la temporalité de la projection de diapositives et de la vidéo, ou dans l'espace de l'image et de l'installation. Image et son dialoguent, ou suspendent leur concordance pour permettre de mieux voir, ou de mieux entendre. *Entre l'écoute et la parole* : avant d'en faire le titre de la présente exposition, Esther Shalev-Gerz a intitulé ainsi deux de ses œuvres. L'une en 2002, magnifique portrait en deux temps d'une femme entre deux cultures, deux lieux, deux temporalités (*White Out – Entre l'écoute et la parole*) ; l'autre en 2005, impressionnante installation qui commémorait les soixante ans de la libération du camp de concentration d'Auschwitz-Birkenau (*Entre l'écoute et la parole : derniers témoins, Auschwitz 1945-2005*). Entre ce qui est articulé et ce qui est entendu, il y a l'image dit Jacques Rancière, c'est-à-dire le lieu où la rencontre avec le spectateur devient possible : « On n'est pas devant, on n'est pas à la place de. On est toujours *entre*. La chose est à entendre en deux sens : *être entre*, c'est appartenir à un certain type de communauté, une communauté construite, précaire, qui ne se définit pas en termes d'identité commune, mais en termes de partage possible. Mais ce qui est à partager est lui-même pris dans un partage, lui-même en voyage entre deux êtres, deux lieux, deux actes. Ce qu'on peut appeler image, c'est proprement le mouvement de cette translation. »[2]

« Être entre » présuppose également l'inconfort de n'être jamais entièrement à sa place ; c'est être à la fois ici et là, à la fois dans et hors de ce qui est vu, ou fait, ou dit. « Être entre » implique, forcément, le mouvement, le déplacement. Et par conséquent, la question du lieu. Du lien des lieux entre eux. De notre rapport à eux. Dans *Anges inséparables : la maison éphémère pour Walter Benjamin* (2000) comme dans *Still/Film* (2009), Esther Shalev-Gerz filme et photographie l'intervalle entre des lieux, se déplace de l'un à l'autre pour tenter de capter le lien possible entre Weimar d'une part et Buchenwald de l'autre, entre Alytus où vécut sa mère et Vilnius où elle-même est née. Comme si le temps du trajet d'un lieu à l'autre permettait également de capter ce que furent ces lieux dans

1
Jacques Rancière, « Le travail de l'image », *Esther Shalev-Gerz*, Fage Éditions/Éditions du Jeu de Paume, Lyon/Paris 2010, p. 12.

2
Ibid, p. 12.

un autre temps, pour d'autres que nous. Comme des portraits de paysages qui feraient écho aux portraits de gens. Déjà dans ses tout premiers travaux photographiques, Esther Shalev-Gerz travaille ces allers-retours entre deux lieux, mais cette fois-ci au sein d'une même image, à la pliure entre deux réalités. Ainsi dans *Juste un ciel* (1987-1989), l'artiste photographie la ville de Jérusalem – qu'elle a quittée en 1984 – sous différents angles puis superpose ces images, juxtaposant ainsi des espaces disjoints dans la réalité. Ou plus tard, dans *Daedal(us)* (2003), un projet réalisé avec la complicité des habitants d'un quartier de Dublin, des photographies de façades sont projetées sur d'autres bâtiments, collusion entre deux lieux et deux temps – celui de la prise de vue, celui de sa projection. « Être entre », c'est aussi être entre deux ou plusieurs langues, toutes plus ou moins présentes, toutes liées à des contextes particuliers, mais qui, de ce fait, voyagent. Lituanien, russe, hébreu, yiddish, allemand, anglais, français pour ce qui est de l'artiste. Arabe, persan, hébreu, yiddish, français et anglais pour ce qui est de Rola Younes, la jeune femme dont le portrait dialogue avec celui de Jacques Rancière dans l'installation vidéo *D'Eux* (2009), et dont les chants donnent corps aux différentes langues et aux affects qu'elles véhiculent dans l'espace de l'installation.

Les Portraits des histoires (1998-2008), *White Out – Entre l'écoute et la parole* (2002), *Est-ce que ton image me regarde ?* (2002), *First Generation* (2004), *Entre l'écoute et la parole : derniers témoins, Auschwitz 1945-2005* (2005), *D'Eux* (2009), *Le dernier déclic* (2010) : tout l'œuvre d'Esther Shalev-Gerz peut être assimilé à un travail incessant sur la question du portrait. Le plus souvent filmés en plan fixe, ses interlocuteurs répondent à des questions, racontent, sont suspendus dans l'instant qui précède la parole, ou dans celui de l'écoute – écoute des mots des autres ou de leurs propres énoncés, devenus « autres » eux aussi par la distance instaurée par le dispositif filmique. L'une des formes les plus saisissantes de « portrait » se trouve dans l'installation *MenschenDinge – L'aspect humain des choses* (2004-2006). Invitée à créer un projet pour le Mémorial du camp de concentration de Buchenwald, Esther Shalev-Gerz choisit de faire parler les professionnels du musée – le directeur, un historien, un archéologue, une restauratrice et une photographe – qui sont en contact quotidien avec les objets trouvés sur le terrain du camp. Ils racontent leur rencontre à la fois professionnelle, personnelle et imaginaire avec ces objets créés ou détournés par les détenus. C'est donc par le portrait de personnes situées dans le présent que s'esquisse en filigrane le portrait de celles et ceux qui ont façonné ces objets, signes d'humanité au sein d'un système concentrationnaire destiné à la leur ôter entièrement. Comme le formule Georges Didi-Huberman dans *Écorces* : « On ne peut donc jamais dire : il n'y a rien à voir, il n'y a plus rien à voir. Pour savoir douter de ce qu'on voit, il faut savoir voir encore, voir malgré tout. Malgré la destruction, l'effacement de toute chose. Il faut savoir regarder comme regarde un archéologue. Et c'est à travers un tel regard – une telle interrogation – sur ce que nous voyons que les choses commencent de nous regarder depuis leurs espaces enfouis et leurs temps enfuis. »[3] Par ses dispositifs, Esther Shalev-Gerz permet précisément ces allers-retours entre passé et présent – le passé est « actualisé » dans le présent de ses protagonistes, plutôt que relégué dans la distance confortable de ce qui n'est plus et qui donc ne nous « regarderait » pas.

Dans l'exposition qu'Esther Shalev-Gerz a conçue pour le Musée cantonal des Beaux-Arts de Lausanne, l'artiste a dessiné un parcours reflétant les différentes périodes de sa production. Des œuvres majeures sont articulées de façon non chronologique, au rythme des salles et des questions qu'elles explorent. Questions de lieux et de paysages, questions de traces mémorielles contenues dans les objets ou les récits, questions de portraits articulés par la parole et le silence. Ainsi, *Juste un ciel* (1987-1989) ouvre l'exposition aux côtés de *Still/Film* (2009), *Livres aspirés par le ciel* (1998) fait écho à *Anges inséparables* (2000) et *MenschenDinge* (2004-2006), tandis que *Entre l'écoute et la parole : derniers témoins, Auschwitz 1945*-2005 (2005) répond à *Est-ce que ton image me regarde ?* (2002). Ailleurs, *White Out* (2002) et *D'Eux* (2009) se déploient chacun dans des espaces propres mais opèrent simultanément comme transition entre les autres travaux. Enfin, les œuvres conçues pour et dans l'espace public sont présentes sous formes de traces documentaires photographiques ou filmées.

Nos remerciements s'adressent tout particulièrement à Esther Shalev-Gerz pour son enthousiasme et son engagement dans ce projet. Celui-ci n'aurait pas été possible sans la collaboration des collectionneurs et institutions qui soutiennent son travail, et des auteurs de cette monographie, Nora M. Alter, Georges Didi-Huberman, Annika Wik et James E. Young, dont les textes ouvrent de nouvelles pistes pour penser son œuvre. Qu'ils trouvent ici l'expression de notre plus vive reconnaissance.

Nicole Schweizer
Musée cantonal des Beaux-Arts/Lausanne

3
Georges Didi-Huberman, *Écorces*, Éditions de Minuit, Paris 2011, p. 61.

*
Unrealized proposals for works in public spaces are marked with an asterisk

Oil on Stone, 1983

Tel Hai
Permanent installation; sculpture in Jerusalem stone, 2.5 × 1.2 × 1.7 m

In 1983, during the Lebanon War, Esther Shalev-Gerz installed the sculpture *Oil on Stone* on the side of a mountain in Galilee, on the historic site of Tel Hai ("The hill of life" in Hebrew). Carved out of a block of white Jerusalem stone, the sculpture consists of a brick wall diagonally cut in two. When seen from a particular viewpoint, a human silhouette pointing north is visible. When seen from other angles, it is simply a wall that has fallen into ruin.

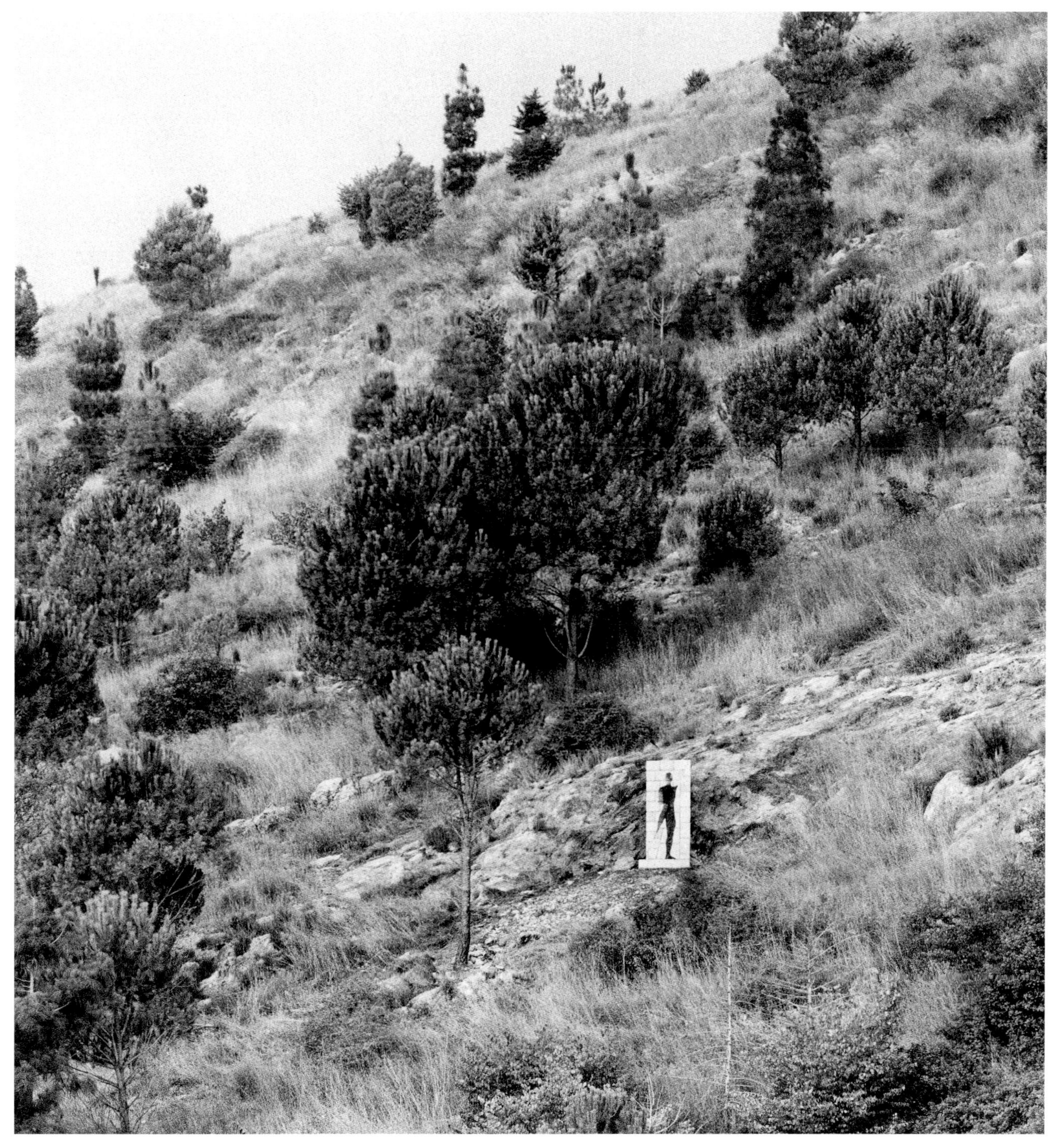

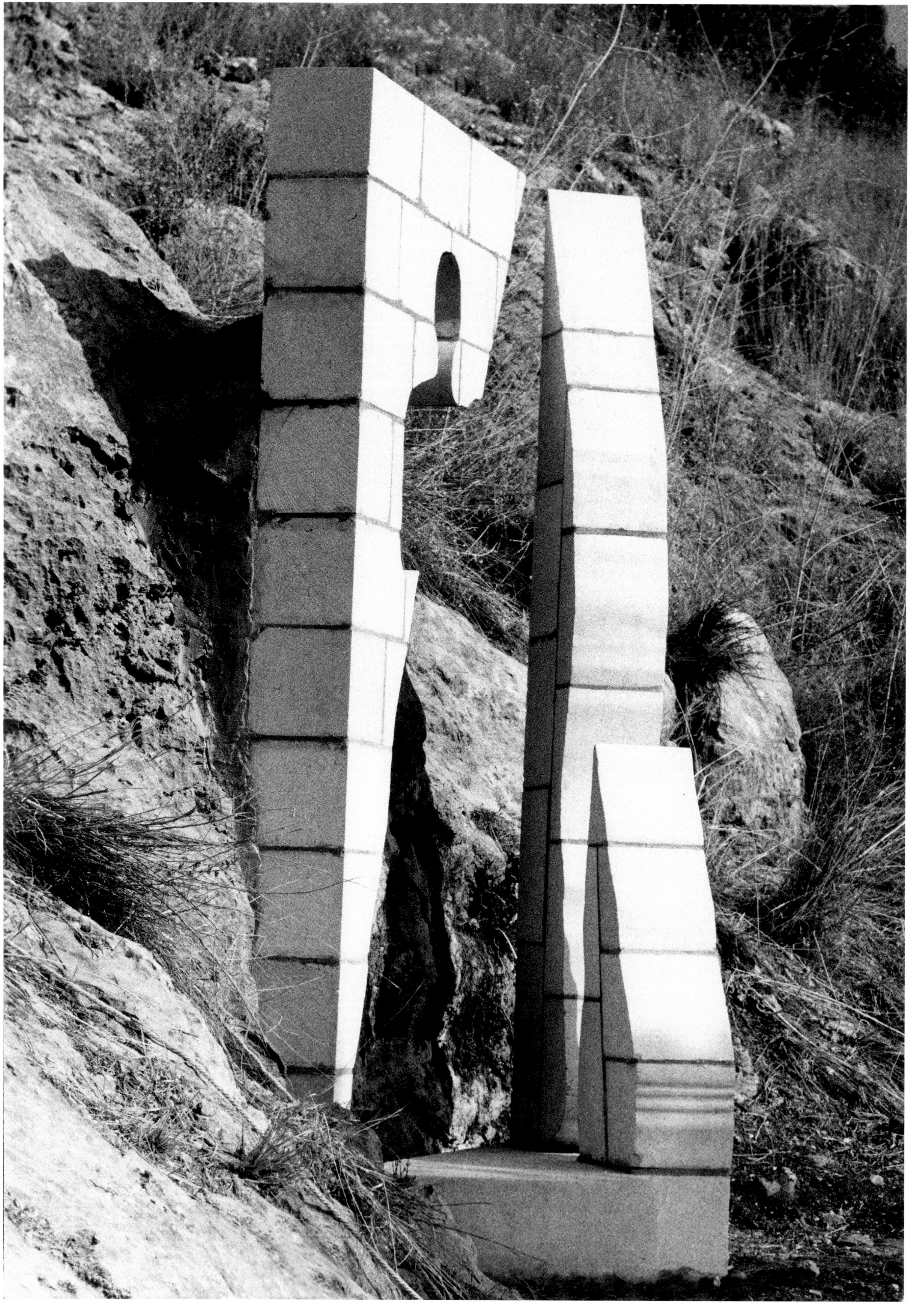

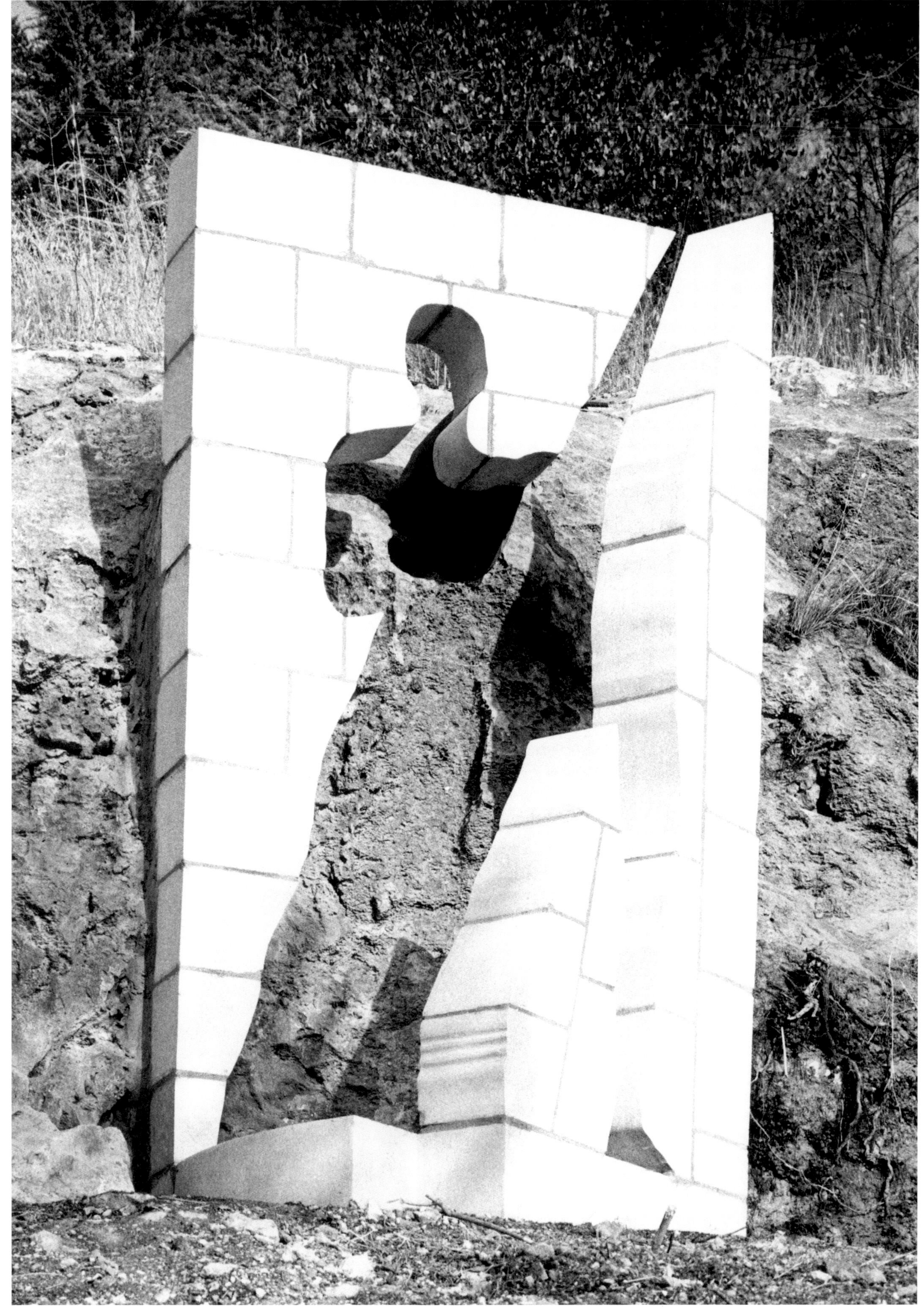

Irreparable, 1986–2000

Black and white and color photographs, dimensions variable

In the *Irreparable* series, Esther Shalev-Gerz questions the possibility of capturing reality through photography. Starting from black and white or color photographs, she cuts rectangles out of the images and relocates them—reinserting them into the same image in a staggered position, or inserting black or white rectangles in their place. By shifting the component parts of the photograph in this way, and introducing a break in its legibility, Shalev-Gerz destabilizes the concordance between reality and its representation.

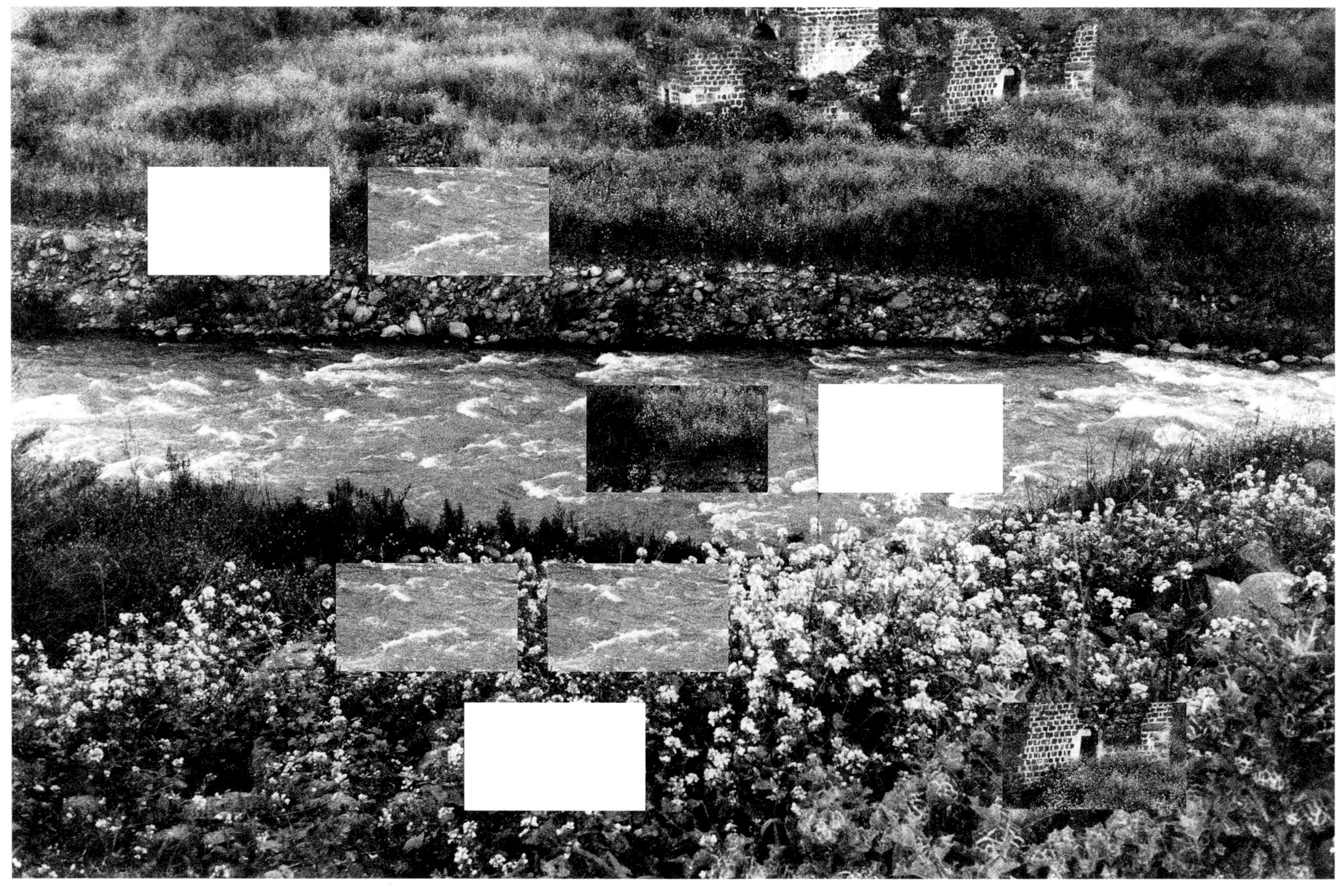

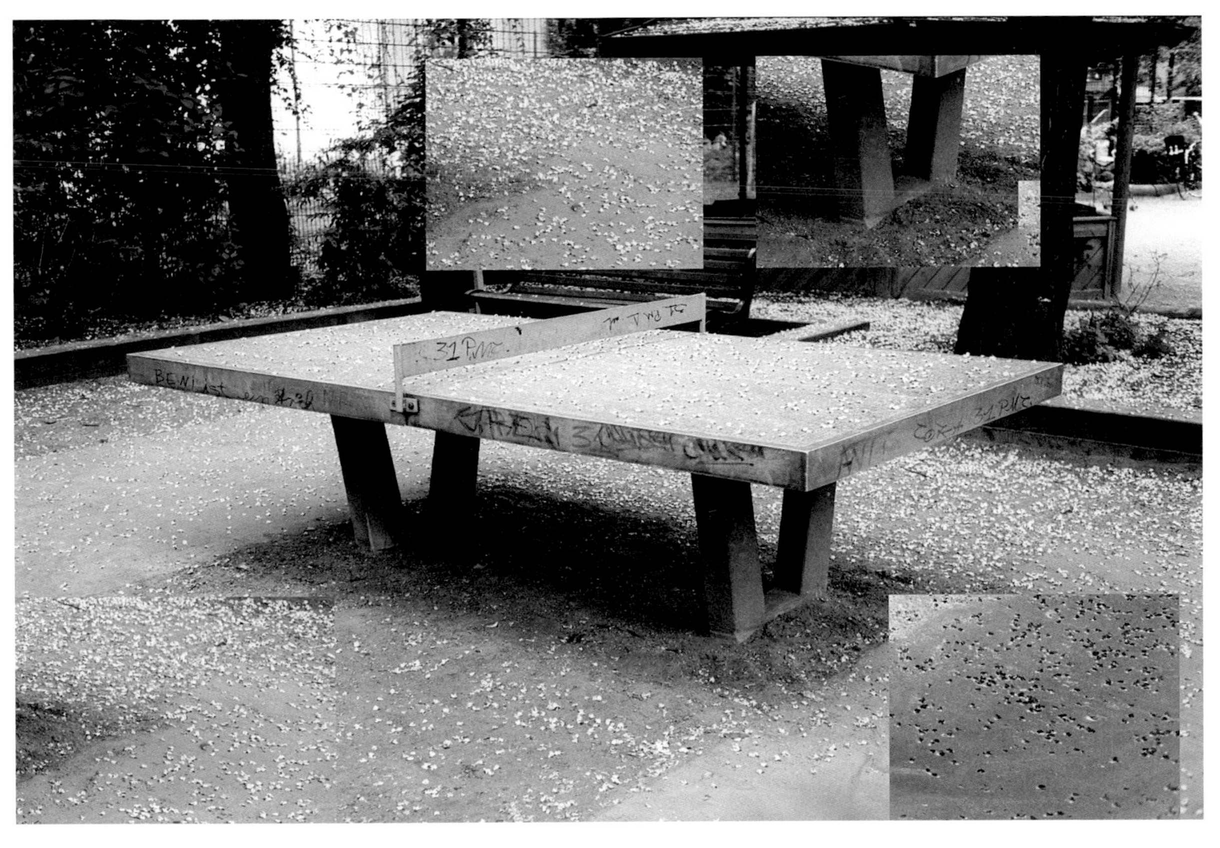

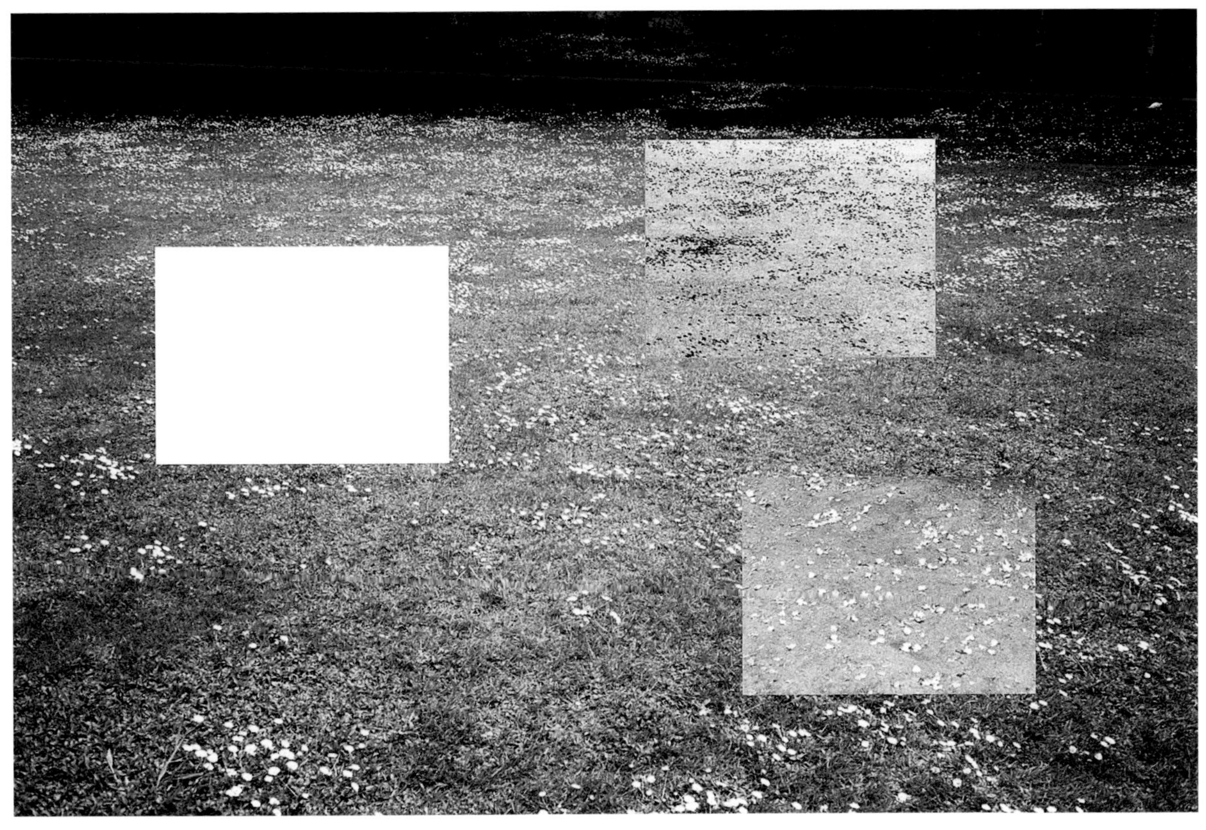

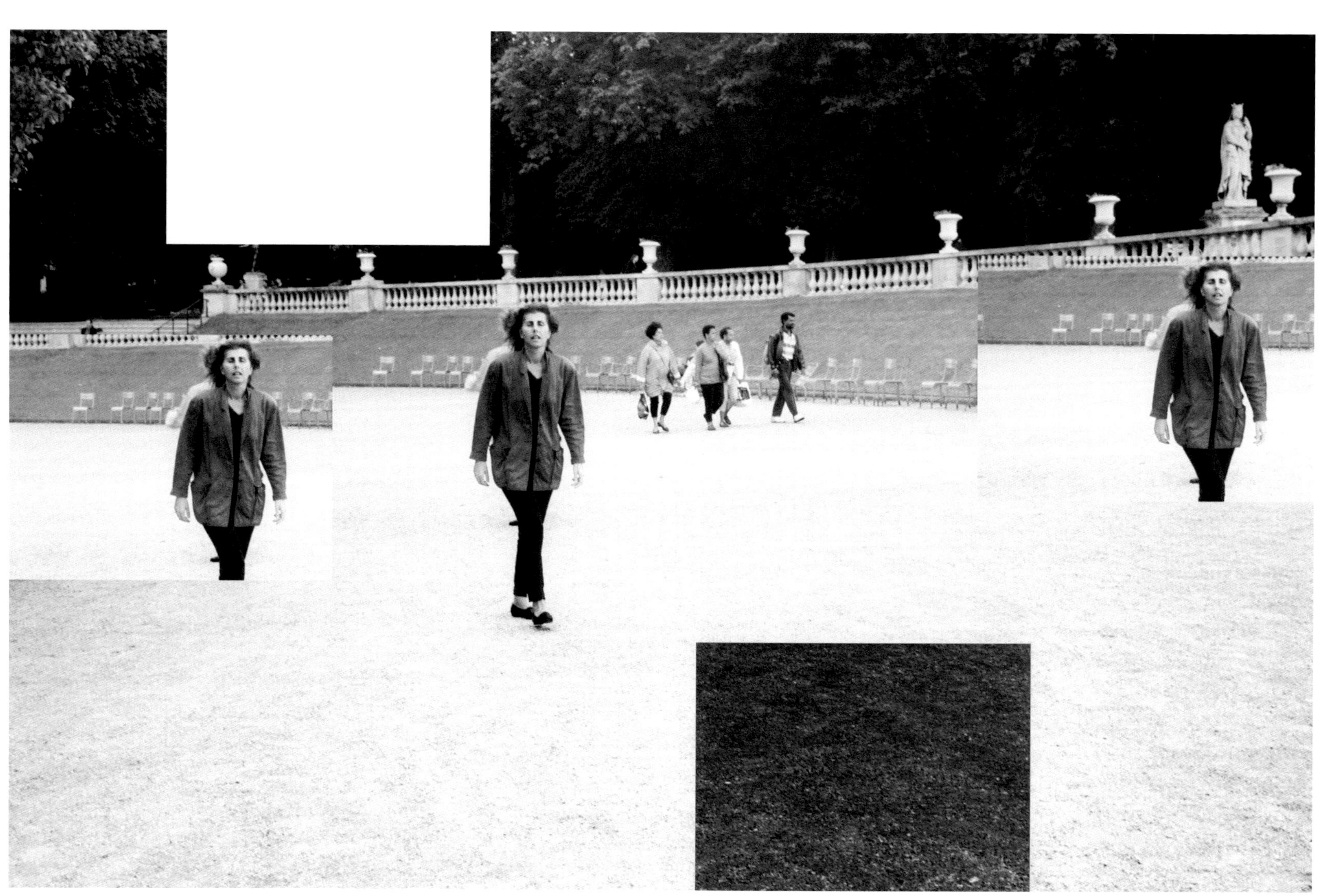

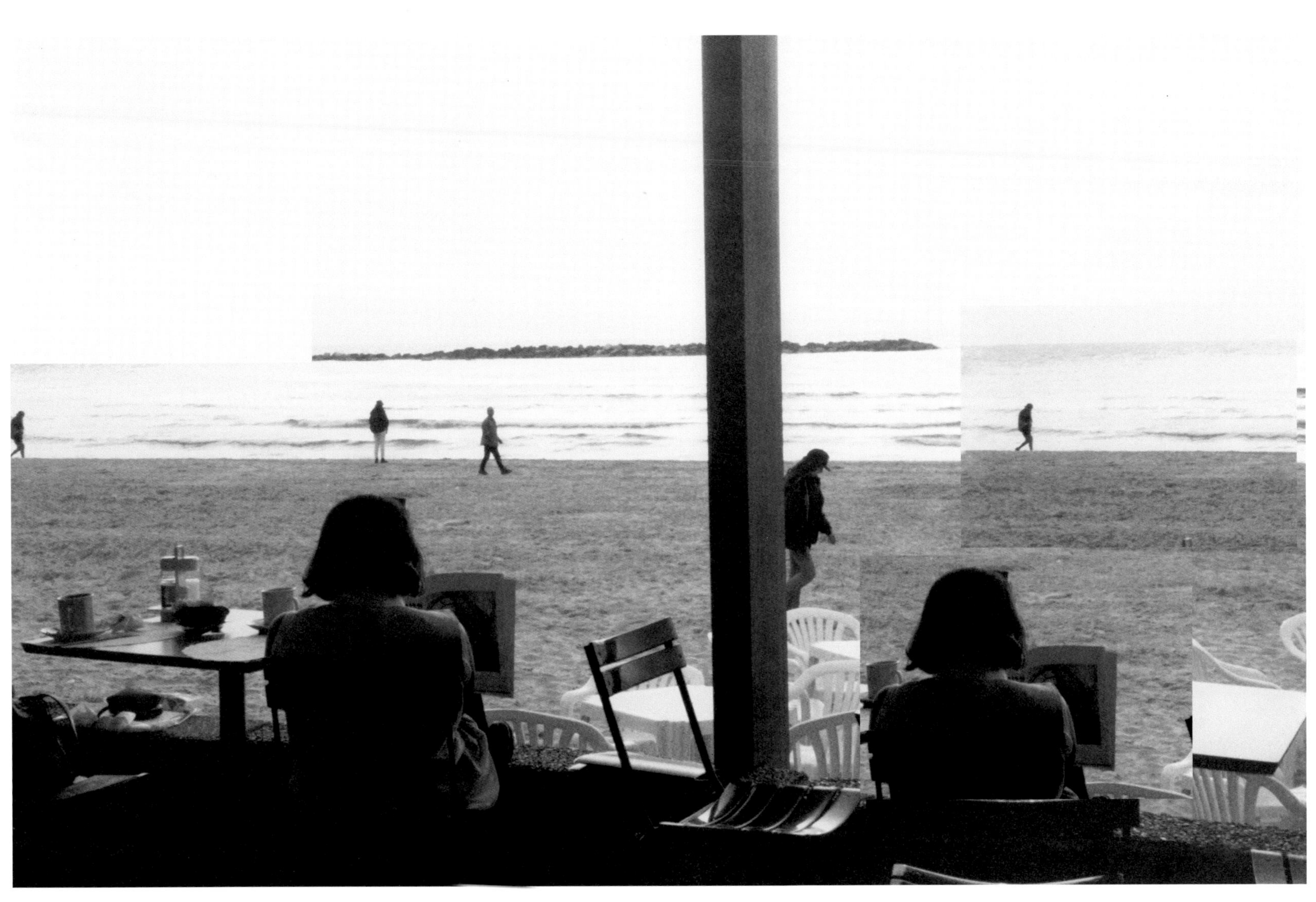

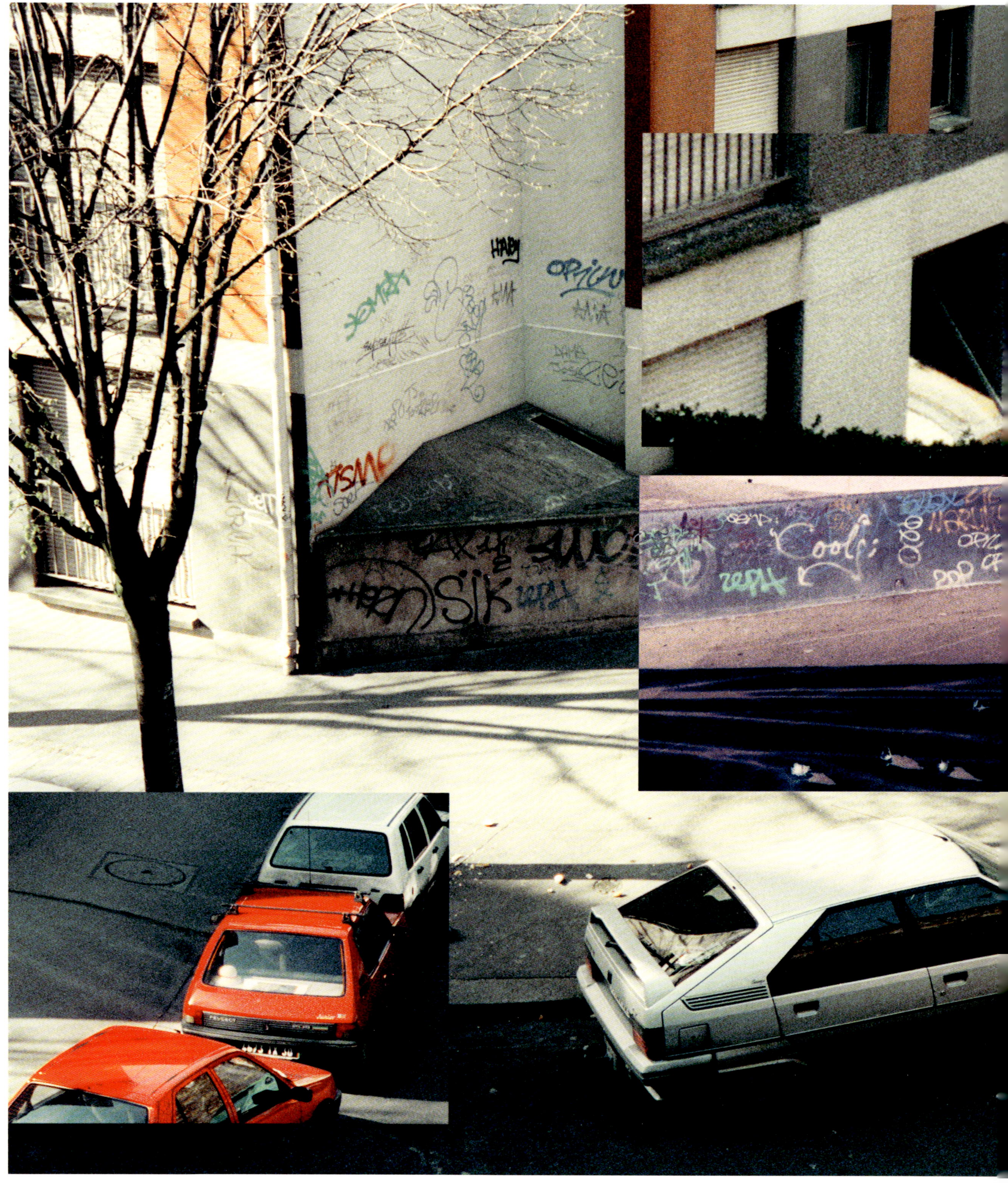
SIK

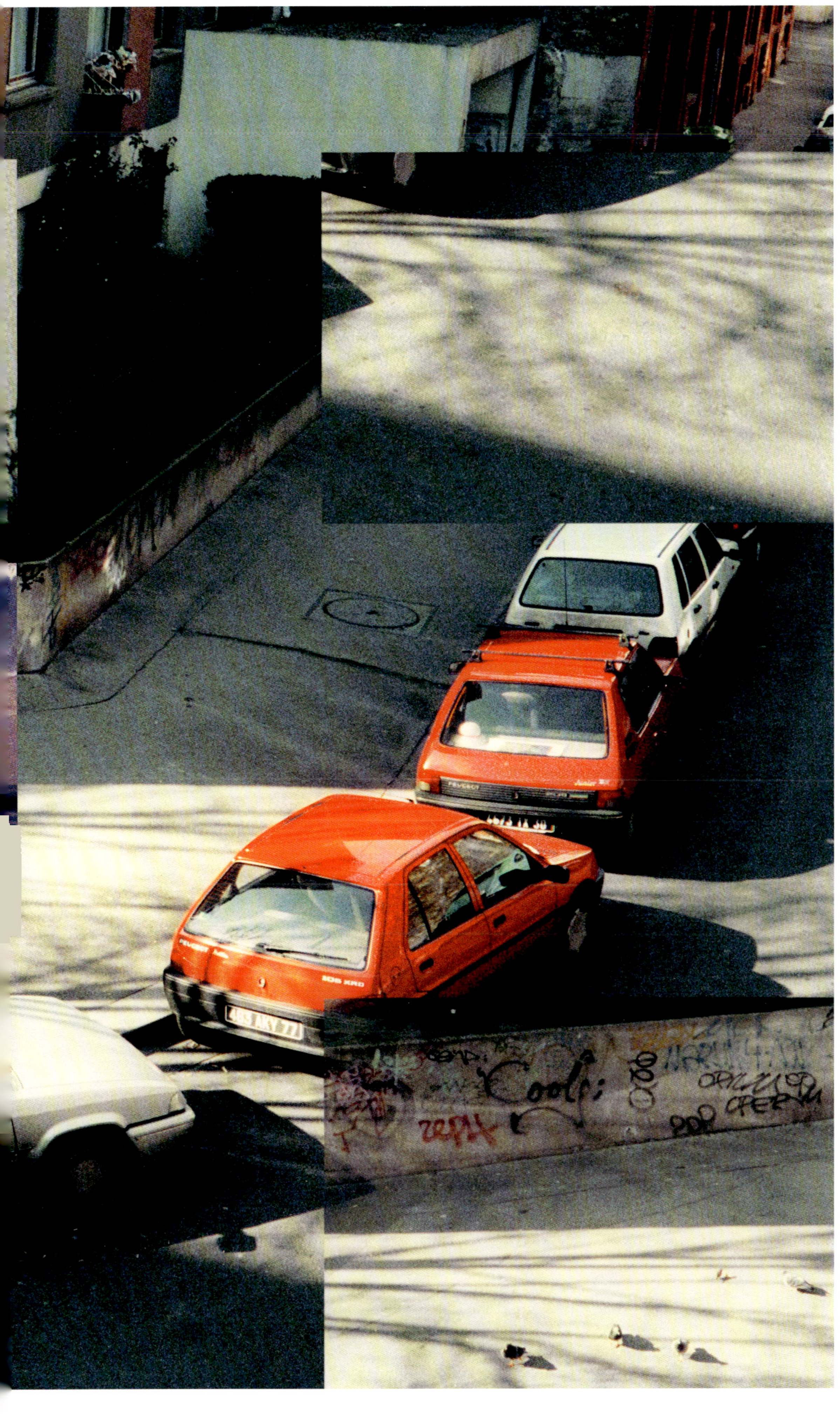
Cool

Monument Against Fascism, 1986–1993
with Jochen Gerz

Hamburg-Harburg
Permanent installation; aluminum column covered with sheets of lead, 12 × 1 × 1 m; 7 metric tons, panel with a text translated into seven languages

The *Monument Against Fascism* commissioned by the city of Hamburg was erected in 1986 on a very busy square in the city. It consisted of a 12-meter column clad in lead. A text reproduced in seven languages invited the inhabitants to inscribe their names on the column. As soon as an accessible part was completely covered with inscriptions, it was lowered into the ground. Since 1993, after seven stages of burial, all that remains visible is the top of the column, and the text that ends with these words: "For in the long run no one will stand up to oppose injustice in our place."

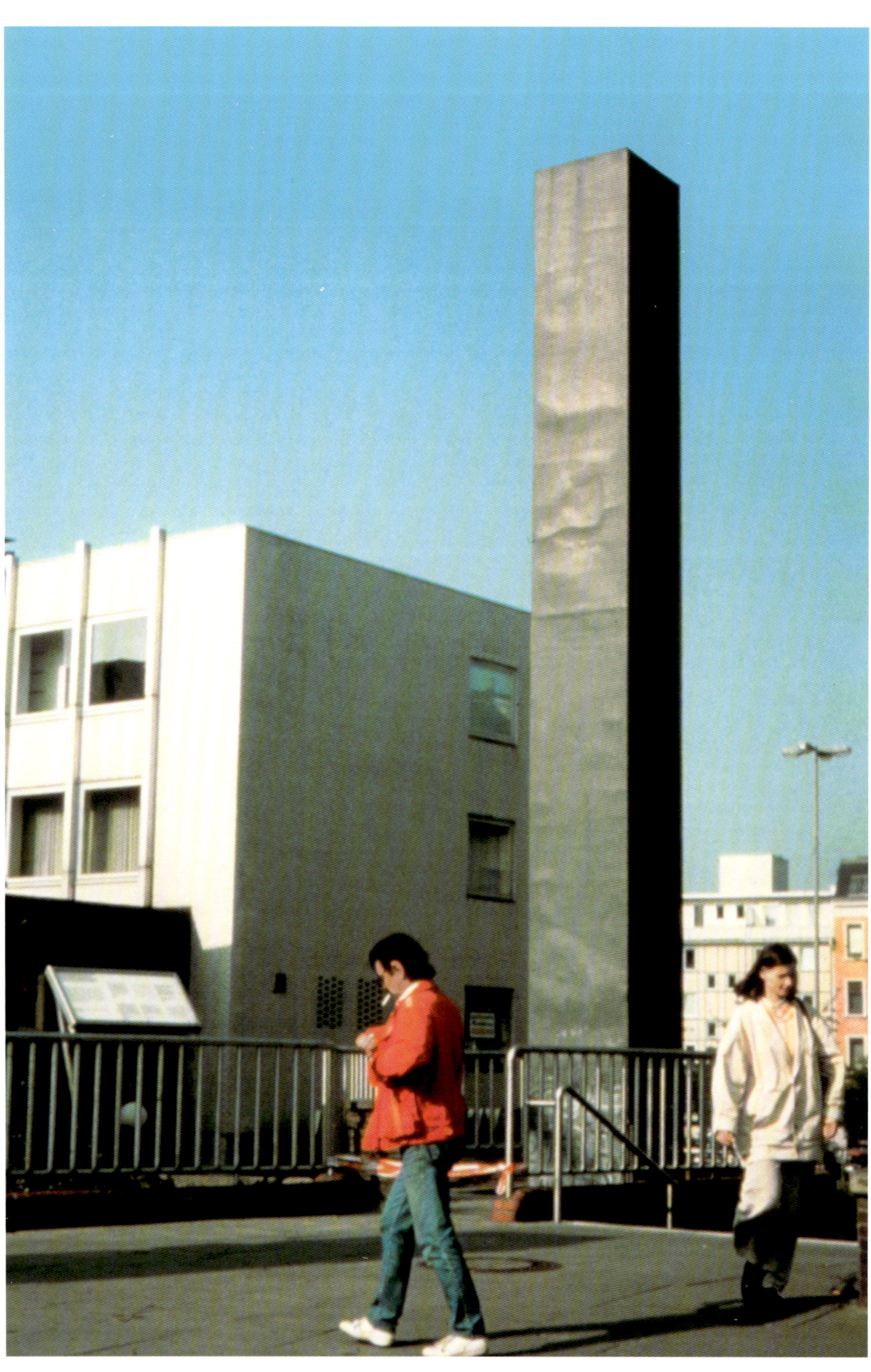

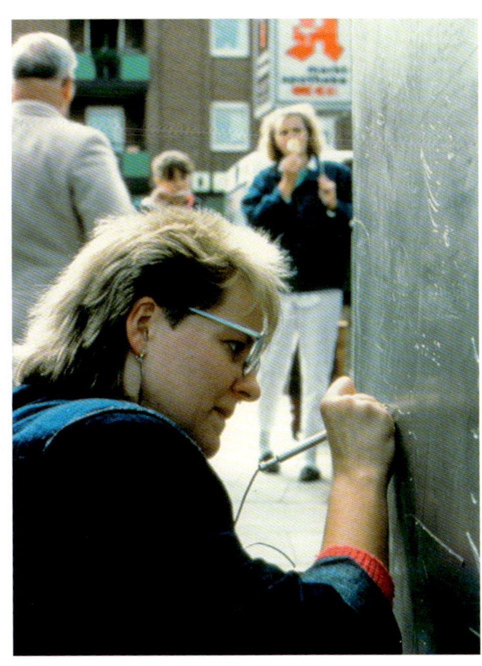

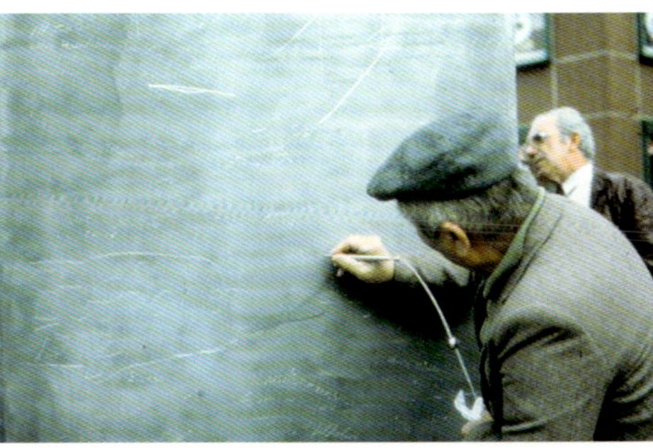

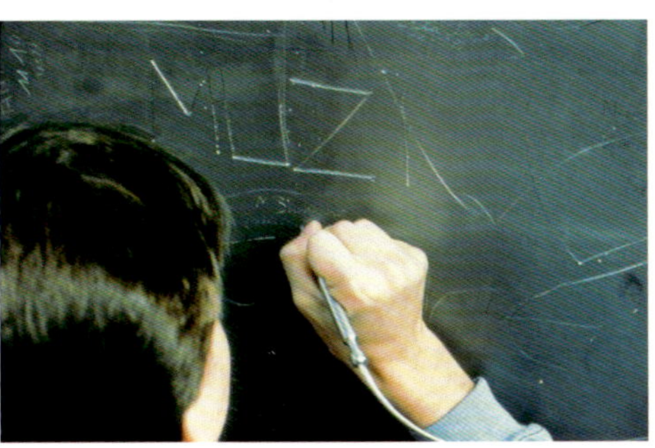

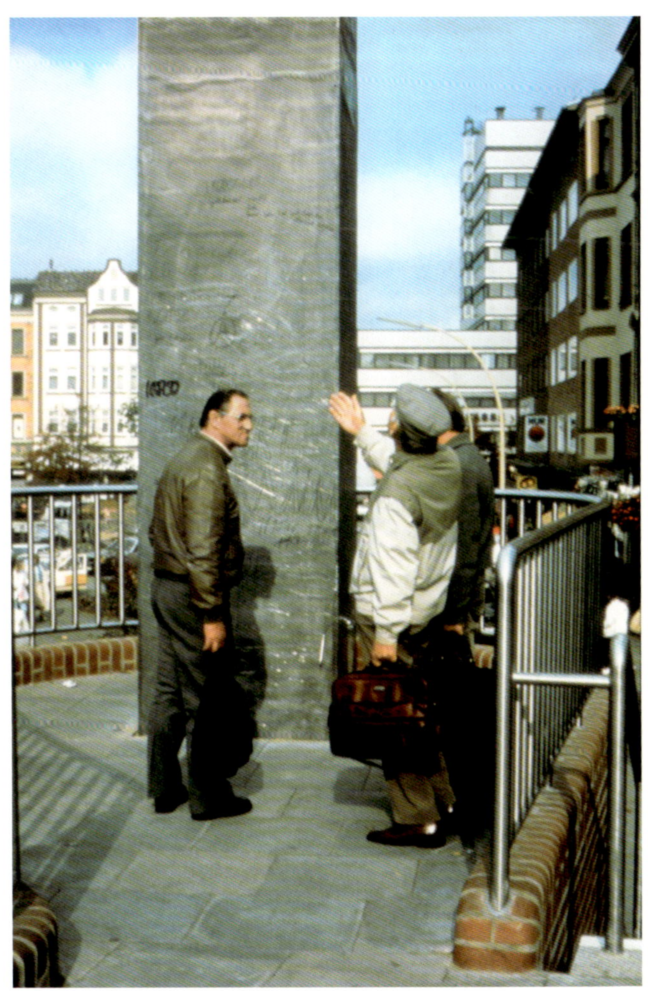

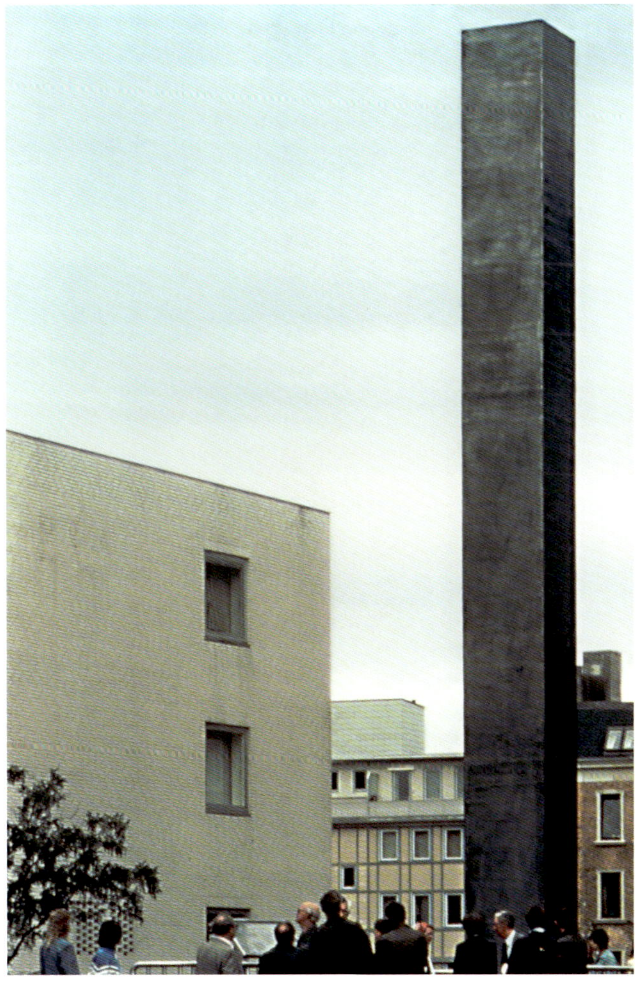

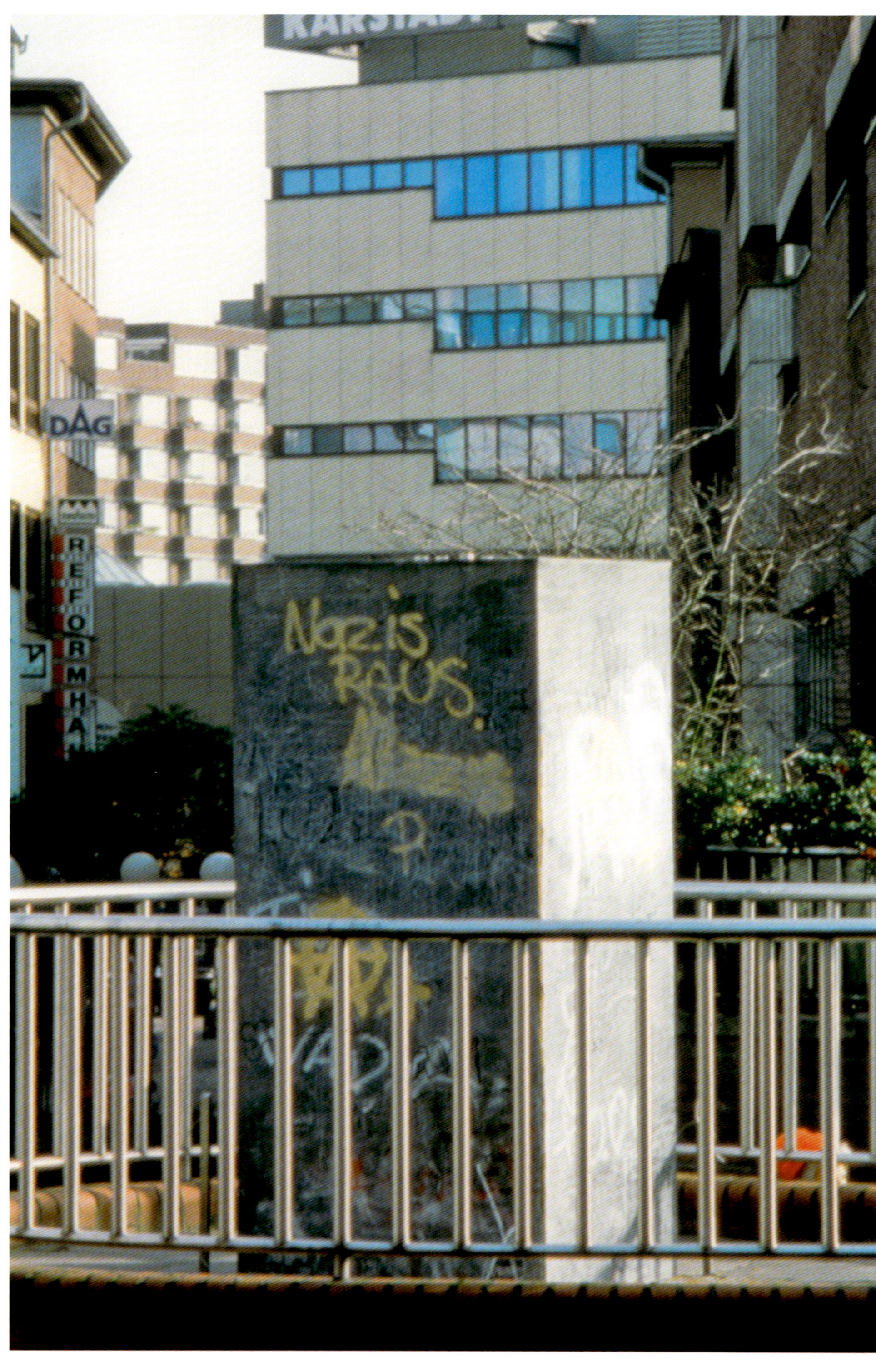
DAG
REFORMHA
Nazis Raus

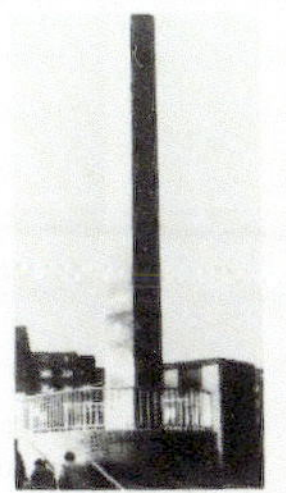

10. Oktober 1986
Einweihung

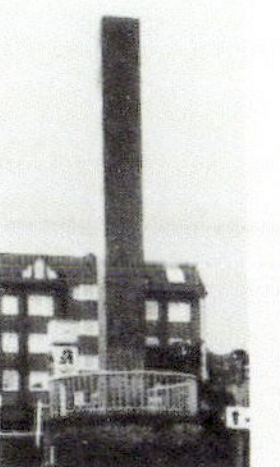

1. September 1987
1. Absenkung

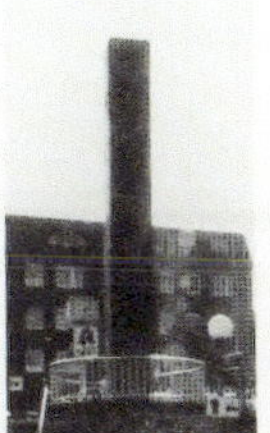

23. Oktober 1988
2. Absenkung

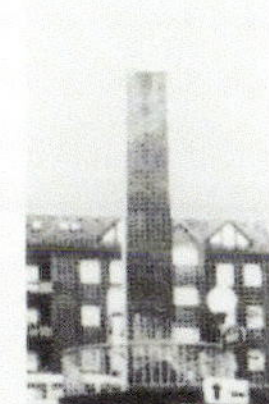

6. September 1989
3. Absenkung

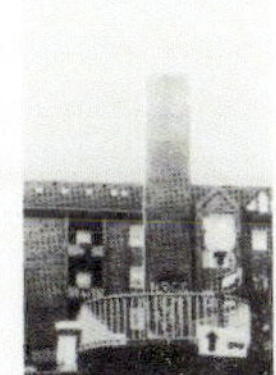

22. Februar 1990
4. Absenkung

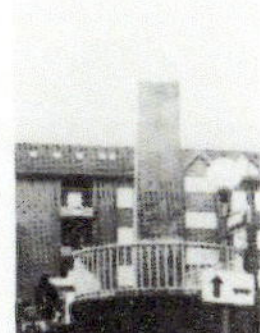

4. Dezember 1990
5. Absenkung

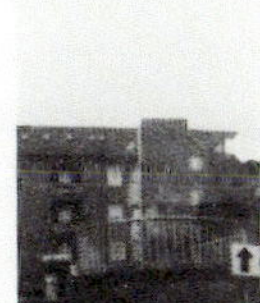

27. September 1991
6. Absenkung

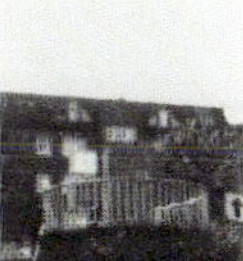

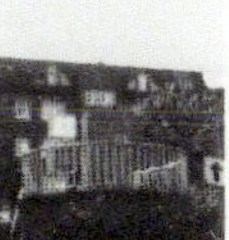

27. November 1992
7. Absenkung

10. November 1993
letzte Absenkung

Wir laden die Bürger von Harburg und die Besucher der Stadt ein, ihren Namen hier unseren eigenen anzufügen. Es soll uns verpflichten, wachsam zu sein und zu bleiben. Je mehr Unterschriften der zwölf Meter hohe Stab aus Blei trägt, um so mehr von ihm wird in den Boden eingelassen. Solange, bis er nach unbestimmter Zeit restlos versenkt und die Stelle des Harburger Mahnmals gegen Faschismus leer sein wird.

Denn nichts kann auf Dauer an unserer Stelle sich gegen das Unrecht erheben.

Harburg'lu Türk hemşerilerimizi ve bu şehrin Türk ziyaretçilerinin isimlerini bizim isimlerimize ilave etmeye çağırıyoruz. Bu bizleri her an uyanık bulunmaya mecbur etsin. 12 metre boyundaki kurşun levhanın üzerinde ne kadar çok imza olursa, onun yere gömülecek kısmı da o kadar uzun olacaktır. Günün birinde o tamamen yere gömülüp kaybolacak ve Harburg'un faşizme karşı uyarma anıtının yeri boş kalacaktır.

Zira, uzun sürede hiçbir şey haksızlığa karşı çıkmada bizim yerimizi alamaz.

We invite the citizens of Harburg, and visitors to the town, to add their names here to ours. In doing so we commit ourselves to remain vigilant. As more and more names cover this 12 metre tall lead column, it will gradually be lowered into the ground. One day it will have disappeared completely, and the site of the Harburg monument against fascism will be empty.

In the end it is only we ourselves who can rise up against injustice.

Nous invitons les citoyens de Harbourg et les visiteurs de cette ville à joindre ici leurs noms aux nôtres. Cela pour nous engager à être vigilants et à le demeurer. Plus les signatures seront nombreuses sur cette barre de plomb haute de douze mètres, plus elle s'enfoncera dans le sol. Et un jour, il disparaîtra entièrement et l'emplacement de ce monument rappèlant l'horreur du facisme sera vide désormais.

Car à la longue, nul ne pourra s'élever à notre place contre l'injustice.

אנדרטה נגד פשיזם
אנו מזמינים את תושבי הרבורג ומבקרי העיר להוסיף שמם לשמנו. בעשותנו זאת אנו מתחייבים להשאר על המשמר. כמה שיותר שמות יכסו את עמוד העופרת בן 12 מטרים, הוא יורד לאיטו לתוך האדמה. יום אחד הוא יעלם לחלוטין ורחבת האנדרטה נגד פשיזם תהייה ריקה.

שהרי רק אנו עצמנו יכולים לקום נגד אי־צדק.

Мы приглашаем жителей и гостей города Гарбурга присоединять свои имена к нашим, что обязывает нас не только быть, но и остаться бдительными. Чем больше подписей будет написано на 12-метровом свинцовом пруте, тем глубже тот будет уходить в землью. Это будет продолжаться до тех пор, пока по истечение времени весь памятник не исчезнет бесследно.

Ведь в конечном итоге ничто и нико кроме нас не может бороться с несправедливостью.

نحن ننادي المو اطنين بهار بورج وزوار المدينة بإضافة إسمهم هنا إلى أسمائنا. فإن ذلك يلزمنا بأن نكون ونظل يقظين. فكلما زادت التوقيعات التي يحملها الصاري من الرصاص وارتفاعه ١٢ مترا. فسوف يزداد الجزء الذي يغرس منه في الأرض. إلى أن يتوارى تماما بعد وقت غير محدد ويصبح موقع نصب هاربورج التذكاري ضد الفاشية خاليا تماما.

فلن يستطيع شيئ على الدوام أن يقوم بدلا عنا بمناهضة الظلم.

Harburgs Mahnmal gegen Faschismus, Krieg, Gewalt – für Frieden und Menschenrechte wurde nach einstimmigem Beschluß der Bezirksversammlung Harburg im Auftrag der Kulturbehörde Hamburg nach dem Konzept von Esther und Jochen Gerz realisiert.

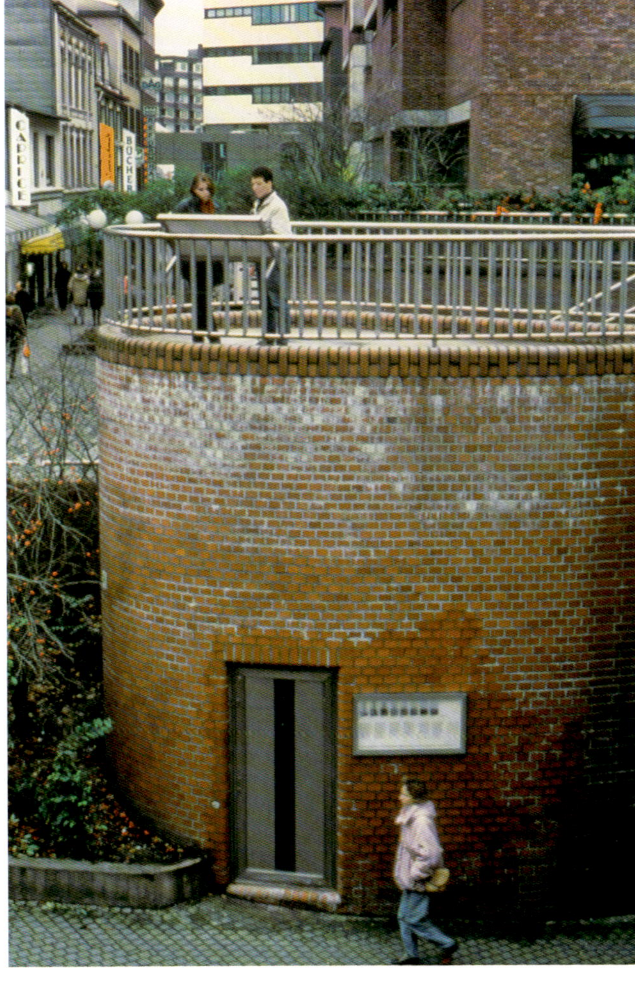

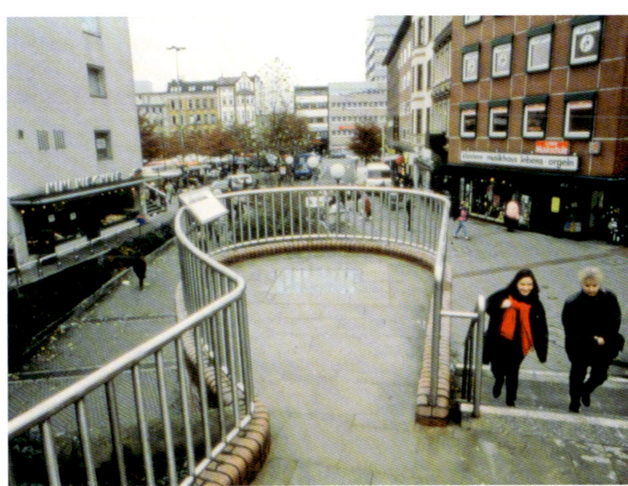

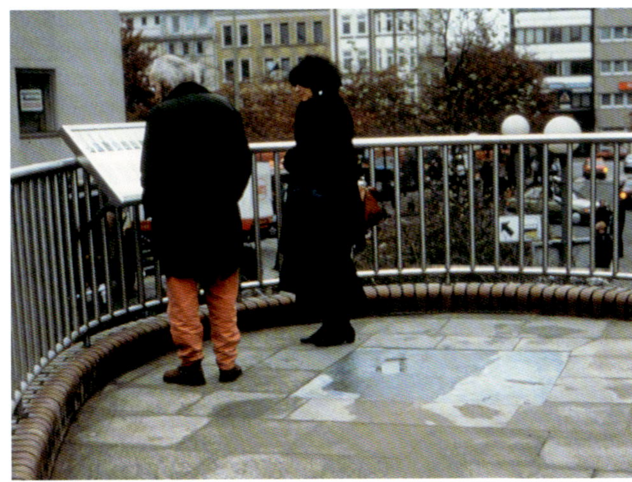

Just One Sky, 1987–1989

Slide show (9 color images), dimensions variable

Esther Shalev-Gerz created the *Just One Sky* series of slides as an echo of the anonymous posters covering the walls of Jerusalem at the time. She photographed the city she left in 1984 from different angles, then superimposed these images over one another, so juxtaposing areas that are not contiguous in reality. The projection of the slides makes it possible to introduce a rhythm, a movement from one image to another, an approach anticipating Shalev-Gerz's video work still to come.

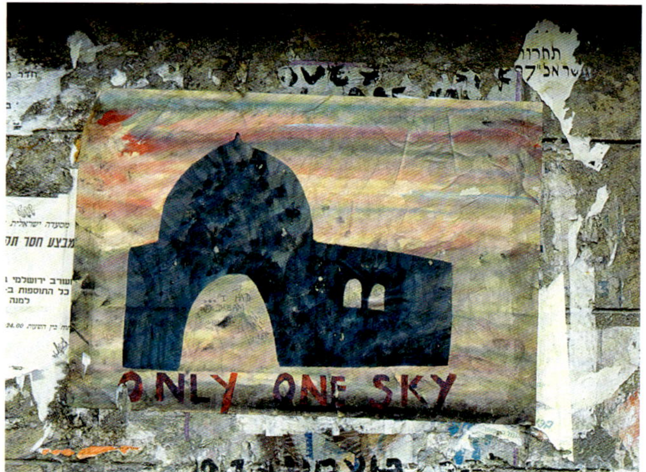

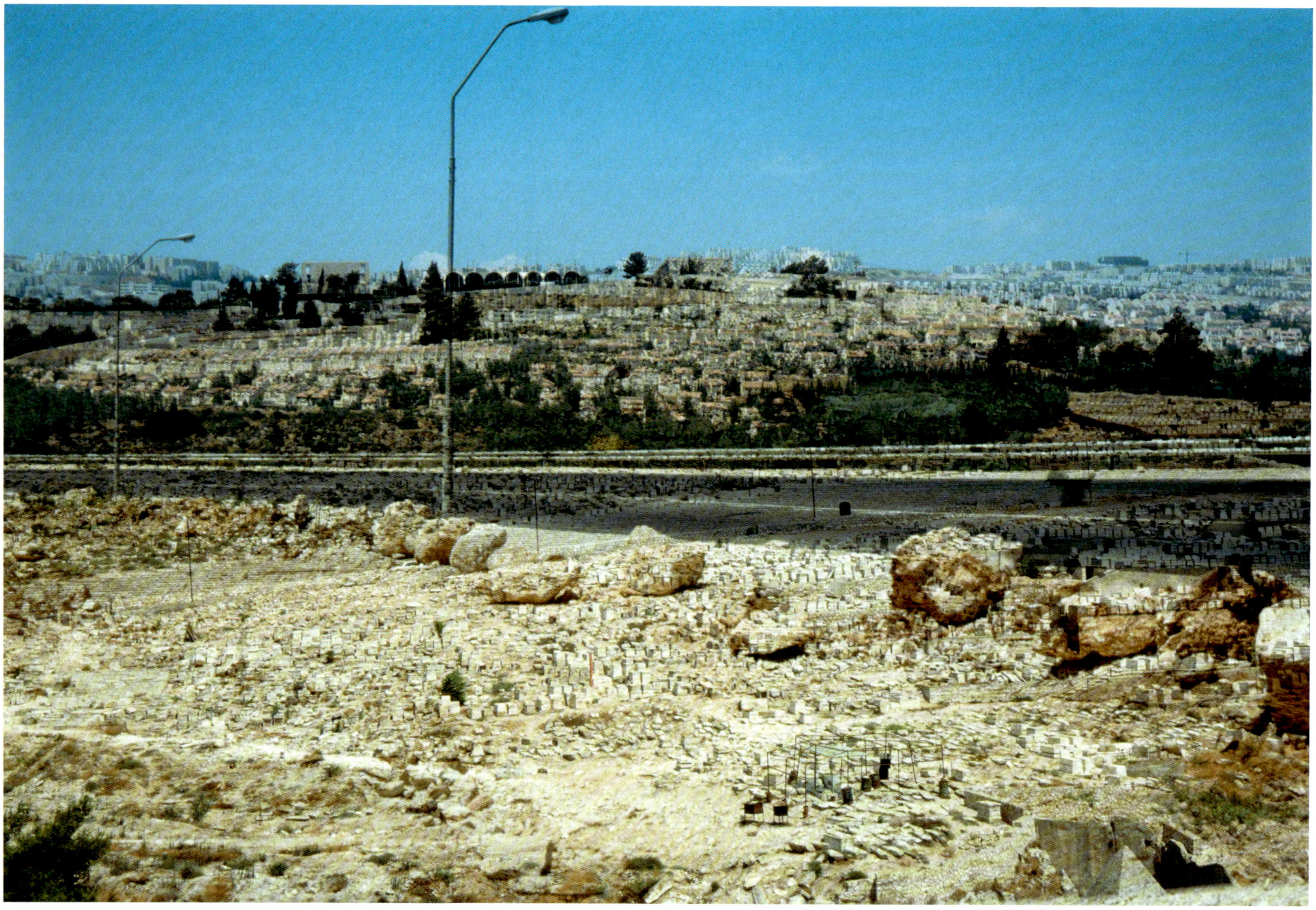

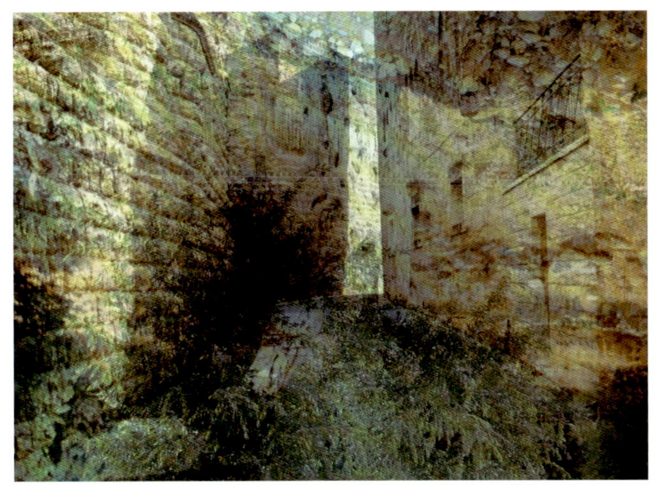

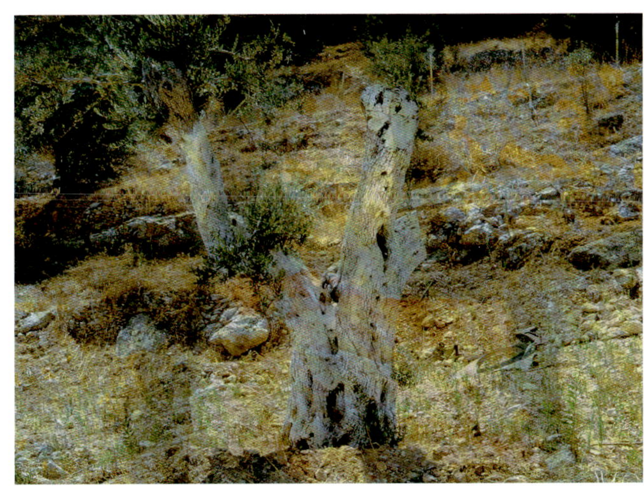

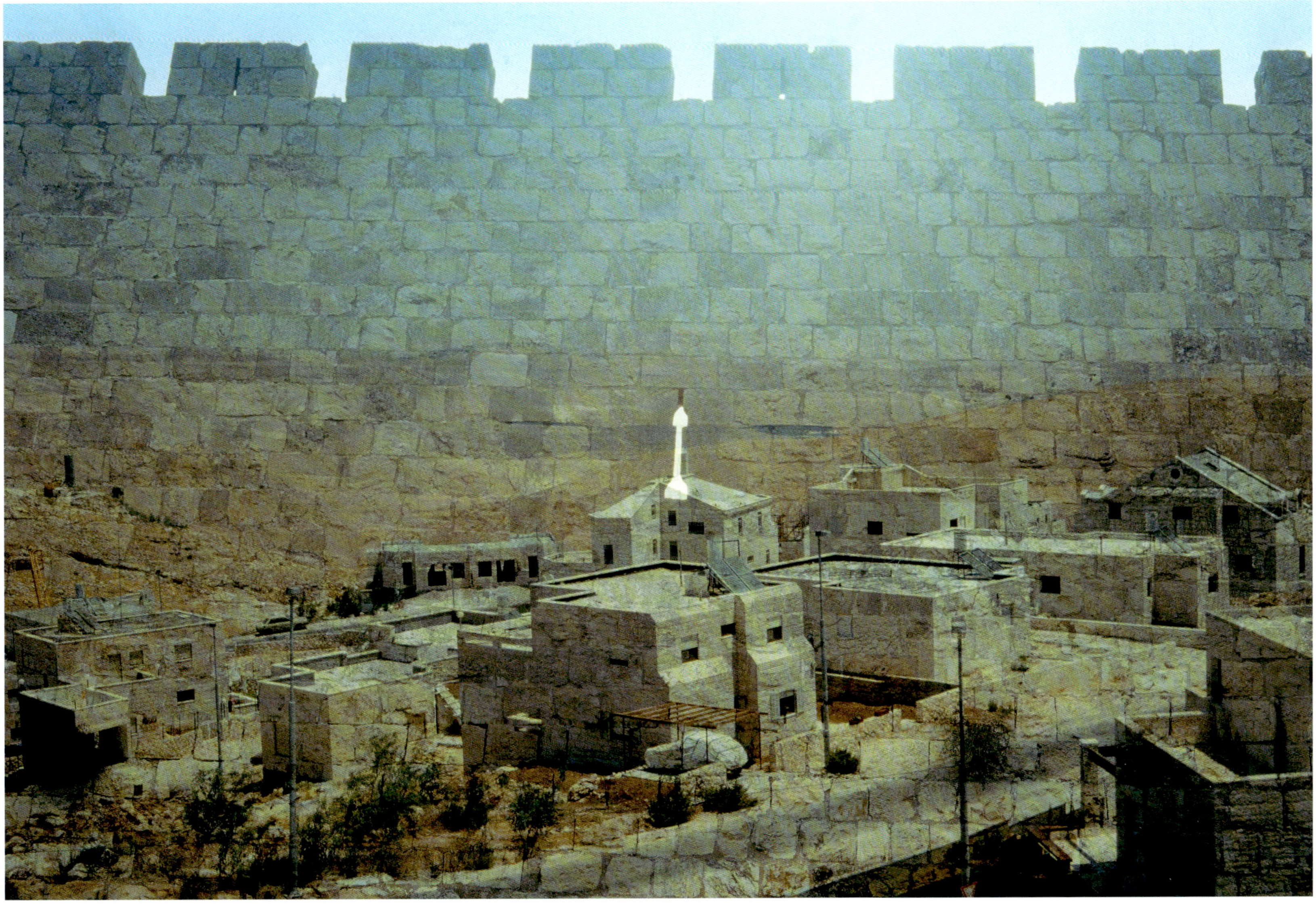

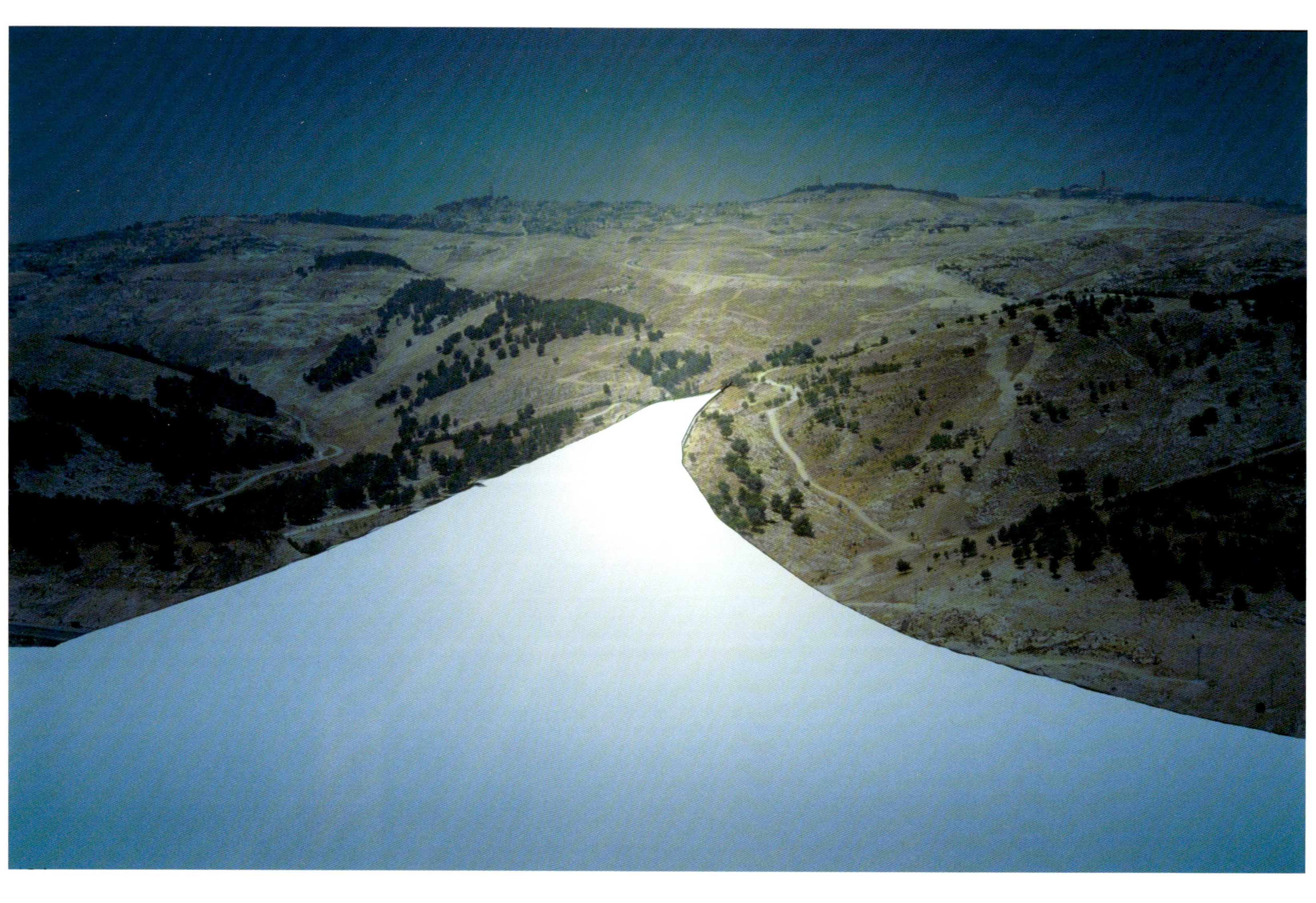

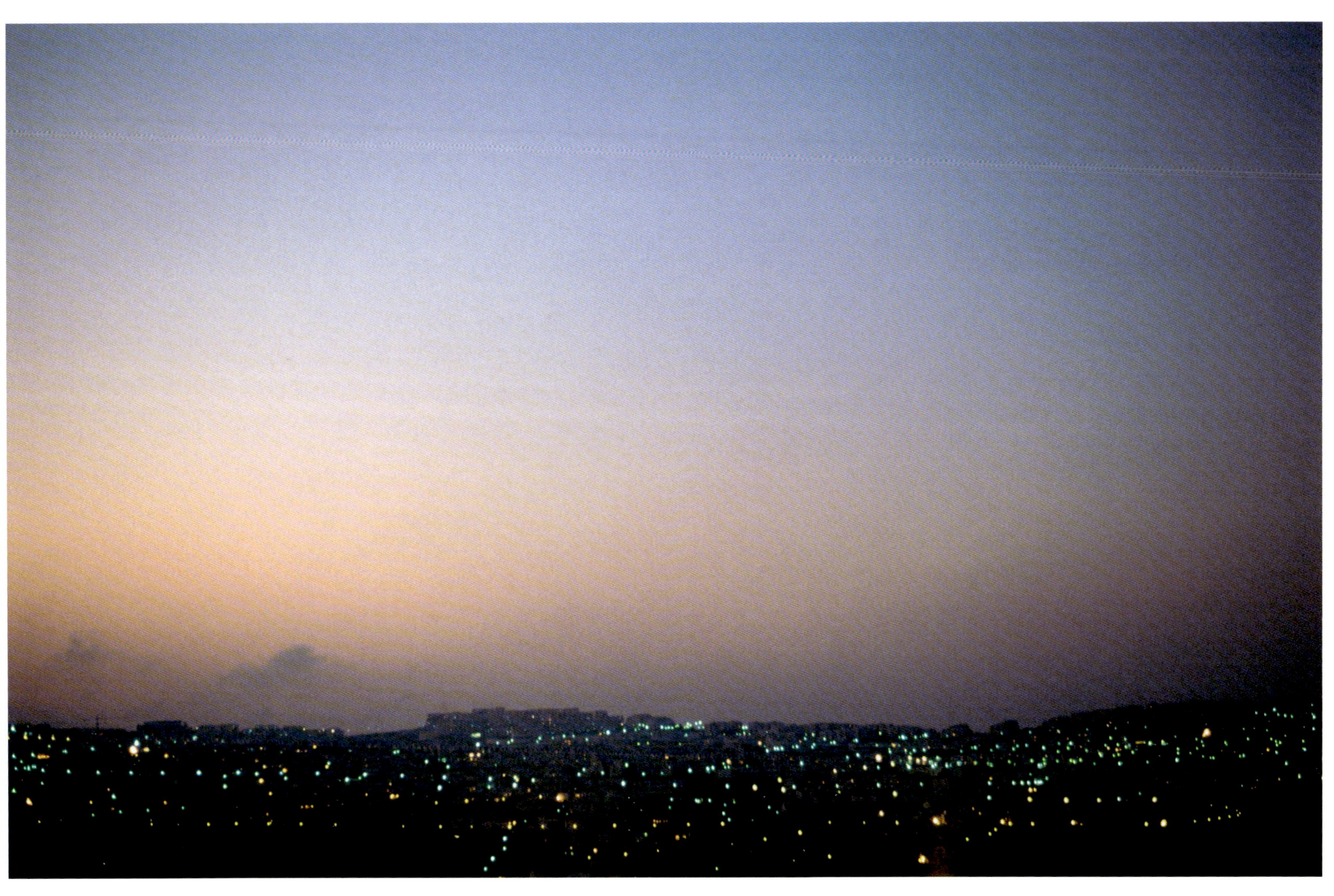

Erase the Past, 1990–1991

Slide show (24 black and white images), dimensions variable

Erase the Past consists of two series of images, and works like a flip book. In both series, part of a room with a portrait on the wall is visible. When these images are flipped through rapidly, just one element remains constant on the same scale: in one series it is the official portrait of Erich Honecker, the Communist leader of the GDR until 1989, and in the other that of Bertolt Brecht.

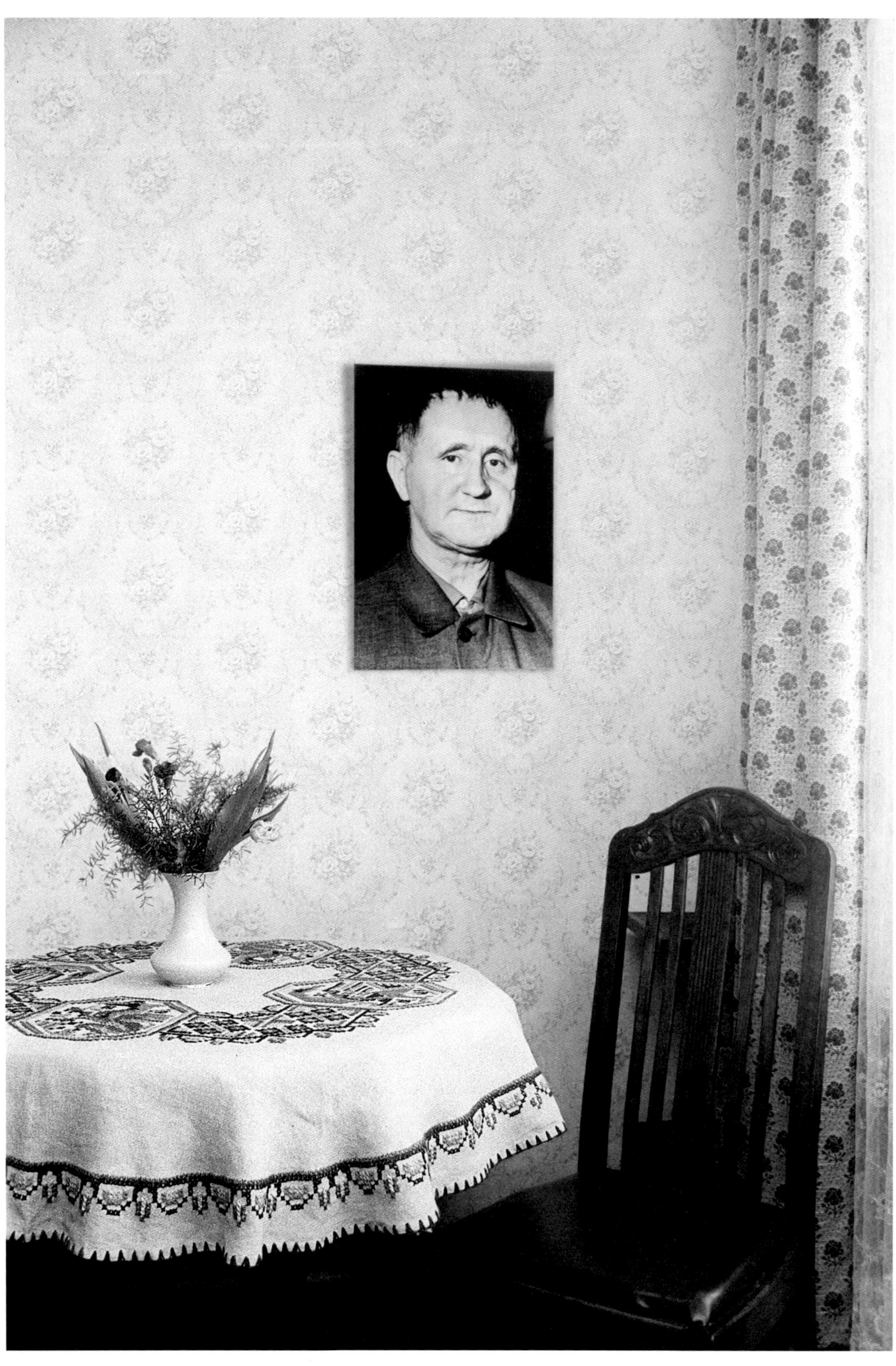

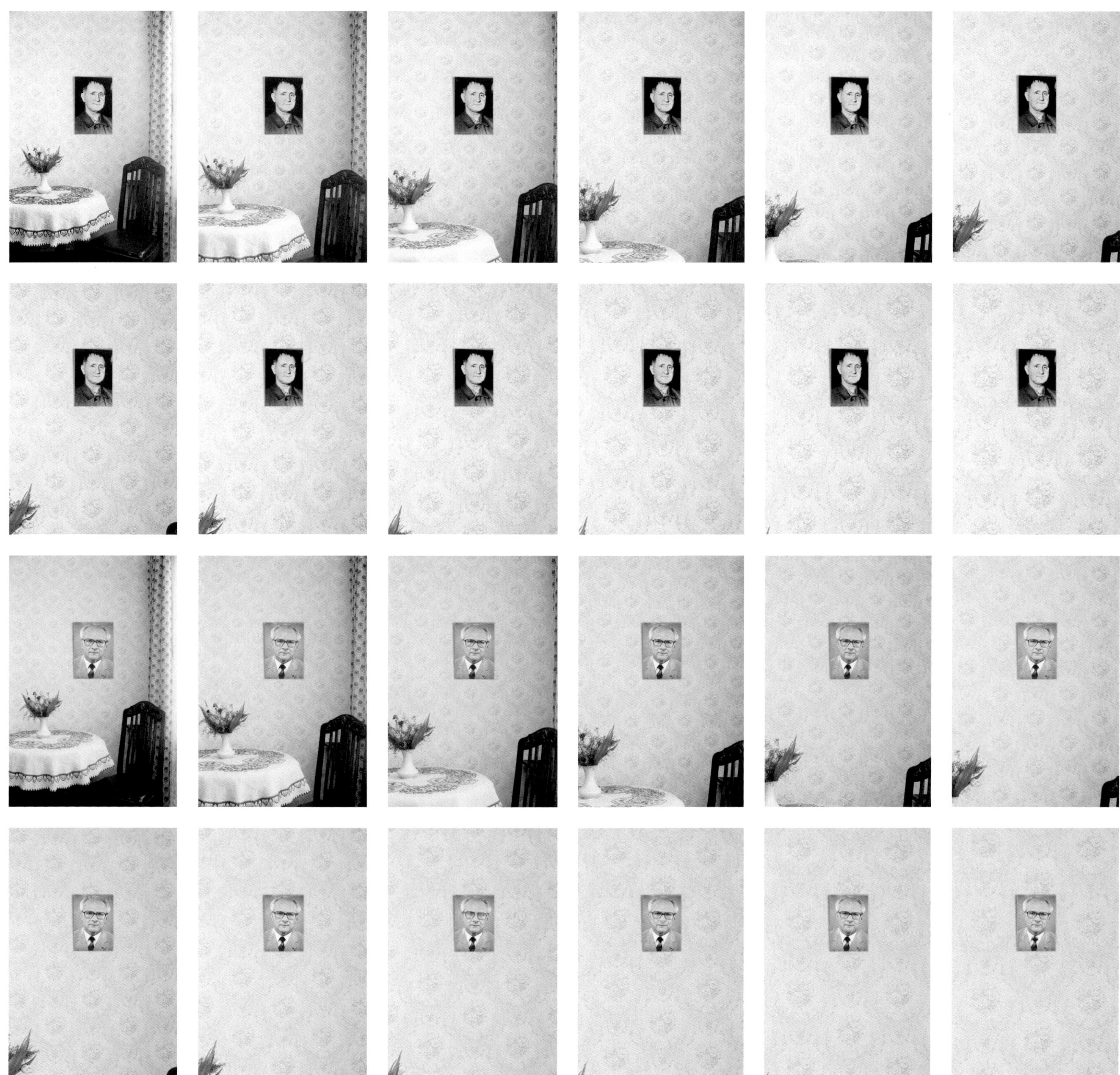

The Dispersal of Seeds, the Collection of Ashes, 1995
with Jochen Gerz

Geneva
Permanent installation; 2 steel columns, 18 m × 20 cm; 3 steel platforms, 40 × 40 cm each

To mark the 50th anniversary of the United Nations Organization, the German government commissioned a work from Esther Shalev-Gerz and Jochen Gerz for the United Nations park in Geneva. Two almost identical masts were erected alongside one another. One is topped by a simple platform, the other by a double platform, symbolizing the possibility of new departures on the one hand, and the need to collect stories on the other. In 1996, a counterpart to this sculpture was unveiled in Marl, Germany.

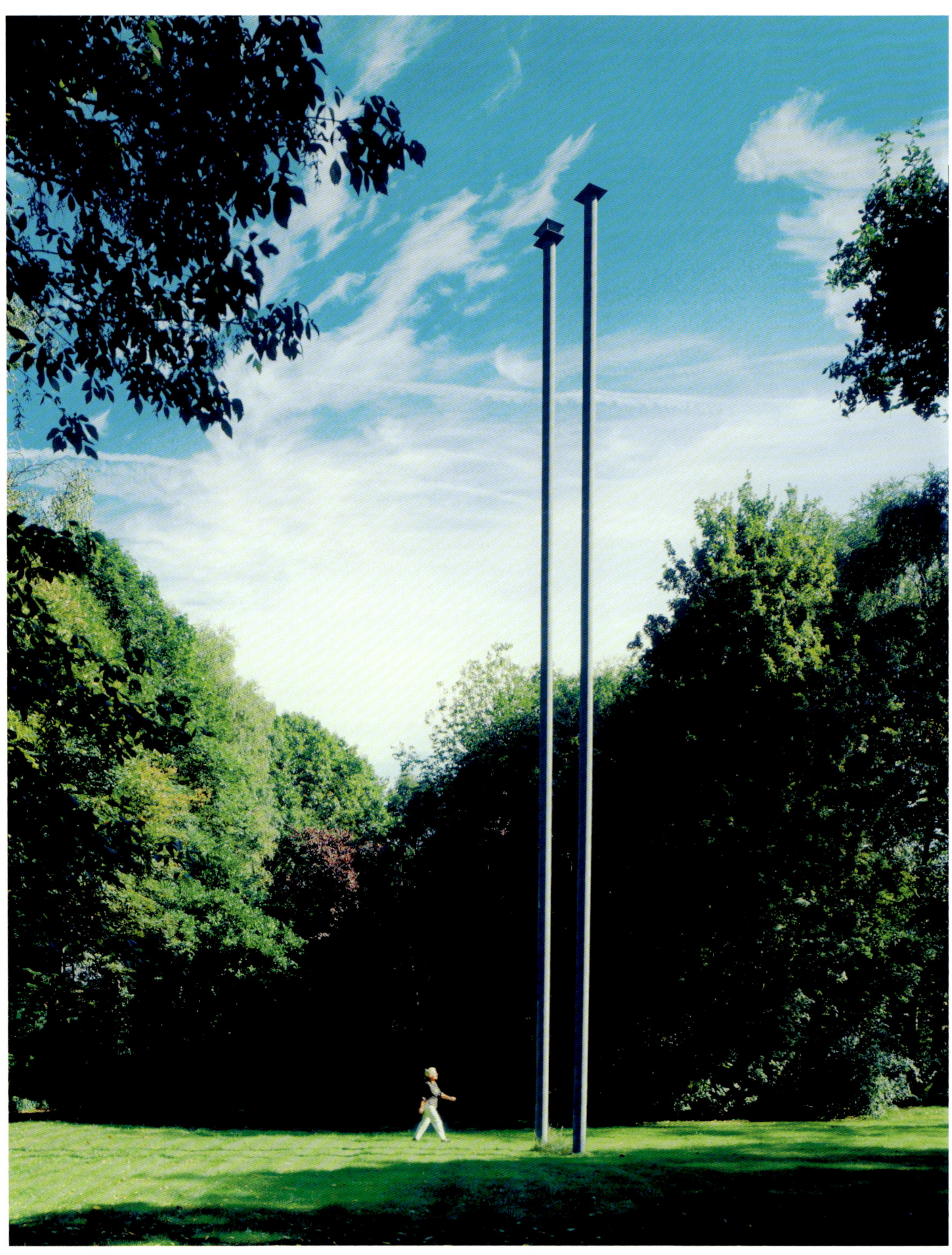

The Geese of Feliferhof, 1996 *
with Jochen Gerz

Graz

In 1996, Esther Shalev-Gerz and Jochen Gerz won a competition launched by the Austrian government to pay tribute to those who opposed the Nazi regime. The artists proposed installing four white flags carrying inscriptions ("Courage is punished by death," "The soldier's fiancée is barbarism," etc.) on the site at Feliferhof where a great many members of the resistance were shot between 1941 and 1945. The project was rejected by the Austrian army, and was never implemented. The polemics were widely reported in the press, which took the matter up several years running.

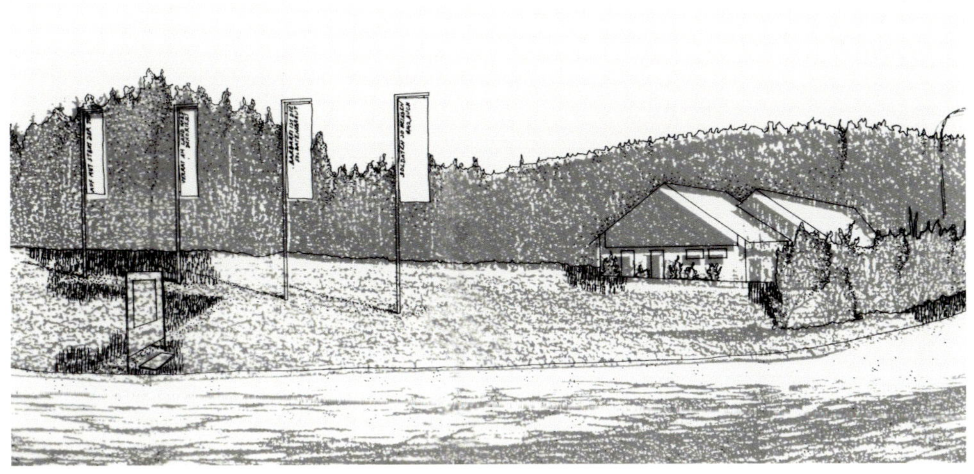

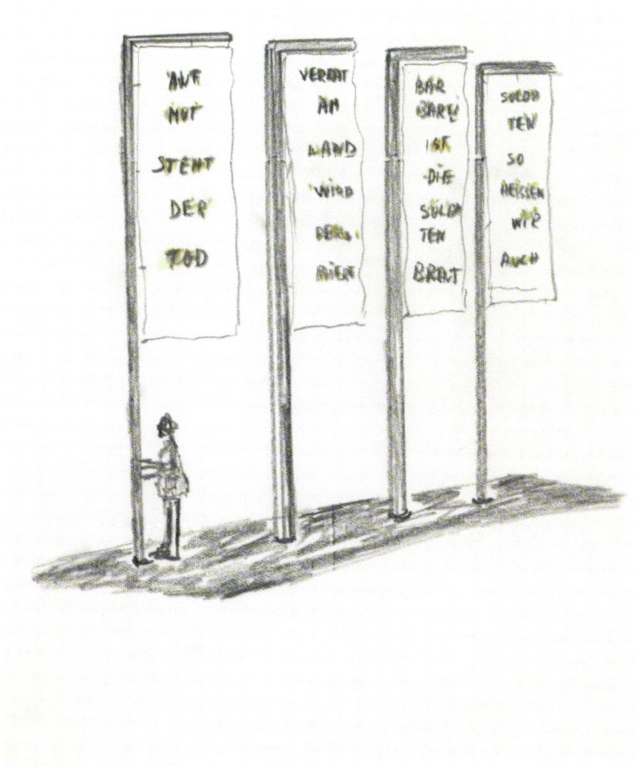

A Gaze at Algeria—Look Only Through Your Eyes, 1997

Internet project and photographs, dimensions variable

A Gaze at Algeria offers a challenge to the Internet as a space of collective awareness. The world was able to see images of Algeria on television and in the press at a turbulent moment in its history, whereas its own inhabitants were unaware that such images were being seen. Using rudimentary webcams, participants in Rome, Paris, Skopje, Sofia, Istanbul, and Bucharest were invited to direct their gaze at Algeria for 60 seconds. Each individual gaze was then simultaneously projected onto screens in each of these countries.

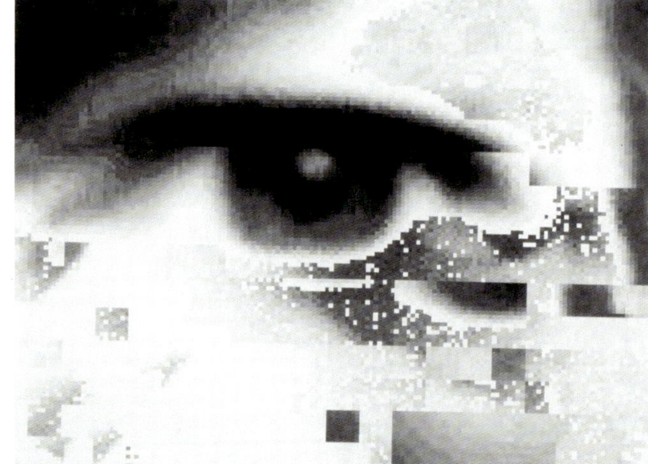

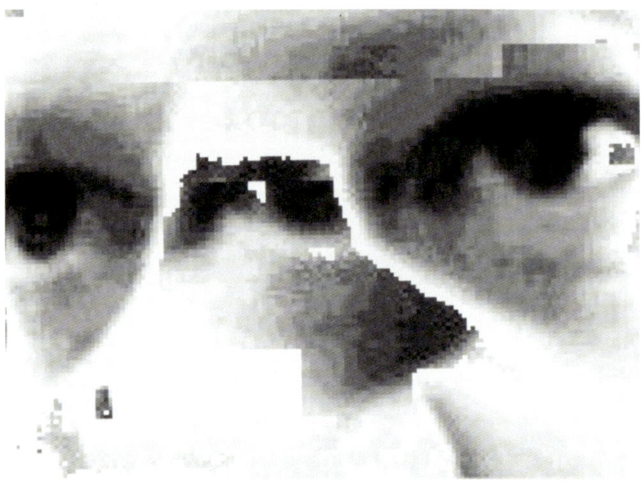

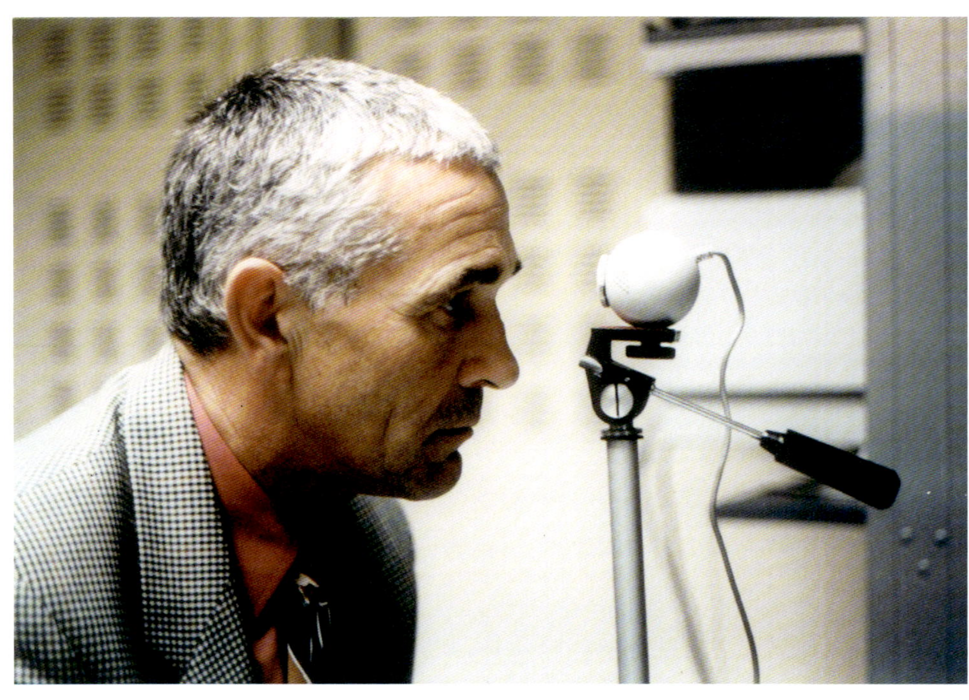

Judengang, 1997–2000

Berlin
Installation; color video projection, with sound, 132 min; color video projection, silent, 5 min.; 43 photographs, dimensions variable

The *Judengang* is the name of a condemned pathway skirting a 19th-century former Jewish cemetery in the Prenzlauerberg district of Berlin. It is said that the Jews did not have the right to access the cemetery through its main entrance because the sight of their funeral processions upset the neighborhood. The Judengang, which has since become a no-man's land, is used by local residents as their backyard. In a video Esther Shalev-Gerz invites them to think up a new use for this place.

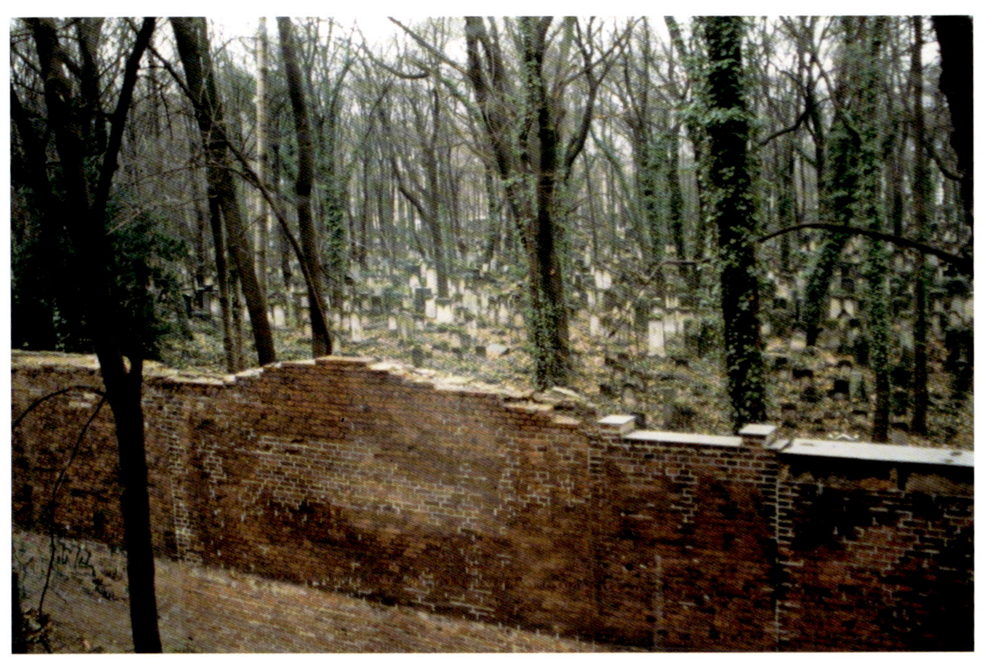

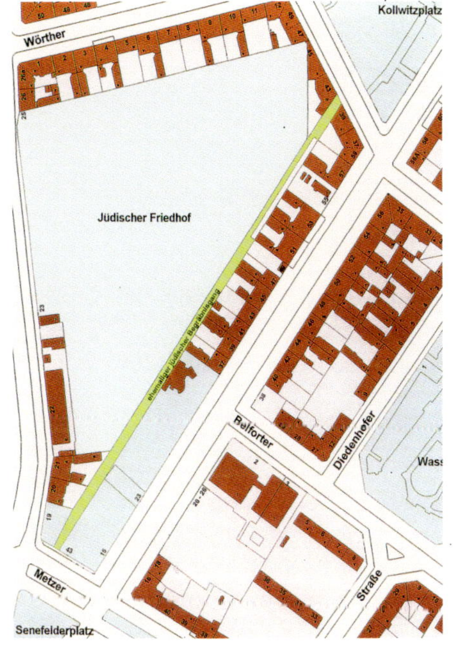

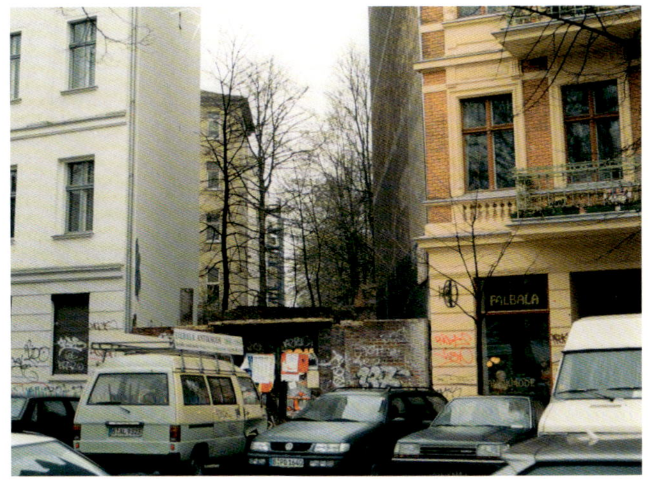

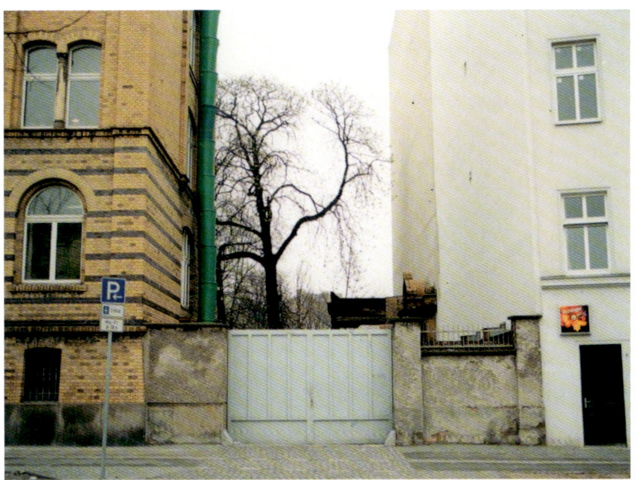

Tower (Without Walls), 1998 *

Jerusalem

In 1998 Esther Shalev-Gerz proposed the intervention *Tower (Without Walls)* to the city of Jerusalem. The project consisted of imagining Jerusalem without city walls, by projecting the image of the streets located on the other side onto the outside of the perimeter wall, in memory of the appropriation of territories by the Jews in Palestine in the 1930s, in the form of villages consisting of towers encircled by walls (Homa u-Migdal). So far the project has not been implemented.

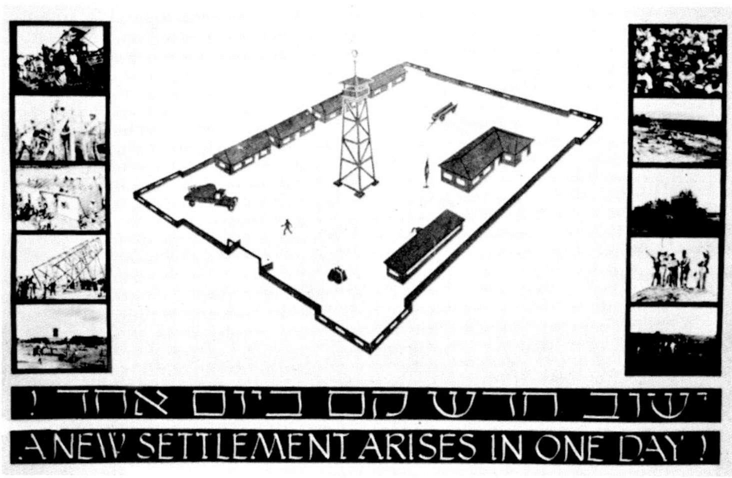

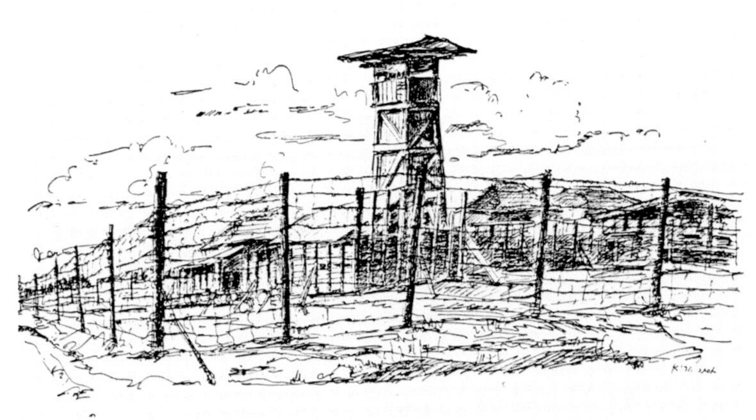

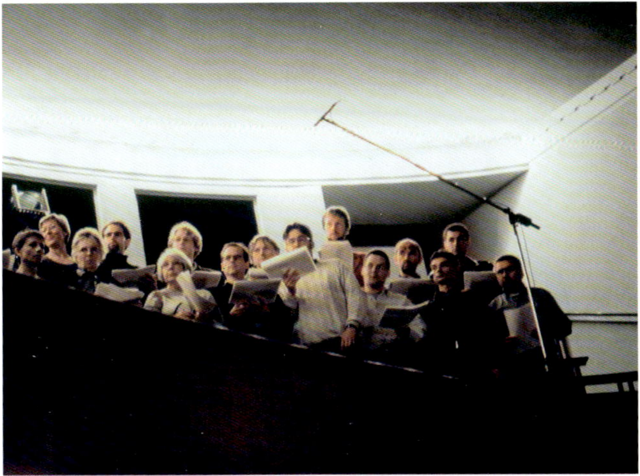

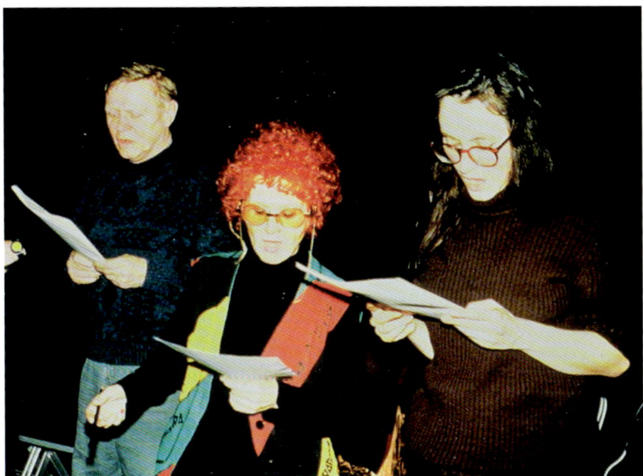

The Berlin Inquiry, 1998
with Jochen Gerz

Berlin
5 theater performances, Hebbel Theater Berlin, Berliner Ensemble, Volksbühne am Rosa Luxemburg Platz, in collaboration with Der Tagesspiegel, ZDF, Deutschland-radio, and SFB-Hörfunk

In 1998 Esther Shalev-Gerz and Jochen Gerz invited the audiences at three theaters in Berlin to re-enact the play *Die Ermittlung (The Investigation)* by Peter Weiss, written in 1965 and based on testimony collected during the Auschwitz trials between 1963 and 1965. How each performance went depended on everyone's participation, thus breaking down the conventional distinctions between spectators/witnesses and actors. Fragments of the project were broadcast in parallel on television and radio and reported in the newspapers.

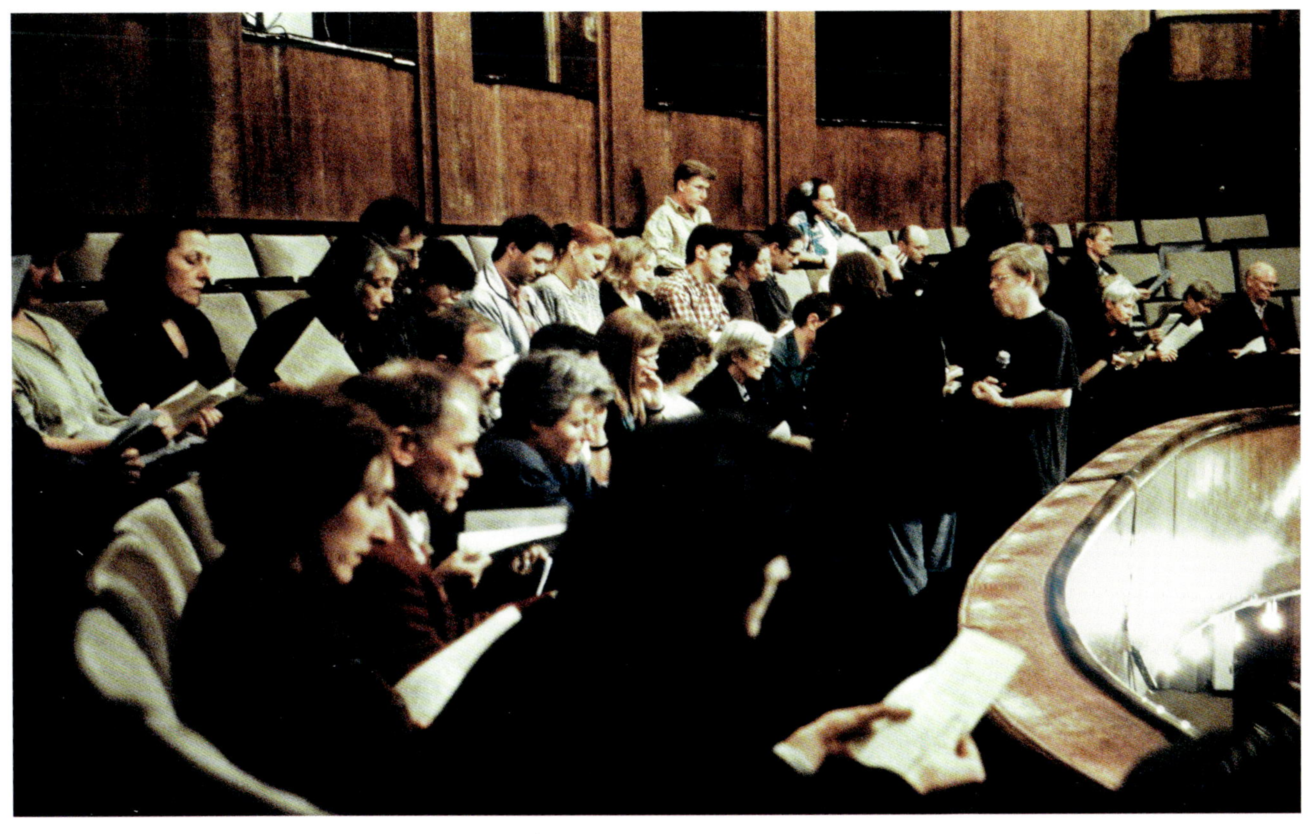

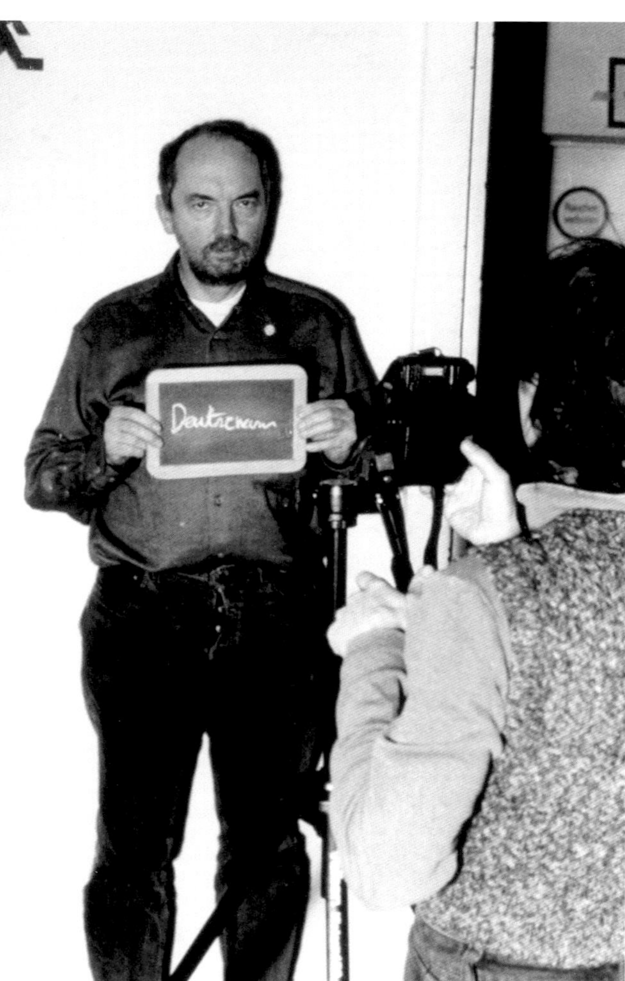

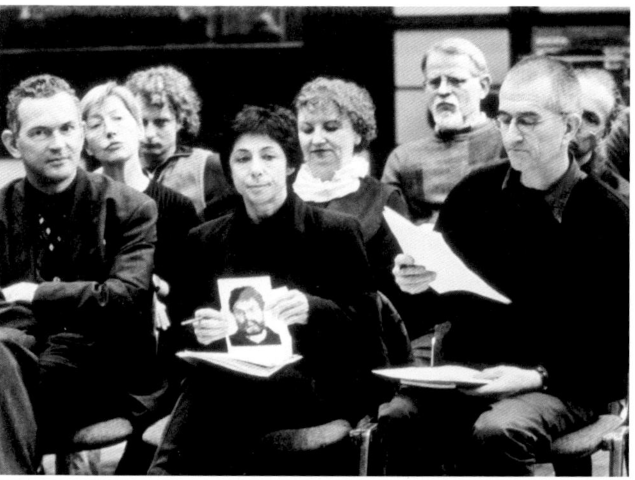

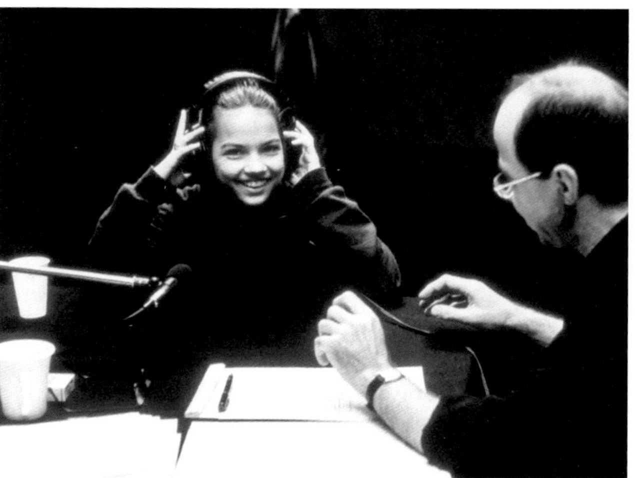

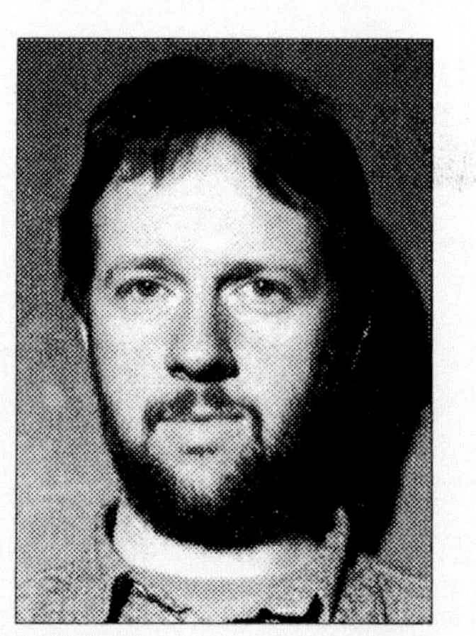

Es wurde ja soviel dummes Zeug geredet
und man wußte doch nie woran man war
Der Prozentsatz war bestimmt
Er richtete sich nach dem Bedarf
an Arbeitskräften

Martin Haesner, Lehrer, Berlin-Lankwitz

DIE BERLINER ERMITTLUNG
Berliner Ensemble, Hebbel-Theater, Volksbühne

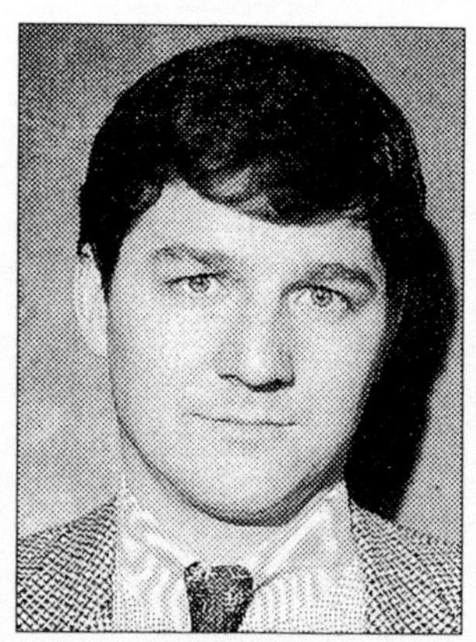

Bei meiner Ankunft fragte ich
Bin ich denn hier richtig
Da hat man gesagt
Hier bist du immer richtig

Ich sah Rauch
Ich dachte mir
das sind die Bäckereien
Ich hatte gehört
da würde Tag und Nacht Brot gebacken

Joachim Rissmann, Hotelier, Berlin-Charlottenburg

DIE BERLINER ERMITTLUNG
Nach einem Oratorium von Peter Weiss
Berliner Ensemble, Hebbel-Theater, Volksbühne

© Werz

In Karlshorst grenzen Welten aneinander

uprogramm des Bundes von 1700 Wohnungen auf 700 reduziert / Genehmigungen ab Jahr 20(

VON MICHAEL BRUNNER

:HTENBERG. Karlshorst sieht in diesen n wie ein kunterbunter Flickenteppich Neben gelben, blauen und grünen Fas- n sanierter Mehrfamilienhäuser leuch- weiße Einfamilienhäuser. Zwischen den vierten Altbauten und den neuen Häu- gähnen dunkelgraue Lücken. Auch dort en Häuser, doch sie sind verlassen. Die terhöhlen sind leer, durch die Dächer Regen, der dunkle Putz der Fassaden kelt. Karlshorster Tristesse.

m die Tristesse auf Dauer zu vertreiben, ßte etwas geschehen: Am besten wäre Investition in großem Stil. Doch un- st hat der Bund als bislang einziger grö- r Investor einen Rückzieher vollführt. der Bundesbaukommission in Bonn die Nachricht, daß der Bund seine Pläne 1700 Wohnungen in Karlshorst revidiert . Tatsächlich hatte der Bundestag ent- eden, das Wohnungsbauprogramm für e Bediensteten von bislang 12 000 auf mehr 9100 Wohnungen zu verringern. mar Kansy, der Vorsitzende der Bundes- kommission, versicherte zwar, Karls- t werde nicht aufgegeben. Doch in Ber- kam an: Der Bund zieht sich aus dem eil der Stadt zurück. Karlshorst ist verlo- Kansy meinte aber: Der Bund baut zwar arlshorst, aber nicht für seine Bedienste- Die neuen Wohnungen und Häuser nen dann nach Bedarf an Interessenten nietet oder verkauft werden.

/enn vom Bund als Bauherr in Karlshorst Rede ist, geht es um eine Fläche von 60 tar Größe zwischen Zwieseler Straße, enicker Allee, Wiesengrundstraße und ngelände. Dort war bis zum Abzug der stgruppe der Russischen Streitkräfte ein ppenteil stationiert. Für die Bebauung es Gebiets hatte das Bundesbauministe- n 1996 einen Städtebaulichen Wettbe- werb ausgelobt, an dem sich 180 Architek- ten beteiligten. Unter den 20 Teilnehmern der zweiten Runde setzte sich der Berliner Architekt Jörg Springer durch. Mit dem Ber- liner Landschaftsplaner Jörg Hollricher legte Springer ein Städtebauliches Konzept vor,

ANZEIGE

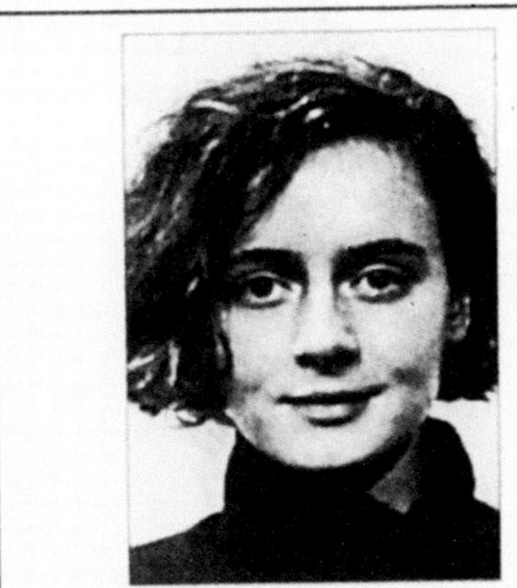

Wir sprechen Ihnen zu diesem großen Verlust
unser aufrichtiges Beileid aus
Auf Wunsch kann Ihnen die Urne
gegen Nachnahme von 15 Mark
zugestellt werden

Wir mußten dafür sorgen
das nicht 2 Häftlinge zur selben Minute starben
und daß die Todesursachen ihrem Alter entsprachen
Demnach durfte ein Zwanzigjähriger nicht
an Herzmuskelschwäche sterben

Ulrike Bollmann-Kramm, Schülerin, Berlin-Schöneberg

© Gerz

DIE BERLINER ERMITTLUNG
Nach einem Oratorium von Peter Weiss
Berliner Ensemble, Hebbel-Theater, Volksbühne

das 1700 Wohnungen in Reihenhäusern und Einfamilienhäusern mit großem Grün- anteil vorsah.

15 Hektar, ein Viertel der von den russi- schen Streitkräften geräumten Fläche, gehö- ren dem Bund. Weitere Grundstückseigen- tümer sind das Land Berlin und nach Ar ben des Lichtenberger Baustadtrats Andi Geisel der russische Staat. Geisel schätzt Wert der Bundesimmobilie auf einen zv stelligen Millionenbetrag. Er hält es für cher, daß 700 Wohnungen gebaut wer Zunächst müsse jedoch Baurecht gescha werden. „Vom Jahr 2000 an will der Be Lichtenberg die Baugenehmigungen e len", sagt Geisel.

Alles wäre gut, wenn da nicht das Ö Boden wäre. Im Norden des Gebiets schen Zwieseler Straße, Robert-Siew Straße und Bahnstrecke (Friedrichsfelc Schöneweide) befand sich nämlich Panzerkaserne der Roten Armee. Umv experten bekommen graue Haare, wenn an die Kosten für die Entsorgung der A sten denken. Unter den Bewohnern Karlshorst gilt es jedenfalls als offenes heimnis, „daß die Russen beim Ölwec einfach die Hähne aufgedreht haben". klar ist derzeit, wie sich die Grundstück gentümer Bund und Berlin die Kosten die Bodensanierung teilen werden.

Bislang ergreifen die 90er Jahre nur gernd Besitz von Karlshorst. An der Zwi ler Straße Ecke Rheinpfalzstraße steht prahlerisches Schild: „Sportpark Karlsh Berlins einzigartige Sportoase im Grün Ein holpriger Weg aus Betonplatten f vorbei an einer Reihe von Garagen und rotteten Baracken zu mehreren Tennis zen. Hat sich der Blick auf die Aschepl geöffnet, fällt rechter Hand ein ansehr saniertes Sportzentrum auf. Wie nal Karlshorst Alt und Neu beieinander lie ist auch direkt an der Zwieseler Straße z hen: An der westlichen Straßenseite ein nagelneues Doppelhaus mit Klinke sade, das in der Lüneburger Heide erst sig wirken würde. Doch 30 Meter d entfernt, hinter der Kasernenmauer, ein riesiger Betonbunker: Dort grenzen Welten aneinander.

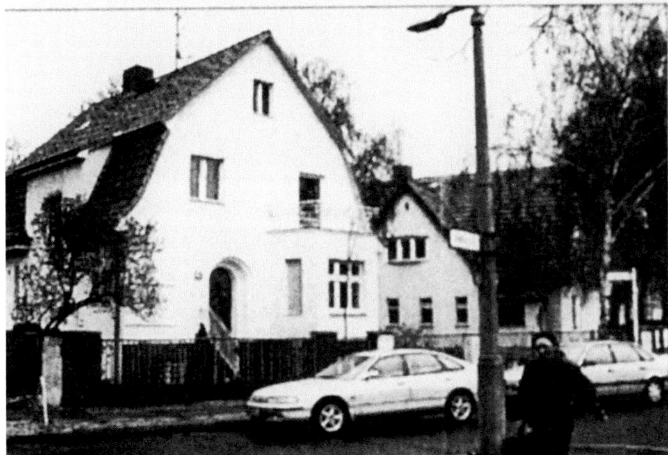

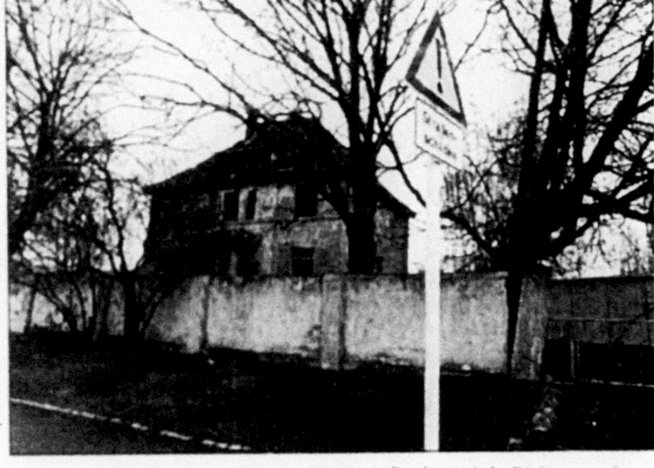

ORT DER GEGENSÄTZE ist Karlshorst. Neben renovierten Häusern wie an der Ehrenfelsstraße (links) finden sich Ruinen wie a eseler Straße.

Fotos: Thilo R

Irreparable 85, 1998

Berlin
Intervention in public space; silkscreen print, 119 × 175 cm with light box

Irreparable 85 offers a link between the past and the present. A luminous panel was installed in homage to the politically committed artist Käthe Kollwitz (1867–1945) on the site of her house, which was destroyed during World War II. The negative of an old photograph of the house has been inserted into the panel. The image of the luminous panel filled with the color blue recurs on the negative, which picks up on the color of the facade of the current building. At night only the negative image of the illuminated house is visible. The work offers an impossible return journey in time.

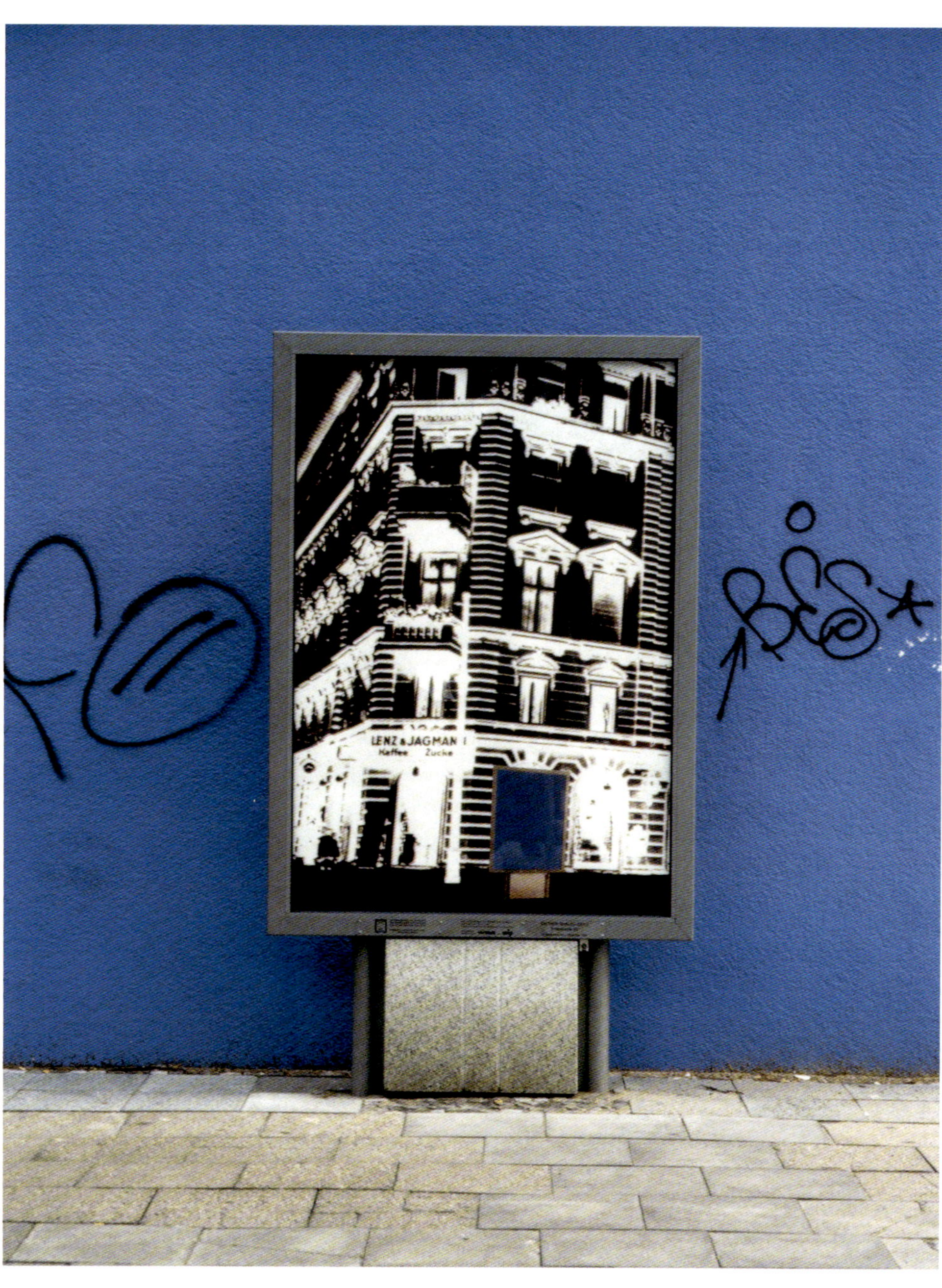

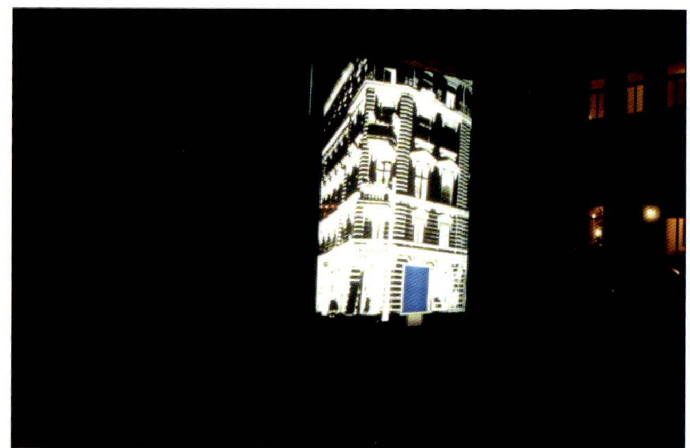

Books Inhaled by the Sky, 1998

Video projection, color, sound, 14 min.

Books Inhaled by the Sky was filmed in the rotunda of the Louviers Museum in Normandy, which has an important, but little consulted, collection of historical and religious works, confiscated from abbeys in neighboring areas during the French Revolution. The backs of the books are filmed increasingly fast in close-up, and the video finishes with a shot of a man throwing books up into the sky—where they remain. The video is part of Esther Shalev-Gerz's thinking about the role of archives, and the iconological relationship between text and image.

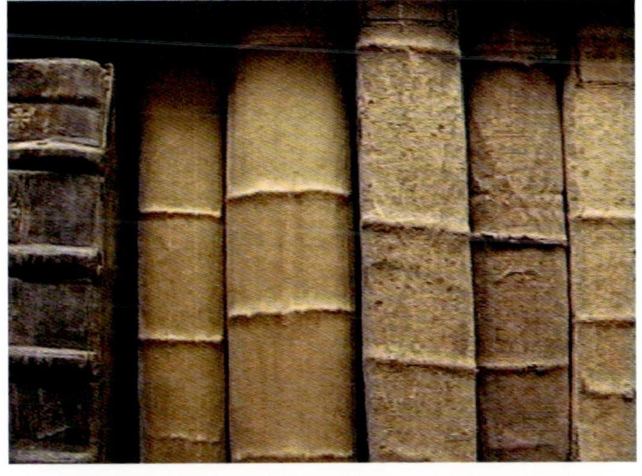
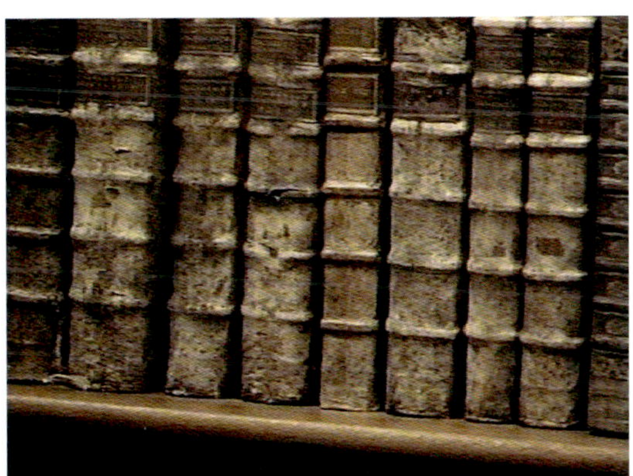
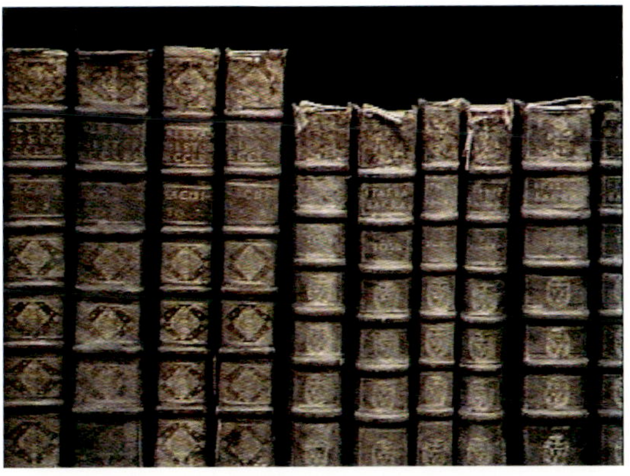
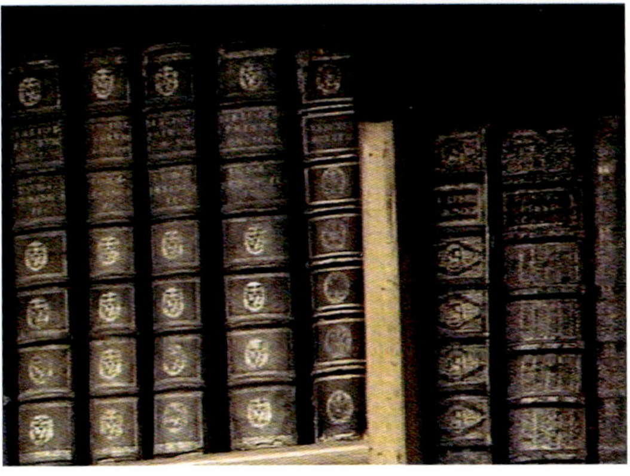
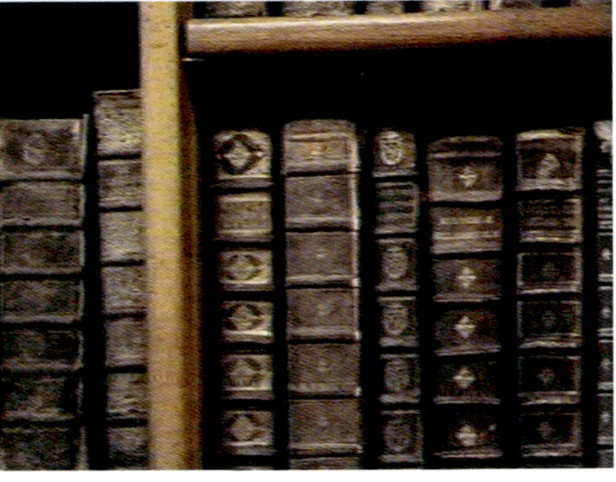

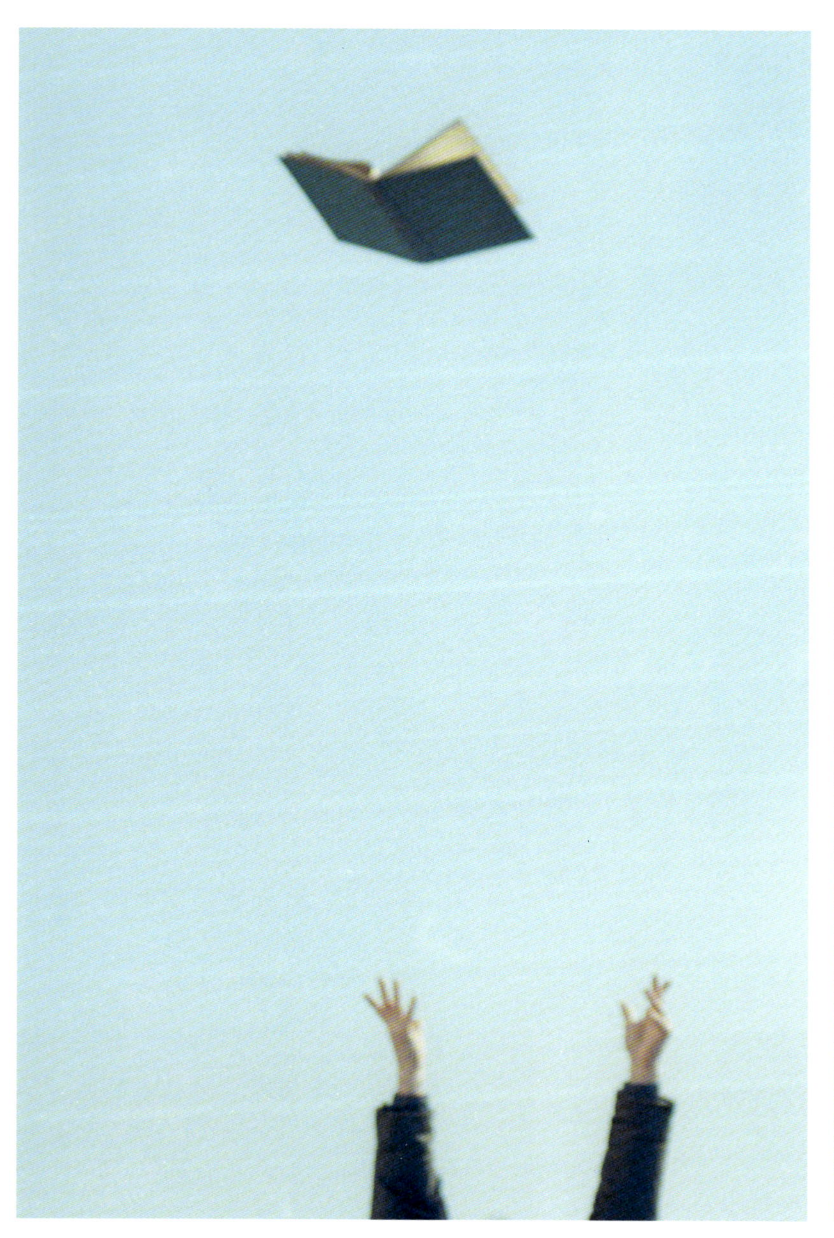
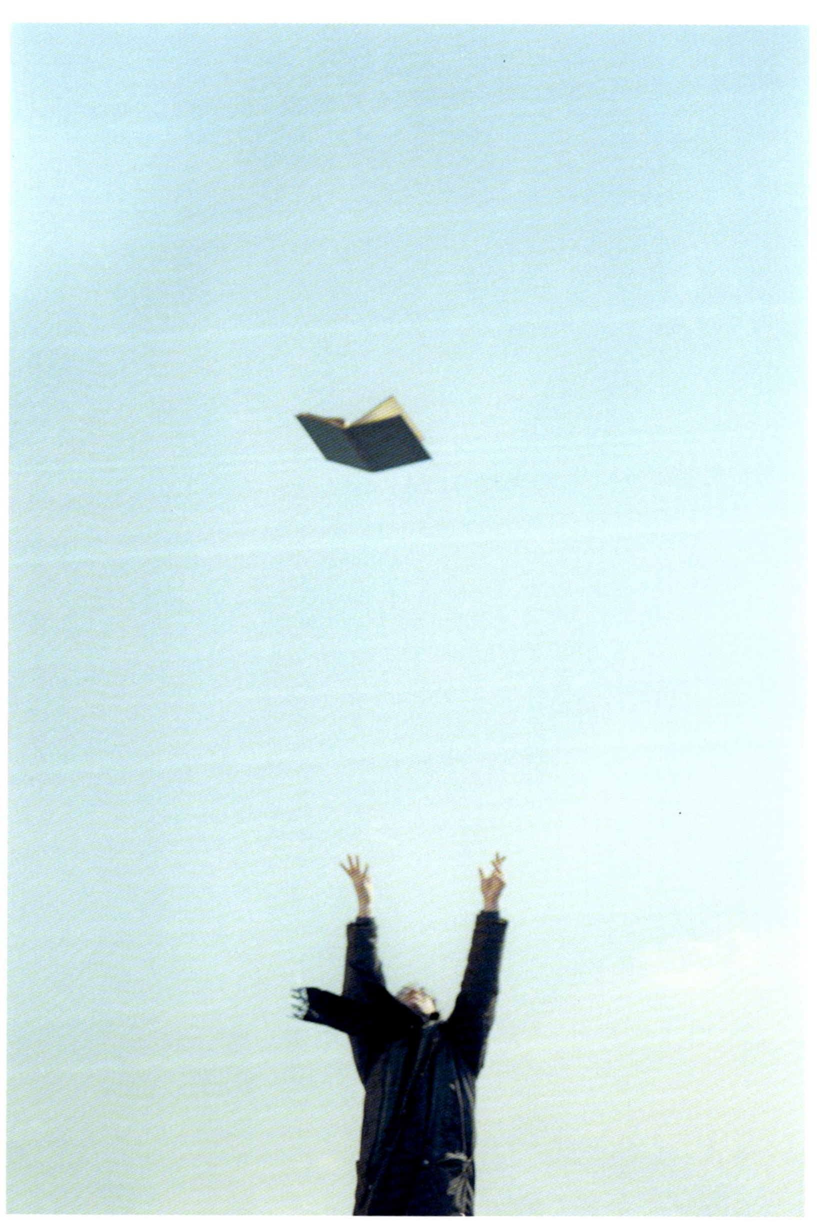

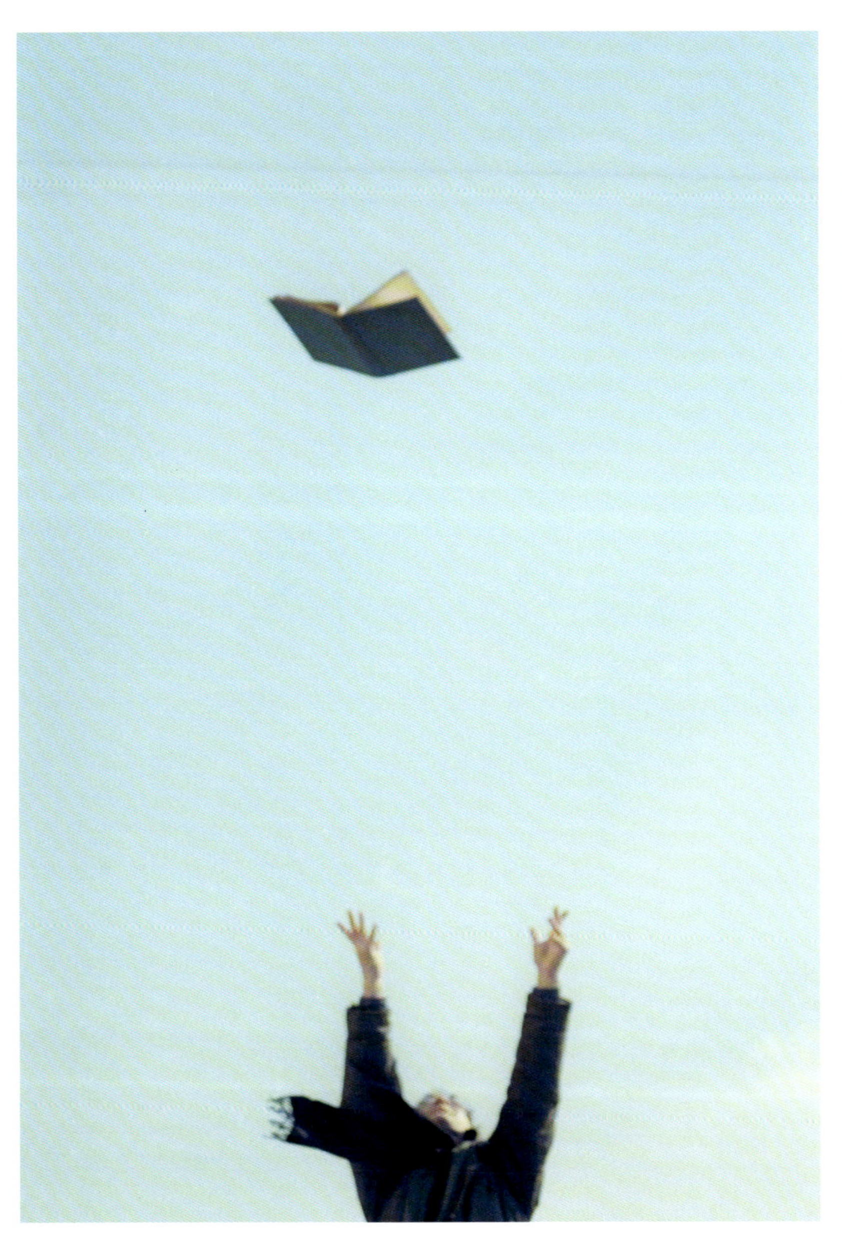

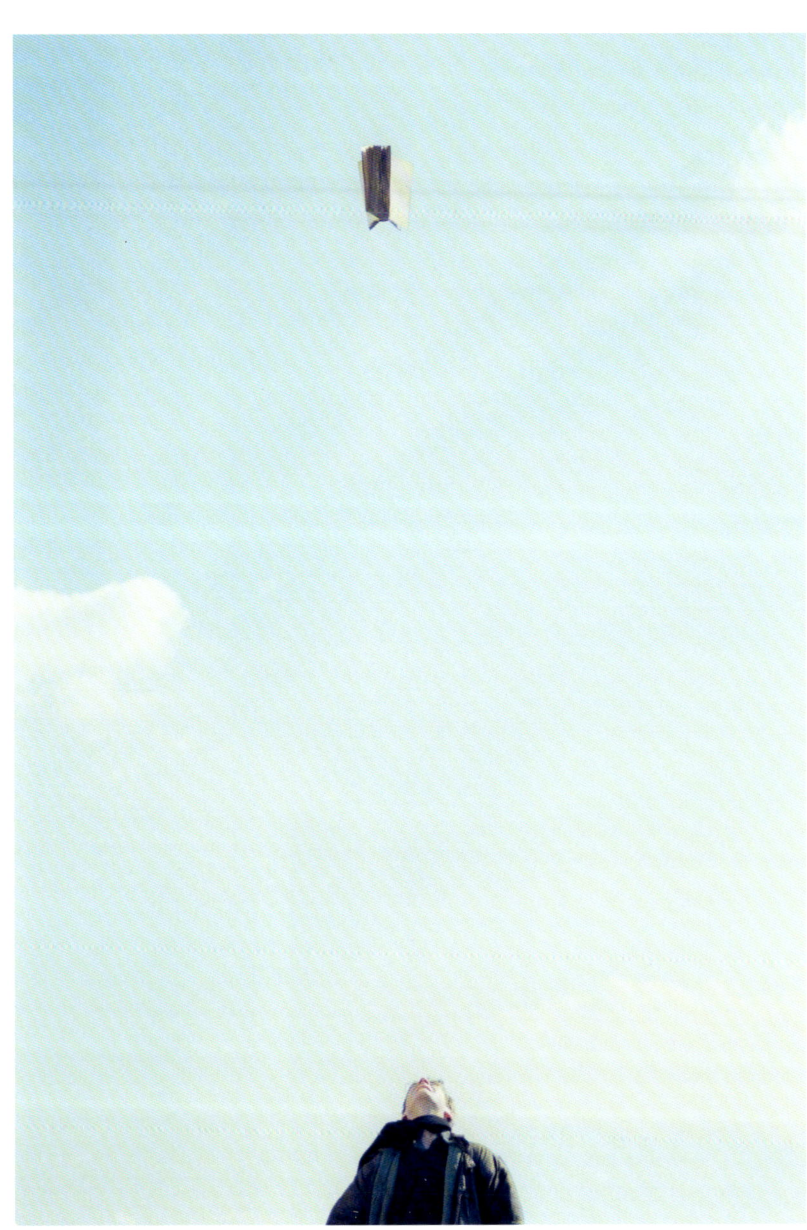

Inseparable Angels: An Imaginary House for Walter Benjamin, 2000

Installation
3 black and white photographs, 70 × 90 cm each; *Angel 10*, 2000–2010: a two-faced electric clock, 120 cm; *Angel 11*: 1 double chair, 82 cm × 65 cm × 43 cm; *Angel 12*: 1 color video, sound, 15 min.

Conceived as an imaginary house for Walter Benjamin, the title of the installation *Inseparable Angels* is a reference to the picture *Angelus Novus* (1920) by Paul Klee. It consists of a video retracing the journey between Weimar and Buchenwald concentration camp, filmed through the window of a taxi. The driver recounts the histories of the places he is passing through. At times the image wobbles, slows down, or becomes double, with texts by Franz Kafka, Heiner Müller, Gershom Sholem, Klee, and Benjamin interposed as voice-overs. All the texts make reference to angels. A clock with two faces, the hands of which turn in opposite directions, a double chair with no back, and three photographs accompany the video.

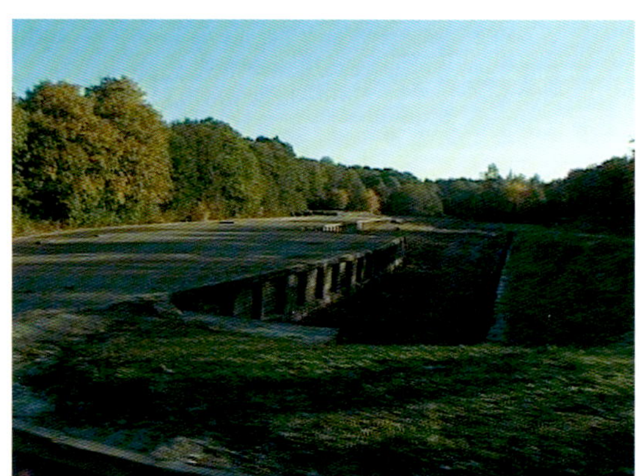

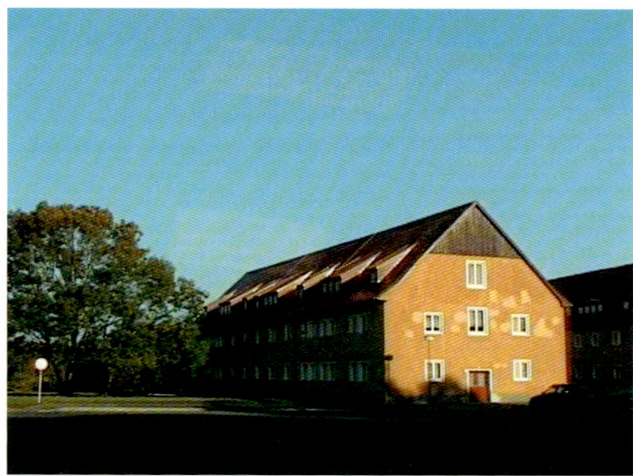

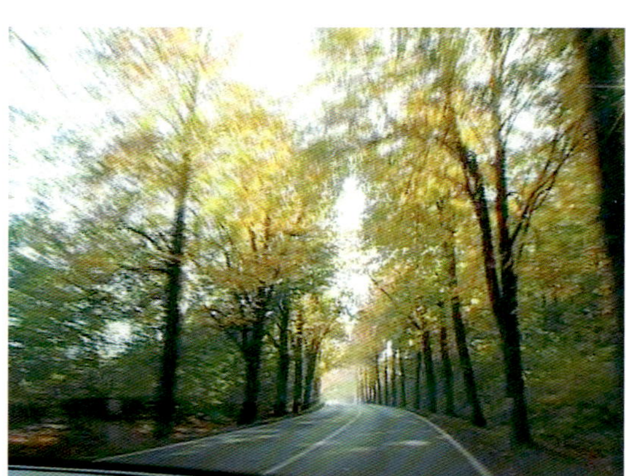

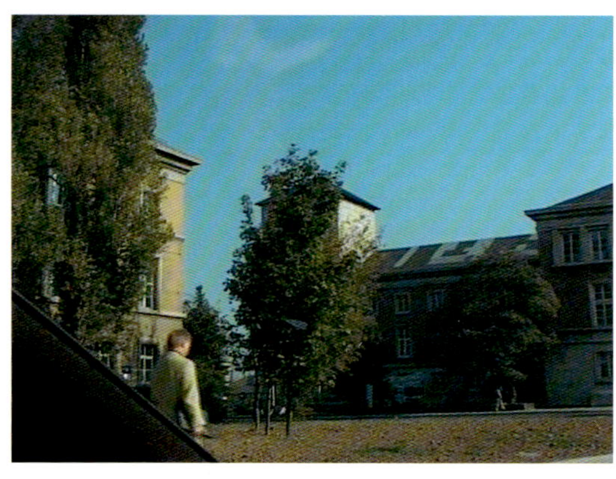

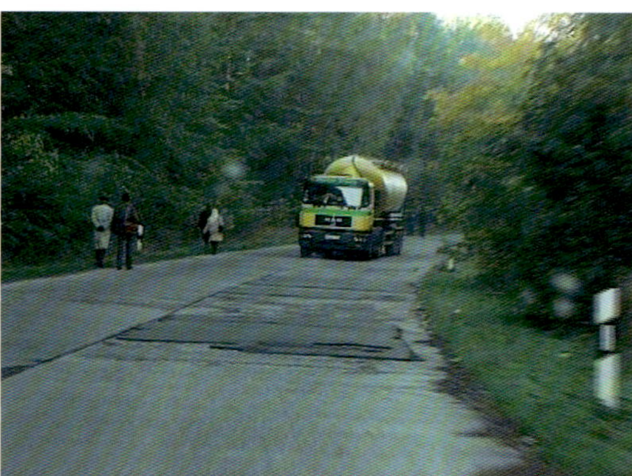

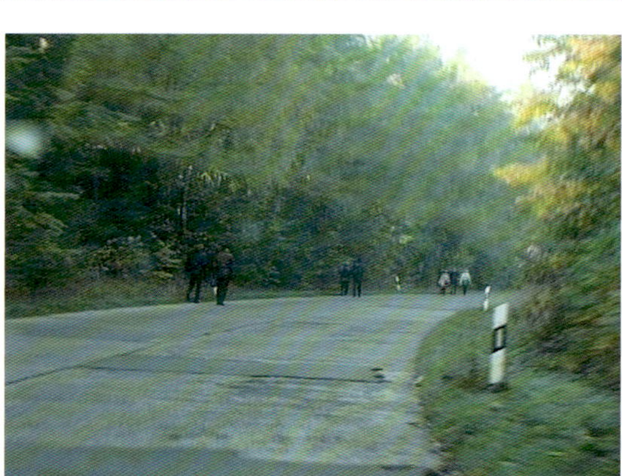

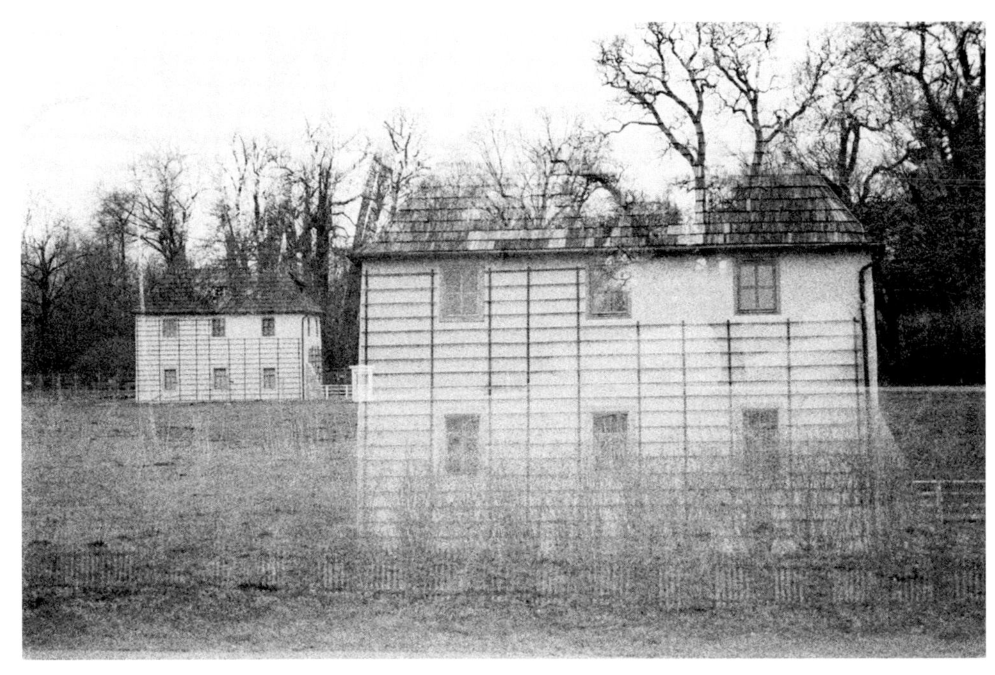

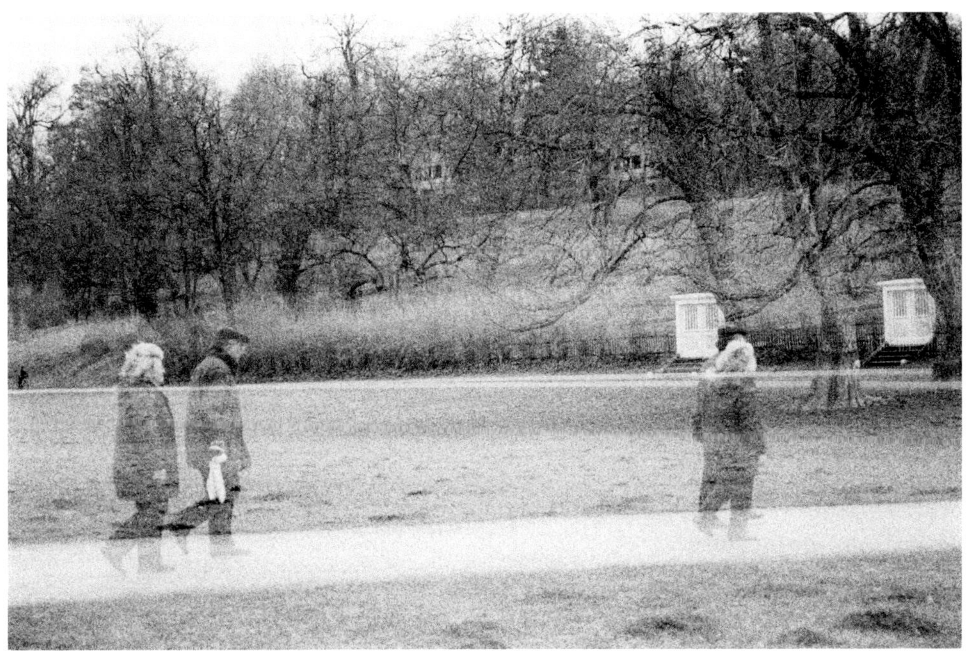

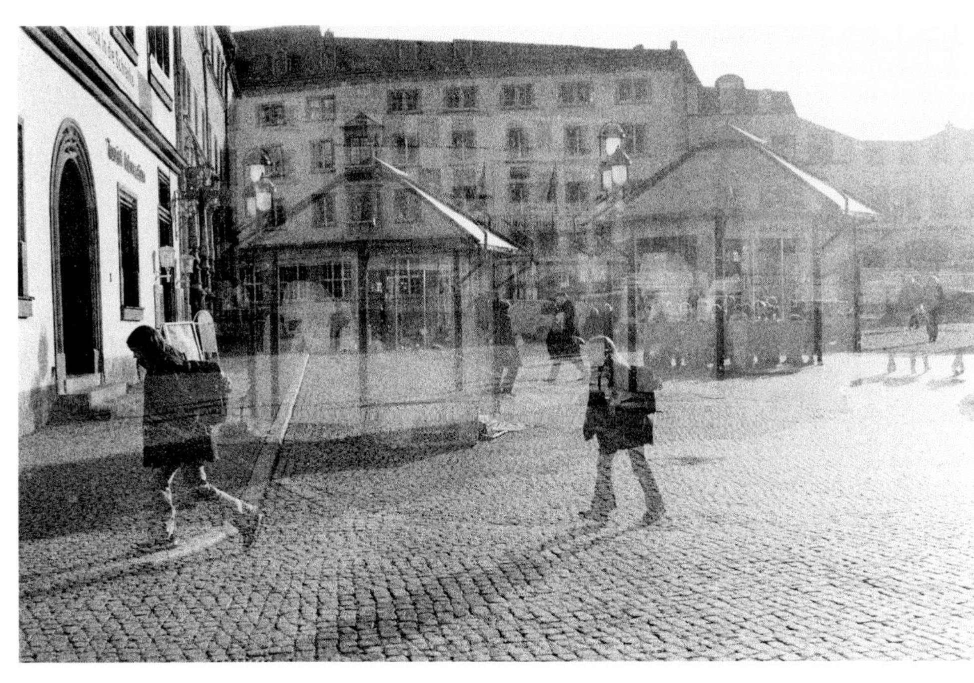

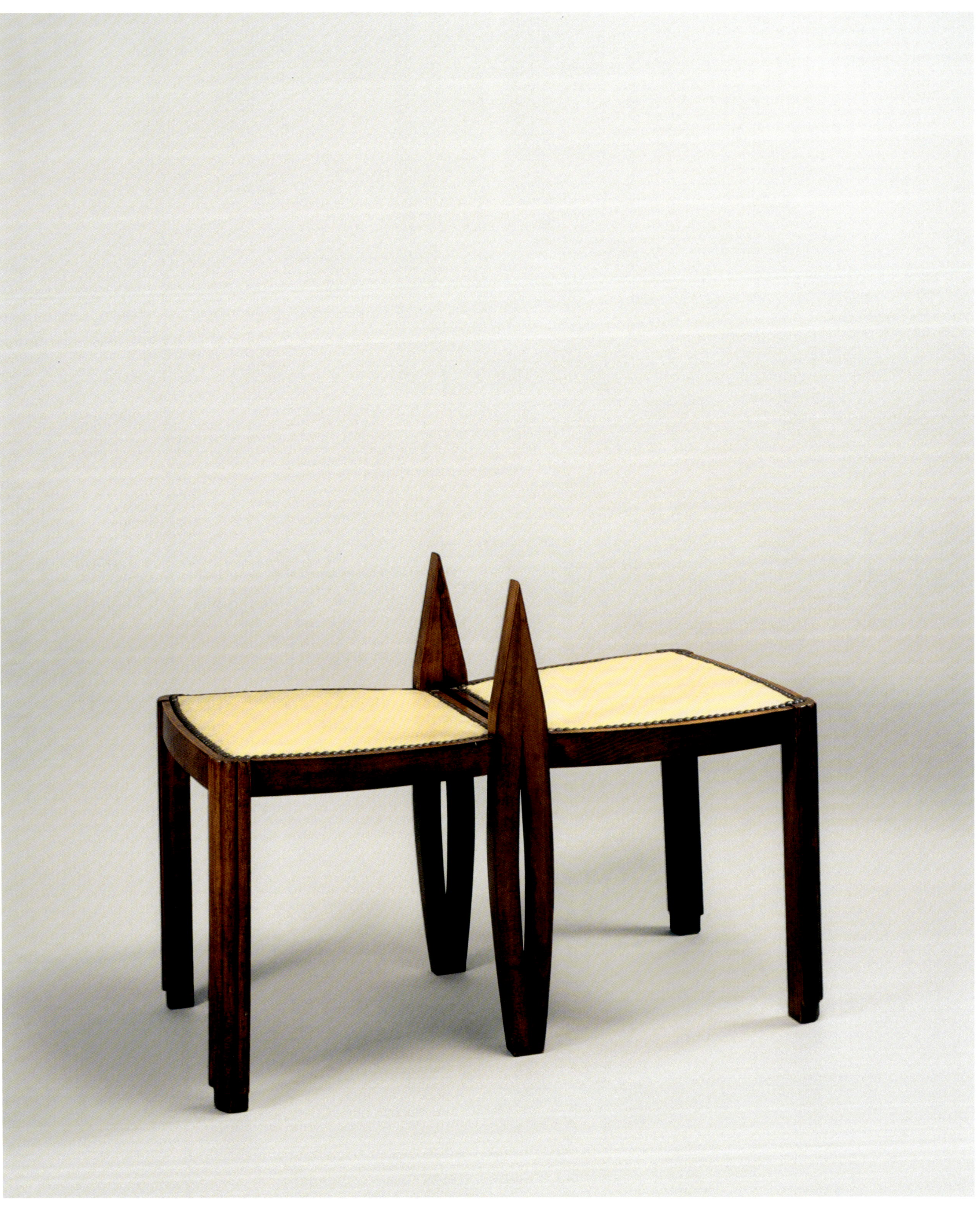

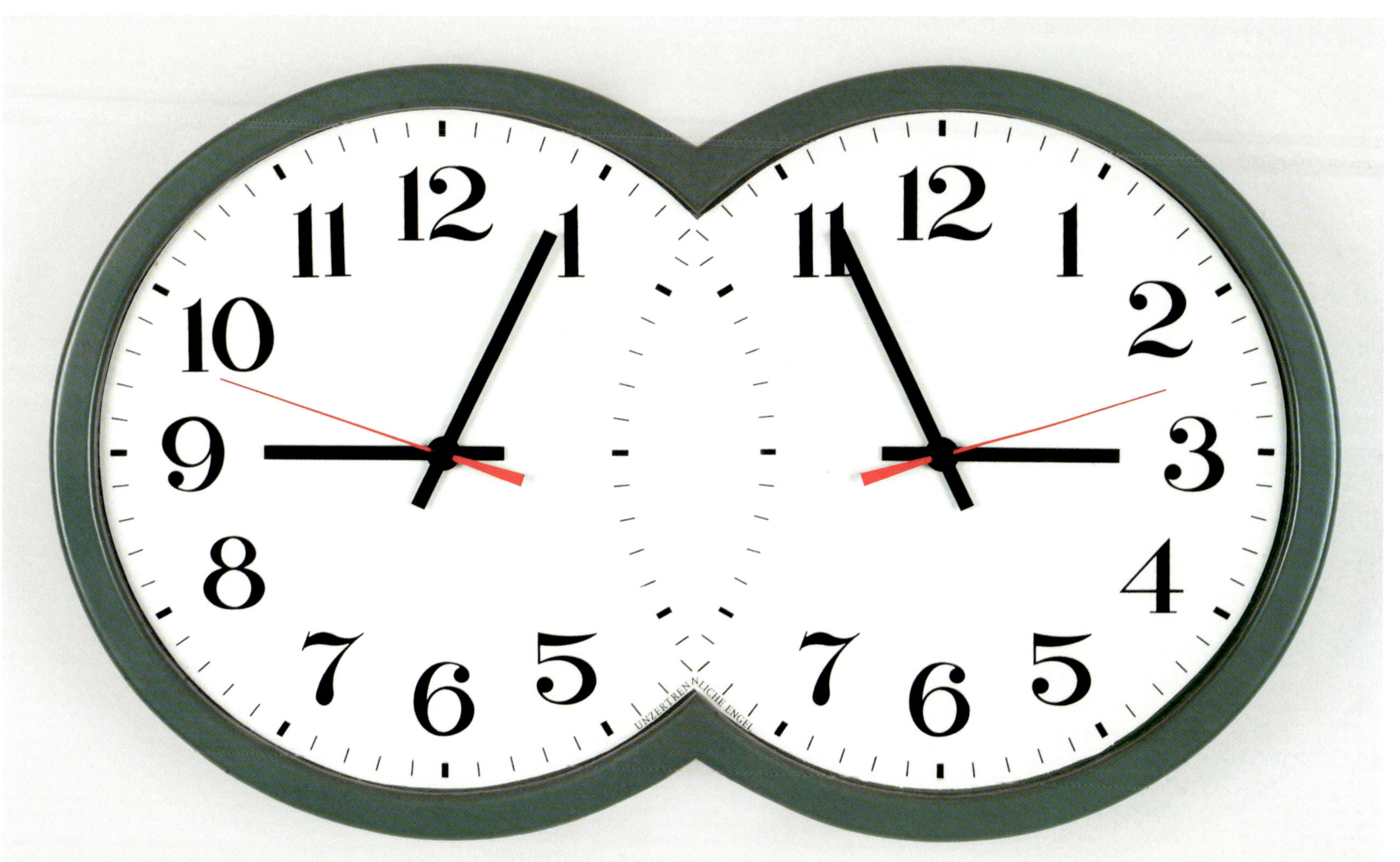
UNZERTRENNLICHE ENGEL

The Inseparables, 2000–2008

Wanas, Sweden
Permanent installation; double-faced clock,
183 × 296 × 35 cm

For the group exhibition *Loss* organized by the Wanas foundation in Sweden, Esther Shalev-Gerz created a new version of the double clock from *Inseparable Angels: An Imaginary House for Walter Benjamin.* Following the exhibition the clock was permanently installed on the facade of the foundation's Kunsthalle, which hosts 49 permanent works designed for public spaces on its site.

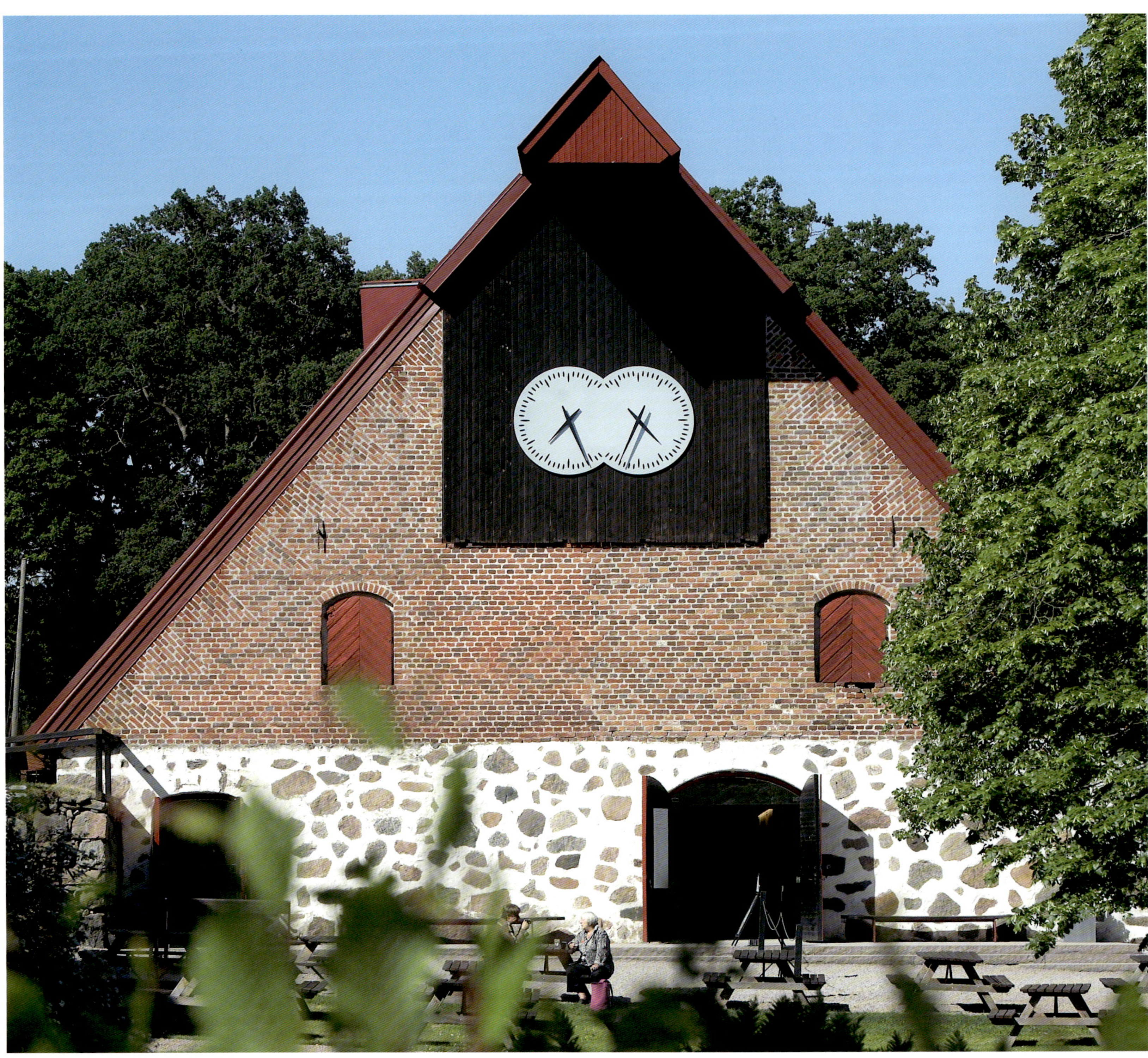

The Judgement. A Philosophical Walk, 2001*

Berlin

In the context of a competition for a monument to the victims of the Nazi military courts, Esther Shalev-Gerz proposed *The Judgement. A Philosophical Walk*. The monument consists of an itinerary marked by luminous Plexiglas flags installed along the route leading to the former place of execution of those condemned to death. One of the two sides of the flags is devoted to the story of the person sentenced, the other to that of the judge, in order to underline the irrefutable link between the two parties.

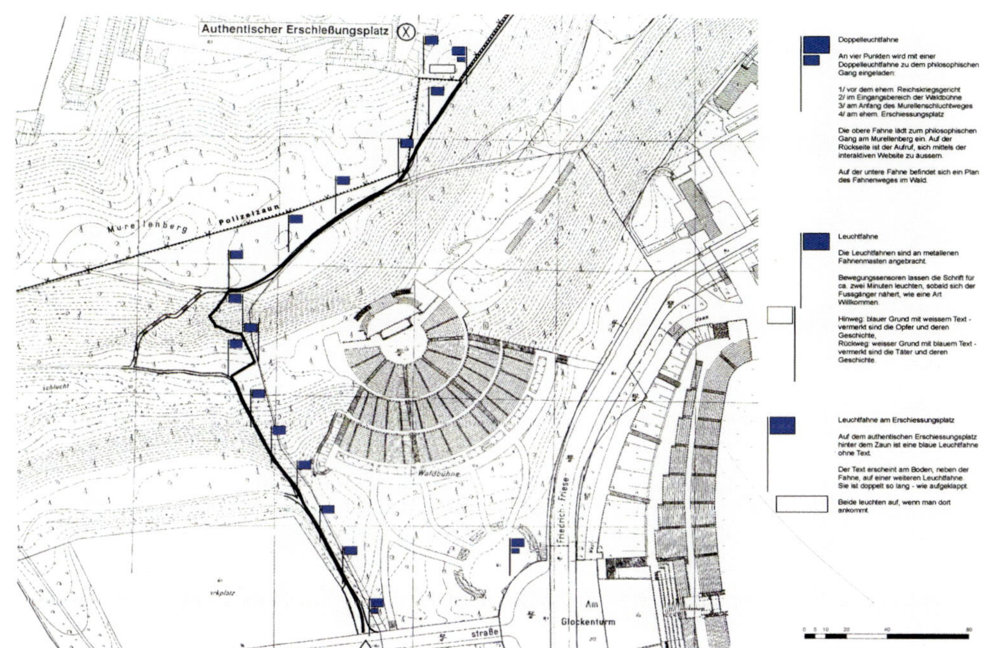

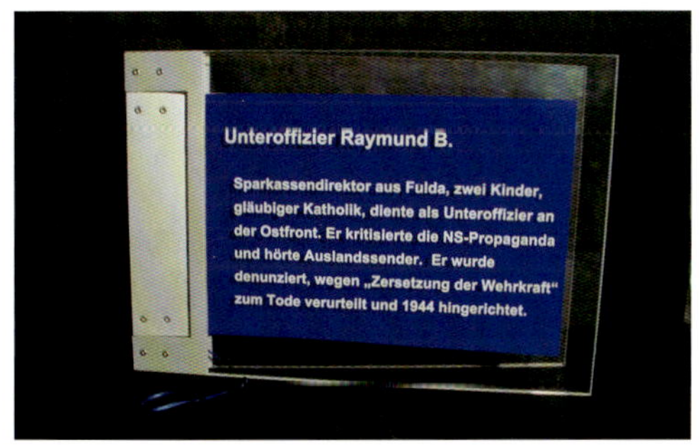

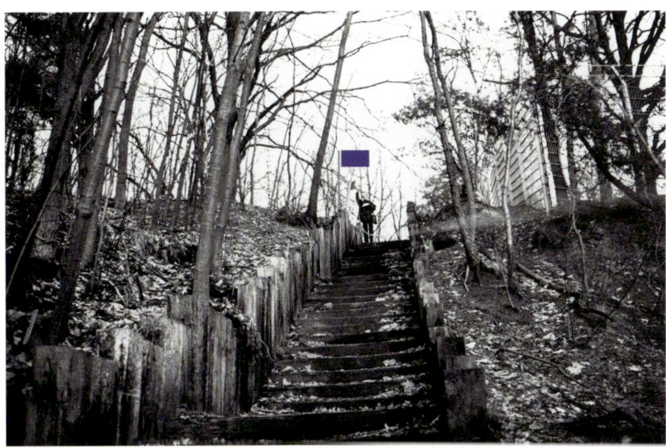

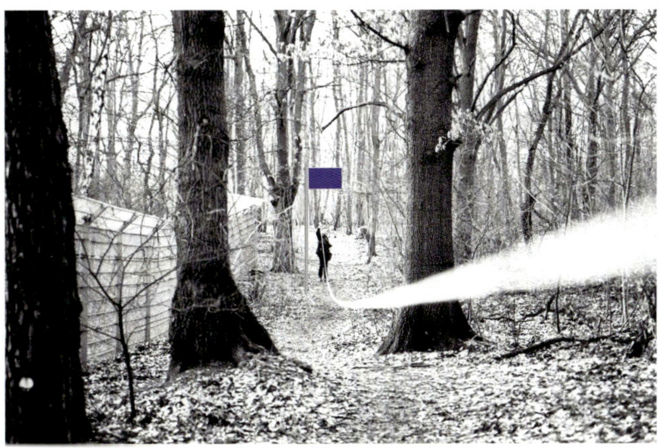

White Out—Between Telling and Listening, 2002

Installation; 2 synchronized video projections, color, sound, 40 min. each; 7 color photographs, Diasec mounted, 80 × 120 cm each; 6 texts laminated onto aluminum, 80 × 120 cm each

White Out—a snowstorm in which one loses one's bearings—is a video installation focusing on Åsa Simma, a woman of Sami origin living in Stockholm. Two videos of Åsa are projected opposite one another, one filmed in Stockholm, the other in her native surroundings in Lapland. In the former, she reacts to quotations conjuring up the Swedish and Sami cultures, in the latter she listens to her own words. A series of photographs from the collection held at the Stockholm history museum, as well as texts, complete the installation.

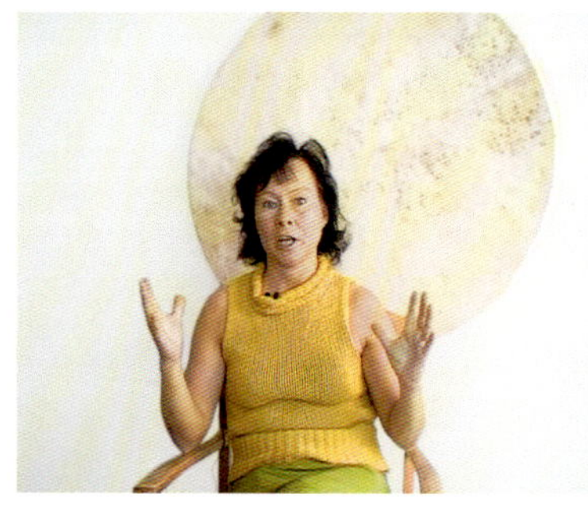
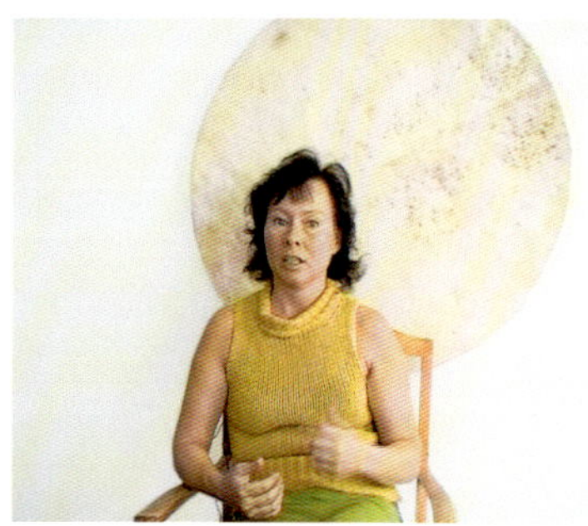
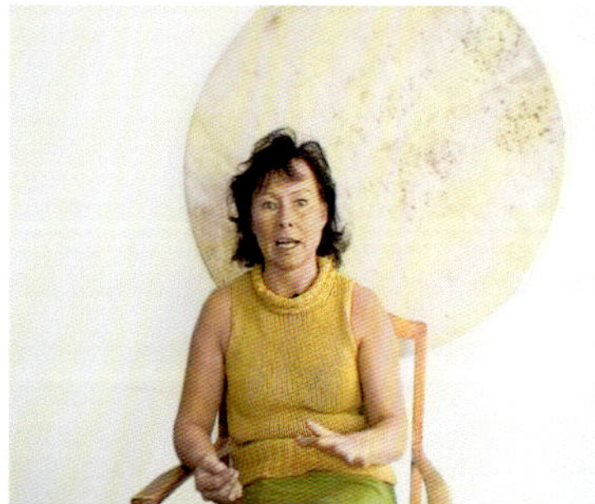
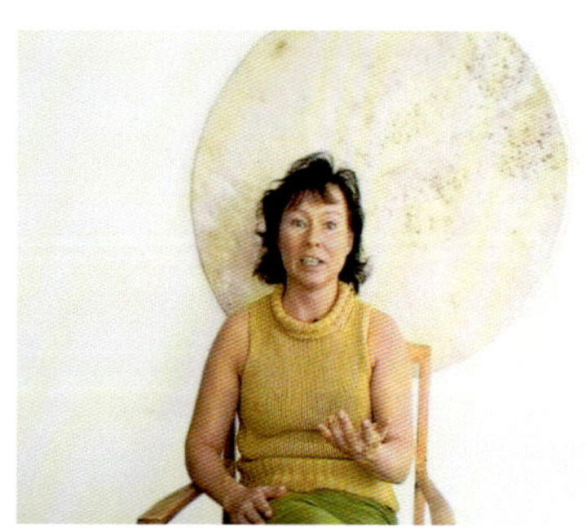

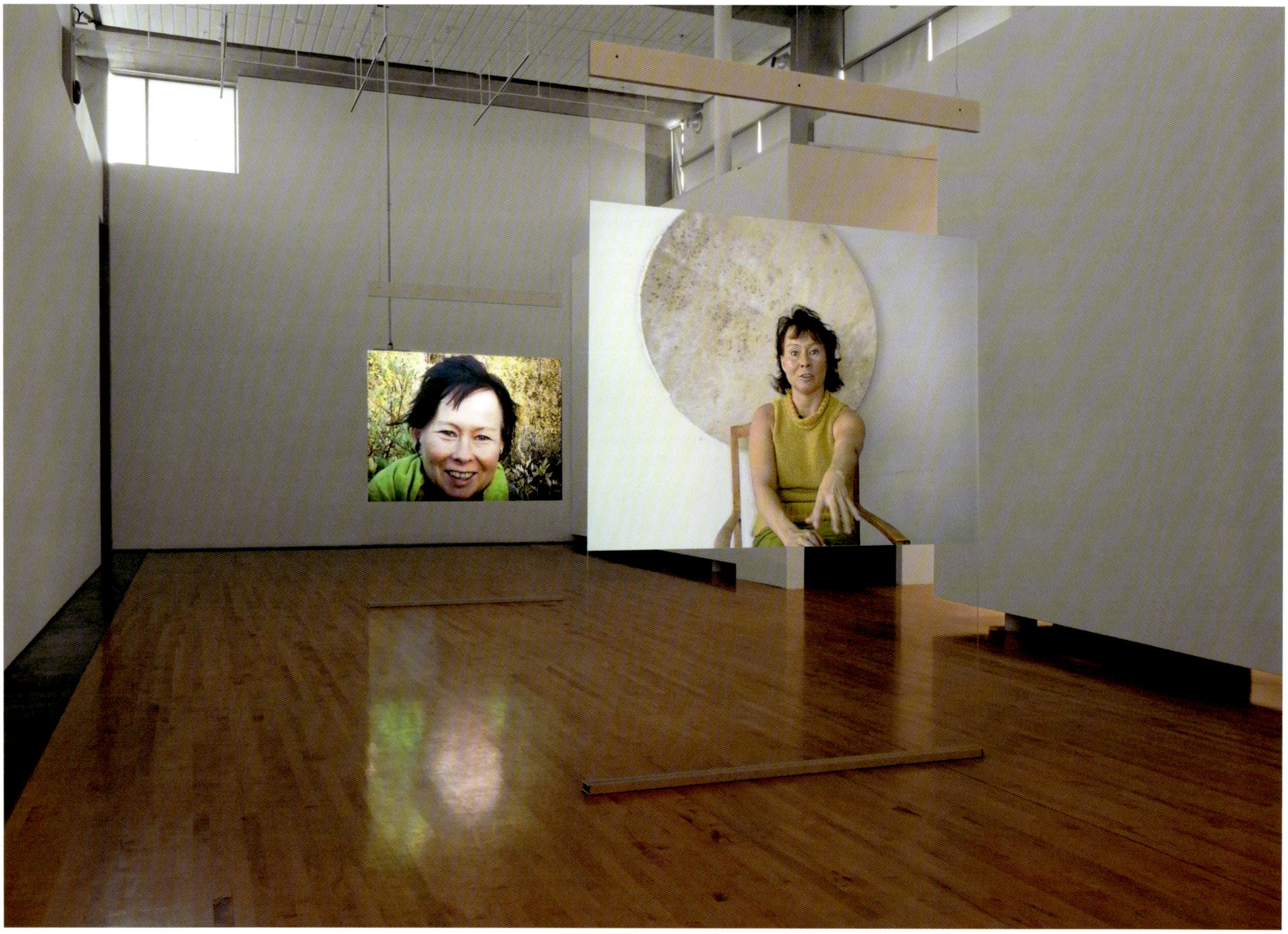

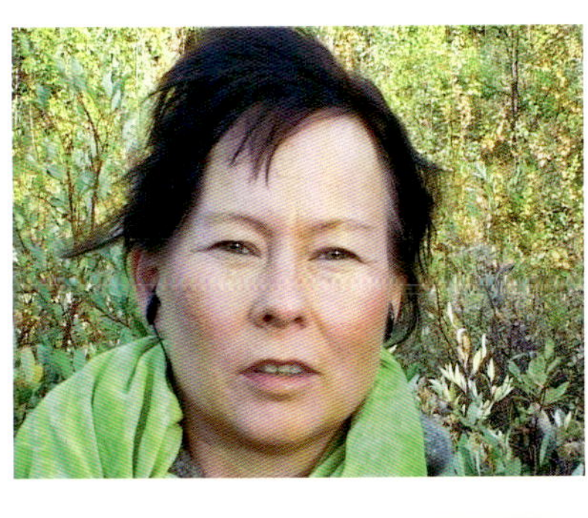
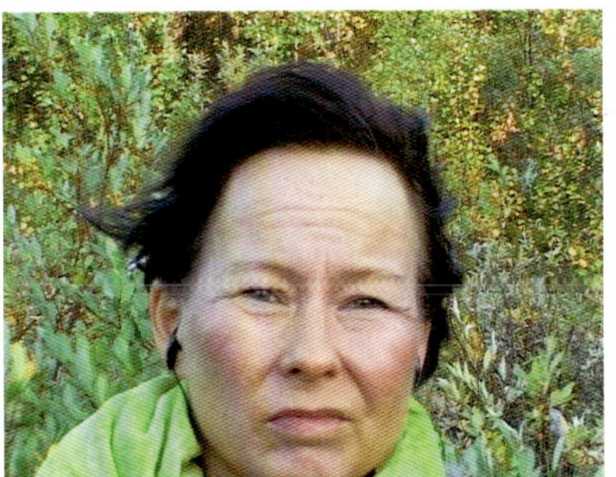
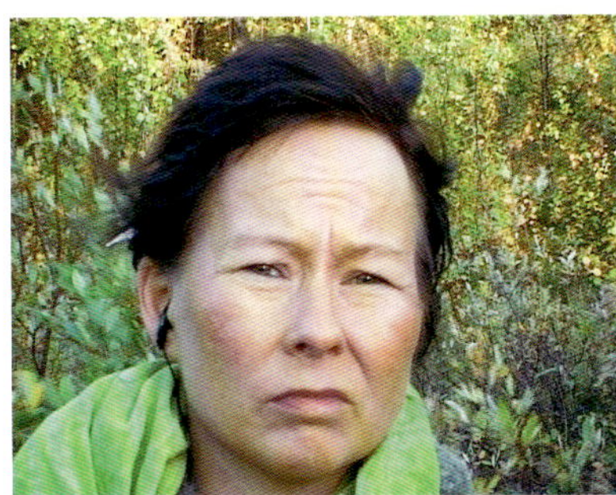
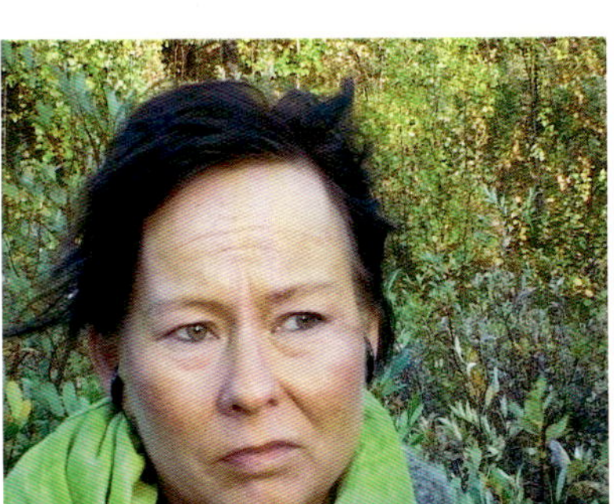

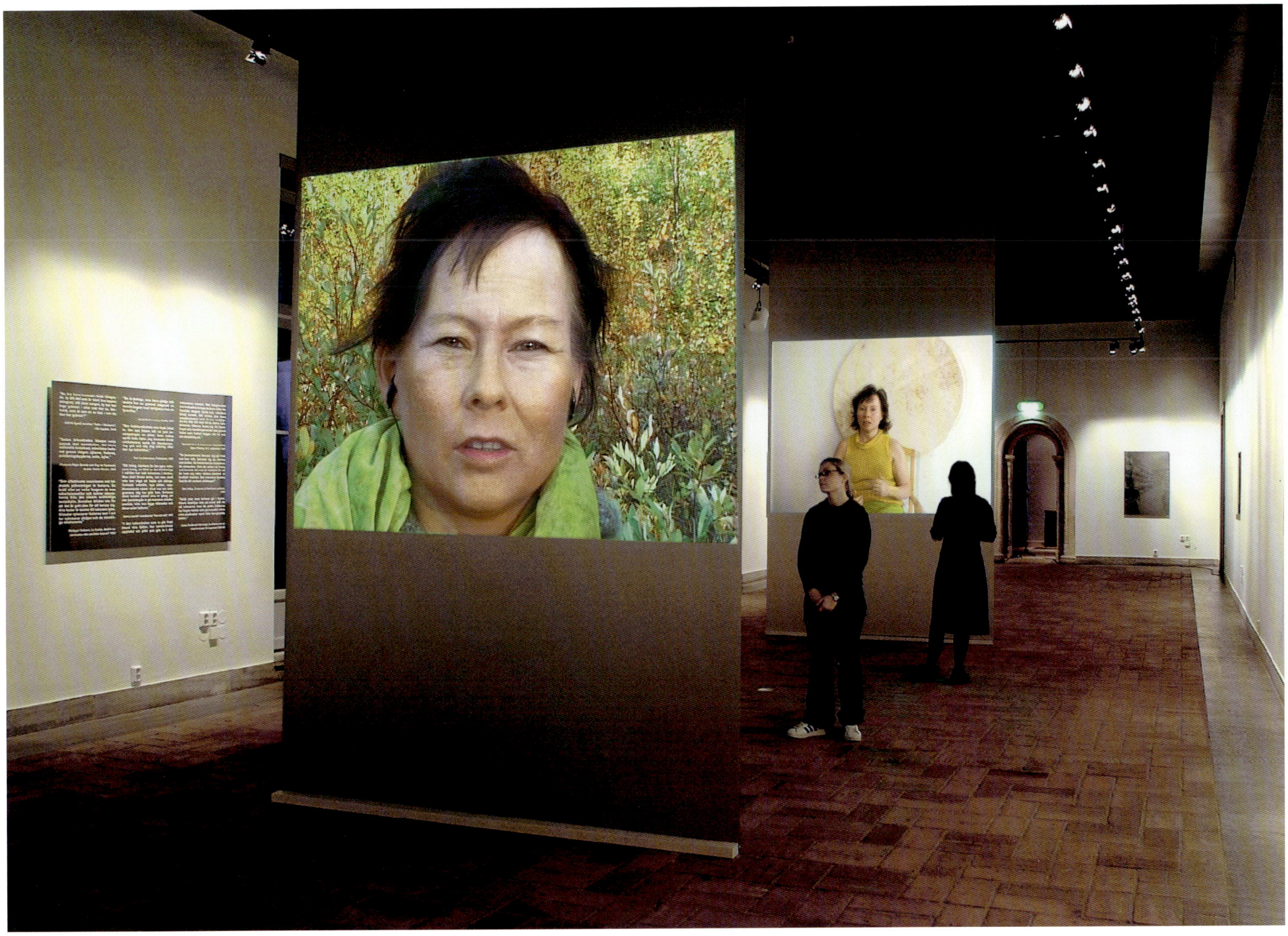

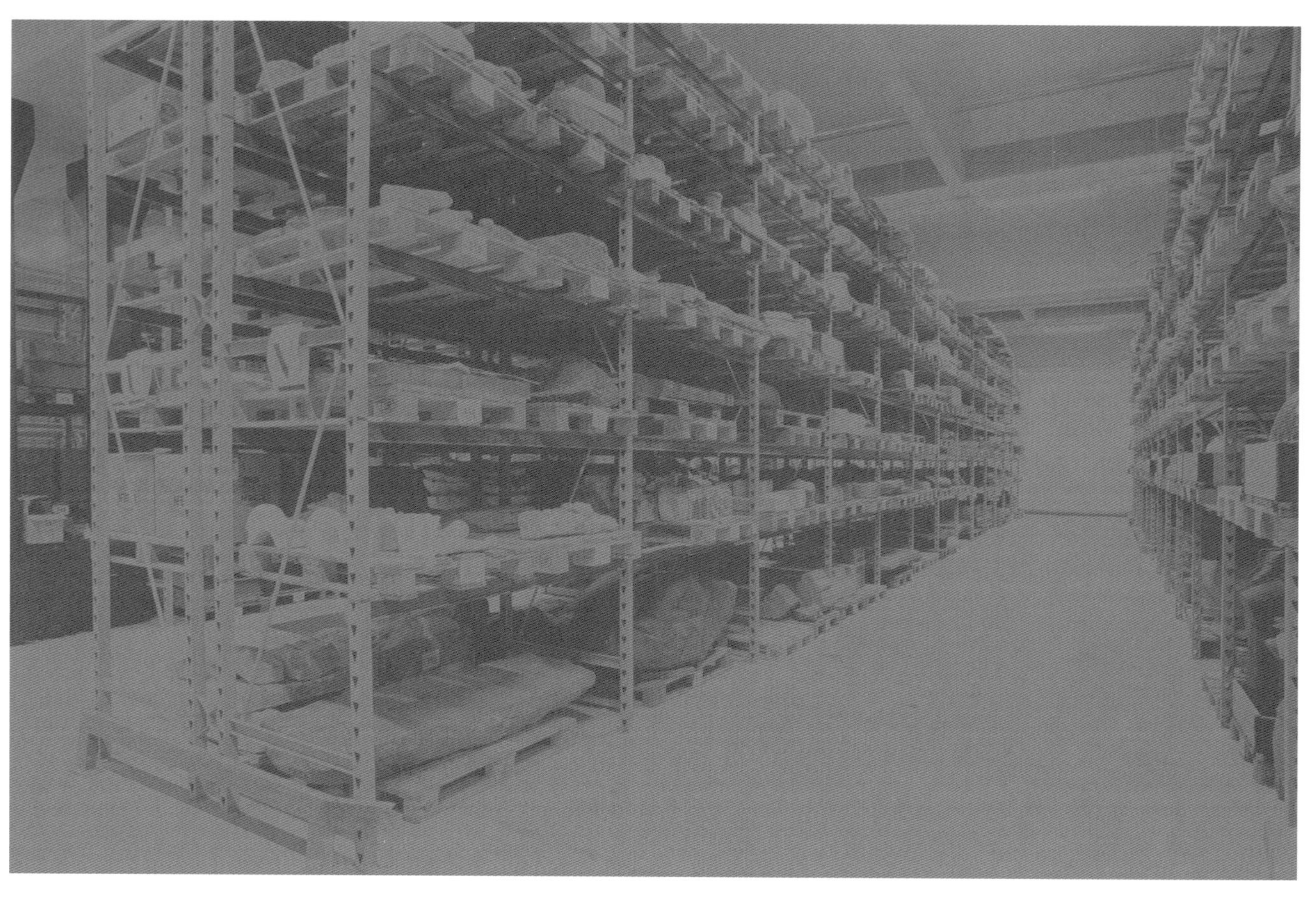

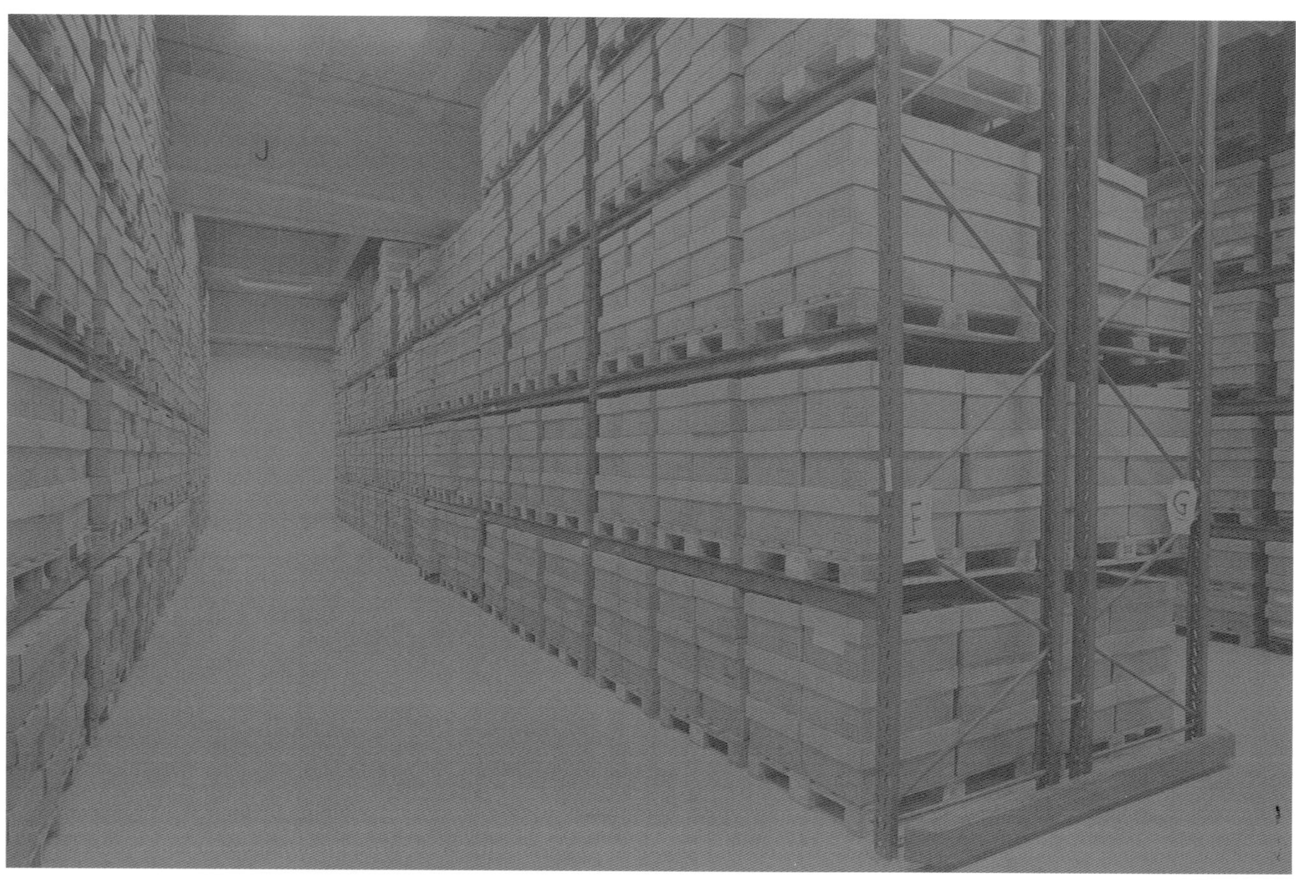
J
G

"They are decent people, but their feelings of joy and sorrow are played out against an ancient background of nervous anxiety as restless as reflected light."

André Bellessort, 1866-1942, French writer, *La Suède*, 1911

"They (Swedish women) become inebriated from pure, clear air, intoxicated with movement, and are radiant. They hold sway over tamed elements. They appear so healthy and so vital that you are grateful to them for fostering within them such elements of potent vivacity. This intensity of physical existence is wondrous to behold!"

Marc Hélys, pseudonym of Marie Léra, 1864-1956, French writer and journalist, *A travers le féminisme suédois*, 1906

"Now, his five thousand reindeer are dispersed, because all that is big for the Lapp will be dispersed; all but the sorrow, because it has no limits - or what do you think, you [Swede] who is one among us – do you think it has limits?"

Alfhild Agrell, 1849-1923, Swedish writer, in the short story "Pako – the Lord", in *A Lappish Book*, 1919

"A force, stronger than the force of nature, a breath of the inexplicable in the world, has put the women in movement. One shall understand this, and one shall not dare to check or close. Yellowed fields of wheat, new cities, blooming states, show us where the road of the emigrants has passed. Maybe Woman shall also once show, that when she penetrated the working field of Man, she wanted to place wilderness and deserts below culture."

Selma Lagerlöf, 1858-1940, Swedish writer, in her speech of women's right to vote, "Home and State", 1911

"The functional era had just blown in. The style of the new times was the scrape off of styles. Its naked language was facts. I immediately translated the language of architecture into the language of literature. I walked around looking for the new Man."

Ivar Lo-Johansson, 1901-1990, Swedish writer, *The Writer* (novel), 1957

"Men as well as women wear trousers. The sexes are not differentiated more than that women wear longer coats over their other clothes and that they have certain red decorations on their heads and belts decorated with tin."

Johan Ferdinand Korningh, *The Story of a Missionary Trip to Lappland 1659-60*

"For centuries every Swede has had to wrestle with solitude, a major national complex; the solitude of individuals isolated by forests, lakes, rivers, depopulation, snow, cold."

François-Régis Bastide, 1926-1996, French writer and diplomat, and Guy de Faramond, French reporter for "Le Monde" in Sweden from 1968 to 1974, *Suède*, Petite Planète, 1954

"In the cultural movement that now passes our mountains, the Lapp Woman has apprehended her duty and joined the working force. With devotion and loyalty they sacrifice a lot for the future happiness and prosperity of the Lapps. To mention all the achievements of these Lapp women is impossible. They all do their share for the great events. The ideas transform into actions and the actions become the foundation on which the people as a collective build its life and its development."

Gustav Z. Hedenström, Swedish journalist, in *Samefolkets Egen Tidning*, No 3, September 1927

"The most effective form of exorcism in the face of the harshness of the climate is recourse to traditional celebrations. For the duration of an evening or an entire week they act as a sort of safety valve and liberate people from their melancholy introversion. At these events the Swedes do not drink for pleasure, but in order to get drunk. All these festivals are linked to the cycle of nature. The climate regulates the festivals, and they in their turn regulate human relationships."

Philippe Ysebaert, *La Suède, Modèle ou caricature des sociétés futures*, 1992

"The women, who just recently have become majority citizens, with social duties and citizens rights, must now also individually and collectively make their contributions. […] The safeguard of the peace in an unsettled world, isn't that worth our efforts? The indifference and the passive attitude of women is one of the foundations of the spreading and strength of militarism."

"The International Socialistic Day of Women", Manifest in *Morgonbris*, Social Democratic Magazine for Women, No 3, March 1931

Does Your Image Reflect Me?, 2002

Installation; 4 synchronized video projections, color, 2 with sound, 2 silent, 38 min. each; 11 color photographs, Diasec mounted, 8 of which 40 × 90 cm and 3 of which 100 × 150 cm; 1 silkscreen, 74 × 100 cm

Pursuing her research into the gap between telling and listening, Esther Shalev-Gerz makes a double portrait, that of a Polish Jewish woman who survived the Bergen-Belsen concentration camp, located not far from Hannover, and that of a German woman who spent the war years in that city. Each of them tells her story, and they listen to one another via interposed images on their television sets. Their stories are about the same period, but different places. The installation places the viewer at the intersecting point of these spoken accounts.

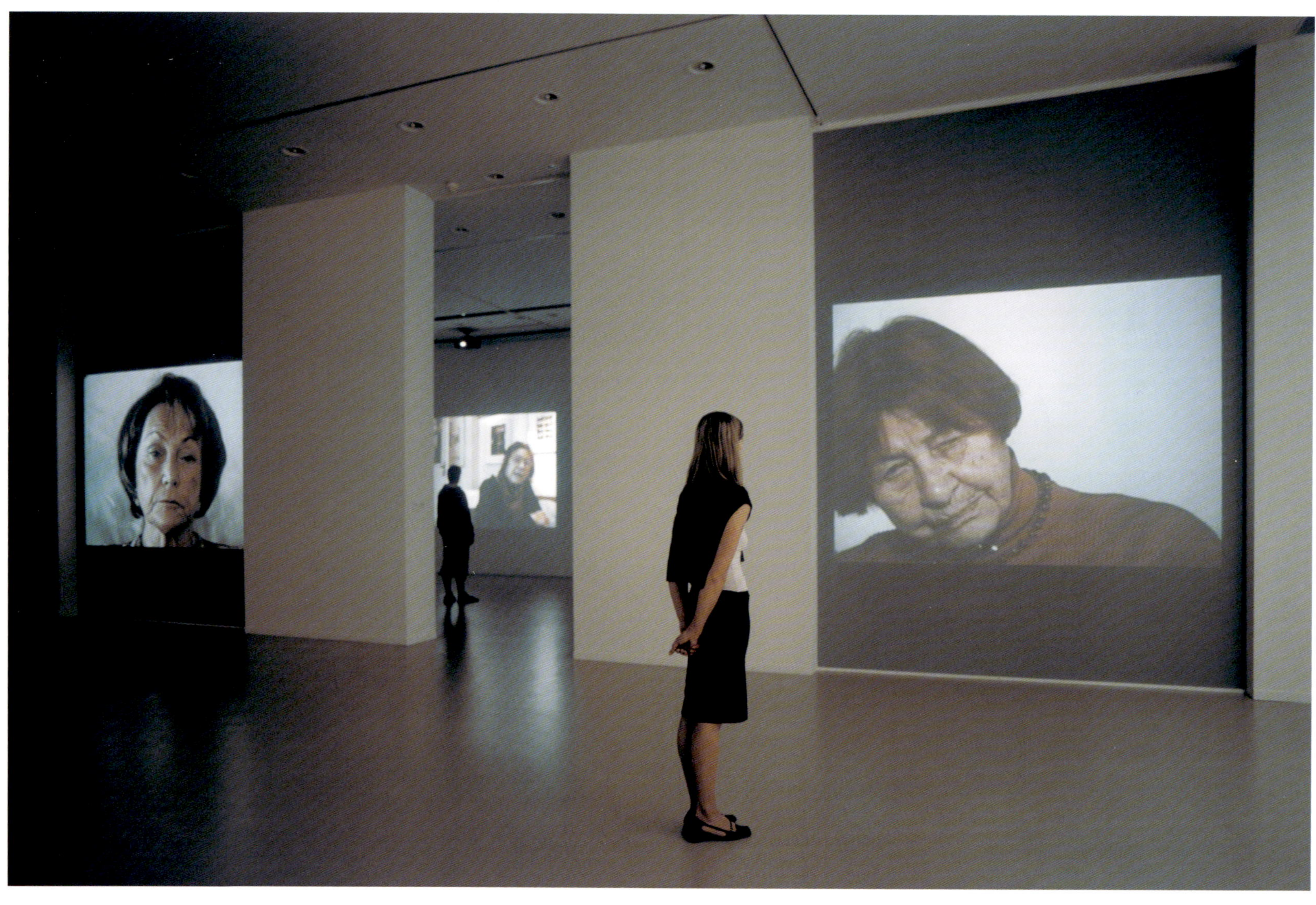

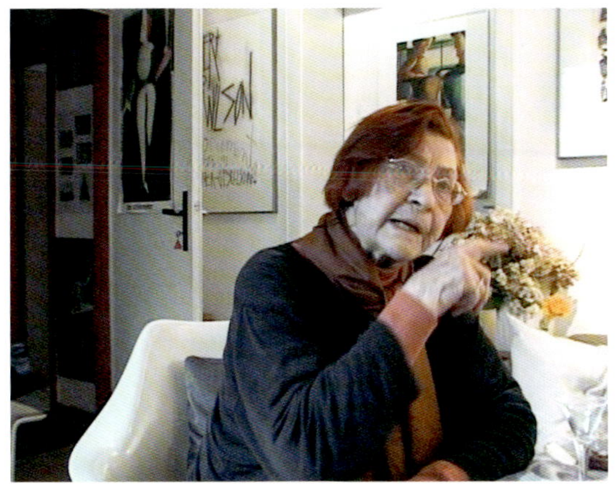
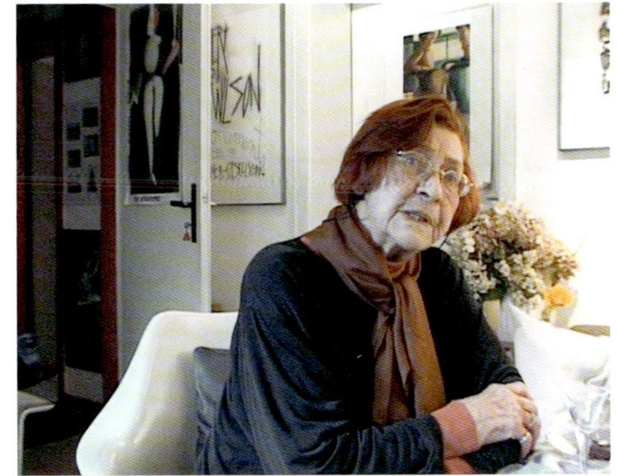
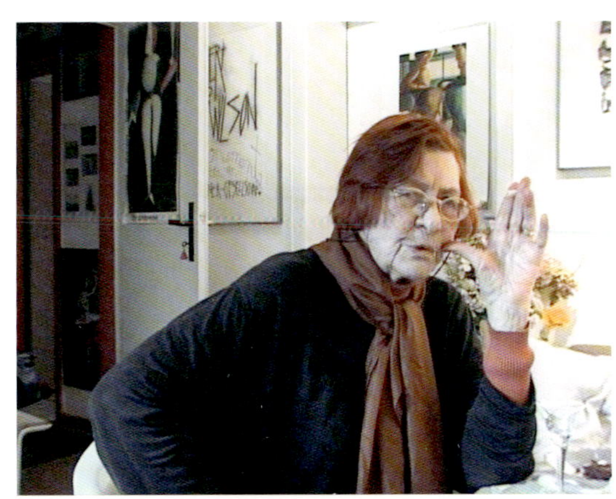
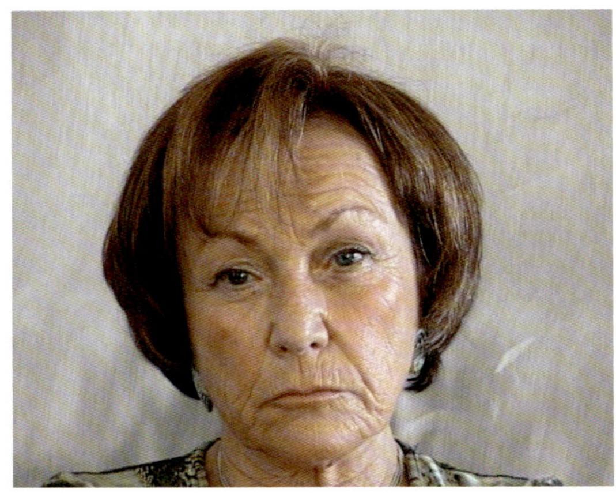
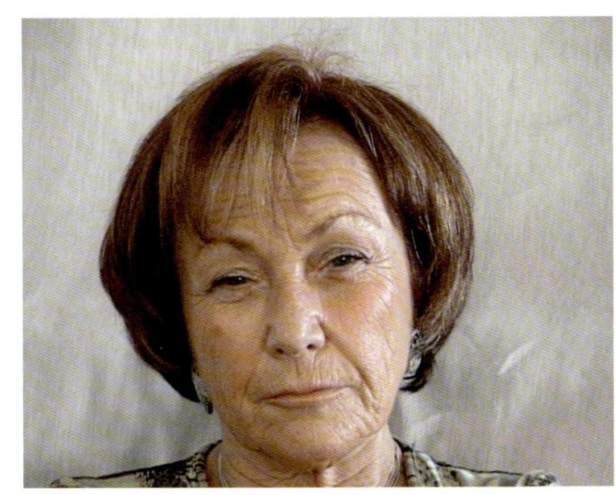
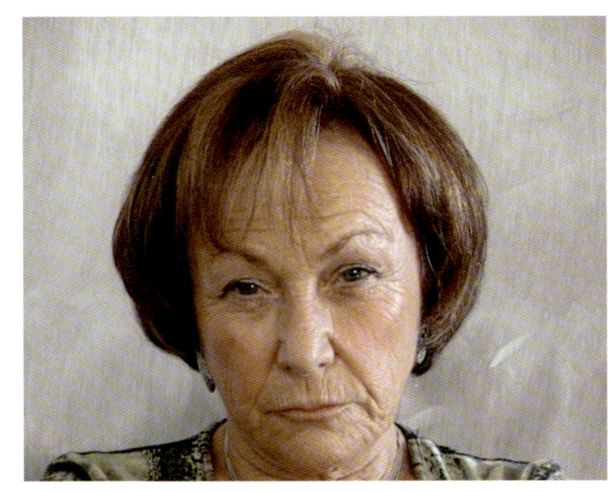
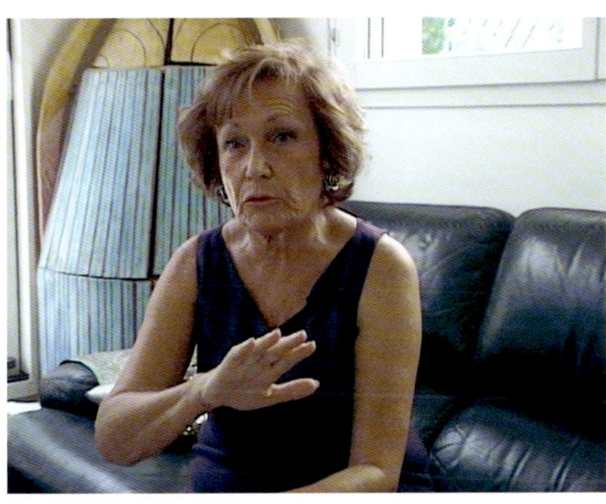
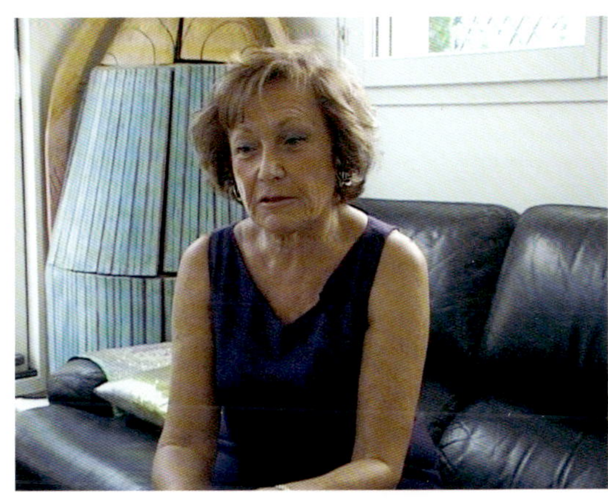
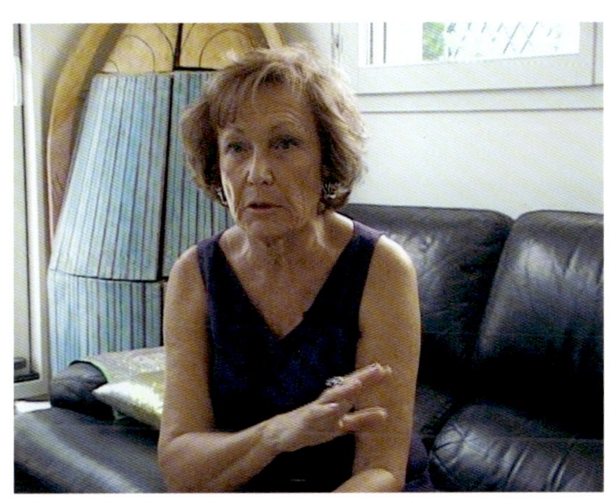
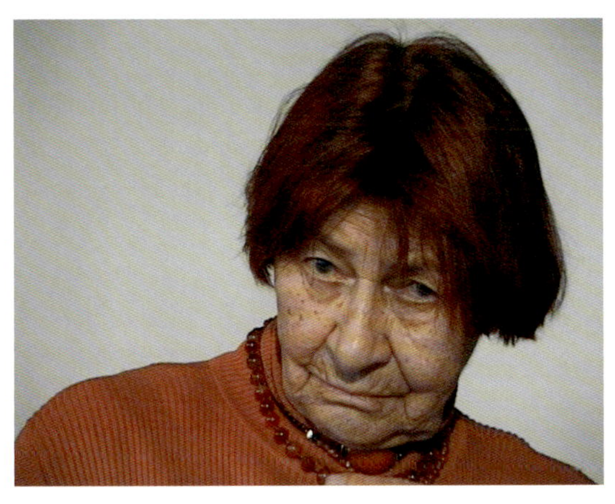
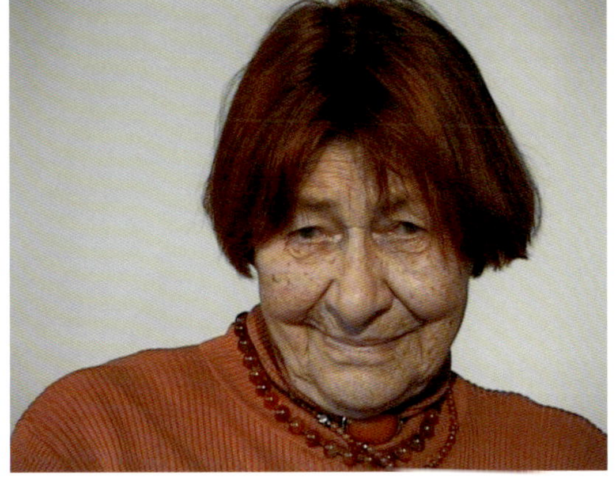
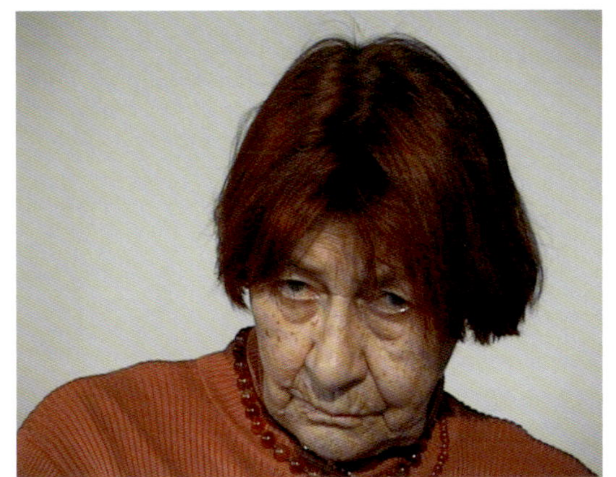

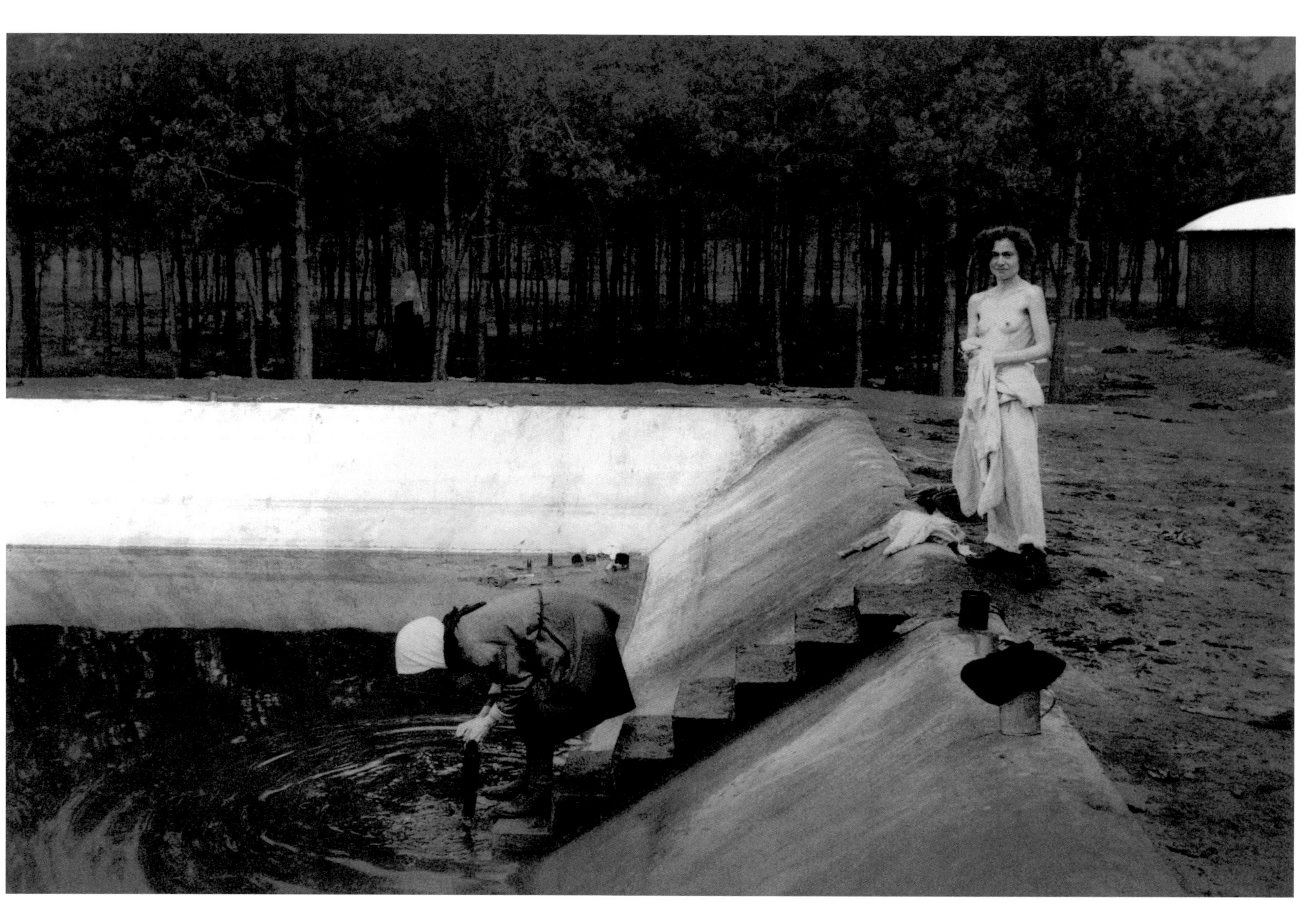

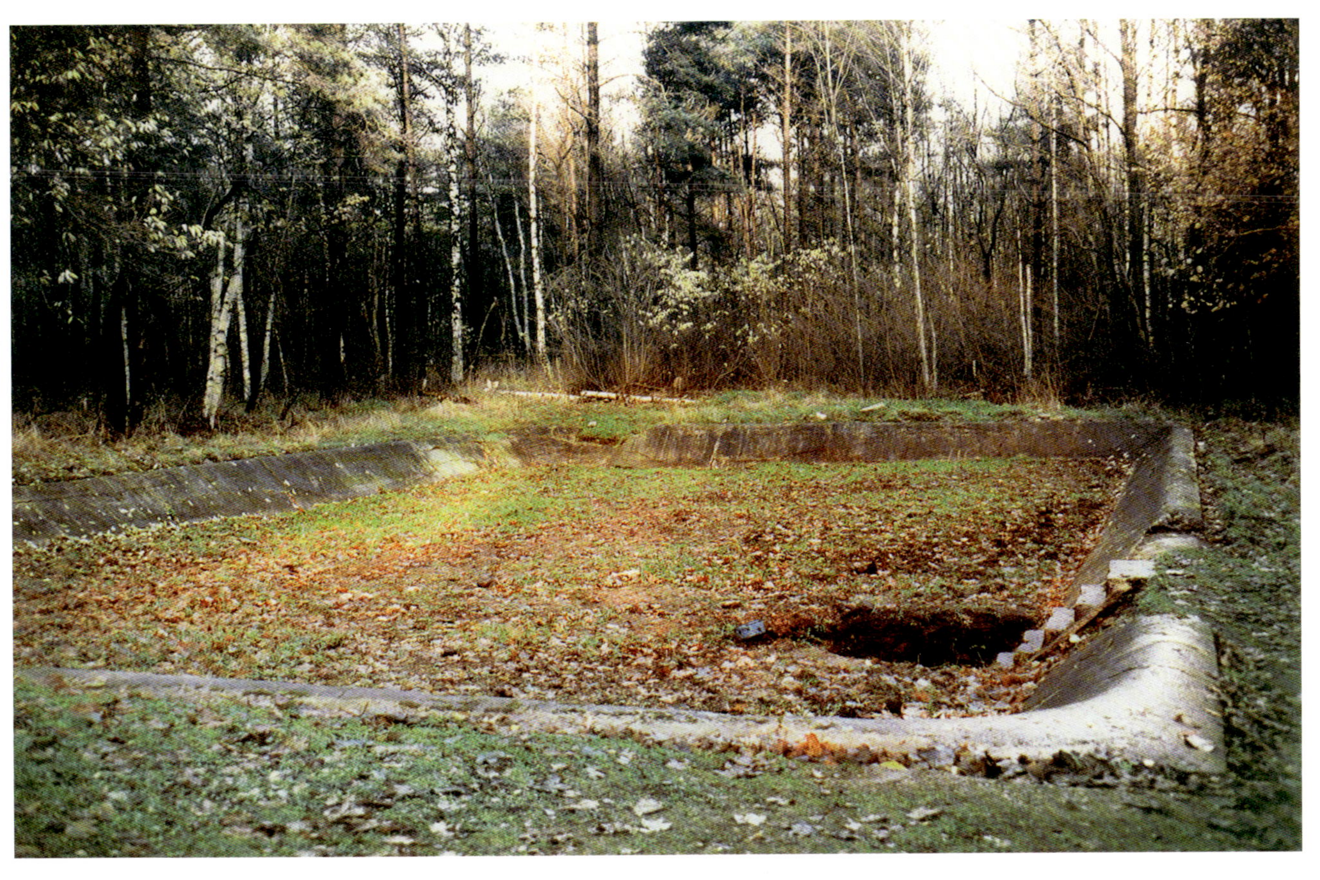

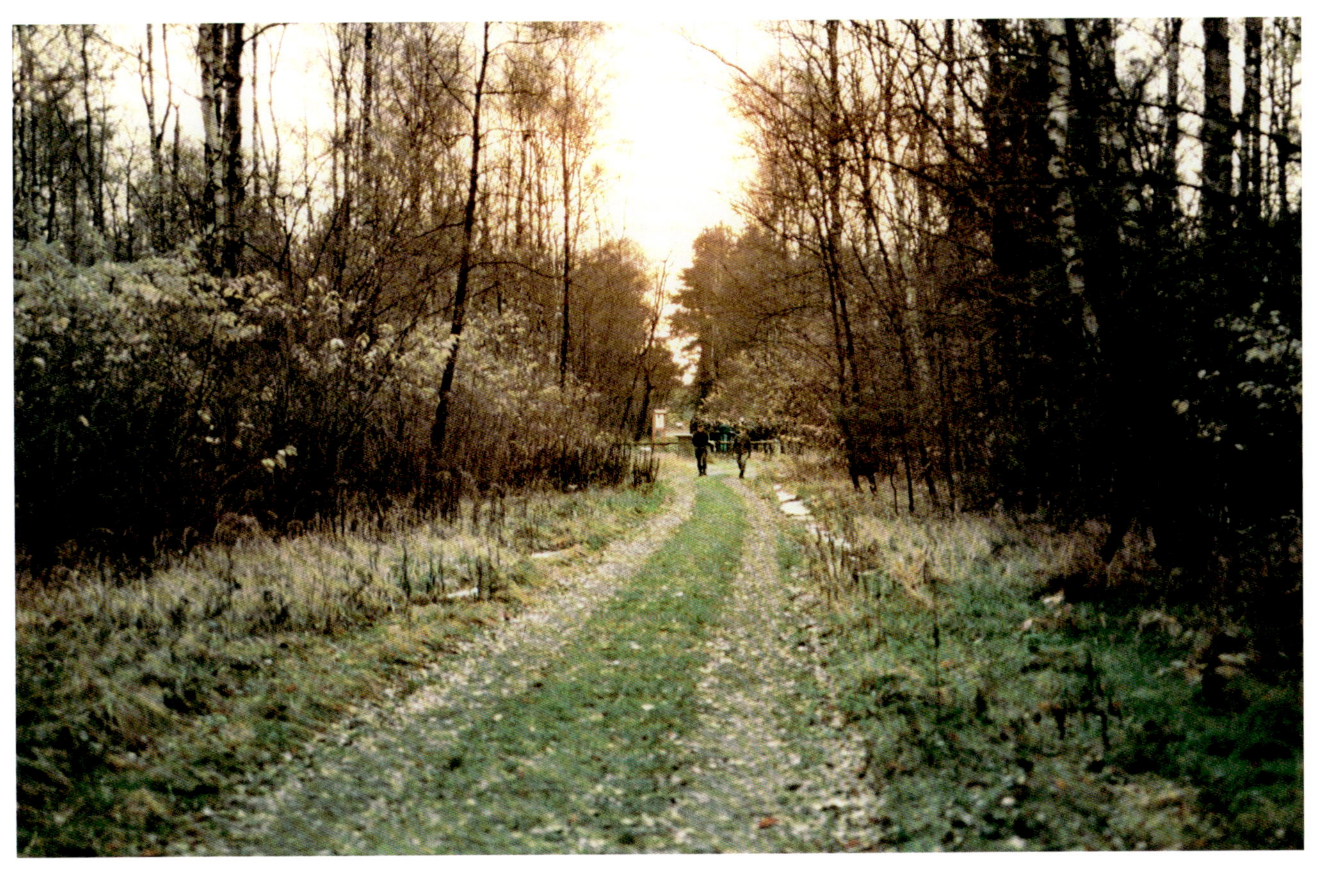

A Thread, 2003–2006

Glasgow
Permanent installation; 10 steel shelters with canopies above them, 300 × 200 × 200 cm each

A Thread is a permanent installation made in collaboration with the recently re-housed inhabitants of the Castlemilk district in the south of Glasgow. The participants were invited to choose their favorite views in the park, which previously belonged to Castlemilk House, and which is adjacent to the new housing. A circular bench covered by a canopy designed by the residents was installed at each viewing point, so drawing an imaginary line through the park.

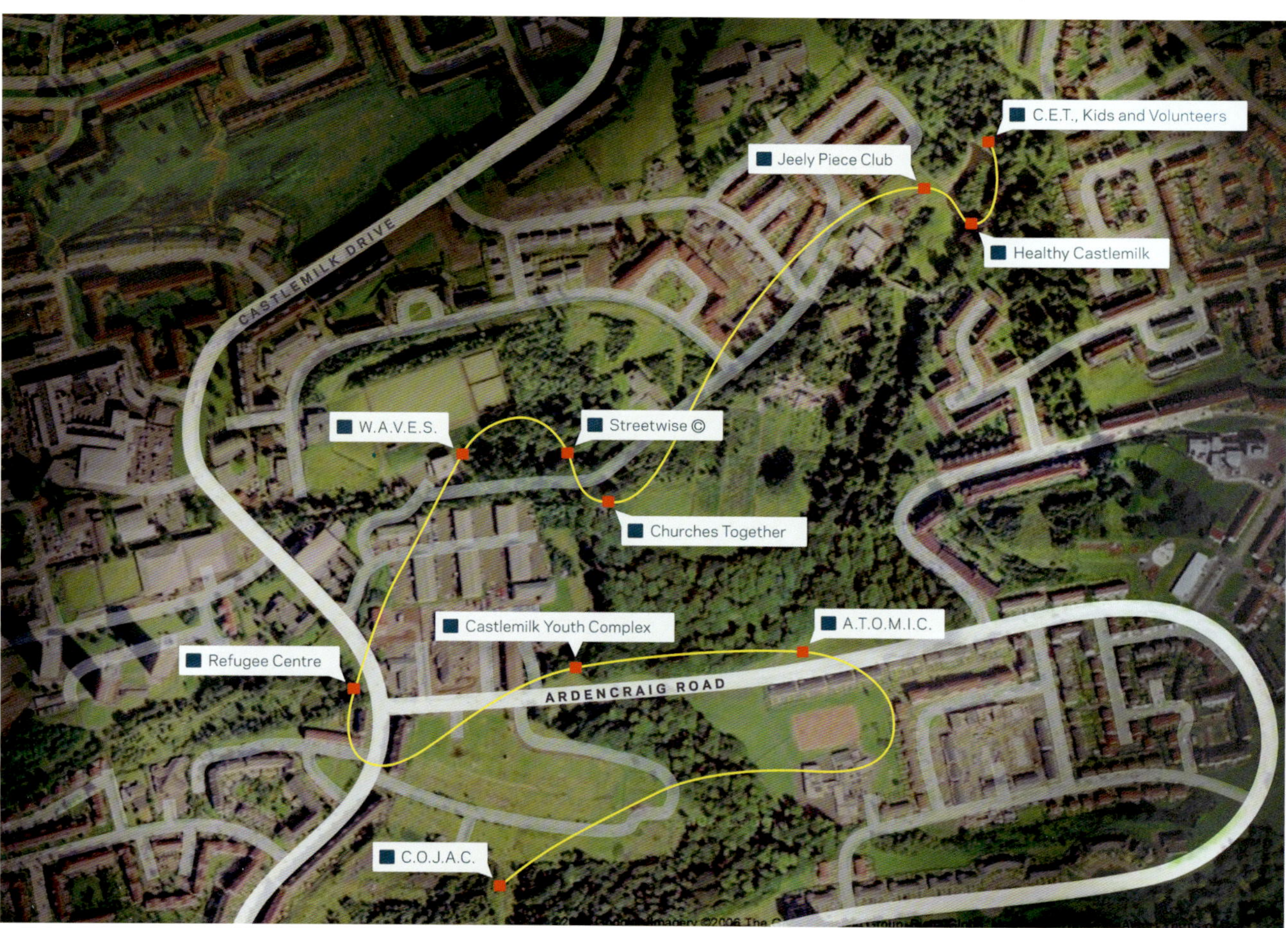

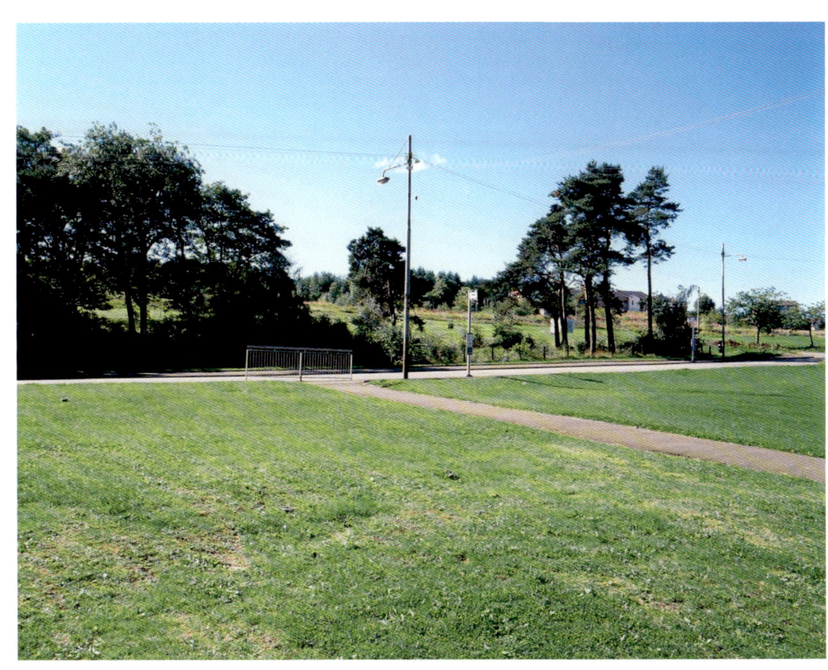
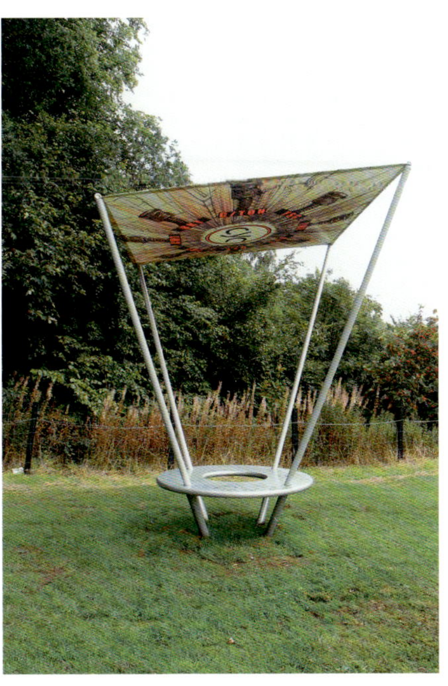
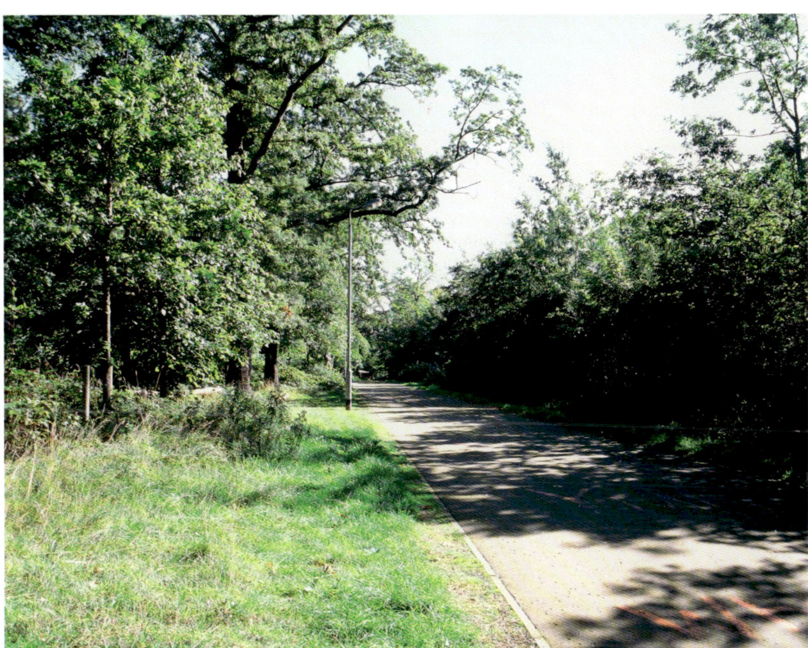
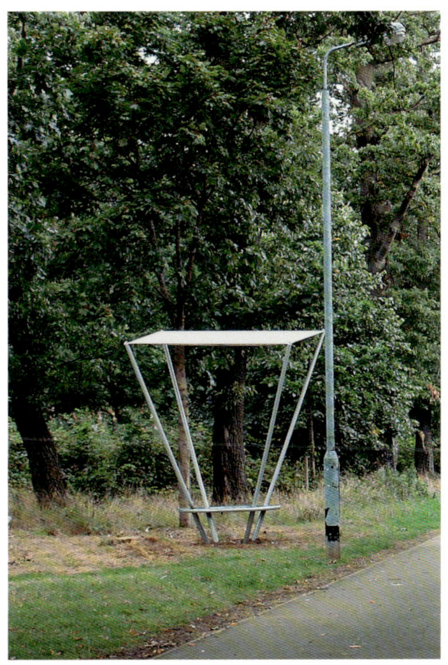
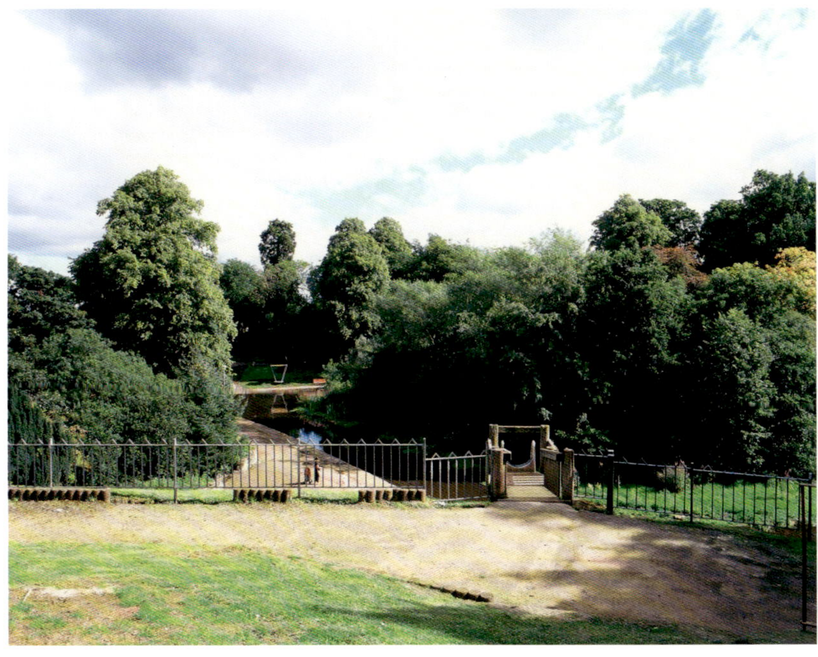
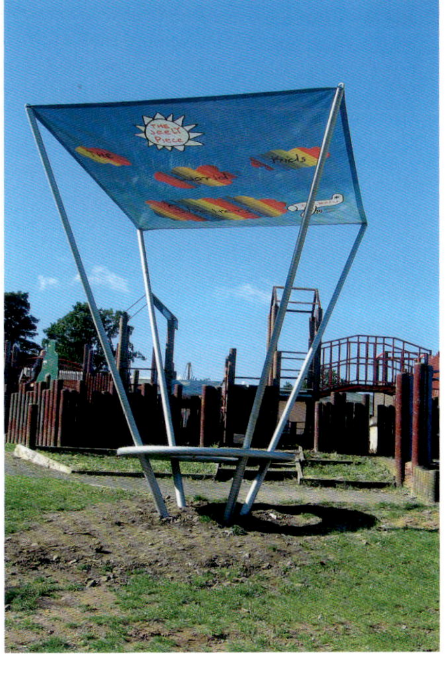

THE "BLANCS SOUCIS"* OF OUR HISTORY GEORGES DIDI-HUBERMAN

"Le blanc souci de notre toile" [The white anxiety of our sail] is the last line of a sonnet written in 1890 and entitled *Salut.* Stéphane Mallarmé placed this poem as an epigraph to his "complete collection of poetry," a collection he was almost finished arranging when death interrupted him in 1898; it was published by Edmond Deman in 1899. Mallarmé wanted this unassuming poem, initially entitled *Toast,* to be set in a small typeface—a preference Deman and subsequent publishers chose to disregard. When it came down to it, it was only about a modest *greeting*: welcoming the listener or the reader, opening the door of the collection. To do so, it was a matter of *rising to one's feet* to "offer this toast while standing," as Mallarmé writes, echoing a toast drunk at the end of a gathering of friends. For through this greeting it was a matter of *recognizing* in others, whoever they were, a shared "white anxiety," which the poet made rhyme with these three words: "Solitude, récif, étoile" [solitude, reef, starry veil].[1] As if the uttering of a poem—or the execution of a partita, or the composition of a picture—was specifically about that recognition of a common concern from the "solitude" of each individual, the "reef" of the work produced, and the "star"—or constellation—that is revealed in our thoughts by looking at it, reading it, or listening to it.

It seems that Esther Shalev-Gerz composes her works—to be looked at, read, and listened to—from a similar gesture. She rises to her feet to give a toast, she works in order to recognize, in herself as in others (for her works never fail to have specific interlocutors), something like a space populated by the *white anxieties of our history.* An installation she came up with in 2005 particularly prompted my desire to write, or, to put it another way, my anxiety, my own "solicitudes," in relation to history and to art. It was entitled *Between Listening and Telling: Last Witnesses, Auschwitz 1945–2005,* and was presented in a huge space in the town hall in Paris, between January and March 2005, as part of the commemorations of the liberation of the camp at Auschwitz.[2] The artist was called on to "put into space," to *exhibit the words* of 60 or so survivors of the Nazi camps: they gave testimony of their experiences in front of the video cameras of four teams of interviewers coordinated by Bénédicte Rochas. The testimony gathered varied in length, according to the requirements of each narrator: between two and nine hours were recorded for each person.

But can we be made into *spectators* of such lengths of time, such words? Is exhibiting spoken words—and specifically words relating to this extreme history—not to threaten them in their very existence, exhibiting them so that they become pure forms devoid of meaning? Is it not consigning them to no longer being addressed to anyone at all, no longer affecting anyone? There was a great risk involved: the risk that an artistic gesture, however elegant it might be, might render this collection of terrible stories inaccessible—or at the very least secondary. Were we not condemned to the bad dilemma of "under-exposing" these words (understating them as documentary epiphenomena of the work itself), or conversely "over-exposing" them (talking them up as archival fetishes), two symmetrical ways of rendering something both *inaudible* and *unwatchable*? Archives as we well know are fashionable in the postmodern art world. But it is very often at the cost of being referred back to an ambiguous use value: either intimidating and auratic, or decorative and unusable—inaccessible in either case.

Well Esther Shalev-Gerz's main concern or *souci*, totally consistent with the ethical and political dimension of her work over the long term, was in fact not to "take" this corpus of spoken words in order to shape it for her own personal use and into her own personal "style," but to *return* it to everyone, to all of us. In short, it was a question of *giving a form to the common good* henceforth constituted by these testimonies that had been brought together. It is not irrelevant that the artist's installation occupied a *communal place*, by which I mean the large hall in the Hôtel de Ville in Paris, and not a private space or an art gallery. Esther Shalev-Gerz's work very much questioned a *res publica* there, that public matter constituted by all of the testimony collected, those fragments of our shared history, before any *res artistica* in the form of a matter for "art buyers," experts or aesthetes. *Between Listening and Telling* is a work of art, quite undoubtedly, but it was a work first conceived outside her own "specialty," her professional body, or her "milieu": hence a "republican" work in the literal meaning of the term.

Not only was the space communal, but in addition Esther Shalev-Gerz had wanted to preserve its usual lighting level, although it was also a question of putting video images in a situation where they could be watched. Would it not have been more effective—and spectacular—to have darkness around these images, as is so often the case in our museums of contemporary art? But the artist wanted to proceed to something like a *communal sharing* of the testimonies, the witnesses, and the *témoignaires* (those to whom the testimonies were addressed), without anything intervening to reduce the *possibilities of coexistence* and meeting between all those involved. So it was that the 60 or so testimonies could be viewed in their entirety in the hall at the Hôtel de Ville at some 60 work stations supplied with individual headphones, so that each viewer or listener had the opportunity to find him/herself, as if one to one, *confronting the image and spoken words of a single witness*, for the actual duration of his/her story. At the same time, the arrangement of the tables devised by Esther Shalev-Gerz—a serpentine arrangement, with each concave curve being occupied by a listening station—placed virtually every viewer *opposite the body and silence of the témoignaire,* or spectator positioned on the other side of the table. Through this very simple device, each person was thus simultaneously kept apart in his/her viewing and listening, but in the communal exhibition space.

[*Translator's note: the word "blanc" can mean white, blank, or space; the word "souci" can mean concern, solicitude, care, or worry. In some cases I have left these words in French as otherwise the author's argument would not make sense.]

1
Stéphane Mallarmé, "Salut" (1893), in Henri Mondor and Georges Jean-Aubry (eds.), *Stéphane Mallarmé. Œuvres complètes,* Gallimard, Paris 1945 (1974 edn.), p. 27. For an English translation of this poem, see http://www.poetryintranslation.com/PITBR/French/Mallarme.htm#_Toc223495070. Last accessed July 4, 2012.

2
Entre l'écoute et la parole: Derniers témoins. Auschwitz 1945-2005, Paris, Mairie de Paris – Mémorial de la Shoah, 2005. See Stefanie Baumann, "Œuvres," in *Esther Shalev-Gerz,* Éditions du Jeu de Paume/Fage Éditions, Paris/Lyon 2010, p. 90–95.

Is not knowing how to keep *the singular and the plural together* exactly what a policy worthy of the name should aim at—just like an artistic decision? [3] The arrangement devised by Esther Shalev-Gerz had another virtue: where usually the plurality of the sound documents and that of the spectators-listeners at an exhibition ends up in a general racket, a composite noise that ruins any concentration in listening, the large hall at the Hôtel de Ville was strangely—but necessarily—silent. Words spoken into the headphones, close to each person's ears: *whispered words,* in a sense. And otherwise the silence of each individual, the *silent listening,* earnest and quite often devastated, the collective silence of the "spectators" of the exhibition. Now to this already prevailing silence the artist wanted to add something like a pause: on three large screens arranged between the blind arcades of the room, there was a loop—going from one screen to the other with a slight time lapse, seven seconds I think[4]—showing a *montage of silences* patiently picked out by the artist from the tens of hours of conversations held with the survivors.

Silences shown with care, since the brief "blank" moments in the speech—when the witness is searching for words, can no longer find them, is disheartened by his/her own description, lets a moved and silent recovery of memory take place, etc.—had been isolated by framing, usually in close-up, centered on the witness's face, and slowed down to half speed. This made it possible to make the *gesture* implied by each of these fragile moments visible. *Edited silences* too, so that a real "atlas of blanks" was constituted from which something like the *gestus*—but a *gestus* as a picture within a picture, so to speak—of the testimonies as such, finally emanates from it. On the basis of Wittgenstein's dictum, it would be possible to put forward the idea that what cannot be talked about should not only be *kept quiet,* but also *shown.* And not only shown, but *edited* as well, according to a visual consistency that Wittgenstein specifically wanted to theorize under the term *Übersicht,* an "overview," the "all-encompassing gaze." [5]

***

Faced with this montage of silences, it would be possible to imagine something like the ultimate version of a famous Hassidic parable. When his people were in danger, the Baal Shem-Tov[6] used to go into a certain forest, stand in front of a certain tree and utter certain words; then the people would survive. Then the descendent of the Baal Shem-Tov, when his people were in danger, also went back to the forest that had been named to him by his ancestor, but he no longer knew exactly which tree he should say the words in front of; he uttered them all the same, looking this way and that, and it sufficed for the people to survive. Later still, the descendent of the descendent went into exile, and nobody any longer knew where the forest was, perhaps it had been transformed into a military camp or a chemical factory; but too bad, the descendent of the descendent uttered the words in his Brooklyn slum, and the people find they survive in spite of everything. Then it came about that the last in the line had completely forgotten the actual words; then he simply told the story, and the people survived in their story.

After Chantal Akerman, who used this parable as the opening to her film *Histoires d'Amérique* (1989)—and I seem to remember that she added some musings about the question of knowing who this story should now be passed on to, as she herself had no child—it might be supposed that Esther Shalev-Gerz, in her montage of silences, is suggesting a *possibility of survival* even in the failure to utter a sentence of the story. All children of survivors know full well the extent to which what is transmitted from one generation to the next is first of all and above all silence. It could also be hypothesized that where Esther Shalev-Gerz—with her husband Jochen Gerz—had imagined her famous *buried monument,*[7] she now lets the silences of a few survivors float in the air, silences that might then form a sort of *hanging monument.* "Gestures of lead" in one instance—since the *Monument Against Fascism* (1986–1993) was covered with lead suspended on an aluminum frame—"gestures of air" here. Inscriptions on the one hand (lead as a surface to print on), the uninscribable in this case (where could these silences be inscribed?). It is the strange seriousness of what floats and does not settle, of what is addressed to us but is not uttered.

Things are, in reality, more complicated than that, I mean, more dialectic. It is not in fact because she had extracted all those moments of silence from the witnesses' stories that Esther Shalev-Gerz actually wanted to isolate them. What she wanted to do was, on the contrary, to really *confront* the silences with the words themselves. Are not the breaths drawn by the flautist moving and meaningful precisely in their physical effort to reconstitute the music of Bach? Would isolating them from that music not render them pointless or abstract? Therefore it would be quite wrong completely to isolate—fetishize—these silences that were collected by the artist, assembled and shown by her, *in sight of the words,* restored in their entirety through the individual viewing and listening devices.

Thus this collection of silences is in no way a monument to silence as such. Or to put it in other words, a monument to the unspeakable nature of the Shoah. More modestly, it gives only the counter-motif—the counter-form, the indent, the lining, the time lapse, albeit effective and striking—of spoken words that are as necessary as they are lacunary (as are the images themselves, moreover). Could it not be said that the puzzle of the slightest sentence uttered will never be finished, terminated, defined? The gaps are really there—not only as absences, but as fundamental *gestures*—and that is what the work of Esther Shalev-Gerz shows. The puzzle will never be completed, from the level of the least fragment of a sentence

3
See Jean-Luc Nancy, *Être singulier pluriel,* Galilée, Paris 1996, p. 15–123.

4
A time lapse the logic of which was initially hard to grasp: it started from the right and "spread" toward the left. In answer to my question about this, Esther Shalev-Gerz spontaneously evoked her two mother tongues: Lithuanian (which is written from left to right) and Yiddish (like Hebrew, written from right to left).

5
Ludwig Wittgenstein, *Remarks on Frazer's "Golden Bough"* (1930–1933), ed. and rev. Rush Rhees, trans. A. C. Miles, Harleston, Norfolk 1991. See Georges Didi-Huberman, *Atlas ou le gai savoir inquiet. L'œil de l'histoire, 3,* Éditions de Minuit, Paris 2011, p. 255–272.

6
Rabbi Baal Shem-Tov (1698–1760) is regarded as the founder of Hassidic Judaism [editor's note].

7
See *Jochen Gerz & Esther Shalev-Gerz: Das Harburger Mahnmal gegen Faschismus,* Verlag Gerd Hatje, Ostfildern 1994.

uttered to that of the whole society of witnesses of history. In 2005, shortly before the completion of the *Between Listening and Telling* project, one of the witnesses suddenly retracted his testimony: he took it back into his own possession, unable to disclose it to those near to him, perhaps waiting until he died for his words to become audible and able to be shared.

***

A silence often appears at the most powerful moment of spoken testimony. A silence often carries—bears in silence—the very intensity of what is being said. That is one of the most compelling motifs of what could be called the cinema of testimony: in the framing and length of the shots, in the trim or cut of the sequences, and finally in the editing, the poetics and ethics of a representation of the spoken word capable of not censuring the "blanks" are truly decided. We see that throughout *Shoah* (1985), the film by Claude Lanzmann, without it being necessary, I feel, to call on the "irrepresentability" of that story or the "transcendency" of those momentarily mute faces.[8] We will no doubt learn a lot about the choices made by Claude Lanzmann on the day when a comparative analysis of the rushes and the edited versions of *Shoah* has been carried out.[9] The great silence of Abraham Bomba, in the "second period" of the film, constitutes in this context a *moment when everything is played out* in terms of the fate of the testimony, between the incomparable strength of what is uttered and its tremendous fragility in being uttered.

Abraham Bomba, you may remember, tells the story of Treblinka with surprising detachment: he formulates his account in faultless sentences pronounced unfalteringly, he therefore seems to be well distanced from his own affects and his remembered images, the words seem to come unprompted, a bit mechanically, in this language (English) which is not however his own, and as if "detached" by a strange syllabic scansion that seems to me to go beyond mere accent. The thing is that the very possibility of bearing witness is conditional on the impersonality of the account, for all that it is given in the first person. It is as if Abraham Bomba could tell the story only if he made his own "I" non-existent, decommissioned it. It is as if the neutrality of his practical gestures—he is busy doing someone's hair in front of Lanzmann's camera—allowed him to articulate his unbearable testimony. When Claude Lanzmann asks him what he "felt" at the time, Abraham Bomba replies with factual data, a way of not answering. When Lanzmann repeats his question, a little later, he answers that feelings had disappeared, another way of precluding his feelings in the hollow of his words. But when he starts to *talk about another man*, to remember another Jewish hairdresser, also from Czestochowa, another man whose fate we will not know—although Bomba obviously does—a terrible silence suddenly catches him by the throat and holds him in its grip for long minutes. The "I" of Abraham Bomba was hermetically sealed up, to be sure; but emotion rises up and leaves him speechless at the very moment when it is someone else—someone like him, a friend—who is evoked, invoked in a sense. Silence definitely does not say "I," and is addressed to that other person. It requires the insistence, oppressive yet necessary, of Lanzmann, then a *detour through a different language*—a few phrases pronounced, as if for himself, in Yiddish—for the testimony to be able to resume.[10]

We could say, with Jean-Luc Nancy, that in these *blank moments*, representation—with the transmission of the story it authorizes—has been "bewildered in the sense of surprised, disconcerted, paralyzed."[11] We could say, with Jacques Rancière, that such moments are part of speech itself and in no way "disconcert" the images: "The irreparable does not forbid words, it modulates them differently. It does not forbid images. Rather, it obliges them to move and to explore new possibilities. The irreparable nature of what took place in no way obliges us to create monuments to absence and to silence. Absence and silence are there anyhow, in any given situation. The question is to know what the people of the present make of them—what they make of words that contain an experience or objects that contain a memory, and of the images that transmit that memory."[12] Well, these suggestions, legitimate as they may well be—each with its special choice of vocabulary—seem very general, as if placed above or set back from the unique experiences they set out to subsume. We then understand that the *"blancs soucis" of the testimony,* as they are so clearly seen in Claude Lanzmann's *Shoah*, or, set out in a different way, in Esther Shalev-Gerz's montages, appeal to contemporary philosophical thinking *as a paradigm.*

A potent paradigm, at the intersection of questions fundamental to both aesthetics and ethics. Would the *screaming silence* of the survivors of the Shoah therefore today occupy a discursive place equivalent to that occupied, throughout the classical period, by the *silent scream* of the famous *Laocoon*? We remember how Lessing, starting from a consideration of the "scream [as a] natural expression of pain,"[13] praised that convention of representation intended to *avoid a gaping appearance* in the sorrowful figure of the antique sculpture: "A gaping mouth is a blot in painting, a hollow in sculpture, which produces the most shocking effect in the world, not to speak of the offputting appearance it gives to the rest of the twisted, grimacing face."[14] We also remember how in Lessing's eyes the image worthy of grief demanded the proposal of a "unique instant," that *fecund instant*, that "pregnant instant" capable of "leaving imagination a free field" and giving birth to the appropriate affective responses in front of this representation of *pathos*.[15]

Finally, we know how Roland Barthes summed up that economy of representation under the heading of what he called a *classic picture*: "The picture (pictorial, theatrical, literary) is a pure cutout, with clean edges, irreversible, incorruptible, which represses into nothingness all the unnamed things

8
As can be read in the book by Aline Alterman, *Visages de* Shoah*: le film de Claude Lanzmann*, Éditions du Cerf, Paris 2006, p. 219–270.

9
See the doctoral research currently being undertaken by Rémy Besson under the direction of Christian Delage at the EHESS (Lhivic) in Paris on *La mise en récit du film* Shoah, as well as his presentation of the installation *Entre l'écoute et la parole* at the EHESS, in the presence of Esther Shalev-Gerz, as part of a seminar session entitled "La place du non articulé dans les témoignages filmés des survivants du génocide juif."

10
See Claude Lanzmann, *Shoah* (1985), Gallimard, Paris 2001, p. 161–169.

11
Jean-Luc Nancy, "La représentation interdite," in *L'Art et la mémoire des camps. Représenter, exterminer*, Éditions du Seuil, Paris 2001, p. 23.

12
Jacques Rancière, "The Work of the Image," in *Esther Shalev-Gerz*, p. 137.

13
Gotthold Ephraim Lessing, *Laocoon: An Essay on the Limits of Painting and Poetry* (1766), trans. Edward Allen McCormick, The Johns Hopkins University Press, Baltimore 1984.

14
Ibid.

15
Ibid.

surrounding it, and promotes everything it causes to enter into its field to essence, to light; this demiurgic discrimination involves high thinking: the picture is intellectual, it wants to say something (moral, social), but also says it knows how it must be said; it is simultaneously significant and propaedeutic, impressive and reflexive, moving and aware of the paths of emotion."[16] As Barthes finds in Diderot—based on Lessing and *Laocoon*—the picture assumes a *pregnant instant* subject "always [to] the Law: the law of society, the law of fighting, the law of sense."[17]

There is no room in such an economy for what Barthes calls the "unnamed"—those *blank instants* now welcomed by Claude Lanzmann in the context of the documentary film, or by Esther Shalev-Gerz in that of the art exhibition. However, by placing Brecht and Eisenstein at the same level of "classicism" as Diderot and Lessing, Barthes deprived himself of understanding the main thing, namely that we go beyond the economy of the "classic picture" only to bring about the breaking of the frames that were developed in the 1920s and 1930s by the arts—pictorial, theatrical, literary, and cinematographic—*of montage and its intervals.* A long way from what Roland Barthes postulates, Brecht's "tableaux" and Eisenstein's "shots" open up the frame and leave room for gaps, silences, cracks in meaning, precisely in that they are edited or assembled, contrasted, given rhythm, and phrased in a certain way. *Laocoon* himself had been able to escape the classic (in reality neoclassical) economy of "convention," as soon as he had no longer been looked at through Lessing's static criteria—the "unique instant" or physiognomic convention—but through the moving criteria of Goethe when he speaks before the sculpture of a vertiginous economy of *transitory moments.*[18]

***

The montage of silences projected by Esther Shalev-Gerz appears in this light straight away: it is a collection of transitory moments. Although in slow motion, every gesture associated with this break in speech is very quickly cut off by the following one, the resulting impression—which nothing softens—being that of *visual discontinuities*, while *the silences persist.* Discontinuities and duration, breaks and persistence: is that not the very status of the words giving testimony? In her installations Esther Shalev-Gerz has never ceased to instigate dialogues, to give shape to *interlocutory situations*: she asks this and that person questions, she confronts faces and points of view, she worries about stories—even simple opportunities to smile—from everyone, she questions objects (like those found in the earth of Buchenwald camp in the work *MenschenDinge—The Human Aspect of Objects*, 2004–2006), practices (like photography), in the prism of each unique story, as in collective history.[19] In doing so, she unceasingly questions transmission right down to its effects of disarray or perdition: one of her installations has the title *White Out* (2002), suggesting the total loss of any sense of direction for anyone trying to find their way in the middle of a snowstorm.[20]

The silences shown and edited by Esther Shalev-Gerz are not simply failures of speech on the part of the witnesses. They are moments of transition, dialectic infills, scansion in the *tempo* of history itself. Therefore they are events in speech, and even authentic *events in the testimony*. Events that are simultaneously *singular and collective,* belonging to the person whose discourse falters, but addressed to all of those who agree, in every failure of discourse, to listen to the burning desire to open still further the limits of what can be said, to go on sharing this *common demand of (hi)story* (and here I am intending the French word "histoire" in its two meanings of historical development requiring us to adopt a position, however discretely, and the historical account, however fragile, required from the testimony). As Gilles Deleuze emphasized so well in *The Logic of Sense,* "there are no private or collective events, no more than there are individuals and universals, particularities and generalities. Everything is singular, and thus both collective and private, particular and general, neither individual nor universal. Which war, for example, is not a private affair? Conversely, which wound is not inflicted by war and derived from society as a whole? Which private event does not have all its coordinates, that is, all its impersonal social singularities?"[21]

Editing her silences, for Esther Shalev-Gerz, meant *showing the break twice:* once the silent break in the witness' speech; the other break, that from one image to the next—one silence to the next—reveals the formal construction of a time dismantled and then reassembled by the artist. Confronting these silences, in the economy of the installation *Between Listening and Telling*, including all of the testimonies uttered, also meant *showing the break with the connection*, a break in the connection (silences in the speech), and a connection in the break (editing of the silences with editing of the words). Then the break is in fact no longer "personal" or individual: its assembly with all the other breaks makes it possible to understand something that travels between all these silences, between all these spoken words, which would be a *community of the break.* "Method," Eisenstein wrote, "is fracture *and* assemblage [made] visible."[22] It is in this that the montage of a few singular breaks straight away appears to be a political decision as much as an aesthetic one, as is indicated to us by Gilles Deleuze commenting on Zola's *La Bête humaine*, or recently by Pierre Zaoui when he wrote in *La Traversée des catastrophes* that a theory of the break is necessary in order to explain "how the most effective, most fruitful, most profound upheavals *for all human beings* can turn out to be the most silent, most imperceptible, least collective."[23]

In what way could what concerns "all human beings" appear in the momentary silence in some unique spoken words, in short in "the least collective" exercise possible, since

16
Roland Barthes, "Diderot, Brecht, Eisenstein" (1973), in Barthes, *Image, Music, Text*, Fontana, New York 1979, p. 69–78.

17
Ibid.

18
Johann Wolfgang von Goethe, "Upon the Laocoon" (1798), in *Essays on Art and Literature (Goethe: The Collected Works, Vol. 3)*, ed. John Gearey, trans. Ellen von Nardroff and Ernest H. von Nardroff, Princeton University Press, Princeton, New Jersey 1994.

19
See *Esther et Jochen Gerz. Raisons de sourire. Le fragment d'Arles*, Actes Sud, Arles 1997; *Esther Shalev-Gerz. Les portraits des histoires. Aubervilliers*, École nationale supérieure des Beaux-Arts/Les Laboratoires d'Aubervilliers, Paris/Aubervilliers 2000; *Esther Shalev-Gerz. Does your image reflect me?*, Sprengel Museum, Hannover 2002; *Esther Shalev-Gerz. First Generation, Multicultural Centre Botkyrka, Fittja 2006; Esther Shalev-Gerz. MenschenDinge—The Human Aspect of Objects*, Stiftung Gedenkstätten Buchenwald und Mittelbau-Dora, Weimar 2006; *Esther Shalev-Gerz. Der letzte Klick*, Museum für Photographie, Braunschweig 2010.

20
See *Esther Shalev-Gerz: Two installations*, Historiska Museet, Stockholm 2002, p. 8–35.

21
Gilles Deleuze, *The Logic of Sense* (1969), ed. Constantin V. Boundas, trans. Mark Lester and Charles Stivale, Columbia University Press, New York 1990.

22
Sergei Eisenstein, "Ermolova" (1937–1939), French trans. A. Zouboff, in François Albera (ed.), *Cinématisme. Peinture et Cinema*, Éditions Complexe, Brussels 1980 (republished in Les Presses du réel, Dijon 2009), p. 224. My italics.

23
Deleuze, *The Logic of Sense*. Pierre Zaoui, *La Traversée des catastrophes. Philosophie pour le meilleur et pour le pire*, Éditions du Seuil, Paris 2010, p. 320.

it in fact breaks the continuity of the dialogue, indeed the social connection with others? That is exactly the question the silences of these witnesses, these *blancs soucis* [blank anxieties] *of testimony*, direct at us here. But what is a *souci* [a worry, a concern, an anxiety] when it comes down to it? It is firstly a *malfunction*, as when one says, faced with a telephone that remains silent for lack of a connection or a failed battery, "il y a un souci" [there is something wrong]. It is the "blanks" in the witness' speech as momentary "breakdowns": in as far as they cause them to fail to say what their position as a witness nonetheless commits them to say. More fundamentally, *souci* is a *torment:* a symptom that can be more painful or less so and crosses and disrupts the normal exercise of any activity whatsoever. The witness' "white solicitudes/blank anxieties" thus signal those moments when they cannot manage to name something, but also the psychological agitation that goes with its cause, and soon the consequence too.

The French word "soucier" comes from a Latin verb that means "to agitate, stir powerfully, trouble, worry, raise, provoke." "Souci" agitates us because—like a tectonic movement—it stirs and brings to the surface whole areas of our consciousness, our language. It infiltrates through all our cracks and comes up—like sulfur fumes—as a "blank" in the space of our thoughts or our words. It is the escape of a fear or an unconscious desire that hampers the coming into operation of our will. How can we not see, in Esther Shalev-Gerz's montage, that the "blanks" in the witnesses' speeches are all emanations of suffering that come, so to speak, to poison their will to tell their story? And as a result they often experience that feeling of unease, impotence, and anguish that takes them back, freezes them, imprisons them mutely in the unbearable nature of a remembered image that fails to be unraveled in words?

The Latin verb that the French word "soucier" is derived from is *sollicitare.* Its physical meaning (to agitate, stir) has given rise to a whole vocabulary of psychological torment, worry, but also—or one might say even—of amorous desire (that is why *sollicitare* also means "to excite, provoke, attract"). *Souci* is torment because it is extended toward the other while the other keeps concealing itself: Therefore it demonstrates the *solicitude* of desire, love, and in general the attention accorded to the world and to others. We know that Martin Heidegger in *Being and Time*, just after dealing with anguish as a "privileged revelation of being there," accorded *souci* (in German, *Sorge*) a quite fundamental place, which was that of "the being of being-there," no less.[24] But to express this legitimate position of preeminence or pre-existence—"*souci* is existentially and a priori 'anterior' to any de facto 'behavior' and 'situation' of being there, which means that it is always already present *in* all behavior and *in* every situation"—Heidegger stated that he was providing against any "concrete anthropology."[25] This would probably have exempted him from engaging in "concrete solicitude" in a historical period—the same one that the testimonies shown by Esther Shalev-Gerz are concerned with—a period when there was "something to get worked up about," as it is expressed in modern parlance. It may be said in passing that the position of Georges Bataille was quite different when, in *Inner Experience*, he joined up the *existence* of each instant to a *demand* set as a concern (*souci*), an unappeasable disquiet in the face of time.[26]

Finally there is a poetic history of solicitude. I will sum it up in three simple factors.[27] The first is that of *beauty:* it is when Malherbe invents this admirable expression of desire or looking at what comes and goes, like a wave, between the given and the withdrawn: "Beauté, mon beau souci, de qui l'âme incertaine / A, comme l'Océan, son flux et son reflux ... "[28] [Beauty, my fine concern, whose uncertain soul / Has, like the Ocean, its ebb and its flow ...] The second factor is the antithesis I started from, that of Mallarmé hailing *le blanc* as a dialectic fill-in for all solicitude: "Solitude, récif, étoile / À n'importe ce qui valut / Le blanc souci de notre toile" [Solitude, reef, and starry veil / To whatever's worthy of knowing / The white anxiety of our sail].[29] The third factor could be that where *montage* takes on both of the two previous terms: it is when Jean-Luc Godard, picking up on and extending Malherbe's choice of words, compares editing, his "beau souci," to a "heartbeat," a "link-up to a gaze," or again to what he names the "highlighting of an unknown woman" when, in working on images, you succeed in "bringing out the soul beneath the mind, the passion behind the scheming, [and in] making the heart prevail over understanding by destroying the notion of space in favor of that of time."[30]

***

The "blancs soucis" of the testimonies themselves bear witness to the *movements of times*—both words in the plural—at work in the narrative of each historical account. They have to do with montages and intervals, fractures and assemblages brought together anachronically according to processes of attraction, or conversely of conflict. Speaking in general about silence in speech, speaking of solicitude outside any "concrete anthropology," does not take us very far, only to fine notions stripped of flesh, stripped of gestures. Looking at Esther Shalev-Gerz's montage, we would have to know how to come back down from the grand paradigms—"the pregnant instant" according to Lessing, "the being of being-there" according to Heidegger—to the small syntagms: in short, to come back down from a philosophy of silence in general to those discrete segments or *strands of silences* we discover here and there in the course of the accounts produced by the witnesses of history.

Thus, confronted with such a montage of silences, at the intersection of two dimensions that everything seems to make opposite: on one side, the *emotion* inherent to what

24
Martin Heidegger, *Being and Time* (1927), trans. trans. John Macquarrie and Edward Robinson, Harper and Row Publishers, New York, rev. ed. 1962.

25
Ibid.

26
Georges Bataille, *Inner Experience* (1943), trans. Leslie Anne Boldt, State University of New York, New York 1988.

27
It is possible to consult the poetic and philosophical collection formed by Richard Millet and Jean-Michel Maulpoix focusing on the motif "Le souci" in *Recueil*, no. 3, 1986, p. 65–170.

28
François de Malherbe, "Dessein de quitter une dame qui ne le contentait que de promesse" (1600), in Antoine Adam (ed.), *Malherbe. Œuvres*, Gallimard, Paris 1971, p. 21.

29
Stéphane Mallarmé, "Salut" (1893), *Stéphane Mallarmé. Œuvres complètes*, p. 27.

30
Jean-Luc Godard, "Montage, My Fine Care" (1956), in *Godard on Godard: Critical Writings by Jean-Luc Godard*, Da Capo Press, Boston 1986.

Georges Bataille called "man's recognition of what dooms him to what is the object of his most powerful horror," an emotion that leads him to the "profound silence introduced by tears"[31]; on the other, the *construction* inherent to what Jacques Rancière, speaking of Jean-Luc Godard, names the "phrasing of history."[32] We understand that this double dimension has to be taken on board in order to understand something in what is transmitted to us by these witnesses who have come from hell. It is there that, for the poet, "the blank indefeasibly returns, a minute ago gratuitous, now certain, to conclude that there is nothing beyond and to authenticate silence."[33] And it is there that the time comes for the historian himself to *break the silence* (to extend the gesture of testimony of all those who were at a moment reduced to silence, but nonetheless broke it) while at the same time agreeing, in accordance with the words of Mallarmé, and without being sure of anything, to *authenticate silence*.[34]

31
Georges Bataille, "[Attraction et répulsion]" (1938), in *Œuvres complètes, II*, Gallimard, Paris 1971, p. 318 and 333.

32
Jacques Rancière, *Le Destin des images*, La Fabrique Éditions, Paris 2003, p. 41–78.

33
Stéphane Mallarmé, "Quant au livre" (1895), in *Stéphane Mallarmé. Œuvres complètes*, p. 387.

34
For editorial reasons, the text presented here is a shortened version of the full text.

BLANCS SOUCIS DE NOTRE HISTOIRE
GEORGES DIDI-HUBERMAN

« Le blanc souci de notre toile » constitue le vers final d'un sonnet écrit en 1890 et intitulé *Salut.* Ce poème fut placé par Stéphane Mallarmé en exergue de son « recueil complet de poésies », recueil qu'il finissait de mettre en ordre lorsque la mort l'interrompit en 1898, et que l'éditeur Edmond Deman fit paraître dès 1899. Mallarmé souhaitait que ce modeste poème, d'abord intitulé *Toast,* ne fût composé qu'en petits caractères – ce que Deman et les éditeurs successifs auront voulu ignorer. Il ne s'agissait, en somme, que de modestement *saluer* : accueillir l'auditeur ou le lecteur, ouvrir la porte du recueil. Il s'agissait, pour cela, de *se lever* pour « porter debout ce salut », comme l'écrit Mallarmé, à l'image d'un toast porté à la fin d'une réunion d'amis. Il s'agissait enfin, par ce salut, de *reconnaître* en autrui, quel qu'il fût, un « blanc souci » partagé, que le poète aura fait rimer avec ces trois mots : « Solitude, récif, étoile. »[1] Comme si la profération d'un poème – ou l'exécution d'une *partita,* ou la composition d'une image – avait pour enjeu même cette reconnaissance d'un souci commun depuis la « solitude » de chacun, le « récif » de l'œuvre produite et l'« étoile » – ou la constellation – qu'y met au jour, dans notre pensée, son regard, sa lecture ou son écoute.

Il semble qu'Esther Shalev-Gerz compose ses œuvres – de regard, de lecture et d'écoute – à partir d'un geste semblable. Elle se lève pour saluer, elle travaille pour reconnaître, en elle-même comme en autrui (car ses œuvres ne vont jamais sans interlocuteurs précis), quelque chose comme un espace peuplé par les *blancs soucis de notre histoire.* Un dispositif inventé par elle en 2005 a particulièrement sollicité mon désir d'écriture ou, dit autrement, mon inquiétude, mes propres « soucis » quant à l'histoire et quant à l'art. Il s'intitule *Entre l'écoute et la parole : derniers témoins, Auschwitz 1945-2005,* et fut présenté dans un vaste espace de la Mairie de Paris, entre janvier et mars 2005, dans le cadre des commémorations de la libération du camp d'Auschwitz[2]. L'artiste était conviée à « mettre en espace », à *exposer la parole* d'une soixantaine de survivants des camps nazis : ils témoignaient de leur expérience devant les caméras vidéo de quatre équipes d'intervieweurs coordonnées par Bénédicte Rochas. Les témoignages recueillis variaient en durée, selon les exigences de chaque narrateur : entre deux et neuf heures enregistrées pour chacun.

Mais peut-on nous rendre *spectateurs* de telles durées, de telles paroles ? Exposer des paroles – et singulièrement des paroles touchant à cette histoire extrême –, n'est-ce pas les menacer dans leur existence même, les exposer à devenir de pures formes vides de sens ? N'est-ce pas les vouer à ne plus s'adresser, à ne plus toucher qui que ce soit ? Le risque était grand : le risque qu'un geste artistique, aussi élégant fût-il, ne vînt rendre inaccessible – ou tout au moins secondaire – ce recueil de terribles récits. N'était-on pas condamné au mauvais dilemme de « sous-exposer » ces paroles (les minorer en tant qu'épiphénomènes documentaires de l'œuvre elle-même) ou, au, contraire, de les « sur-exposer » (les majorer comme fétiches archivistiques), deux façons symétriques de rendre toute chose *inaudible* autant qu'*irregardable* ? L'archive, nous le savons bien, est à la mode dans le monde, postmoderne, de l'art. Mais c'est au prix, bien souvent, d'être renvoyée à une valeur d'usage ambiguë : soit intimidante et auratique, soit décorative et inutilisable – inaccessible dans les deux cas.

Or, le principal *souci* d'Esther Shalev-Gerz, en parfaite cohérence avec la dimension éthique et politique de son travail dans la longue durée, était bien, non pas de « prendre » ce corpus de paroles afin de le modeler à son usage et son « style » personnels, mais bien de le *rendre* à chacun, à nous tous. Il s'agissait, en somme, de *donner une forme au bien commun* que constituent, désormais, ces témoignages réunis ensemble. Il n'est pas sans importance que l'installation de l'artiste ait occupé un *lieu communal,* je veux dire cette grande salle de l'Hôtel de Ville de Paris, et non pas un espace privé ou une galerie d'art. Le travail d'Esther Shalev-Gerz interrogeait bien là une *res publica,* cette chose publique que constitue l'ensemble des témoignages recueillis, ces fragments de notre histoire commune, avant toute *res artistica* en tant qu'affaire d'« amateurs », d'experts ou d'esthètes. *Entre l'écoute et la parole* est une œuvre d'art, sans aucun doute, mais ce fut un travail d'abord pensé hors de sa propre « spécialité », de sa corporation ou de son « milieu ». Une œuvre « républicaine », donc, au sens littéral du terme.

Non seulement l'espace était communal, mais encore Esther Shalev-Gerz avait voulu en préserver la luminosité habituelle, bien qu'il s'agît de mettre des images vidéo en situation d'être regardées. N'eût-il pas été plus efficace – et spectaculaire – de faire le noir autour de ces images, comme on le voit si souvent dans nos musées d'art contemporain ? Mais l'artiste aura voulu procéder à quelque chose comme une *mise en commun* des témoignages, des témoins et des témoignaires (les destinataires des témoignages), sans que rien ne vînt réduire les *possibilités de coexistence* et de rencontre entre chacun. C'est ainsi que la soixantaine de témoignages étaient intégralement visionnables dans la salle de l'Hôtel de Ville sur une soixantaine de postes informatiques munis d'écouteurs individuels, en sorte que chaque spectateur ou auditeur avait la possibilité de se retrouver, comme seul à seul, *face à l'image et à la parole du témoin* singulier, dans la durée réelle de son récit. En même temps, la disposition des tables conçue par Esther Shalev-Gerz – une disposition serpentine, chaque creux étant occupé par un poste d'écoute – plaçait quasiment chaque spectateur *face au corps et au silence du témoignaire,* ou du spectateur, situé de l'autre côté de la table. Par ce dispositif très simple, chacun était donc à la fois esseulé dans son visionnage, dans son écoute, et en commun dans l'espace d'exposition.

Savoir maintenir *ensemble le singulier et le pluriel,* n'est-ce pas exactement ce que doit viser une politique – mais, tout

1
Stéphane Mallarmé, « Salut » (1893), in Henri Mondor et Georges Jean-Aubry (éds.), *Stéphane Mallarmé. Œuvres complètes,* Gallimard, Paris 1945 (éd. 1974), p. 27.

2
Entre l'écoute et la parole : derniers témoins, Auschwitz 1945-2005, Paris, Mairie de Paris – Mémorial de la Shoah, 2005. Voir Stefanie Baumann, « Œuvres », in *Esther Shalev-Gerz,* Éditions du Jeu de Paume/Fage Éditions, Paris/Lyon 2010, p. 90-95.

aussi bien, une décision artistique – digne de ce nom[3] ? Le dispositif inventé par Esther Shalev-Gerz comportait une autre vertu : là où, d'ordinaire, la pluralité de documents sonores et celle des spectateurs-auditeurs d'une exposition aboutit à un brouhaha général, une rumeur composite qui ruine toute concentration de l'écoute, la grande salle de l'Hôtel de Ville était étrangement – mais nécessairement – silencieuse. Paroles dans les casques, au contact des oreilles de chacun : *paroles chuchotées,* en un sens. Et, d'autre part, le silence de chacun, l'*écoute silencieuse,* grave et bien souvent atterrée, le silence collectif des « spectateurs » de l'exposition. Or, à ce silence déjà régnant, l'artiste aura voulu ajouter quelque chose comme un point d'orgue : sur trois écrans de grandes dimensions disposés entre les arcatures de la salle, passait en boucle – d'un écran à l'autre et selon un léger décalage, sept secondes je crois[4] – un *montage de silences* patiemment prélevés par l'artiste sur les dizaines d'heures d'entretiens réalisés avec les survivants.

Silences montrés avec soin, puisque les brefs moments de « blanc » dans la parole – lorsque le témoin cherche ses mots, ne les trouve plus, se décourage de sa propre description, laisse venir à lui une remémoration émue-muette, etc. – avaient été isolés selon un cadrage, en général assez proche, sur le visage du témoin, et ralentis selon un rapport de moitié. Cela permettait de rendre visible le *geste* impliqué par chacun de ces moments fragiles. *Silences montés* également, en sorte que se constituait un véritable « atlas des blancs » d'où, finalement, se dégage quelque chose comme le *gestus* – mais un *gestus* en creux, si je puis dire – des témoignages en tant que tels. Sur la base du *dictum* wittgensteinien, on pourrait proposer l'idée que ce dont on ne peut parler, il faut non seulement *le taire,* mais encore *le montrer.* Et non seulement le montrer, mais encore *le monter,* selon une cohérence visuelle que Wittgenstein, précisément, aura voulu théoriser sous le nom d'*Übersicht,* la « vue synoptique », le « regard embrassant »[5].

***

On pourrait imaginer, devant ce montage de silences, quelque chose comme la version ultime d'une célèbre parabole hassidique. Lorsque son peuple était en danger, le Baal Shem-Tov[6] allait dans une certaine forêt, se plaçait devant un certain arbre et prononçait certaines paroles ; alors, le peuple survivait. Puis, le descendant du Baal Shem-Tov, quand son peuple était en danger, retournait lui aussi dans cette forêt que lui avait nommée son aïeul, mais il ne savait plus devant quel arbre exactement prononcer les paroles ; il les prononçait quand même, en regardant ici et là, et cela suffisait pour que le peuple survive. Plus tard encore, le descendant du descendant s'est exilé, plus personne ne sait où se trouve la forêt, elle a peut-être été transformée en camp militaire ou en usine chimique ; mais tant pis, le descendant du descendant, prononce les paroles dans son taudis de Brooklyn, et le peuple se sent survivre malgré tout. Puis, il arrive au dernier venu d'avoir complètement oublié les paroles elles-mêmes ; alors, il raconte simplement l'histoire, et le peuple survit dans son histoire.

Après Chantal Akerman qui a utilisé cette parabole en ouverture de son film *Histoires d'Amérique* (1989) – et je crois me souvenir qu'elle y ajoute une réflexion sur la question de savoir à qui, désormais, transmettre cette histoire, elle qui n'a pas d'enfant –, on pourrait supposer qu'Esther Shalev-Gerz, dans son montage de silences, vient suggérer une *possibilité de survivance* jusque dans l'échec à prononcer une phrase sur l'histoire. Tous les enfants de survivants savent bien à quel point ce qui se transmet, d'une génération à l'autre, c'est d'abord et avant tout le silence. On pourrait aussi faire l'hypothèse que, là où Esther Shalev-Gerz – avec son mari Jochen Gerz – avait imaginé son fameux *monument enterré*[7], elle fait désormais flotter dans l'air les silences de quelques survivants, silences qui formeraient alors une sorte de *monument en suspens...* « Gestes de plomb » d'un côté – puisque le *Monument contre le fascisme* (1986-1993) était recouvert de plomb tendu sur un bâti d'aluminium –, « gestes d'air » ici. Inscriptions d'un côté (le plomb comme surface typographique), l'ininscriptible ici (où inscrire ces silences ?). C'est l'étrange gravité de ce qui flotte et ne se fixe pas, de ce qui s'adresse à nous et ne se prononce pas.

Les choses, en réalité, sont plus compliquées que cela, je veux dire : plus dialectiques. Ce n'est pas parce qu'elle a extrait tous ces moments de silence dans les récits des témoins qu'Esther Shalev-Gerz a voulu, pour autant, les isoler. Ce qu'elle a voulu, au contraire, c'est bien les *confronter* aux paroles elles-mêmes. Les prises de souffle du flûtiste ne sont-elles pas émouvantes et signifiantes précisément dans leur lutte physique pour restituer la musique de Bach ? Les isoler de cette musique, n'est-ce pas les rendre vaines ou abstraites ? On aurait donc bien tort d'isoler complètement – de fétichiser – ces silences qui furent recueillis par l'artiste, montés et montrés par elle, *en regard des paroles* intégralement restituées à travers les dispositifs de visionnage et d'écoute individuels.

Ainsi, cette collection de silences n'a rien d'un monument au silence comme tel. Ou, dit autrement, d'un monument à l'indicibilité de la Shoah. Elle ne donne, plus modestement, que le contre-motif – la contre-forme, le creux, la doublure, le laps, mais efficaces et marquants – de paroles aussi nécessaires que lacunaires (comme le sont, par ailleurs, les images elles-mêmes). Ne pourrait-on dire que le puzzle de la moindre phrase prononcée ne sera jamais achevé, terminé, défini ? Les lacunes sont bien là – non seulement comme défauts, mais comme *gestes* fondamentaux –, et c'est ce que montre l'œuvre d'Esther Shalev-Gerz. Le puzzle ne sera jamais complété, depuis le niveau du moindre fragment de phrase prononcée jusqu'à celui de la société tout entière des témoins de

3
Voir Jean-Luc Nancy, *Être singulier pluriel,* Galilée, Paris 1996, p. 15-123.

4
Décalage dont la logique était d'abord difficile à saisir : c'est qu'il partait de droite et se « propageait » vers la gauche. En réponse à ma question sur ce point, Esther Shalev-Gerz évoque spontanément sa double langue maternelle : lituanienne (qui s'écrit de gauche à droite) et yiddish (qui s'écrit, comme l'hébreu, de droite à gauche).

5
Ludwig Wittgenstein, *Remarques sur « Le Rameau d'or » de Frazer* (1930-1933), trad. J. Lacoste, L'Âge d'Homme, Lausanne 1982, p. 14-21. Voir Georges Didi-Huberman, *Atlas ou le gai savoir inquiet. L'œil de l'histoire, 3,* Éditions de Minuit, Paris 2011, p. 255-272.

6
Le rabbin Baal Shem-Tov (1698-1760) est considéré comme le fondateur du judaïsme hassidique. [N.E.]

7
Voir *Jochen Gerz & Esther Shalev-Gerz : das Harburger Mahnmal gegen Faschismus,* Hatje, Ostfildern 1994.

l'histoire. En 2005, peu avant l'achèvement du projet *Entre l'écoute et la parole*, l'un des témoins s'est tout à coup dédit : il a repris son témoignage par-devers lui, incapable de s'en ouvrir à ses proches, attendant peut-être de mourir pour que sa parole devienne audible et partageable.

***

Un silence apparaît souvent au plus fort de la parole qui témoigne. Un silence porte souvent – supporte en silence – l'intensité même de ce qui se dit. C'est là l'un des motifs les plus puissants de ce qu'on pourrait nommer le cinéma de témoignage : dans le cadrage et la durée des plans, dans la chute ou *cut* des séquences, dans le montage enfin se décident véritablement la poétique et l'éthique d'une représentation de la parole capable de n'en pas censurer les « blancs ». On voit cela tout au long de *Shoah* (1985), le film de Claude Lanzmann, sans qu'il soit nécessaire, me semble-t-il, d'en appeler à l'« irreprésentabilité » de cette histoire ou à la « transcendance » de ces visages momentanément muets[8]. On en apprendra sans doute beaucoup sur les choix de Claude Lanzmann le jour où l'analyse comparée des *rushes* et des montages de *Shoah* aura été menée[9]. Le grand silence d'Abraham Bomba, dans la « seconde époque » du film, constitue à ce titre un *moment où tout se joue* quant au destin du témoignage, entre son incomparable force d'énoncé et son immense fragilité d'énonciation.

Abraham Bomba, on s'en souvient, raconte Treblinka avec un détachement surprenant : il formule son récit avec des phrases impeccables prononcées sans faille, il semble donc à bonne distance de ses propres affects et de ses images réminiscentes, les mots semblent venir tout seuls, un peu mécaniquement, dans cette langue (l'anglais) qui n'est pourtant pas la sienne, et comme « détachés » par une étrange scansion syllabique qui va au-delà, me semble-t-il, d'un simple accent. C'est que la possibilité même de témoigner a pour condition l'impersonnalité du récit pourtant décliné à la première personne. C'est comme si Abraham Bomba ne pouvait raconter cela qu'à rendre son propre « je » inexistant, désaffecté. C'est comme si la neutralité de ses gestes techniques – il est en train de coiffer quelqu'un devant la caméra de Lanzmann – lui permettait d'articuler son insoutenable témoignage. Quand Claude Lanzmann lui demande ce qu'il « éprouvait » alors, Abraham Bomba répond avec des données de faits, façon de ne pas répondre. Quand Lanzmann réitère, un peu plus tard, sa question, il répond que les sentiments avaient disparu, autre façon de forclore ses sentiments dans le creux de sa parole. Mais, alors qu'il commence de *parler d'un autre homme,* d'évoquer un autre coiffeur juif, lui aussi de Czestochowa, un autre homme dont nous ne saurons pas ce qu'il est devenu – mais Bomba le sait évidemment –, un terrible silence tout à coup le prend à la gorge qui, pendant de longues minutes, ne le lâchera plus. Le « je » d'Abraham Bomba était hermétiquement rempardé, certes ; mais l'émotion surgit et le laisse coi au moment même où c'est un autre – un semblable, un ami – qui est évoqué, en un sens invoqué. Le silence, décidément, ne dit pas « je », et c'est à l'autre qu'il s'adresse. Il faudra l'insistance, oppressante et nécessaire, de Lanzmann, puis un *détour par une autre langue* – quelques phrases prononcées, comme pour soi-même, en yiddish – pour que le témoignage puisse reprendre son cours[10].

On pourrait dire, avec Jean-Luc Nancy, que dans ces *blancs moments* la représentation – avec la transmission du récit qu'elle autorise – a été « interdite au sens de surprise, interloquée, médusée »[11]. On pourrait dire, avec Jacques Rancière, que de tels moments font partie de la parole elle-même et n'« interdisent » en rien les images : « L'irréparable n'interdit pas la parole, il la module différemment. Il n'interdit pas les images. Il les oblige plutôt à bouger, à explorer des possibles nouveaux. Le caractère irréparable de ce qui a eu lieu n'oblige en rien à élever des monuments à l'absence et au silence. L'absence et le silence sont là, de toute façon, dans toute situation donnée. La question est de savoir ce que les présents en font, ce qu'ils font des mots qui contiennent une expérience, des choses qui en retiennent le souvenir, des images qui la transmettent. »[12] Or, ces propositions, pour légitimes qu'elles soient – chacune avec son choix particulier de vocabulaire –, apparaissent bien générales, comme placées au-dessus ou en retrait des expériences singulières qu'elles ont pour ambition de subsumer. On comprend alors que les *« blancs soucis » du témoignage,* comme on les voit si clairement dans *Shoah* de Claude Lanzmann ou, autrement distribués, dans les montages d'Esther Shalev-Gerz, sollicitent la pensée philosophique contemporaine *à titre de paradigme.*

Puissant paradigme, au croisement de questions fondamentales pour l'esthétique comme pour l'éthique. Le *silence criant* des survivants de la Shoah occuperait-il donc, aujourd'hui, une place discursive équivalente à celle occupée, durant toute l'époque classique, par le *cri silencieux* du célèbre *Laocoon* ? On se souvient comment Lessing, à partir d'une considération sur le « cri [comme] expression naturelle de la douleur »[13], louait dans le personnage douloureux de la sculpture antique cette convenance de la représentation destinée à *éviter la béance* : « Une bouche béante est, en peinture, une tache, en sculpture un creux, qui produisent l'effet le plus choquant du monde, sans parler de l'aspect repoussant qu'elle donne au reste du visage tordu et grimaçant. »[14] On se souvient aussi comment l'image digne de la douleur exigeait, aux yeux de Lessing, la mise en avant d'un « unique instant », cet *instant fécond,* cet « instant prégnant » capable de « laisser un champ libre à l'imagination » et de donner naissance aux convenables réponses affectives devant cette représentation du *pathos*[15].

On sait, enfin, comment Roland Barthes a résumé cette économie de la représentation sous le chef de ce qu'il appelait un *tableau classique* : « Le tableau (pictural, théâtral, littéraire)

8
Comme on le lit dans l'ouvrage d'Aline Alterman, *Visages de* Shoah : *le film de Claude Lanzmann*, Éditions du Cerf, Paris 2006, p. 219-270.

9
Voir la recherche de doctorat actuellement menée par Rémy Besson sous la direction de Christian Delage à l'EHESS (Lhivic) sur *La mise en récit du film* Shoah, ainsi que sa présentation à l'EHESS, en présence d'Esther Shalev-Gerz, de l'installation *Entre l'écoute et la parole* dans le cadre d'une séance de séminaire intitulée « La place du non articulé dans les témoignages filmés des survivants du génocide juif ».

10
Voir Claude Lanzmann, *Shoah* (1985), Gallimard, Paris 2001, p. 161-169.

11
Jean-Luc Nancy, « La représentation interdite », in *L'Art et la mémoire des camps. Représenter, exterminer,* Éditions du Seuil, Paris 2001, p. 23.

12
Jacques Rancière, « Le travail de l'image », in *Esther Shalev-Gerz,* 2010, p. 11.

13
Gotthold Ephraim Lessing, *Laocoon* (1766), trad. A. Courtin (1866) revue par J. Bialostocka, Hermann, Paris 1990, p. 45.

14
Ibid., p. 51.

15
Ibid., p. 55-56.

est un découpage pur, aux bords nets, irréversible, incorruptible, qui refoule dans le néant tout son entour, innommé, et promeut à l'essence, à la lumière, tout ce qu'il fait entrer dans son champ; cette discrimination démiurgique implique une haute pensée: le tableau est intellectuel, il veut dire quelque chose (de moral, de social), mais aussi il dit qu'il sait comment il faut le dire; il est à la fois significatif et propédeutique, impressif et réflexif, émouvant et conscient des voies de l'émotion. »[16] Comme Barthes le repère chez Diderot – à partir de Lessing et du *Laocoon* –, le tableau suppose un *instant prégnant* soumis « toujours [à] la Loi: loi de la société, loi de la lutte, loi du sens. »[17]

Il n'y a pas de place, dans une telle économie, pour ce que Barthes appelle l'« innommé » — ces *blancs instants* désormais accueillis par Claude Lanzmann dans l'espace du cinéma documentaire ou par Esther Shalev-Gerz dans celui de l'exposition artistique. En plaçant Brecht et Eisenstein au même plan de « classicisme » que Diderot et Lessing, Barthes se privait cependant de comprendre l'essentiel, à savoir qu'on ne dépasse l'économie du « tableau classique » qu'à mettre en œuvre la brisure des cadres que développèrent, dans les années 1920 et 1930, les arts – picturaux, théâtraux, littéraires et cinématographiques – *du montage et de ses intervalles.* Bien loin de ce que postule Roland Barthes, les « tableaux » de Brecht et les « plans » d'Eisenstein ouvrent le cadre et laissent leur place aux béances, aux silences, aux fêlures du sens, dans la mesure même où ils sont montés, contrastés, rythmés et phrasés d'une certaine façon. Le *Laocoon* lui-même avait su échapper à l'économie classique (en réalité néoclassique) de la « convenance », dès lors qu'il n'avait plus été regardé à travers les critères statiques de Lessing – l'« unique instant » ou la convenance physiognomonique – mais à travers ceux, mobiles, de Goethe quand il parle, devant la sculpture, d'une économie vertigineuse de *moments transitoires*[18].

***

Le montage de silences projetés par Esther Shalev-Gerz apparaît d'emblée sous cet angle: c'est un recueil de moments transitoires. Bien que ralenti, chaque geste lié à ce suspens dans la parole se voit bien vite coupé par le suivant, l'impression qui en résulte – et que rien ne vient apaiser – étant celle de *discontinuités visuelles* alors que *durent les silences.* Discontinuités et durées, failles et persistances: n'est-ce pas là le statut même de la parole qui témoigne? Esther Shalev-Gerz n'a jamais cessé, dans ses dispositifs artistiques, de susciter des dialogues, de mettre en forme des *situations interlocutoires*: elle pose des questions aux uns et aux autres, elle confronte les visages et les points de vue, elle s'inquiète des histoires – voire des simples occasions de sourire – de chacun, elle interroge des objets (comme ceux retrouvés dans la terre du camp de Buchenwald dans l'œuvre *MenschenDinge*, 2004-2006), des pratiques (comme la photographie), au prisme de chaque histoire singulière comme de l'histoire collective[19]. Ce faisant, elle questionne sans relâche la transmission jusque dans ses effets de déroute ou de perdition: l'une de ses installations s'intitule *White Out* (2002), expression qui désigne la perte du sens de l'orientation pour quelqu'un qui tente de trouver son chemin au milieu d'une tempête de neige[20].

Les silences montrés et montés par Esther Shalev-Gerz ne sont pas simplement des défauts de la parole des témoins. Ce sont des moments de transition, des chevilles dialectiques, des scansions dans le *tempo* de l'histoire elle-même. Ce sont donc des événements dans la parole, et même d'authentiques *événements du témoignage.* Événements tout ensemble *singuliers et collectifs,* propres à celui dont le discours défaille mais adressés à tous ceux qui acceptent d'écouter, dans chaque défaillance du discours, le désir brûlant d'ouvrir toujours plus les limites du dicible, de partager encore cette *commune exigence de l'histoire* (et j'entends « histoire » dans les deux sens du devenir historique exigeant nos prises de position, si discrètes soient-elles, et du récit historique exigé à partir du témoignage, si fragile soit-il). Comme Gilles Deleuze l'a bien souligné dans *Logique du sens,* « il n'y a pas d'événements privés, et d'autres collectifs; pas plus qu'il n'y a de l'individuel et de l'universel, des particularités et des généralités. Tout est singulier, et par là collectif et privé à la fois, particulier et général, ni individuel ni universel. Quelle guerre n'est pas l'affaire privée, inversement quelle blessure n'est pas de guerre, et venue de la société tout entière? Quel événement privé n'a pas toutes ses coordonnées, c'est-à-dire toutes ses singularités impersonnelles sociales? »[21]

Monter ses silences, pour Esther Shalev-Gerz, c'était *montrer deux fois la fêlure*: une fois la fêlure silencieuse dans la parole du témoin, une autre fois la fêlure qui, d'une image l'autre – d'un silence l'autre –, révèle la construction formelle d'un temps démonté puis remonté par l'artiste. Confronter ces silences, dans l'économie de l'installation *Entre l'écoute et la parole,* à l'intégralité des témoignages prononcés, c'était aussi *montrer la fêlure avec le lien,* fêlure dans le lien (silences dans la parole) et lien dans la fêlure (montage des silences avec montage des paroles). Alors, en effet, la fêlure n'est plus « personnelle » ou individuelle: son montage avec toutes les autres rend possible la compréhension de quelque chose qui passe entre tous ces silences, entre toutes ces paroles, et qui serait une *communauté de la fêlure.* « La méthode, écrivait Eisenstein, c'est la fracture *et* l'assemblage [rendus] visibles. »[22] C'est en cela que le montage de quelques fêlures singulières apparaît d'emblée comme une décision politique autant qu'esthétique, comme nous l'indiquent Gilles Deleuze commentant *La Bête humaine* de Zola ou, récemment, Pierre Zaoui lorsqu'il écrit, dans *La Traversée des catastrophes,* qu'une théorie de la fêlure est nécessaire pour expliquer « comment les bouleversement les plus effectifs, les plus féconds, les plus profonds *pour tous les hommes* peuvent

16
Roland Barthes, « Diderot, Brecht, Eisenstein » (1973), in Éric Marty (éd.), *Roland Barthes. Œuvres complètes, IV. 1972-1976,* Éditions du Seuil, Paris 2002, p. 339.

17
Ibid., p. 341 et 343.

18
Johann Wolfgang von Goethe, « Sur Laocoon » (1798), trad. J.-M. Schaeffer, *Écrits sur l'art,* Klincksieck, Paris 1983 (rééd. Flammarion, Paris 1996), p. 165-178.

19
Voir *Esther et Jochen Gerz. Raisons de sourire. Le fragment d'Arles,* Actes Sud, Arles 1997 ; *Esther Shalev-Gerz. Les portraits des histoires. Aubervilliers,* École nationale supérieure des Beaux-Arts/Les Laboratoires d'Aubervilliers, Paris/Aubervilliers 2000 ; *Esther Shalev-Gerz. Est-ce que ton image me regarde ?,* Sprengel Museum, Hanovre 2002 ; *Esther Shalev-Gerz. First Generation,* Multicultural Centre Botkyrka, Fittja 2006 ; *Esther Shalev-Gerz. MenschenDinge–The Human Aspect of Objects,* Stiftung Gedenkstätten Buchenwald und Mittelbau-Dora, Weimar 2006 ; *Esther Shalev-Gerz. Der letzte Klick,* Museum für Photographie, Braunschweig 2010.

20
Voir *Esther Shalev-Gerz : Two Installations,* Historiska Museet, Stockholm 2002, p. 8-35.

21
Gilles Deleuze, *Logique du sens,* Éditions de Minuit, Paris 1969, p. 178.

22
Sergeï Mikhaïlovitch Eisenstein, « Ermolova » (1937-1939), trad. A. Zouboff, in François Albera (éd.), *Cinématisme. Peinture et cinéma,* Éditions Complexe, Bruxelles 1980 (rééd. Les Presses du réel, Dijon 2009), p. 224. Je souligne.

s'avérer les plus silencieux, les plus imperceptibles, les moins collectifs. »[23].

En quoi ce qui concerne « tous les hommes » pourrait-il apparaître dans le silence momentané de quelques paroles singulières, bref, dans l'exercice « le moins collectif » qui soit puisqu'il brise, justement, la continuité du dialogue voire le lien social avec autrui ? Telle est, exactement, la question que nous adressent ici les silences de ces témoins, ces *blancs soucis du témoignage.* Mais qu'est-ce qu'un souci, au juste ? C'est, d'abord, un *dysfonctionnement,* comme lorsqu'on dit, devant un téléphone qui reste muet, par défaut de connexion ou batterie en panne, « il y a un souci ». Ce sont les « blancs » de la parole du témoin en tant que « pannes » momentanées : en tant qu'ils le font échouer à dire ce que sa position de témoin, pourtant, l'engage à dire. Plus fondamentalement, le souci est un *tourment* : un symptôme plus ou moins douloureux qui vient traverser, inquiéter, l'exercice normal d'une activité quelconque. Les « blancs soucis » du témoin signalent donc ces moments où il ne parvient pas à nommer quelque chose, mais aussi la perturbation psychique qui en marque la cause et, bientôt, la conséquence aussi.

Notre français « soucier » vient d'un verbe latin qui signifie « remuer, agiter fortement, troubler, inquiéter, soulever, provoquer »... Le souci nous agite parce qu'il remue et soulève – tel un mouvement tectonique – des pans entiers de notre conscience, de notre langage. Il s'infiltre par toutes nos fêlures et survient – telle une fumée de soufre – comme un « blanc » dans l'espace de nos pensées ou de nos paroles. C'est l'échappée d'une angoisse ou d'un désir inconscient qui contrarie la mise en mouvement de notre volonté. Comment ne pas voir, dans le montage d'Esther Shalev-Gerz, que les « blancs » dans la parole des témoins sont autant d'émanations du souffrir qui viennent, pour ainsi dire, empoisonner leur volonté de récit ? Et qu'il en résulte souvent chez eux ce sentiment de malaise, d'impouvoir et d'angoisse qui les ramène, les fixe, les emprisonne muettement dans l'insoutenable d'une image réminiscente échouant à se délier en paroles ?

Le verbe latin d'où vient notre français « soucier » est le verbe *sollicitare.* Son sens physique (agiter, remuer) aura donné lieu à tout un vocabulaire du tourment psychique, de l'inquiétude, mais aussi – ou pour cela même – du désir amoureux (voilà pourquoi *sollicitare* veut également dire « exciter, provoquer, attirer »). Le souci est tourment parce qu'il est tendu vers l'autre quand l'autre ne cesse de se dérober : il manifeste donc la *sollicitude* du désir, de l'amour et, en général, de l'attention accordée au monde et à autrui. On sait que Martin Heidegger, juste après avoir traité de l'angoisse en tant que « révélation privilégiée de l'être-là », posait dans *Être et temps* le souci *(Sorge)* à une place tout à fait fondamentale, qui était celle de « l'être de l'être-là », pas moins[24]. Mais, pour dire cette légitime position de prééminence ou de préexistence – « le souci est existentiellement et aprioriquement "antérieur" à tout "comportement" et à toute "situation" facticiels de l'être-là, ce qui signifie qu'il est toujours-déjà présent *en* tout comportement et *en* toute situation » –, Heidegger déclarait se prémunir contre toute « anthropologie concrète »[25]. Ce qui l'aura probablement exempté du « souci concret » à se faire dans une période historique – celle-là même dont les témoignages montrés par Esther Shalev-Gerz ont le souci –, une période où il y avait « de quoi s'en faire » (du souci), comme on le dit couramment. Tout autre fut, soit dit en passant, la position de Georges Bataille quand il ajointait, dans *L'Expérience intérieure,* l'*existence* de chaque instant à une *exigence* posée comme souci, comme inquiétude inapaisable devant le temps[26].

Il y a, enfin, une histoire poétique du souci. Je la résumerai en trois simples moments[27]. Le premier est celui de *la beauté* : c'est lorsque François de Malherbe invente cette admirable expression du désir ou du regard comme ce qui va et vient, comme une vague, entre le donné et le retiré : « Beauté, mon beau souci, de qui l'âme incertaine / A, comme l'Océan, son flux et son reflux... »[28]. Le deuxième moment est l'antithèse d'où je suis parti, celle de Mallarmé saluant *le blanc* comme cheville dialectique de tout souci : « Solitude, récif, étoile / À n'importe ce qui valut / Le blanc souci de notre toile. »[29] Le troisième moment pourrait être celui où *le montage* assume l'un et l'autre des deux précédents termes : c'est lorsque Jean-Luc Godard, reprenant et prolongeant la formule de Malherbe, compare le montage, son « beau souci », à un « battement de cœur », un « raccordement sur un regard » ou encore ce qu'il nomme la « mise d'une inconnue en évidence » lorsque, dans le travail sur les images, on parvient à « faire ressortir l'âme sous l'esprit, la passion derrière la machination, [et à] faire prévaloir le cœur sur l'intelligence en détruisant la notion d'espace au profit de celle du temps. »[30]

***

Les « blancs soucis » du témoignage témoignent eux-mêmes de *mouvements de temps* – mouvements pluriels et temps pluriels – à l'œuvre dans la diégèse de chaque récit historique. Ils sont affaire de montages et d'intervalles, de fractures et d'assemblages anachroniquement réunis selon des processus d'attraction ou, au contraire, de conflits. Parler en général du silence dans la parole, parler du souci hors de toute « anthropologie concrète » ne nous amène pas très loin, seulement à de belles notions dénuées de chair, dénuées de gestes. Il faudrait, regardant le montage d'Esther Shalev-Gerz, savoir redescendre des grands paradigmes – « l'instant prégnant » selon Lessing ou « l'être de l'être-là » selon Heidegger – vers les petits syntagmes : descendre, en somme, depuis une philosophie du silence en général vers ces discrets segments ou *brins de silences* que nous découvrons, ici et là, au fil des récits produits par les témoins de l'histoire.

23
Gilles Deleuze, *Logique du sens,* p. 180-189 et 373-386. Pierre Zaoui, *La Traversée des catastrophes. Philosophie pour le meilleur et pour le pire,* Éditions du Seuil, Paris 2010, p. 320.

24
Martin Heidegger, *Être et Temps* (1927), trad. R. Boehm et A. de Waelhens, Gallimard, Paris 1964, p. 226-240.

25
Ibid., p. 236-237.

26
Georges Bataille, *L'Expérience intérieure* (1943), *Œuvres complètes, V,* Gallimard, Paris 1973, p. 83.

27
On pourra consulter le recueil poétique et philosophique constitué par Richard Millet et Jean-Michel Maulpoix autour du motif « Le souci » dans *Recueil,* n°3, 1986, p. 65-170.

28
François de Malherbe, « Dessein de quitter une dame qui ne le contentait que de promesse » (1600), in Antoine Adam (éd.), *Malherbe. Œuvres,* Gallimard, Paris 1971, p. 21.

29
Stéphane Mallarmé, « Salut » (1893), p. 27.

30
Jean-Luc Godard, « Montage, mon beau souci » (1956), in Alain Bergala (éd.), *Jean-Luc Godard par Jean-Luc Godard, I. 1950-1984,* Cahiers du cinéma, Paris 1985 (éd. 1998), p. 93.

Nous serions donc, face à un tel montage de silences, à la croisée de deux dimensions que tout semble opposer : d'un côté, l'*émotion* particulière inhérente à ce que Georges Bataille nommait « la reconnaissance par l'homme de ce qui le voue à ce qui est l'objet de son horreur la plus forte », émotion qui le mène au « silence profond introduit par les larmes. »[31] D'un autre côté, la *construction* inhérente à ce que Jacques Rancière, parlant de Jean-Luc Godard, nomme le « phrasé de l'histoire. »[32] On comprend qu'il faut assumer cette double dimension pour comprendre quelque chose dans ce que nous transmettent ces témoins venus de l'enfer. C'est là que, pour le poète, « indéfectiblement le blanc revient, tout à l'heure gratuit, certain maintenant, pour conclure que rien au-delà et authentiquer le silence. »[33] Et c'est là que, pour l'historien lui-même, vient le temps de *rompre le silence* (pour prolonger le geste de témoignage de tous ceux qui furent, à un moment, réduits au silence mais qui le rompirent malgré tout) tout en acceptant, selon la formule mallarméenne, et sans être sûr de rien, d'*authentiquer le silence*[34].

31
Georges Bataille, « [Attraction et répulsion] » (1938), in *Œuvres complètes, II*, Gallimard, Paris 1971, p. 318 et 333.

32
Jacques Rancière, *Le Destin des images*, La Fabrique, Paris 2003, p. 41-78.

33
Stéphane Mallarmé, « Quant au livre » (1895), in *Œuvres complètes*, p. 387.

34
Ce texte, pour des raisons éditoriales, est ici présenté dans une version écourtée.

IN-BETWEEN: THE CUT
ANNIKA WIK

In extreme close-up, the camera moves across a face. The intimate perspective allows the viewer to discover every tiny cell in the skin. The camera follows a furrow in the surface of the skin as though it was leading the viewer's gaze to a crucial point. Wrinkles appear as lines that shape a landscape. The placement of the camera ascribes meaning to each part of the face. The nuances of color in the skin are emphasized; the same goes for its structure. Strands of hair are depicted so closely that they become nearly unrecognizable because of their size. The movements of the face are explored, and give it life.

This manner of depicting traces and movements in people's faces is a method that recurs frequently in Esther Shalev-Gerz's work. She moves in close proximity to the faces she depicts, and it is as though, with the camera's help, she is searching for places to "open people up."

In *First Generation* (2004) the faces she films in extreme close-up are shown as a site-specific work on a glass façade in Botkyrka, outside of Stockholm, Sweden. As a viewer, one sees the moving portraits directly from the street. Close, close and in constant motion, it is a display of faces that belong to people who exist in the area where the work is on display.

A close-up intensifies through its size; it limits and directs the viewer's attention. The film theorist Jacques Aumont emphasized the way a close-up exerts power through its size and varies in its distance, and how it materializes or creates a metaphorical sense of visual touch.[1] As early as the 1920s, Jean Epstein wrote that the close-up is the soul of the film, but that without motion it gives up its essence.[2] At that time, there was an ongoing, lively film-theoretical debate on the close-up and its connection to the human face. When Walter Benjamin wrote about the aura in modern mechanical reproduction just over a decade later, he argued that it was under threat and that it was retreating to its last refuge—the face of man.[3] In the late 1940s, the Hungarian author and film theorist Béla Balázs wrote about the human face and how our sense of space is cut out by an isolated face:

> Even if we had just seen the same face in the middle of a crowd and the close-up merely separated it from the others, we would still feel that we have suddenly been left alone with this one face to the exclusion of the rest of the world. Even if we have just seen the owner of the face in a long shot, when we look into the eyes in a close-up, we no longer think of that wide space, because the expression and significance of the face has no relation to space and no connection with it. Facing an isolated face takes us out of space, our consciousness of space is cut out ...[4]

In *First Generation*, the separation of the face from the spatial is given multiple layers of meaning. The people depicted are in the crowd we may have just seen at a distance; they are those wandering around in the place where the work is on display. The people belong to the place, but the dislocation of the site-specific work shows that it is more complex than this. Their spatial belonging is problematized through the aesthetic aspects of the work. The people who are shown in the glass façade lose, as Balázs says, their connection to place in some way. To get it back, and to experience the work in its entirety, the viewer must go into the building. She must get in, past the facade. Once inside the building, the people's stories can be heard; inside, the portraits are given voices. Because the people's images and their stories have been separated from one another and placed in a construct of space-time, the viewer is invited to step into a space in-between, a place between image and sound, between a person's appearance and her story.

Here there is an interesting dislocation of sound and image that is characteristic of Esther Shalev-Gerz. In encounters with her artistic practice, the cinematic aspects of this type of dislocation have come to interest me a great deal. I want to understand what kind of space she offers the viewer. What exists there? How do these spaces come into being? How can I understand them? As a film scholar, I find a series of cinematic references interesting in order to approach this aspect of Shalev-Gerz's art. One of these is Ingmar Bergman's *Persona* (1966), but it would be just as illuminating to use specific scenes in films by Alain Resnais, Jean-Luc Godard, Agnes Varda, Michelangelo Antonioni, or Rainer Werner Fassbinder in order to discern cinematic perspectives that I find interesting in Shalev-Gerz's artistic methods.

In Ingmar Bergman's *Persona*, a drama is enacted between two women. Elisabeth Vogler is a renowned actress who suddenly falls into existential doubt during one of her appearances on stage, and she decides to stop speaking. She is placed in a nursing ward, where nurse Alma is designated her personal carer. After some time, the director of the ward sends both women to a place in the countryside with the thought that Elisabeth will regain her strength and become well again. In all respects, the film is about the assumptions of the film medium. It is a meta-film in the most literal sense, in which Bergman explores the materiality of film and its aesthetic qualities. Throughout the movie, it is revealed that a film is made up of parts that are connected in order to form a whole, which, according to Sergei Eisenstein for example, is greater than the sum of its parts.[5] In contrast with Béla Balázs's confidence in the individual take, in Eisenstein's view the cinematic qualities are not captured in the takes but rather in the combination of the parts. While for Balázs close-ups are, in a sort of magic or religious way, revealing and more truthful than other cinematic images because they show what the eye cannot perceive, for Eisenstein, the single image or take can never function as that which is specific to the film

1
Jacques Aumont, *The Image*, British Film Institute, London 1997, p. 103–104.

2
Jean Epstein, " Magnification and Other Writings," trans. Stuart Liebman, *October*, vol. 3 (Spring, 1977), p. 9–25.

3
Walter Benjamin, "The Work of Art in the Age of Mechanical Reproduction," in Hannah Arendt (ed.), *Illuminations*, Schocken Books, New York 1968, p. 226.

4
Béla Balázs, *Theory of the Film (Character and Growth of a New Art)*, Roy Publishers, New York 1953, p. 61.

5
Sergei Eisenstein, "Béla Forgets the Scissors," in Richard Taylor and Ian Christie (ed.), *The Film Factory: Russian and Soviet Cinema in Documents*, Harvard University Press, Cambridge, Massachusetts 1988, p. 145–149.

medium.[6] For him, "the expressive effect of cinema is the result of juxtapositions."[7] It is the joining of the parts, the editing, the montage that is specific to film.

In one of *Persona*'s most emblematic sequences, in an analogous way, Bergman combines the two women's faces. With this combined image, Bergman manages to bring out the ambivalence or even the contradiction that shows how, at the same time, the combined portrait depicts two women who become one, and the different sides of one woman. Seen from a more formalistic perspective, the combination is brought forward *in* the image rather than between the images; it ends up within the image instead of being made invisible through editing. In classic Hollywood film, with its seamless continuity editing, the viewer is always invited into a safe place in the diegesis of the film. In Bergman's high modernist and reflexive film, the viewer is offered no such comfortable position. She is constantly confronted by or reflected in the images.

The method that Bergman uses to expose the materiality of the film and show the many faces of man in *Persona* is similar to the way Esther Shalev-Gerz avails herself of the logic of film as an artistic tool in order to "open people up" and get their stories to emerge. I see similarities in the portrayals of the space between sound and image, outside and inside, and the depicted and his or her story, but where Bergman exposes the materiality of film, parts and cuts in the film itself, Shalev-Gerz opens up in her work a mental and truly physical space, a place, a time, into which she invites the viewer. She invites the viewer to physically and spatially step into the place where the cut or the juxtaposition of a film takes place. In an effort to clarify and illustrate the methodological similarities I am talking about, I will take the liberty of dwelling a bit longer upon Bergman's film and a specific scene in it.

After some time in the countryside, Alma begins to find comfort in being the one who speaks, with Elisabeth as the self-appointed mute listener. She abandons her integrity more and more, and becomes more and more outspoken. One evening, after a few glasses of wine, she confides in Elisabeth a memory of a sexual adventure that has played a great role in her emotional life. In one of the most erotic scenes in cinematic history, Bergman makes use of the power and boundlessness of the viewer's own imagination. He lets Alma tell her whole adventure without resorting to depicting the sex act or the orgy in a flashback. Instead, the viewer, along with Elisabeth herself, must imagine what is described without images from the event. In contrast to classically formalistic narrative, such as the use of shot reverse shot, the viewer is denied reaction shots according to the alternating pattern that usually accompanies dialogue. Instead, the monologue begins with a long shot that includes both the speaker and the listener. Then we go from various long shots into close-ups of Alma, who speaks, with only one shot of Elisabeth in-between. We make our way deeper and deeper into her secret and her mind. We are given no image to change to, or breathe in; rather, the suspense builds gradually through closer and closer shots. Close-ups of Elisabeth follow like some sort of delayed reaction shots, which do not change in rhythm with the delivery of the story. The difference between the listener and the speaker is underscored when, in the scene, we see close-ups of an ear (hearing), and when an arm becomes a silhouette that conceals the eyes (the gaze) of Elisabeth (the listener). Sound and image are separated, and the parts that are usually united are emphasized one by one and in different layers.[8] The images underscore the ear by depicting it in profile; consciousness of the eyes is raised when they are obscured. The characters represent the speaker and the listener, and seeing and hearing are reflected back onto the viewer. The scene is strong in its content, and at the same time it is very material, formalistic, and technical in its presentation. The position that Bergman assigns to the viewer stands in direct opposition to the safe place that continuous editing offers. Instead, the viewer lands in a position where she is confronted by the reflexive character of the image, in a space for imagination, confrontation, and self-reflection.

In several of Esther Shalev-Gerz's video works, the viewer is offered spaces of this kind, but transferred from film to spatial interpretation. When the viewer of *First Generation* is met with extreme close-ups outside the building, and then, only when she has entered the building, hears the sound, this creates a dislocation that is similar to the erotic scene in *Persona*. First we can see, then we can hear, and between the two we are offered space to reflect and bring along our own experience. The time that passes between the moment the viewer sees the people's faces on the outside in *First Generation*, until she finds herself inside the building and hears their stories, leaves space for her to integrate her own experiences into the story. The distance between image and sound activates a temporal and spatial in-between that corresponds to an intended intermediate process, which, from a film-theory perspective can be said to be what is cut away in the editing of a film. Shalev-Gerz uses, so to speak, the logic of the cinematic apparatus in a spatial structure to artistically open up the person, or the image of the person, in order to reach her story so that we in the space between can link another's experience to our own.

The dislocation of time and place in order to create a space where the viewer can integrate her own experience can also be clearly seen in *White Out—Between Telling and Listening* (2002), where a Sami woman by the name of Åsa Simma tells her story in one place, only to listen to it later in a different place. When she is standing in the environment that her life story is about, it is as though she is seriously listening to her own story. The filming of this process, Simma listening to herself, creates a physical and mental place in which the viewer watches Simma's insight while at the same time she is able to reflect on her own life story. Where does it take place? How does it sound? Have I listened properly to my own story?

6
Béla Balázs, "The Future of Film," in Taylor and Christie (ed.), *The Film Factory*, p. 144–145. Eisenstein's text from footnote number five is a response to this text by Béla Balázs.

7
Eisenstein, "Béla Forgets the Scissors," p. 147.

8
For a film-theoretical discussion of the eye as more spatially adapted and the ear as more temporally, how sound supplies temporality to the images in *Persona*, see Michel Chion, *Audio-Vision: Sound on Screen*, Columbia University Press, New York 1994.

The focus in *Does Your Image Reflect Me?* (2002) is on two women's life stories; two stories whose origins are in experiences from two different positions during the Second World War. Their memories and stories are passed on and filmed, in order to then be played for and shown to the other. The other is, in turn, filmed as she listens. As a viewer, it becomes obvious how entwined the story is with the person who tells it; how physical the memory is and what strength it takes to bring the story out of the body. In the same way, it becomes obvious what a physical experience it is to take part in someone else's direct experience.

This idea of the story's rootedness in the body, and the strength it takes to have to return to an experience in order to turn it into a story, is also conveyed in *Between Listening and Telling: Last Witnesses, Auschwitz 1945–2005* (2005). Here, Shalev-Gerz focuses, in the part of the work that is film-based, on the moment when a person is about to start telling a story, the second before the story leaves the body. If not as close as in *First Generation*, she finds herself, with her camera, close enough to capture the body's effort reflected in the face. She captures the moment when the person is forced to relive a part of the experience in order to tell her story so that someone else can take part in it. The film portraits are constant reminders to the visitors in the exhibition space that the testimonies they listen to stem from real people with real bodily experiences and memories that are just as difficult to live with as to recall.

When the work *Sound Machine* (2008) was exhibited in Norrköping and at the Moderna Muséet in Stockholm, the visitor encountered the sound outside the building and then was met, inside the building, by the moving images that the sound could be said to have originated from. Sound and image are thus reunited only when the visitor has visited both places, both the inside and the outside. The dislocation of sound and image is problematized on several levels in the work. A similar dislocation of time and space in *First Generation* is created for the viewer in *Sound Machine*. It is a space for listening and for experiencing a multilayered mental and bodily act.

The sounds that meet the audience outside the buildings are sounds that women who worked in the textile industry in Norrköping heard when they were employed there earlier in their lives. Inside, these women are shown listening to the sounds in front of a landscape of machinery. The industry was shut down many years ago. The women have moved on in their careers, and the machines have grown silent. The women that Shalev-Gerz has depicted were pregnant during the time they worked at that place. In this way, one can say that the sound was inscribed even in the next generation, and as such it also draws attention to the order in which our senses come into being: that, as fetuses, we first develop our hearing and that sight comes later—something upon which Slavoj Žižek bases his psychoanalytic readings of, for example, David Lynch's *Mulholland Drive* (2001) and *Blue Velvet* (1986), Coppola's *The Conversation* (1974), and Bergman's *Persona*.[9] In *Sound Machine*, there is also a historical dimension that is brought forth by the dislocation of sound and image; namely, the fact that the machines have long since become silent, that the factories have been shut down, and that the textile industry has moved to other parts of the world.

Esther Shalev-Gerz looks for methodological ways to explore and artistically give shape to people's direct experiences. As part of this method, it seems necessary to create a place in space-time for the viewer to tread, and Shalev-Gerz constructs this place by reifying space according to the logic of film editing. In these and other video works she uses the cinematic apparatus and its logic to create space and time for the viewer to reflect the experiences of the other in her own. As a method, then, it is not a matter of how she works with cuts in her own films but how she gives form to what fits into a cut. The edited-away space that exists in a cinematic narrative—the time that exists between images, distance, translocations—is what she creates in time and space and what she invites the viewer to explore in her works.

This interest in opening up the image—literally cutting something out to bring forth something else—is a common thread through Esther Shalev-Gerz' work. In the slide series *Just One Sky* (1987–1989), there is a picture of Jerusalem in which part of the slide has been cut away with a sharp knife. A sharp edge in the picture bears witness to this harsh treatment in order to remove part of the picture, and the edge as well as what has been cut away from the motif tells a whole story. In the video work *Inseparable Angels: An Imaginary House for Walter Benjamin* (2000), it is not easy to discern the cut. It is there, but the result in the moving images creates a certain amount of confusion. Here, a cut or a shift in the strip of film has caused the contours in the film to smear. This makes it seem alternately like a double exposure and as though something is quite simply missing. Something has been cut away, and with that, the characteristic inadequacy of memory is visible, reflected in the aesthetics. In the series *Irreparable* (1986–2000), Photoshop has been used to cut away or lift out parts of the image. The parts have then been placed somewhere else in the image. The result can be seen as a collage, but the manner in which it has been done, in the form of a series, is more reminiscent of a montage. Even in her sculptural work, the scissors and the cut are absolutely central. The sculpture *Oil on Stone* (1983) is built from a prototype in the form of a two-dimensional card that has been cut in two. The card has then been pulled apart and made figural. By way of the cut and the turn, a movement has been written into the sculpture. In the transfer from image to sculpture, the image has been opened up just as it has been in her video works; and by way of the viewer's presence, a spatiotemporality that is

9
Interestingly presented by Slavoj Žižek in *The Pervert's Guide to Cinema*, P. Guide, London 2006.

typical of Shalev-Gerz has been written in. Just as with several of her video works, the viewer must move around the work in order to experience it in its entirety, its movement, and its extension in time.

These reflections on Shalev-Gerz's method of cutting, dislocating, and uniting lead once again to Sergei Eisenstein and his theories of juxtaposition and montage, this time to Eisenstein's 1937 reading of Gotthold Ephraim Lessing's 1766 study of the *Laocoon*.[10] Lessing argued in his classic text that every form of art has its own specific properties and can best reach its capacity if the artist makes maximal use of these possibilities while simultaneously realizing their limits. In this argument, he praised sculpture and painting for their spatial qualities and poetry for its extension in time. In his text, Eisenstein extends Lessing's example in order to argue that film involves a compromise between the qualities of these art forms, and he advances his argument by illustrating that connecting and montage, which, in his eyes, characterize film, existed long before film existed as a form of art.[11] Or, as Eisenstein expresses it:

> When we say that in the fundamental structures of film aesthetics there is retained the unique nature of the cinematic phenomenon—the creation of motion out of the collision of two motionless forms—we are not dealing with natural, physical movement but with something that has to do with the way our perceptions work. This is not only the primary phenomenon of cinematic technique ... For strictly speaking what occurs in this case is not movement; instead, our consciousness displays its ability to bring together *two separate phenomena* into a *generalized image*: to merge two *motionless* phases into an *image of movement.*[12]

The quotation is interesting in relation to both Shalev-Gerz's still and moving works: the way a movement or the image of a movement can be seen to be written into the work no matter the medium. In the moving works discussed above, where sound and image have been separated in various ways, it is, as we have seen, up to the viewer to step in, between the parts, and bring them together. This task is also obvious in the work *On Two* (2009). Here, apparently disparate phenomena have been placed side by side and front and back in the image; two people with different backgrounds, two islands in completely different parts of the world, different languages, texts, and life stories. The young Lebanese student of philosophy Rola Younes stands in the frame beside the French philosopher Jacques Rancière. Two islands are depicted in the background of the image, behind Younes and Rancière: Ile Seguin outside of Paris, and Cortes Island off the west coast of Canada. He reads a passage from his book *The Emancipated Spectator*[13]; she speaks and sings in a few of the many languages she has command of. Both are filmed against a green screen. They are not in the same room or context. They have different backgrounds and life stories. It is up to the viewer to find links, form a dialogue between the two, and create an equal worth between dualities. Their backgrounds, languages, and stories become parts that the viewer must put together into a whole that is greater than its parts, a montage that in many ways is handed over to the viewer to complete.

To round out this reflection on Esther Shalev-Gerz's work from a film studies perspective, I will return one last time to *Persona*. Before the women's faces are combined, there is a long scene in two parts. The scene is about Elisabeth's sense of being a mother, and it is a story that, on the soundtrack, is told exactly the same way twice, by Alma. Even the choice of shots is identical, with the sole difference being that it is first Elisabeth, the listener, whom we see portrayed, and then it is Alma, the speaker. Both versions of the story conclude with an extreme close-up. We take part in the same story from the perspectives of the speaker and the listener, and depending on whether we see them as two different women or two sides of one woman, we are given images of someone seriously listening to her own story, someone listening to herself.

Thus we begin and end in extreme close-up, and in-between them, comparisons between Bergman's way of depicting, in *Persona*, people's ability or inability to listen to themselves, and Shalev-Gerz's methods, where, in a place between time and space and using the logic of film as a tool, she portrays people and opens them up in order to bring forth their histories and life stories, for both the people themselves and the viewer to listen to.

10
Sergei Eisentstein, "Laocoon," in Michael Glenny and Richard Taylor (ed.), *Selected Works Vol. II: Towards a Theory of Montage*, I.B. Tauris, London 2010, p. 109–202.

11
Ibid.

12
Ibid., p. 119.

13
Jacques Rancière, *The Emancipated Spectator*, Verso Books, London 2009.

ENTRE-DEUX: LE MONTAGE
ANNIKA WIK

La caméra parcourt un visage en très gros plan. Le spectateur découvre chaque pore, chaque cellule de la peau qui lui est ainsi détaillée. La caméra suit un sillon de la surface cutanée, comme si elle voulait amener le regard du spectateur vers un lieu important. Les rides apparaissent comme des lignes qui font sens. Le positionnement de la caméra donne une signification à chaque partie du visage. Les nuances de la peau, la variation de ses couleurs sont accentuées. Sa structure aussi. Un cheveu devient presque impossible à reconnaître, tant il est filmé de près et tant sa taille devient incongrue. Les mouvements du visage sont explorés, et celui-ci prend vie.

Mettre ainsi en images les sillons et les mouvements du visage humain est une méthode récurrente dans l'œuvre d'Esther Shalev-Gerz. Elle se meut au plus près des visages qu'elle reproduit ; on a l'impression qu'avec sa caméra, elle recherche l'endroit par lequel elle pourra entrer à l'intérieur des gens qu'elle filme. Dans *First Generation* (2004), projet *in situ*, elle utilise une façade en verre d'un bâtiment de Botkyrka, ville de la banlieue de Stockholm, pour projeter des visages qu'elle a filmés en très gros plan. Le spectateur voit ces portraits en mouvement depuis la rue ; des portraits en gros plan et en mouvement permanent, ceux d'habitants du quartier.

Du fait de sa taille, le gros plan intensifie, il limite et cible l'attention. Le théoricien du cinéma Jacques Aumont explique en quoi, par sa taille, le gros plan est un défi ; comment il joue sur les distances et matérialise, c'est-à-dire crée, une sensation métaphorique de toucher visuel[1]. Dès les années 1920, Jean Epstein écrit que le gros plan est l'âme du film, mais que, sans mouvement, il perd son essence[2]. À cette époque, le débat est vif entre théoriciens du cinéma quant au pourquoi et au comment du gros plan et à sa relation avec le visage humain. Lorsque Walter Benjamin, une dizaine d'années plus tard, écrit sur l'aura à l'ère de la reproductibilité technique, c'est pour dire que cette aura est menacée et que son dernier refuge est le visage humain[3]. À la fin des années 1940, l'écrivain et théoricien du cinéma de nationalité hongroise Béla Balázs écrit sur le visage humain et souligne que notre sens de l'espace est érodé par la vision d'un visage isolé :

> « Lorsque le visage d'une personne que l'on vient de voir au sein d'un groupe est soudain séparé de son environnement pour être ainsi mis en relief, alors c'est comme si nous étions brutalement placés en tête à tête avec cette personne. Même si nous l'avons vue auparavant dans un certain cadre, nous n'y pensons plus dès que nous en découvrons le visage en gros plan. Car *l'expression* d'un visage et *la signification* de cette expression n'ont *aucun lien, aucun rapport avec le cadre en question*. Face à un visage isolé, nous ne percevons pas le lieu. Notre sens de l'espace est érodé. »[4]

Dans *First Generation*, la séparation entre le visage et le lieu prend plusieurs sens. Les personnes représentées se trouvaient peut-être dans le groupe que nous venons d'apercevoir, ce sont elles qui se promènent là où l'œuvre est exposée. Elles forment un tout avec le lieu, mais la décomposition de l'œuvre *in situ* montre que la réalité est plus complexe que cela. Leur appartenance spatiale se trouve problématisée par les choix esthétiques de l'œuvre. Comme le dirait Balázs, les visages projetés sur la façade en verre perdent, d'une certaine façon, leur lien avec l'espace. Pour retrouver ce lien, et pour vivre l'œuvre dans son entier, le spectateur doit entrer dans le bâtiment. Il doit y entrer en passant derrière la façade. Une fois à l'intérieur, on entend les récits des personnes, les portraits y gagnent une voix. Du fait de la séparation entre images et récits et de l'utilisation d'une construction spatio-temporelle, ce qui est proposé au spectateur, c'est d'entrer dans un espace intermédiaire, un espace entre image et son, entre l'apparence d'un être humain et son histoire.

Se retrouve ici un décalage intéressant entre image et son, caractéristique de l'œuvre d'Esther Shalev-Gerz. Dans ma rencontre avec son œuvre, ce sont les aspects filmiques de ce type de décalage qui m'intéressent. Je veux comprendre quels sont ces espaces qu'elle offre au spectateur. Qu'y trouve-t-on ? Comment se forment-ils ? Comment pouvons-nous les comprendre ? En tant que spécialiste du cinéma, un grand nombre de références cinématographiques me paraissent intéressantes pour aborder cet aspect de la pratique d'Esther Shalev-Gerz. L'une de ces références est le film *Persona* d'Ingmar Bergman (1966), mais il aurait été tout aussi éclairant d'utiliser certaines scènes tirées de films d'Alain Resnais, de Jean-Luc Godard, d'Agnès Varda, de Michelangelo Antonioni ou de Rainer Werner Fassbinder pour analyser les perspectives cinématographiques dans l'œuvre d'Esther Shalev-Gerz.

Dans *Persona* d'Ingmar Bergman, un drame se joue entre deux femmes. Elisabeth Vogler est une actrice reconnue qui, au cours d'une représentation théâtrale, tombe soudain dans un profond doute existentiel et décide de ne plus parler. Elle est admise dans un service de soins où une infirmière prénommée Alma devient sa garde-malade personnelle. Après un temps, la chef de service envoie les deux femmes à la campagne où Elisabeth est censée reprendre des forces et guérir. À tous égards, ce film est un film sur les conditions qui sous-tendent le médium filmique lui-même. C'est un « méta-film » au sens littéral du terme, dans lequel Bergman explore la matérialité du film et ses propriétés esthétiques. Il est une mise à nu de la façon dont une œuvre cinématographique est composée de parties qui forment un tout. Un tout qui, selon Sergueï Eisenstein par exemple, est plus grand que la somme de ses parties[5]. À la différence de Béla Balázs qui croit à la prise de vue en tant que telle, chez Eisenstein les qualités filmographiques ne proviennent pas de la prise de

1
Jacques Aumont, *L'image*, Nathan, Paris 1990, p. 105-108.

2
Jean Epstein, « Grossissement », in *Bonjour Cinéma*, Éditions de la Sirène, Paris 1921, p. 93-108.

3
Walter Benjamin, « L'œuvre d'art à l'époque de sa reproductibilité technique », in *Œuvres, vol. III*, Gallimard, Paris 2000 (1939), p. 269-316.

4
Béla Balázs, « Das Gesicht des Menschen », in *Der Film. Werden und Wesen einer neuen Kunst*, Globus Verlag, Vienne 1949, p. 60-92.

5
Sergueï Eisenstein, « Béla oublie les ciseaux », in *Kinogazeta*, 10 août 1927, p. 3, repris in Sergueï Eisenstein, *Au-delà des étoiles*, UGE, Paris 1974, p. 157-165.

vue en elle-même mais de l'assemblage de ses composantes. Alors que pour Balázs, les gros plans sont, de façon quasi magique ou religieuse, révélateurs et plus vrais que d'autres plans puisqu'ils montrent ce que l'œil ne peut percevoir, chez Eisenstein, ce n'est jamais ni l'image seule, ni la prise de vue isolée qui font la spécificité d'un film[6]. Pour lui, l'expressivité d'un film est le résultat des assemblages effectués[7]. C'est l'assemblage des parties, le découpage, le montage, qui lui confèrent sa spécificité.

Dans l'une des séquences les plus emblématiques de *Persona*, Bergman fait se fondre, de façon analogique, les visages des deux femmes. Avec cette image fusionnée, Bergman réussit à faire naître l'ambivalence, ou même peut-être la contradiction, de ce portrait qui montre à la fois deux femmes devenir une, mais aussi les différentes facettes d'une seule et même femme. D'un point de vue formel, il est clair que la transformation des deux visages en un seul est bien *dans* l'image, et non entre les images. Cette transformation est même soulignée par l'image au lieu d'être rendue invisible par le montage. Dans le récit hollywoodien classique, avec son système de « montage continu », de narration « sans couture », le spectateur est en permanence invité à s'installer confortablement dans la diégèse du film. Dans le film éminemment moderniste et réflexif de Bergman, un tel confort n'est pas offert au spectateur. Celui-ci est sans arrêt confronté par les images ou reflété par elles.

La méthode que Bergman utilise pour mettre à nu la matérialité du film et montrer les nombreuses facettes de l'être humain dans *Persona* est semblable à la façon dont Esther Shalev-Gerz se sert de la logique cinématographique comme outil artistique pour « ouvrir les gens » et faire émerger leurs histoires. Je vois des points communs avec Bergman dans l'utilisation qu'elle fait de l'espace entre image et son, entre intérieur et extérieur, entre portrait et histoire ; mais là où Bergman révèle la matérialité du film, ses différentes composantes et ses intervalles, Esther Shalev-Gerz ouvre dans ses installations un espace tant mental que physique, un lieu, un temps où le spectateur est invité à pénétrer. Elle invite le spectateur à entrer, tant sur le plan physique que spatial, dans ce qui, dans un film, est le lieu du montage. Pour tenter d'expliciter et d'illustrer ces similarités méthodologiques, je m'arrêterai encore une fois sur le film de Bergman déjà cité et sur une scène en particulier.

Après avoir passé quelques temps à la campagne, Alma commence à prendre du plaisir à être celle qui parle, avec Elisabeth dans le rôle choisi d'auditrice muette. Peu à peu, Alma relâche ses défenses et devient de plus en plus franche et directe. Un soir, après quelques verres de vin, elle confie à Elisabeth le souvenir d'une aventure sexuelle qui a joué un grand rôle dans sa vie émotionnelle. Dans l'une des scènes les plus érotiques de l'histoire du cinéma, Bergman se sert de la force et de l'infinie capacité d'imagination du spectateur. Il laisse Alma raconter toute son aventure sans tomber dans la facilité de représenter l'acte sexuel ou l'orgie par un flashback. Au lieu de cela, le spectateur, tout comme Elisabeth, doit se représenter lui-même ce qui est raconté, sans l'aide d'images. La forme choisie pour le récit est tout sauf classique. Bergman ne recourt pas au procédé du champ/contrechamp. Il refuse de montrer au spectateur les réactions d'Elisabeth et ne suit pas le modèle de plans alternés habituellement utilisé lorsqu'il s'agit de mettre un dialogue en images. Au contraire, le monologue d'Alma commence par un plan large qui englobe les deux protagonistes. Nous passons ensuite de différents plans larges à des gros plans d'Alma parlant, seulement interrompus par un unique plan d'Elisabeth. Nous pénétrons de plus en plus profondément à l'intérieur de son secret et à l'intérieur d'Alma elle-même. Aucune autre image ne nous est accordée, ni pour changer de point de vue, ni pour prendre une respiration. La tension croît progressivement au fur et à mesure de la multiplication de plans de plus en plus rapprochés. Des gros plans d'Elisabeth se succèdent comme une sorte d'illustration décalée de ses réactions, mais ils ne suivent pas le rythme du récit. La différence entre celle qui écoute et celle qui parle est soulignée par le choix de présenter des gros plans d'une oreille – l'écoute – et de la silhouette d'un bras qui cache les yeux – le regard – d'Elisabeth, l'auditrice. Le son et l'image sont séparés et les composantes qui, normalement, devraient être assemblées sont présentées ici chacune séparément et en différentes couches[8]. Les images soulignent l'oreille en nous montrant un profil. Elles nous font prendre conscience des yeux en nous les cachant. Les protagonistes représentent l'orateur et l'auditeur. La vue et l'audition se réfléchissent sur le spectateur. C'est une scène forte de par son contenu et, en même temps, très matérielle, formaliste et technique sur le plan de sa représentation cinématographique. La position que Bergman assigne au spectateur est à l'opposé du confort offert par le « montage continu ». Chez lui, le spectateur est confronté au caractère réflexif de l'image, dans un espace dévolu à l'imagination, à la confrontation et à l'auto-réflexion.

Dans plusieurs des œuvres vidéo d'Esther Shalev-Gerz, des espaces de cet ordre sont également offerts au spectateur, mais transférés de l'univers cinématographique à une configuration spatiale. Lorsque le spectateur de *First Generation* est confronté à des gros plans très rapprochés à l'extérieur du bâtiment, et qu'il n'entend le son qu'une fois à l'intérieur, un décalage se crée qui ressemble à la scène érotique dans *Persona*. On voit d'abord, et l'on entend ensuite. Entre les deux, la possibilité de réfléchir et d'intégrer notre propre expérience est offerte. Dans *First Generation,* le temps qui s'écoule entre l'instant où le spectateur voit les visages des gens de l'extérieur et celui où il se retrouve dans le bâtiment et entend leurs récits laisse un espace qui permet d'intégrer sa propre expérience à l'histoire qui nous est

6
Béla Balázs, « Produktive und reproduktive Filmkunst », in *Die Filmtechnik*, n°12, 1926, repris in Béla Balázs, *Schriften zum Film. Band 2 : "Der Geist des Films". Kritiken und Aufsätze 1926-1931*, Carl Hanser, Munich 1984, p. 209-212. Le texte d'Eisenstein cité dans la note ci-dessus est une réponse à ce texte de Béla Balázs.

7
Sergueï Eisenstein, « Béla oublie les ciseaux », p. 157-167.

8
Pour une discussion théorique sur l'œil comme adapté à l'espace et l'oreille davantage au temps, et sur la façon dont le son apporte une temporalité aux images dans *Persona*, voir Michel Chion, *L'Audio-vision. Son et image au cinéma*, Nathan, Paris 1990.

racontée. La distance entre l'image et le son active un intervalle spatio-temporel – un interlude voulu – qui, d'un point de vue cinématographique, peut être considéré comme équivalent à ce qui est coupé lors du montage. En d'autres termes, Esther Shalev-Gerz utilise la logique cinématographique dans une structure spatiale pour « ouvrir » les protagonistes de ses œuvres – ou leur image – et accéder ainsi à leur histoire afin que, dans cet intervalle, nous puissions créer un lien entre notre propre expérience et celle des autres.

Dans *White Out – Entre l'écoute et la parole* (2002), on retrouve clairement cette idée de décalage spatio-temporel destiné à créer un espace de réflexion pour le spectateur. Une femme saami, nommée Åsa Simma, raconte son histoire dans un lieu donné, pour ensuite l'écouter dans un autre lieu. Lorsqu'elle se retrouve dans l'environnement qui constitue le cadre de l'histoire qu'elle raconte – celle de sa vie – on la voit écouter avec attention sa propre histoire. En filmant Åsa Simma qui s'écoute elle-même, l'installation vidéo ouvre un espace physique et mental qui permet au spectateur de saisir ce qui se passe chez elle et qui, parallèlement, lui offre la possibilité d'y réfléchir. Où se déroule l'histoire ? Comment résonne-t-elle ? Ai-je bien écouté ma propre histoire ?

Dans *Est-ce que ton image me regarde ?* (2002), ce sont les récits de vie de deux femmes qui forment le point central de l'œuvre, deux histoires qui ont leurs origines dans des expériences vécues selon deux positions différentes pendant la Seconde Guerre mondiale. Leurs récits sont filmés séparément, puis montrés à chacune d'entre elles. Chacune est ensuite filmée écoutant le récit de l'autre. Le spectateur découvre alors à quel point chaque récit est lié à celle qui le raconte, et à quel point le processus de remémoration est non seulement mental mais également physique. Raconter – faire sortir de soi cette histoire – demande à ces femmes une énergie considérable. De la même façon, il ressort clairement qu'écouter le récit de quelqu'un peut être une expérience physiquement éprouvante.

Cet ancrage corporel du récit et l'énergie nécessaire à transformer un vécu en récit apparaît également dans l'œuvre *Entre l'écoute et la parole : derniers témoins, Auschwitz 1945-2005* (2005). Esther Shalev-Gerz se concentre ici, dans la partie filmique de l'œuvre, sur l'instant où une personne prend son élan avant de se mettre à raconter, cet instant précis qui précède le moment où le récit va quitter le corps. Même si elle ne filme pas ici d'aussi près que dans *First Generation*, sa caméra est suffisamment proche pour capter l'effort corporel qui se reflète sur le visage au moment où la personne est amenée à revivre une partie de son histoire afin que quelqu'un d'autre puisse y accéder. Les portraits filmés rappellent aux visiteurs que les témoignages qu'ils écoutent proviennent de personnes réelles, avec des expériences corporelles et des souvenirs réels, dont il est aussi difficile de se souvenir que de vivre avec.

Lorsque l'œuvre *Sound Machine* (2008) a été montrée à Norrköping et au Moderna Museet de Stockholm, le visiteur était accueilli par du son à l'extérieur du bâtiment, pour découvrir ensuite, une fois à l'intérieur, les images en mouvement d'où les sons provenaient à l'origine. Ici encore, le son et l'image n'étaient donc réunis que lorsque le visiteur était passé par les deux étapes, extérieure et intérieure. Le décalage entre son et image est ici problématisé à plusieurs niveaux. En utilisant un décalage similaire à celui de *First Generation,* Esther Shalev-Gerz crée un intervalle spatio-temporel comparable qui génère un espace ouvert à l'intégration des expériences des visiteurs.

Les sons qui accueillent les visiteurs à l'extérieur sont les bruits que les ouvrières de l'industrie textile de Norrköping entendaient au quotidien dans l'usine. À l'intérieur, une vidéo montre les femmes qui écoutent ces sons, devant un arrière-plan de machines. L'usine est désormais fermée depuis de nombreuses années. Les femmes qui y travaillaient ont changé de métier et les machines se sont tues. Shalev-Gerz a choisi de faire le portrait de femmes enceintes à l'époque où elles y travaillaient. D'une certaine façon, les sons qu'elles y entendaient ont donc été transmis à la génération suivante et, dans ce sens, la configuration spatiale de l'œuvre attire l'attention sur l'ordre dans lequel nos sens se développent : le fœtus commence par entendre, la vue n'arrive que plus tard. C'est d'ailleurs l'un des éléments sur lequel Slavoj Žižek base ses lectures psychanalytiques de *Mullholland Drive* (2001) et de *Blue Velvet* (1986) de David Lynch, de *The Conversation* (1974) de Coppola et, bien sûr, de *Persona* de Bergman[9]. Il y a aussi, dans *Sound Machine*, une dimension historique soulignée par le décalage entre son et image, à savoir le fait que les machines se sont tues depuis longtemps, que les usines ont fermé et que l'industrie textile est allée s'installer dans d'autres régions du monde.

Dans son œuvre, Esther Shalev-Gerz recherche des façons d'explorer et de représenter les expériences directes des gens. Un aspect essentiel de sa méthodologie consiste à créer un lieu spatio-temporel réservé au spectateur. Elle construit ce lieu en matérialisant l'intervalle existant dans la logique du montage cinématographique. Dans les installations vidéo dont nous avons parlé et dans d'autres, elle utilise la logique cinématographique pour donner au spectateur l'espace et le temps nécessaires pour réfléchir à l'expérience des autres à travers la sienne. Sa méthode ne consiste donc pas à réfléchir sur la façon de découper ni de monter ses propres films, mais bien sur la façon de donner forme à ce qui s'insère dans le montage. L'espace qui disparaît au montage dans le récit cinématographique – le temps qui existe entre les images, les distances, les déplacements – est ce qu'elle façonne sur un plan spatio-temporel et qu'elle nous invite à explorer dans ses œuvres.

Cet intérêt à ouvrir l'image – à littéralement couper quelque chose pour faire apparaître autre chose – constitue

9
Voir la présentation de Slavoj Žižek dans *The Pervert's Guide to Cinema*, P. Guide, Londres 2006.

un fil rouge dans l'œuvre d'Esther Shalev-Gerz. Dans la série de diapositives *Juste un ciel* (1987-1989), une partie d'une image de Jérusalem a été découpée et enlevée au couteau. Le bord saillant témoigne du traitement brutal infligé à la diapositive pour la mutiler et cette incise, comme ce qui a été enlevé, raconte toute une histoire. Dans l'œuvre *Anges inséparables: la maison éphémère pour Walter Benjamin* (2000), le montage est difficile à distinguer de prime abord. Il est là, mais ce que l'on voit dans ces images en mouvement crée une certaine confusion. C'est le montage ou le décalage de la bande vidéo qui fait que les contours des images sont flous. Ce qui donne alternativement l'impression soit d'une double exposition, soit tout simplement qu'il manque quelque chose. Quelque chose a été coupé, et le choix esthétique vient souligner le caractère lacunaire de la mémoire. Dans la série *Irréparable* (1986-2000), Esther Shalev-Gerz a utilisé le logiciel Photoshop pour couper ou extraire des composantes de l'image. Celles-ci ont ensuite été intégrées ailleurs dans l'image. Le résultat peut être considéré comme une sorte de collage, mais la manière dont il a été effectué, sous forme de série, fait plutôt penser à un montage. Même dans son travail sculptural, les ciseaux et le montage occupent une place centrale. La sculpture *Huile sur pierre* (1983) est construite à partir d'un prototype ayant la forme d'une carte en deux dimensions qui a été coupée en deux. La carte a ensuite été dissociée et rendue figurative. Par la découpe et la torsion, un mouvement a été conféré à la sculpture. En passant du statut d'image à celui de sculpture, l'image, au même titre que les œuvres vidéos décrites plus haut, s'est ouverte et, du fait de la présence du spectateur, s'inscrit dans une spatio-temporalité caractéristique du travail d'Esther Shalev-Gerz. Comme dans ses installations vidéo, le spectateur doit se mouvoir autour de la sculpture pour l'appréhender dans son ensemble, en saisir les mouvements et les implications temporelles.

Ces réflexions sur la façon dont Esther Shalev-Gerz coupe, décale et assemble nous ramène une fois encore à Serguei Eisenstein et à ses théories sur l'assemblage et le montage, en particulier à son analyse de l'étude du *Laocoon* écrite en 1766 par Gotthold Ephraim Lessing[10]. Dans ce texte devenu un classique, Lessing argumentait que chaque forme artistique a ses qualités propres et réalise son potentiel lorsque l'artiste utilise ces spécificités au maximum tout en étant conscient des limites de ces dernières. Dans ce raisonnement, il louait la sculpture et la peinture pour leurs qualités spatiales et la poésie pour sa capacité d'extension dans le temps. Dans son texte, Eisenstein part de l'exemple de Lessing pour argumenter que le cinéma allie les qualités de ces différentes formes d'art, et il approfondit son argumentation en précisant que l'assemblage et le montage, qui sont, selon lui, les caractéristiques premières du cinéma, existaient bien avant que ce dernier ne devienne une forme d'art[11]. Comme Eisenstein l'écrit lui-même:

« Lorsque nous disons que, dans la structure fondamentale de l'esthétique cinématographique, est conservée la nature unique du phénomène filmique – la création du mouvement à partir de deux formes immobiles –, c'est parce que nous n'avons pas affaire à un mouvement physique naturel mais à quelque chose qui touche la manière même dont fonctionne notre perception. Ceci n'est pas seulement le phénomène technique de base de l'art cinématographique ; car ce qui se passe là n'est pas, stricto sensu, un mouvement. Ce qui se passe, c'est que notre conscience montre sa capacité à assembler *deux phénomènes séparés* en *une image unique* ; à fusionner deux phases immobiles en *une représentation du mouvement.* »[12]

Cette citation est intéressante par rapport aux œuvres d'Esther Shalev-Gerz, que ce soit ses œuvres fixes ou ses images en mouvement. Car elle permet de comprendre comment un mouvement ou l'image d'un mouvement peut s'inscrire dans une œuvre, quel que soit son médium. Dans ses œuvres en mouvement où le son et l'image ont été séparés de différentes façons, c'est au visiteur d'entrer dans l'intervalle entre les deux et de les assembler. Cette tâche est aussi évidente dans *D'Eux* (2009) où des phénomènes apparemment disparates sont présentés côte à côte sur l'image. Deux personnes d'origines diverses, deux îles appartenant à des parties du monde totalement différentes, des langues, des textes et des récits de vie différents. La jeune étudiante en philosophie libanaise Rola Younes est aux côtés du philosophe français Jacques Rancière. Deux îles sont reproduites en arrière-plan, derrière eux: l'île Seguin, près de Paris, et l'île Cortes sur la côte ouest du Canada. Il lit un passage de son livre *Le Spectateur émancipé*[13], elle parle et chante dans quelques-unes des nombreuses langues qu'elle maîtrise. Les deux sont filmés sur fond vert. Ils ne sont pas dans la même pièce ni dans le même contexte. Ils ont des parcours différents, des vies différentes. C'est au spectateur de trouver les liens, d'établir un dialogue entre les deux protagonistes et de créer une égalité entre les dualités. Leurs parcours, leurs langues et leurs histoires sont des parties que le spectateur doit assembler pour créer un tout qui soit plus grand que ses parties, un montage dont la réalisation finale est confiée au spectateur.

Pour conclure ces réflexions sur l'œuvre d'Esther Shalev-Gerz du point de vue de la théorie du cinéma, je reviens une dernière fois à *Persona*. Le fusionnement des visages des deux femmes est précédé d'une longue scène en deux parties. La scène traite du rapport d'Elisabeth à la maternité, et le récit est raconté deux fois de suite par Alma exactement de la même manière. Le choix des plans est également identique, la seule différence étant que l'on voit d'abord Elisabeth, celle qui écoute, et ensuite Alma, celle qui parle. Les deux versions du récit s'achèvent toutes les deux par un gros plan très

10
Sergueï Eisenstein, « Laocoon », in *Selected Works : Towards a Theory of Montage*, vol. 2, I.B. Tauris, Londres 2010, p. 109-202.

11
Ibid., p. 109-202.

12
Ibid., p. 119.

13
Jacques Rancière, *Le Spectateur émancipé*, La Fabrique, Paris 2009.

rapproché. Nous participons au même récit du point de vue de celle qui écoute puis du point de vue de celle qui parle et, selon que nous les voyons comme deux femmes différentes ou comme les deux facettes d'une même femme, les images qui nous sont proposées sont celles de quelqu'un qui écoute attentivement sa propre histoire, quelqu'un qui s'écoute elle-même.

Nous terminons donc comme nous avons commencé, par des gros plans très rapprochés avec, entre les deux, des comparaisons entre la façon dont Bergman représente la capacité ou l'incapacité des gens à s'écouter eux-mêmes dans *Persona,* et les méthodes d'Esther Shalev-Gerz qui, avec la logique cinématographique pour outil et le recours aux intervalles spatio-temporels, fait le portrait de personnes afin de présenter une histoire et un vécu qu'eux-mêmes et les spectateurs pourront écouter.

SPACES FOR DEEP MEMORY: ESTHER SHALEV-GERZ AND THE FIRST COUNTER-MONUMENTS

JAMES E. YOUNG

In 1981, Maya Lin—a 21-year old architecture student at Yale University—won an open, blind competition for the *Vietnam Veterans' Monument*, to be sited on the national mall in Washington, DC. In her minimalist, "negative-form" design, Maya Lin openly acknowledged her debt to both Sir Edwin Lutyens's *Memorial to the Missing of the Somme* (1924) in Thiepval, France; and to Georges-Henri Pingusson's *Memorial to the Martyrs of the Deportation* (1962) on the île de la Cité in Paris. Both were precursors to the "counter-monument" realized so brilliantly by Lin, both articulations of uncompensated loss and absence, represented by carved-out pieces of landscape, as well as by the visitor's descent downward (and inward) into memory.[1]

Carved into the ground, a black wound in the landscape and an explicit counterpoint to Washington's prevailing white, neo-classical obelisks and statuary, Maya Lin's design articulated loss without redemption, and formalized a national ambivalence surrounding the memory of American soldiers sent to fight and die in a war the country now abhorred. In Maya Lin's words, she "imagined taking a knife and cutting into the earth, opening it up, an initial violence and pain that in time would heal."[2] That is, she opened a space in the landscape that would open a space within us for memory. "I never looked at the memorial as a wall, an object," Maya Lin has said, "but as an edge to the earth, an opened side." Instead of a positive V-form (like a jutting elbow or a flying-wedge military formation), she opened up the V's obverse space, a negative-space to be filled by those who come to remember America's fallen soldiers.

After the dedication of Maya Lin's *Vietnam Veterans' Monument* in 1982, a generation of young German memorial artists seemed to find in it a contrarian memorial vernacular for the expression of their own national shame and ambivalence toward memory of the Holocaust; they also found a memorial medium for their revulsion against traditionally authoritarian, complacent, and self-certain national shrines. Preoccupied with absence and irredeemable loss, and with a broken and irreparable world, these artists and architects would arrive at their own, counter-memorial architectural vernacular to express the breach in their faith in civilization without mending it. Eventually, counter-memorial artists and architects such as Esther Shalev-Gerz, Jochen Gerz, Horst Hoheisel, Micha Ullman, and Daniel Libeskind (among others) would acknowledge that Maya Lin's design for the Vietnam Veterans' Monument broke the mold that made their own counter-memorial work possible.

How amazing then, that in 1983, without yet having seen or heard about the *Vietnam Veterans' Monument*, Esther Shalev would uncannily counterpoint her nation's own memorial tradition in *Oil on Stone* (Tel Hai, 1983)—what must be called the "other" first counter-monument of its generation. Immigrating to Israel as an 8-year old from Vilnius in 1957, Esther Shalev (like others in her generation), lived through a succession of wars, including the 1967 Six-Day War, the Yom Kippur War of 1973, the Litani invasion of 1978, and the Lebanon War of 1982. But it was this last war, the Israeli invasion of Lebanon in June 1982, a desperate attempt to run the PLO and its rockets out of Lebanon and away from Israel's northern border, that broke an entire generation's heart and national spirit. The aerial bombardment of Beirut, the Christian Phalangists' mass murder of Palestinians in the Sabra and Shatilla refugee camp under Israel's guard, and the death of an Israeli university student and peace demonstrator in a grenade attack by an Israeli counter-demonstrator led to mass demonstrations and the eventual resignation of then-defense minister, Ariel Sharon.

An entire generation of Israeli writers, artists, and academics—already war-weary and skeptical of the government's rationale for Israel's first "war of choice"—would now challenge not just the war but also their own young nation's founding myths and narratives, especially as they seemed to buttress the government's war claims and continued occupation of the West Bank. Israeli soldier-poets and playwrights suddenly began to evoke Holocaust imagery in their depictions of young Palestinian and Lebanese victims of Israel's invasion. Authors like Amos Oz and A.B. Yehoshua publicly upbraided Prime Minister Menachem Begin for comparing Yasser Arafat in Beirut to Adolph Hitler in his Berlin bunker.[3] A rising school of Israeli academics, "the New Historians," openly began to question the State's founding fathers' version of the 1948 War of Independence and the subsequent Palestinian refugee crisis.

In 1982, Esther Shalev took part in a large exhibition of contemporary art, *Here and Now*, at the Israel Museum in Jerusalem. In her piece, *Oil on Metal*, Shalev took a large sheet of steel folded to be free-standing, and cut out a laser-etched human figure, inspired by Picasso, she would later say. The figure is absent, an empty space in the oil-painted metal sheet. Invited the next year to participate in a large outdoor landscape exhibition at Tel Hai in northern Galilee, Shalev fabricated this same "missing figure" in a mortared wall of white stone blocks, which had been cut from a single large slab of Jerusalem stone. She installed *Oil on Stone* on a wild, rocky hillside, just north of and entirely visible from the national shrine to Yoseph Trumpeldor, an early Zionist pioneer and military hero killed while defending a small Jewish settlement at Tel Hai in 1920. According to Yael Zerubavel, "When the State of Israel was founded, Tel Hai was established as an Israeli national 'myth of beginning,' representing the pioneering era in Israeli history ... [T]o the Jewish community in Palestine, the battle at Tel Hai symbolized a major transformation of Jewish national character and the emergence of a new spirit of heroism and self-sacrifice."[4] As the national site of Israel's transformational myth of origins, Tel Hai would now become the site of yet another transformation in national consciousness.

1
See Maya Lin, *Boundaries*, Simon & Schuster, New York 2000, p. 49. Lin's reference to the Pingusson memorial in Paris came in a private conversation with the author.

2
Lin, *Boundaries*, p. 49.

3
See James E. Young, "When Soldier Poets Remember the Holocaust," *Writing and Rewriting the Holocaust*, Indiana University Press, Bloomington & Indianapolis 1988, p. 134–146. See also Amos Oz, "Hitler kvar met, adoni rosh hamemshalah [Hitler's Already Dead, Mr. Prime Minister]," reprinted in *Chatziat Gevul: Shirim Mimilhemet Levanon* [Border Crossing: Poems from the Lebanon War], Sifriat Poalim, Tel Aviv 1983. Also, Yehuda Bauer, "Fruits of Fear," *Jerusalem Post*, June 3, 1982, p. 8; and Ze'ev Mankowitz, "Beirut Is Not Berlin," *Jerusalem Post*, August 4, 1982, p. 8.

4
Yael Zerubavel, "New Beginning, Old Past: The Collective Memory of Pioneering in Israeli Culture," Laurence J. Silberstein (ed.), *New Perspectives on Israeli History*, New York University Press, New York & London 1991, p. 193. Also see Zerubavel's excellent full-length study, *Recovered Roots: Collective Memory and the Making of Israeli National Tradition*, University of Chicago Press, Chicago & London 1995.

Permanently installed in 1983, Shalev's *Oil on Stone* planted its missing human figure as a counterpoint to both the surrounding natural landscape and the white Jerusalem stone blocks composing *The Roaring Lion*, sculptor Abraham Melnikov's memorial to the legendary Trumpeldor, designed in the blocky Assyrian-style of its time, and dedicated at Tel Hai in 1934. By installing *Oil on Stone* within the sightlines of *The Roaring Lion*, Shalev physically and visually countered this national memorial with another kind of memorial, challenging the fixed, heroic idealization of Trumpeldor with a work of sculpture that changes as visitors move around it. In its two carved out panels of stone blocks, placed at 45-degrees to each other, the absent human silhouette seems to move as one passes by, changing form, before seeming to crumble into fallen ruins. In its spatial dialogue with the national memorial to Yoseph Trumpeldor, *Oil on Stone* turns itself from a free-standing negative-form sculpture into a national counter-memorial par excellence—the other great "counter-monument" of its generation—challenging (but not negating) the fixed memory of Israel's national origins.

The Vanishing Monument in Harburg

Other notable artists also participated in the Tel Hai open-air exhibition, including Israeli artist Misha Ullman, whose installation *Sky* consisted of a trench dug into the hillside, an early negative-form monument and meditation on absence. Years later, Ullman would become renowned for his eloquent *Book Burning Memorial, Bibliotek*, a room of empty bookshelves built beneath Berlin's Bebelplatz. His description of the empty library later echoed the pit he had dug out at Tel Hai: "It begins with the void that exists in every pit and will not disappear. You could say that emptiness is a state, a situation formed by the sides of the pit: the deeper it is, the more sky there will be and the greater the void. In the library containing the missing books, that void is more palpable."[5]

At the Tel Hai exhibition, Esther Shalev met another artist, Jochen Gerz, a Berlin-born conceptual artist of erasure and self-effacement. This was 1983, and a match was made between the Israeli artist whose patience with her national narrative and its shrines had run out, and the German artist whose skepticism of monumental and other fixed art forms seem to have been bred into him. By 1972, Jochen Gerz had already mounted an exhibition—*Exit/Dachau*—which offered an explicit critique of Germany's attempt to memorialize its victims, suggesting that in its pedagogical rigidity, the national memorial at Dachau was actually an extension of the authoritarian principles whose victims it would now claim to memorialize. Thus, matched in the "holy land," and married soon after, Esther Shalev-Gerz and Jochen Gerz would collaborate on what is commonly regarded as their generation's first and greatest counter-monument to the victims of Nazi Germany: the vanishing *Monument Against Fascism, War, and Violence—and for Peace and Human Rights* in Harburg-Hamburg, Germany (1986–1993).

In fact, in Germany the issues surrounding Holocaust memorialization come into the sharpest, most painful relief. In the land of what Saul Friedländer has called "redemptory anti-Semitism," the possibility that art might redeem mass murder with beauty (or with ugliness), or that memorials might somehow redeem this past with the instrumentalization of its memory, continues to haunt a postwar generation of memory-artists.[6] Moreover, artists in Germany are both plagued and inspired by a series of impossible memorial questions: How does a state incorporate shame into its national memorial landscape? How does a state recite, much less commemorate, the litany of its misdeeds, making them part of its reason for being? Under what memorial aegis does a nation remember its own barbarity? Where is the tradition for memorial mea culpa? By 1989, Germany's "Jewish question" had morphed into a two-pronged memorial question: How does a nation mourn the victims of a mass-murder perpetrated in its name? How does a nation re-unite itself on the bedrock memory of its horrendous crimes?

Further complicating Germany's memorial equation was the postwar generation's deep distrust of monumental forms in light of their systematic exploitation by the Nazis. In their eyes, the didactic logic of monuments—their demagogical rigidity and certainty of history—continued to recall too closely traits associated with fascism itself. A monument against fascism, therefore, would have to be monument against itself: against the traditionally didactic function of monuments, against their tendency to displace the past they would have us contemplate—and finally, against the authoritarian propensity in monumental spaces that reduces viewers to passive spectators. Rather than attempting to resolve such memorial questions, Esther Shalev-Gerz and Jochen Gerz would now strive for their formal articulation.

Within months of meeting Esther at Tel Hai in 1983, Jochen Gerz had been invited as one of six artists to propose a design in Hamburg for a *Monument Against Fascism, War, and Violence—and for Peace and Human Rights*, a tortuously convoluted title for a kind of "Holocaust monument." According to Esther, when Gerz first broached this invitation with her, she replied by gesturing out of her window to Israel's own monument-strewn landscape. "What do we need with another monument? We have too many already. What we need is one that disappears."[7] Here she agreed to work with Gerz toward finding a form that challenged the monument's traditional illusions of permanence, its authoritarian rigidity. The resulting collaboration between Shalev-Gerz and Gerz would thus combine a traditional Jewish skepticism of material icons and a postwar German suspicion of monumental forms. "What we did not want," they declared, "was an enormous pedestal

5
Quoted in Ellie Armon Azoulay, "The Accidental Sculptor," *Ha'aretz*, September 27, 2009.

6
Saul Friedländer, *Nazi Germany and the Jews*, vol. 1: *The Years of Persecution, 1933–1939*, HarperCollins, New York 1997, p. 3.

7
See James E. Young, *At Memory's Edge: After-Images of the Holocaust in Contemporary Art and Architecture*, Yale University Press, New Haven & London 2000, p. 128.

with something on it presuming to tell people what they ought to think."[8] Theirs would be a self-abnegating monument, literally self-effacing, and it won the competition for the Hamburg-Harburg *Monument Against Fascism, War, and Violence—and for Peace and Human Rights*.

Unveiled in Harburg in 1986, this 12-meter high, one-meter square pillar was made of hollow aluminum plated with a thin layer of soft, dark lead. An inscription near its base read in seven languages:

> We invite the citizens of Harburg, and visitors to the town, to add their names here to ours. In doing so, we commit ourselves to remain vigilant. As more and more names cover this 12-meter-tall lead column, it will gradually be lowered into the ground. One day it will have disappeared completely, and the site of the Harburg monument against fascism will be empty. In the end, it is only we ourselves who can rise up against injustice.

Wary that such memorials had too often served as substitutes for intervention rather than as calls for action, the artists reminded visitors that it was we, not our monuments, who would have to rise up against injustice.

With audacious simplicity, Esther and Jochen's counter-monument would thus flout nearly every cherished memorial convention: its aim was not to console but to provoke; not to remain fixed but to change; not to be everlasting but to disappear; not to be ignored by its passersby but to demand interaction; not to remain pristine but to invite its own violation; not to accept graciously the burden of memory but to throw it back at the town's feet. How better to remember a now-absent people than by a vanishing monument? After several lowerings over the next seven years, the *Monument Against Fascism* itself vanished on November 10, 1993, with its last sinking. Nothing is left above ground but the top surface of the monument, even as a section of the sunken monument itself is partly visible through a glass window into its underground chamber, suggesting its having been internalized by the earth. On its complete sinking, the artists hoped that it would return the burden of memory to those who came looking for it. Now all that stands here are the memory-tourists, forced to rise and to remember for themselves.

Between Listening and Telling

Whether opening up spaces for dialogue between sculptures in the landscape, or opening up the space in a cityscape previously occupied by a now-vanished monument, Esther Shalev-Gerz lives and creates by a singular credo: "You have to open up spaces."[9] Moreover, in her words, "Spatial constructions are not static. They are persistently transformed and redefined by the people that 'practice' the space they are in."[10] In her extraordinary 2005 installation at the Hôtel de Ville in Paris, *Between Listening and Telling: Last Witnesses, Auschwitz 1945–2005*, Shalev-Gerz visually plumbed the depths of what may be the most profoundly elusive of all memory-spaces: that space between a survivor's deep memory of traumatic experience and its verbal articulation.

Holocaust historian Saul Friedländer has drawn a clear distinction between what he terms "common memory" and "deep memory" of the Holocaust: common memory as that which "tends to restore or establish coherence, closure, and possibly a redemptive stance," and deep memory as that which remains essentially inarticulable and unrepresentable, that which continues to exist as unresolved trauma just beyond the reach of meaning.[11] Not only are these two orders of memory irreducible to each other, Friedländer says, but "Any attempt at building a coherent self founders on the intractable return of the repressed and recurring deep memory."[12] That is, to some extent, every common memory of the Holocaust is haunted by that which it necessarily leaves unstated, its coherence a necessary but ultimately misleading evasion.

As his sole example of deep memory, Friedländer refers to the last frame of Art Spiegelman's Holocaust cartoon, *Maus: A Survivor's Tale*, in which the dying father addresses his son, Artie, by the name of Richieu, Artie's brother who died in the Holocaust before Artie was even born.[13] The still apparently unassimilated trauma of his first son's death remains inarticulable—and thereby deep—and so is represented here only indirectly as a kind of manifest behavior. But this example is significant for Friedländer in other ways, as well, coming as it does at the end of the survivor's life. For Friedländer wonders, profoundly I think, what will become of this deep memory after the survivors are gone. "The question remains," he says, "whether at the collective level [...] an event such as the Shoah may, after all the survivors have disappeared, leave traces of a deep memory beyond individual recall, which will defy any attempts to give it meaning."[14] The implication is that, beyond the next generation's artistic and literary representations of it, such deep memory may be lost to history altogether.

In fact, there is another moment in Spiegelman's *Maus* that may also exemplify a survivor's deep memory and its untranslatability into narrative. It occurs during a session between Artie and his psychotherapist, Pavel, who like Artie's father, is a Holocaust survivor. Here Spiegelman seems also to be asking how we write the stories of the dead without filling in their absence. In a way, the co-mixture of image and narrative allows the artist to do just this, to make visible crucial parts of memory-work usually lost to narrative alone, such as the silences and spaces between words. In a series of four frames, Art listens as Pavel compares all that is written about the Holocaust to the absolute silence of the dead, the absence

8
From Claude Gintz, "'L'Anti-Monument' de Jochen & Esther Gerz," *Galeries Magazine*, no. 19, June–July 1987, p. 87.

9
"There Is No Together Place Here: A Conversation between Esther Shalev-Gerz and Moira Jeffrey," *Esther Shalev-Gerz: A Thread*, Centre for Contemporary Arts, Glasgow 2008, p. 45.

10
Ibid., p. 53.

11
Saul Friedländer, "Trauma, Transference, and 'Working Through' in Writing the History of the Shoah," *History and Memory*, no. 4, Spring–Summer, 1992, p. 41.

12
Ibid., p. 41

13
Art Spiegelman, *Maus: A Survivor's Tale*, vols. I and II, Pantheon, New York 1986, 1991, vol. II, p. 135.

14
Friedländer, "Trauma, Transference, and 'Working Through,'" p. 41.

of the dead victims' stories. How to show a necessary silence? Pavel suggests that because "life always takes the side of life [...] the victims who died can never tell THEIR side of the story, so maybe it's better not to have any more stories." To which Art responds in the next panel, "Uh-huh. Samuel Beckett once said: 'Every word is like an unnecessary stain on silence and nothingness.'" This is followed by a panel without words, only Art and his therapist sitting silently, smoking and thinking, a moment in the therapeutic context as fraught with significance as narrative itself. This is not silence as an absence of words but silence as something that actively passes between two people—the only frame in the two volumes without words or some other sign denoting words. In the next panel, Art gesticulates, "On the other hand, he SAID it." Pavel replies in the same panel, "He was right. Maybe you can use it in your book."[15]

Conceived to mark the 60th anniversary of the Red Army's liberation of Auschwitz, *Between Listening and Telling* turned the elegant space of the Hôtel de Ville's Grande Salle outside-in, taking an interior space and inviting visitors to further interiorize the spaces between survivors' videotaped words. What was commemorated here would not be the physical liberation of survivors from the camp, but the non-liberation of survivors from their own internal memories. Being freed from Auschwitz is not tantamount to being freed from one's memory of what happened there. But how to show this?

In 2005, a team of videographers recorded the testimonies of some 60 Auschwitz survivors living in Paris, in which they described their lives before, during, and after their internment. Leaving these taped interviews unedited, Shalev-Gerz showed them on 60 small monitors and DVD players, with headphones, allowing viewers to watch and listen to any of the audiovisual testimonies they chose, as they sat in four parallel rows of tables and chairs running the length of the Grande Salle. At the end of the room, on three large screens mounted side-by-side, a single silent video of the survivors was projected, but with a seven-second time lapse clip showing only the slow-motion faces of survivors in the silent spaces between their words.

It is the space between words, the artist suggests, when memory remains wholly internal and still alive in the mind. Words may be necessary when one wants to share memory, but they also inevitably fix memory into a sound, an idea that it was not when it remained wholly internal and unverbalized. Without words, or between words, our eyes are drawn to the survivors' faces and eyes, where we can see them remembering, without knowing what is being remembered. Here we become witnesses to the survivors' inward search for memory, witnesses to their search for language commensurate to their memory, witnesses to their inability to find such language, witnesses to the pain such memory now re-inflicts on them. We watch as memory remains within, as it finds expression in facial contortions, but not in speech. Whereas writers and speakers must necessarily break silence in order to represent it, silence remains audibly and visually palpable here. Silence that cannot exist in print except in blank pages is now accompanied by the image of one who is silent, who cannot find the words, who may have no words for such memory. In this installation, we are witness to the speaking and to the not-speaking. This is how Shalev-Gerz shows us not only the profound space between listening and telling, but also the untraversible space between a survivor's memory and her verbal testimony. It is almost as if, once verbalized, such memory is no longer the survivor's memory at all, but now only our own.

15
Spiegelman, *Maus*, p. 45.

ESPACES DE LA MÉMOIRE ENFOUIE – ESTHER SHALEV-GERZ ET LES PREMIERS ANTI-MONUMENTS

JAMES E. YOUNG

En 1981, Maya Lin – une étudiante de 21 ans en architecture à l'Université de Yale – remporta un concours anonyme pour le *Monument pour les vétérans du Vietnam*, destiné à être érigé sur le National Mall de Washington. Son projet minimaliste, « en réserve », renvoyait ouvertement au *Mémorial des disparus de la Somme* de Sir Edwin Lutyens à Thiepval en France (1924) comme au *Mémorial des martyrs de la déportation* de Georges-Henri Pingusson sur l'île de la Cité à Paris (1962). Ces derniers furent en effet les véritables précurseurs de cet « anti-monument » si brillamment mis au point par Maya Lin, que ce fut par leur formalisation de la perte et de l'absence irréparables dans les morceaux manquants de paysage, ou par la descente du visiteur au tréfonds – et comme à l'intérieur – de la mémoire[1].

Entaillant le sol, blessure noire dans le paysage en contrepoint explicite au blanc néoclassique des obélisques et de la statuaire de Washington, le projet de Maya Lin traduisait la perte sans rédemption et l'ambivalence nationale autour de la mémoire des soldats américains qu'on avait envoyés se battre et mourir dans une guerre désormais détestée de tout le pays. Pour reprendre les termes de Maya Lin, elle « imaginai[t] avoir pris un couteau pour découper la terre et l'éventrer, une violence et une souffrance inaugurales destinées à disparaître avec le temps. »[2] Autrement dit, elle avait ouvert un espace dans le paysage qui devait à son tour ouvrir en nous un espace pour la mémoire. « Je n'ai jamais envisagé le mémorial comme un mur ou un objet, déclare-t-elle, mais comme une saillie dans la terre, un bord ouvert. » Au lieu de créer une forme en V positive (comme un coude saillant ou des avions militaires en formation), elle en a ouvert l'espace en réserve, espace négatif que rempliront ceux venus se souvenir des soldats tombés pour l'Amérique.

Après l'inauguration du *Monument pour les vétérans du Vietnam* de Maya Lin en 1982, toute une jeune génération d'artistes allemands spécialisés dans les mémoriaux semble y avoir vu une forme d'anticonformisme susceptible de faire écho à l'expression de leur propre honte nationale et à leur attitude ambivalente face à la mémoire de l'Holocauste ; ils allaient par la même occasion y trouver la confirmation de leur rejet des monuments nationaux, traditionnellement autoritaires, complaisants et prétentieux. Préoccupés par l'absence et la perte irrémédiable, mais aussi par un monde brisé et irréparable, ces artistes et ces architectes allaient aboutir à leur propre architecture anti-monumentale pour exprimer la fêlure de leur foi en la civilisation, sans chercher à la ressouder. Et en effet, des artistes et architectes de l'anti-monument comme Esther Shalev-Gerz, Jochen Gerz, Horst Hoheisel, Micha Ullman et Daniel Libeskind – pour ne citer que ceux-là – allaient bientôt reconnaître que le concept du *Monument pour les vétérans du Vietnam* de Maya Lin avait ouvert la voie de leur propre œuvre anti-monumentale.

Il est donc tout à fait surprenant qu'en 1983, sans même avoir vu ni entendu parler du *Monument pour les vétérans du Vietnam*, Esther Shalev ait elle-même fait une œuvre en contrepoint à sa propre tradition mémorielle nationale avec *Huile sur pierre* (Tel Hai, 1983) œuvre qu'il convient de présenter comme « l'autre » premier anti-monument de sa génération. Ayant quitté Vilnius pour Israël en 1957 à l'âge de huit ans, Esther Shalev – comme d'autres de la même génération – a connu une succession de conflits dont la Guerre des Six Jours de 1967, la Guerre du Kippour de 1973, l'Opération Litani en 1978 et la Guerre du Liban en 1982. Mais c'est cette dernière, l'invasion israélienne du Liban en juin 1982, tentative désespérée d'expulser l'OLP et ses missiles du Liban pour les repousser le plus loin possible de la frontière nord d'Israël, qui a brisé le cœur et l'esprit de cohésion de toute une génération. Le bombardement aérien de Beyrouth, le massacre de Palestiniens par les Phalangistes Chrétiens dans les camps de réfugiés de Sabra et Chatila sous autorité israélienne, ainsi que la mort d'un étudiant pacifiste israélien dans l'attaque à la grenade d'un contre-manifestant du même pays, provoquèrent d'énormes manifestations et aboutirent à la démission d'Ariel Sharon, alors Ministre de la défense.

Toute une génération d'écrivains, d'artistes et d'universitaires israéliens déjà lasse de la guerre et sceptique devant la logique gouvernementale qui avait conduit à la première « guerre choisie » d'Israël allait non seulement s'opposer au conflit mais aussi remettre en cause les mythes et récits fondateurs de la jeune nation, alors même qu'elle avait semblé jusque-là soutenir le gouvernement et la poursuite de l'occupation des « Territoires ». Les poètes-soldats et dramaturges israéliens s'étaient soudain mis à évoquer l'imagerie de l'Holocauste dans leurs descriptions des jeunes victimes palestiniennes et libanaises de l'invasion israélienne. Des auteurs comme Amos Oz et A. B. Yehoshua condamnèrent publiquement le Premier Ministre Menachem Begin pour avoir comparé Yasser Arafat dans Beyrouth à Adolf Hitler dans son bunker berlinois[3]. Une école montante d'intellectuels israéliens, les « Nouveaux historiens », commença à remettre ouvertement en question la version des pères fondateurs de l'État sur la Guerre d'Indépendance de 1948 et la crise des réfugiés palestiniens qui s'ensuivit.

En 1982, Esther Shalev participa à une grande exposition d'art contemporain, *Here and Now*, au Musée d'Israël de Jérusalem. Pour son œuvre intitulée *Huile sur pierre*, Shalev avait pris une grande feuille de tôle qu'elle avait pliée de manière à la faire tenir sur la tranche et dans laquelle elle avait découpé au laser une figure humaine inspirée de Picasso – comme elle l'expliquerait plus tard. La figure est absente ; elle est un espace vide dans la tôle enduite de peinture à l'huile. Invitée l'année suivante à participer à une vaste exposition en plein air à Tel Hai dans le nord de la Galilée, Shalev avait reproduit la même « figure manquante » sur un mur de mortier en pierres

1
Voir Maya Lin, *Boundaries*, Simon & Schuster, New York, 2000, p. 49. C'est lors d'une conversation privée que Lin fit référence au mémorial de Pingusson à Paris.

2
Maya Lin, *Boundaries*, p. 49.

3
Voir James E. Young, « When Soldier Poets Remember the Holocaust », *Writing and Rewriting the Holocaust*, Indiana University Press, Bloomington & Indianapolis, 1988, p. 134–146. Voir également Amos Oz, « Hitler kvar met, adoni rosh hamemshalah ["Hitler est mort, Monsieur le Premier Ministre"] », réimprimé in *Chatziat Gevul: Shirim Mimlhemet Levanon* [« Traversée des frontières : poèmes de la Guerre du Liban »], Sifriat Poalim, Tel Aviv, 1983. Et aussi Yehuda Bauer, « Fruits of Fear », *Jerusalem Post*, 3 juin 1982, p. 8 ; et Ze'ev Mankowitz, « Beirut Is Not Berlin », *Jerusalem Post*, 4 août 1982, p. 8.

blanches, elles-mêmes issues d'un unique bloc de pierre de Jérusalem. Elle installa *Huile sur pierre* sur un flanc de colline rocailleux et sauvage, au nord et complètement visible depuis le monument national à Yoseph Trumpeldor, l'un des tout premiers pionniers du sionisme et héros de l'armée tué alors qu'il défendait une petite colonie juive à Tel Hai en 1920. Selon Yael Zerubavel, « Lorsque l'État d'Israël fut fondé, Tel Hai fut instauré comme un "mythe originel" national en Israël qui représentait l'ère des pionniers dans l'histoire du pays… Pour la communauté juive de Palestine, la bataille de Tel Hai était le symbole d'une transformation majeure de l'appartenance juive nationale et de l'émergence d'un nouvel esprit héroïque et sacrificiel. »[4] Site national du mythe originel de la mue d'Israël, Tel Hai allait devenir le lieu d'un nouveau stade de la conscience nationale.

Installé de façon pérenne en 1983, *Huile sur pierre* imposait sa silhouette humaine manquante en contrepoint, à la fois, du paysage naturel environnant et des blocs de pierre blanche de Jérusalem qui composaient le *Lion rugissant*, monument dédié au légendaire Trumpeldor par le sculpteur Abraham Melnikov, dessiné dans le style assyrien rocailleux de son époque et consacré à Tel Hai en 1934. En installant *Huile sur pierre* à l'intérieur des limites du site du *Lion rugissant*, Shalev contredisait le monument national tant physiquement que visuellement avec un mémorial d'une toute autre sorte, remettant en question l'idéalisation héroïque et figée de Trumpeldor par le biais d'une œuvre sculpturale qui changeait au gré des mouvements du visiteur autour d'elle. Dans ces deux panneaux de blocs de pierre évidés et placés à 45° l'un de l'autre, la silhouette humaine absente semble se mouvoir lorsque l'on passe près d'elle, changeant de forme avant de donner l'impression de s'écrouler pour tomber en morceaux. De par son dialogue spatial avec le monument national à Trumpeldor, *Huile sur pierre* passe d'une sculpture en réserve à un anti-monument national *par excellence** (l'autre « anti-monument » important de sa génération) défiant – sans l'ignorer – la mémoire figée des origines d'Israël.

Le monument disparaissant de Harbourg-Hambourg

D'autres artistes de tout premier plan participèrent à l'exposition à ciel ouvert de Tel Hai, parmi lesquels Micha Ullman dont l'installation *Sky* consistait en une tranchée creusée à flanc de colline, l'un des premiers monuments en réserve, méditation sur l'absence. Des années plus tard, Ullman allait se faire connaître pour son éloquent *Book Burning Memorial, Bibliotek* [« Mémorial des livres brûlés, bibliothèque »], une salle entourée d'étagères vides creusée sous la Bebelplatz de Berlin. Sa description d'une bibliothèque vide faisait écho au puits qu'il avait creusé à Tel Hai : « Cela commence avec le vide qui, dans chaque puits, existe et ne disparaîtra jamais. On pourrait dire du vide qu'il est un état, une situation provoquée par les bords du puits : plus il est profond, plus il y aura de ciel et plus il y aura de vide. Dans la bibliothèque des livres disparus, le vide est plus palpable. »[5]

Lors de l'exposition de Tel Hai, Esther Shalev fait la rencontre du berlinois Jochen Gerz, artiste conceptuel de l'oubli et de l'effacement de soi. C'était en 1983 et un lien s'est formé entre l'artiste israélienne, dont la patience envers le récit national et ses hauts lieux avait atteint ses limites, et l'artiste allemand, dont le scepticisme non seulement devant l'art monumental mais aussi devant l'art sous toutes ses formes semblait caractéristique. En 1972, Jochen Gerz avait déjà monté une exposition – *Exit/Dachau* – qui critiquait de façon explicite la tentative allemande de rendre hommage à la mémoire de ses victimes, suggérant que, du fait de sa rigidité pédagogique, le mémorial de Dachau n'était en réalité qu'un prolongement des principes autoritaires dont avaient souffert les victimes auxquelles il était censé rendre hommage. S'étant ainsi trouvés en « Terre Sainte » et mariés peu de temps après, Esther Shalev-Gerz et Jochen Gerz allaient collaborer sur ce que l'on considère généralement comme le premier et le plus important des anti-monuments de leur génération, érigé à la mémoire des victimes de l'Allemagne nazie : il s'agit de l'éphémère *Monument contre le fascisme, la guerre et la violence – pour la paix et les droits de l'homme* à Harbourg-Hambourg en Allemagne (1986-1993).

En fait, en Allemagne, les questions entourant le souvenir de l'Holocauste sont particulièrement vives et douloureuses. Au pays de « l'antisémitisme rédempteur », comme l'a nommé Saul Friedländer, le risque que l'art serve à expier le génocide par la beauté (ou la laideur), ou que les mémoriaux servent en quelque sorte à racheter un tel passé à travers l'instrumentalisation de son souvenir, continue à hanter la génération des artistes d'après-guerre[6]. De surcroît, en Allemagne, les artistes sont à la fois tourmentés et inspirés par un ensemble de questions impossibles sur la mémoire : comment un État intègre-t-il la honte dans son paysage mémoriel national ? Comment un État récite-t-il, plus qu'il ne commémore, la litanie de ses méfaits pour qu'ils finissent par faire partie de sa raison d'être ? Sous quelle égide mémorielle une nation doit-elle se souvenir de sa propre barbarie ? Y a-t-il quelque part une tradition de coulpe mémorielle ? En 1989, la « question juive » de l'Allemagne s'était muée en une question de mémoire à double tranchant : comment une nation fait-elle le deuil des victimes d'un meurtre de masse qu'elle a perpétré en son nom ? Comment une nation peut-elle se réunifier sur les fondations du souvenir de ses crimes ignobles ?

Sans compter que, pour compliquer un peu plus l'équation mémorielle allemande, la génération d'après-guerre avait fait preuve d'une profonde méfiance vis-à-vis des formes monumentales systématiquement exploitées par les nazis. À leurs yeux, la logique didactique des monuments – leur rigidité démagogique et leurs certitudes historiques – rappelait

4
Yael Zerubavel, « New Beginning, Old Past : The Collective Memory of Pioneering in Israeli Culture », sous la direction de Laurence J. Silberstein, *New Perspectives on Israeli History*, New York University Press, New York et Londres 1991, p. 193. Voir également du même auteur l'excellente étude en profondeur : *Recovered Roots: Collective Memory and the Making of Israeli National Tradition*,University of Chicago Press, Chicago et Londres 1995.

* En français dans le texte original [NdT].

5
Cité dans Ellie Armon Azoulay, « The Accidental Sculptor », *Ha'aretz*, 27 septembre 2009.

6
Saul Friedländer, *Nazi Germany and the Jews*, Vol. 1, *The Years of Persecution*, 1933, 1939, HarperCollins, New York 1997, p. 3.

encore trop les caractéristiques mêmes du fascisme. Ainsi, un monument contre le fascisme aurait-il à se présenter d'abord comme un monument contre lui-même : contre la fonction traditionnellement didactique des monuments, contre leur tendance à déplacer le passé qu'ils auraient dû nous donner à contempler – et en définitive, contre la propension autoritaire des espaces monumentaux à réduire le visiteur à un simple spectateur passif. Plutôt que de chercher à résoudre de telles questions mémorielles, Esther Shalev-Gerz et Jochen Gerz allaient s'évertuer à en trouver l'articulation formelle.

Quelques mois après avoir rencontré Esther à Tel Hai en 1983, Jochen Gerz se trouva invité avec six autres artistes à proposer, pour la ville de Hambourg, un concept de *Monument contre le fascisme, la guerre et la violence – pour la paix et les droits de l'homme*, intitulé allemand pour le moins torturé renvoyant à une sorte de « monument à l'Holocauste ». D'après Esther, lorsque Jochen accepta d'abord cette invitation avec elle, elle répondit en montrant les monuments qu'Israël avait éparpillés dans son paysage. « Qu'est-ce qu'on a à faire d'un énième monument ? On en a déjà trop. Ce qu'il nous faut aujourd'hui, c'en est un qui disparaisse. »[7] Dès lors, elle accepta de travailler avec Gerz pour trouver une forme susceptible de remettre en question tant l'illusion de pérennité traditionnellement véhiculée par le monument que sa raideur autoritaire. Leur collaboration associerait ainsi le traditionnel scepticisme juif devant les emblèmes et la suspicion allemande d'après-guerre devant toute forme monumentale. « Ce que nous voulions éviter, déclarèrent-ils, c'était d'avoir un énorme piédestal avec quelque chose dessus qui préjuge de ce que les gens doivent penser. »[8] Leur monument serait un monument d'abnégation, voué, littéralement, à s'effacer. Il remporta le concours.

Inauguré à Harbourg en 1986, ce pilier carré d'un mètre de côté et douze de haut était composé de plaques d'aluminium recouvertes d'une fine pellicule noire et tendre de plomb. On pouvait lire à sa base une inscription en sept langues :

> « Nous invitons les citoyens de Harbourg et les visiteurs de cette ville à joindre ici leurs noms aux nôtres. Cela pour nous engager à être vigilants et à le demeurer. Plus les signatures seront nombreuses sur cette barre de plomb haute de douze mètres, plus elle s'enfoncera dans le sol. Et un jour, elle disparaîtra entièrement et la place de ce monument contre le fascisme sera vide. Car à la longue, nul ne pourra s'élever à notre place contre l'injustice. »

Conscients que ce genre de monuments servait plus souvent de substitut à toute forme d'intervention que d'encouragement à l'action, les artistes y rappelaient que c'est à nous, et non à nos monuments, de nous dresser contre l'injustice.

Avec une simplicité audacieuse, l'anti-monument d'Esther et Jochen allait ainsi fouler au pied pratiquement toutes les conventions du mémorial : son but n'était pas de consoler mais de provoquer ; non de rester figé mais d'évoluer ; non de durer indéfiniment mais de disparaître ; non d'être ignoré par les passants mais d'appeler leur intervention ; non de demeurer virginal mais d'inviter à sa propre profanation ; non d'accepter de bonne grâce le fardeau de la mémoire mais de le laisser tomber à ses pieds. Quoi de mieux pour se souvenir d'un peuple désormais absent qu'un monument qui disparaît ? Après plusieurs abaissements consécutifs au cours des sept années qui suivirent, le *Monument contre le fascisme,* lui-même, disparut le 10 novembre 1993 lors d'un dernier enfouissement. Il n'en reste rien sur le sol, hormis la face supérieure du pilier, même si une partie du monument enfoui demeure visible à travers une vitre dans une pièce souterraine, laissant comprendre qu'il a pénétré dans le sol. Au moment de son enfouissement ultime, les artistes imaginaient ainsi retourner le fardeau de la mémoire à ceux qui étaient venus le regarder. Désormais, il ne reste plus ici que des touristes, poussés à se soulever et à se souvenir pour eux-mêmes.

Entre l'écoute et la parole

Que ce soit en ouvrant des espaces de dialogue entre les sculptures dans le paysage ou en ouvrant l'espace urbain auparavant occupé par un monument maintenant disparu, Esther Shalev-Gerz vit et crée au gré d'un crédo singulier : « Il faut ouvrir les espaces. »[9] Sans compter, pour reprendre ses termes, que « les constructions spatiales ne sont pas statiques. Elles évoluent constamment et sont redéfinies par les gens qui "pratiquent" l'espace dans lequel ils se trouvent. »[10] Pour son installation extraordinaire de 2005 à l'Hôtel de Ville de Paris, intitulée *Entre l'écoute et la parole : derniers témoins, Auschwitz 1945-2005*, Shalev-Gerz sondait visuellement les profondeurs de ce qui est peut-être le plus indéfinissable de tous les lieux de mémoire : cet espace entre la mémoire enfouie de l'expérience traumatique d'un survivant et son énonciation dans le langage.

Historien de l'Holocauste, Saul Friedländer a opéré une distinction claire entre ce qu'il appelle la « mémoire commune » et la « mémoire enfouie » de l'Holocauste : la mémoire commune, soit ce qui « a tendance à restaurer ou à établir une cohérence, une clôture et éventuellement une possible position rédemptrice », et la mémoire enfouie, soit ce qui reste essentiellement inarticulable et irreprésentable, ce qui continue d'exister sous la forme d'un trauma irrésolu juste en deçà du sens[11]. Non seulement ces deux types de mémoires sont irréductibles l'un à l'autre mais, nous dit Friedländer, « toute tentative de construire un moi cohérent se prend les pieds dans un sévère retour du refoulé et une mémoire enfouie

7
Voir James E. Young, *At Memory's Edge : After-Images of the Holocaust in Contemporary Art and Architecture*, Yale University Press, New Haven et Londres 2000, p. 128.

8
Tiré de Claude Gintz, « "L'anti-Monument" de Jochen et Esther Gerz », *Galeries Magazine*, n°19, juin-juillet 1987, p. 87.

9
« There Is No Together Place Here : A Conversation between Esther Shalev-Gerz and Moira Jeffrey », *Esther Shalev-Gerz: A Thread*, Centre for Contemporary Arts, Glasgow 2008, p. 45.

10
Ibid., p. 53.

11
Saul Friedländer, « Trauma, Transference, and "Working Through" in Writing the History of the Shoah », *History and Memory*, n°4, printempsété 1992, p. 41.

récurrente. »[12] Autrement dit, d'une certaine manière, toute mémoire commune de l'Holocauste est hantée par ce qui en est nécessairement laissé informulé, et sa cohérence est en définitive une fuite aussi illusoire qu'indispensable.

Pour seul exemple de mémoire enfouie, Friedländer évoque la dernière vignette de la bande dessinée sur l'Holocauste de Art Spiegelman, *Maus. Un survivant raconte*, dans lequel le père mourant s'adresse à son fils, Artie, en l'appelant Richieu, du nom du frère d'Artie mort en camp de concentration avant même la naissance de ce dernier[13]. Le traumatisme apparemment toujours vif de la mort de son premier fils demeure impossible à formuler – il est enfoui – et il est donc ici représenté indirectement seulement par une sorte de lapsus. Mais, pour Friedländer, cet exemple est aussi significatif du fait qu'il surgit à la fin de la vie du survivant. Car Friedländer se pose, profondément je crois, la question de ce que va devenir cette mémoire enfouie lorsque les survivants auront tous disparu. « La question demeure, dit-il, de savoir si à un niveau collectif [...] un événement comme la *Shoah* peut, après que tous les survivants aient disparu, laisser des traces de mémoire enfouie au-delà du souvenir individuel, qui continue de défier toute tentative de leur donner un sens. »[14] L'implication étant qu'au-delà de ses représentations artistiques et littéraires par la prochaine génération, une telle mémoire enfouie pourrait très bien disparaître à jamais.

En fait, il y a un autre moment dans le *Maus* de Spiegelman qui montre la mémoire enfouie du survivant et ce qu'elle a d'intraduisible dans la forme du récit. Ce moment intervient pendant une séance entre Artie et son psychothérapeute, Pavel, qui, comme le père d'Artie, est un survivant des camps. Là, Spiegelman semble également poser la question de la manière dont nous écrivons les récits des morts sans pouvoir en combler l'absence. D'une certaine façon, le mélange d'images et de récit permet précisément à l'artiste de le faire, de rendre visible des parties essentielles du travail de la mémoire que l'on perd généralement dans un simple récit, comme les silences et les temps morts entre les paroles. Dans une succession de quatre vignettes, Art écoute Pavel comparer tout ce qui a été écrit sur l'Holocauste au silence absolu des morts, l'absence même des victimes mortes dans tous ces récits. Comment montrer un silence qui s'impose? Pavel laisse entendre que du fait que « la vie est toujours du côté de la vie [...] les victimes qui sont mortes ne peuvent jamais raconter LEUR point de vue sur le récit, et donc sans doute vaut-il mieux ne plus avoir de récit du tout. » Ce à quoi Art répond dans la vignette suivante : « Ah bon ? Samuel Beckett a dit un jour : "Les mots sont comme une tache inutile sur le silence et le néant." » Vignette suivie d'une autre, sans dialogues cette fois, où l'on voit Art et son thérapeute assis en silence, fumant et réfléchissant, moment dans le contexte thérapeutique aussi chargé de sens que le récit lui-même. Il ne s'agit pas là du silence comme absence de paroles, mais du silence comme quelque chose qui se produit positivement entre deux personnes. Des deux volumes de la bande dessinée, c'est la seule vignette sans dialogues ni autres signes indiquant une parole. Dans la vignette suivante, Art gesticule : « En même temps, il l'a DIT. » Pavel réplique dans la même vignette : « Il n'avait pas tort. Peut-être pourriez-vous vous en servir dans votre livre. »[15]

Conçu pour marquer le soixantième anniversaire de la libération du camp d'Auschwitz-Birkenau par l'Armée Rouge, *Entre l'écoute et la parole* mit sens dessus dessous l'espace élégant de la Grande Salle de l'Hôtel de Ville de Paris, investissant l'espace intérieur et invitant les visiteurs à intérioriser encore davantage les espaces laissés entre les paroles filmées des survivants. Ce qui était commémoré là, ce n'était pas la libération physique des survivants hors du camp, mais le fait que les survivants n'aient jamais été libérés de leurs souvenirs intimes. Être libéré d'Auschwitz ne revenait pas à être libéré des souvenirs de tout ce qui s'y était passé. Mais comment montrer cela ?

En 2005, une équipe de vidéastes a enregistré les témoignages d'une soixantaine de survivants d'Auschwitz résidant à Paris, témoignages dans lesquels ils décrivaient leur vie avant, pendant et après leur internement. Sans monter aucun des entretiens vidéo, Esther Shalev-Gerz les présenta sur soixante petits moniteurs avec un lecteur DVD et un casque afin de permettre aux spectateurs de regarder et d'écouter les témoignages audiovisuels qu'ils désiraient, assis sur quatre rangées parallèles de tables et de chaises disposées sur toute la longueur de la Grande Salle. À l'extrémité de la pièce, sur trois grands écrans disposés les uns à côté des autres, une vidéo des survivants était projetée sans le son. Elle était constituée de séquences d'une durée de sept secondes où l'on ne voyait que les visages des survivants, au ralenti, dans l'intervalle de silence entre leurs paroles.

C'est l'espace entre les mots, ainsi que le suggère l'artiste, lorsque le souvenir demeure intérieur et qu'il vit encore dans l'esprit. Les paroles peuvent être nécessaires lorsqu'on veut partager un souvenir, mais elles contribuent aussi inévitablement à figer la mémoire dans des sons, contrairement à ce qui se passait quand elle était encore entièrement intérieure et informulée. Ne parlant pas, ou saisis entre leurs paroles, les visages et les regards des survivants attirent notre regard qui les voit se rappeler, sans savoir ce qu'ils se rappellent. Nous sommes témoins de la recherche intérieure des survivants dans leur mémoire, témoins de leur quête d'un langage à la mesure de leur souvenir, de leur capacité à trouver un tel langage, de la souffrance qu'un tel souvenir leur inflige à nouveau. Nous regardons la mémoire qui demeure à l'intérieur se traduire en expressions grimaçantes, mais pas en paroles. Alors que les écrivains et les présentateurs doivent nécessairement briser le silence pour pouvoir le représenter, le silence demeure ici palpable tant à l'image qu'au son. Ce silence, qui ne pourrait exister imprimé que

12
Saul Friedländer, « Trauma, Transference, and "Working Through"... », p. 41.

13
Art Spiegelman, *Maus. Un survivant raconte*, volumes I et II, Éditions Flammarion, Paris, 1998, volume II, p. 135.

14
Saul Friedländer, « Trauma, Transference and "Working Through"... », p. 41.

15
Art Spiegelman, *Maus*, p. 45.

sous la forme de pages vierges, s'accompagne désormais de l'image de quelqu'un de silencieux, qui ne trouve pas les mots, qui n'a peut-être pas de mots pour un tel souvenir. Dans cette installation, nous sommes confrontés au parlant et au non parlant. Voilà comment Esther Shalev-Gerz nous montre non seulement la profondeur de l'espace entre l'écoute et la parole, mais aussi l'espace infranchissable entre la mémoire d'un survivant et son témoignage verbal. C'est un peu comme si, une fois mise en mots, une telle mémoire n'était plus du tout la mémoire du survivant mais désormais seulement la nôtre.

Daedal(us), 2003

Intervention in public spaces and installation;
15 color photographs, Diasec mounted,
108 × 80 cm each, and 15 color photographs,
65 × 53 cm each

Developed with the participation of the residents of a down-at-heel district in north-east Dublin, *Daedal(us)* existed first as a temporary intervention in public spaces, before taking the form of a photographic installation. Photographs of 12 facades are projected onto 12 buildings standing in the vicinity. Producing a simultaneous effect of displacement and recognition, this labyrinth is an invitation to discover different places in the district and to reappropriate the space of the city.

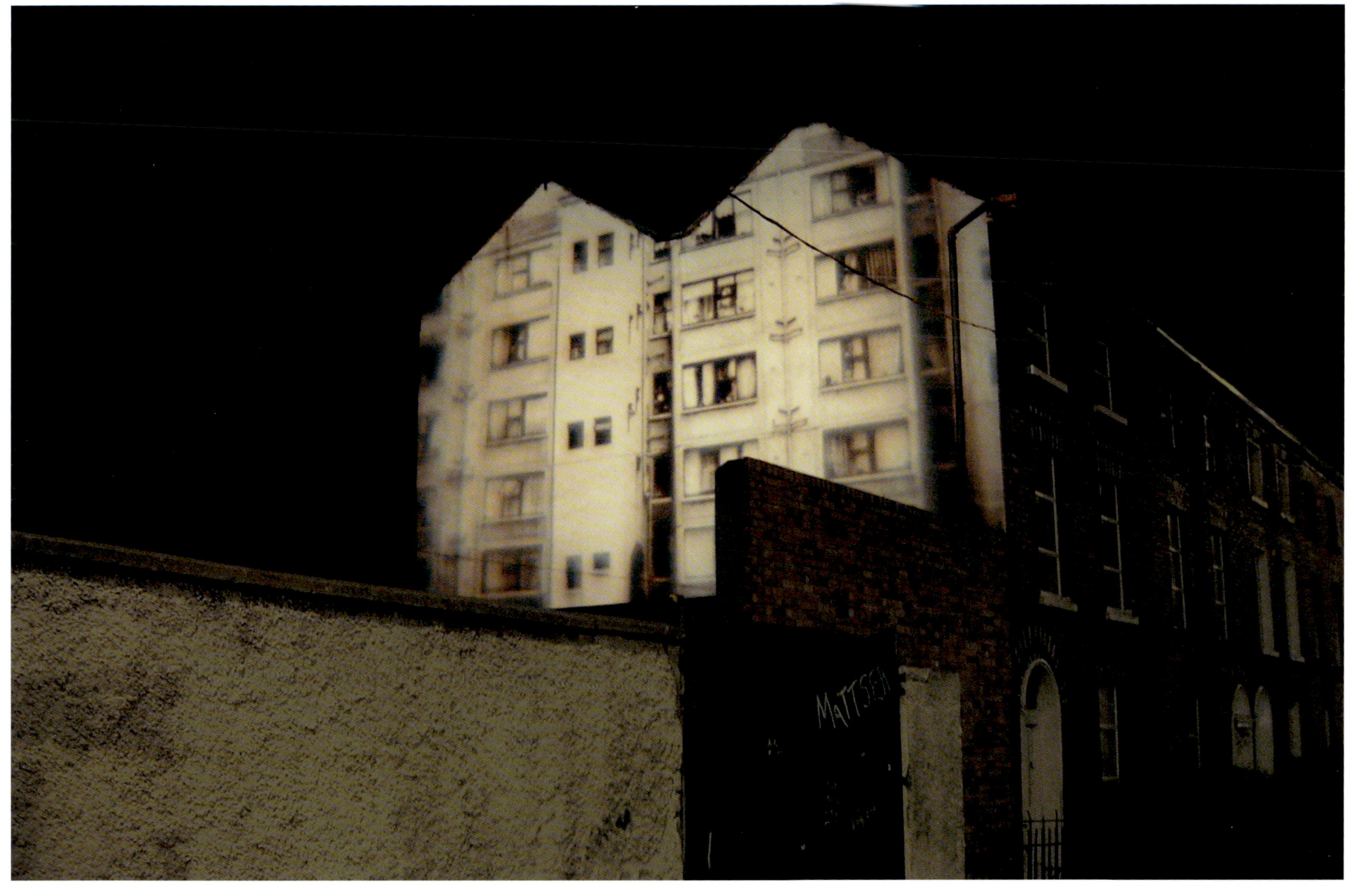

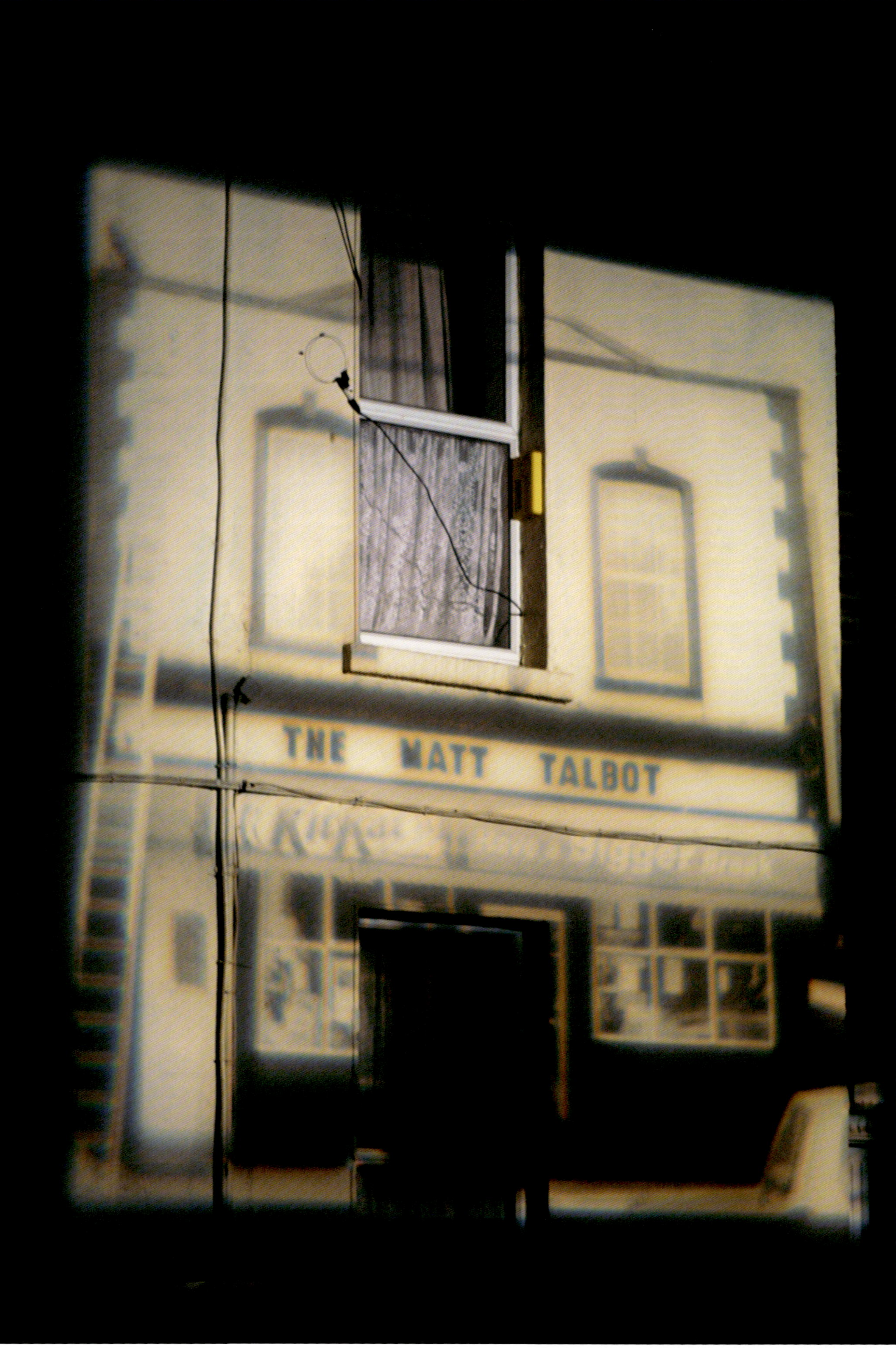
THE MATT TALBOT

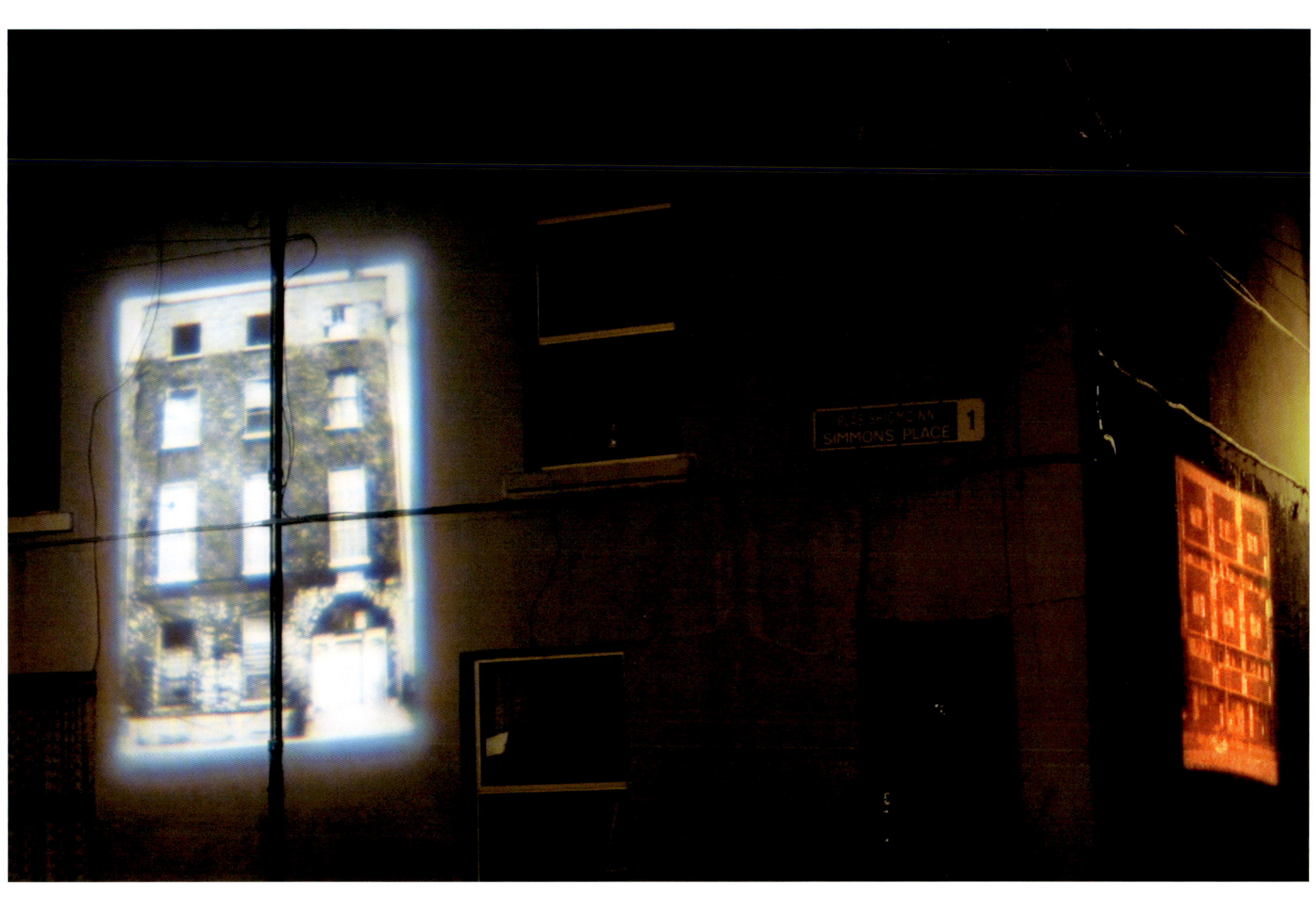
SIMMONS PLACE
1

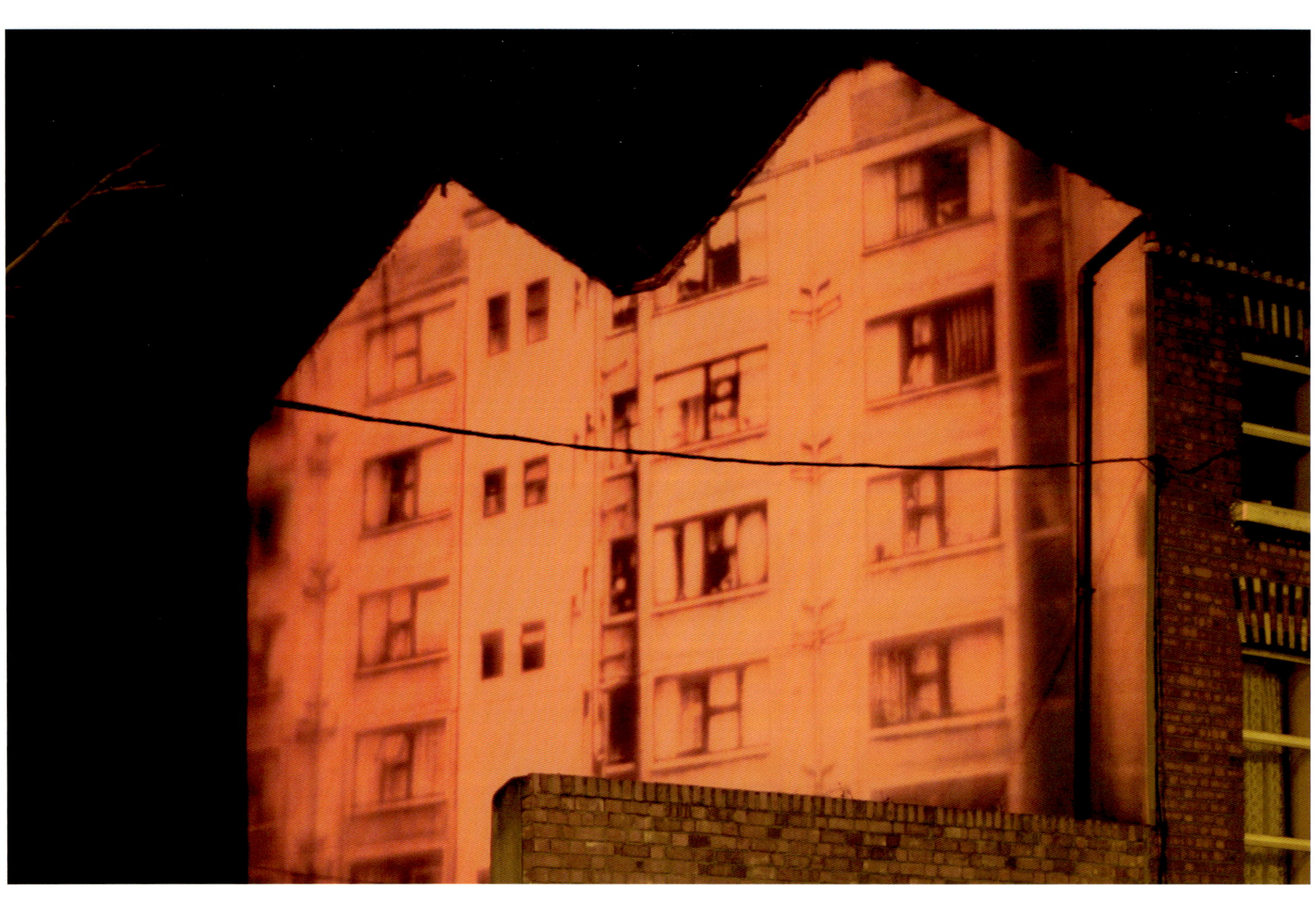

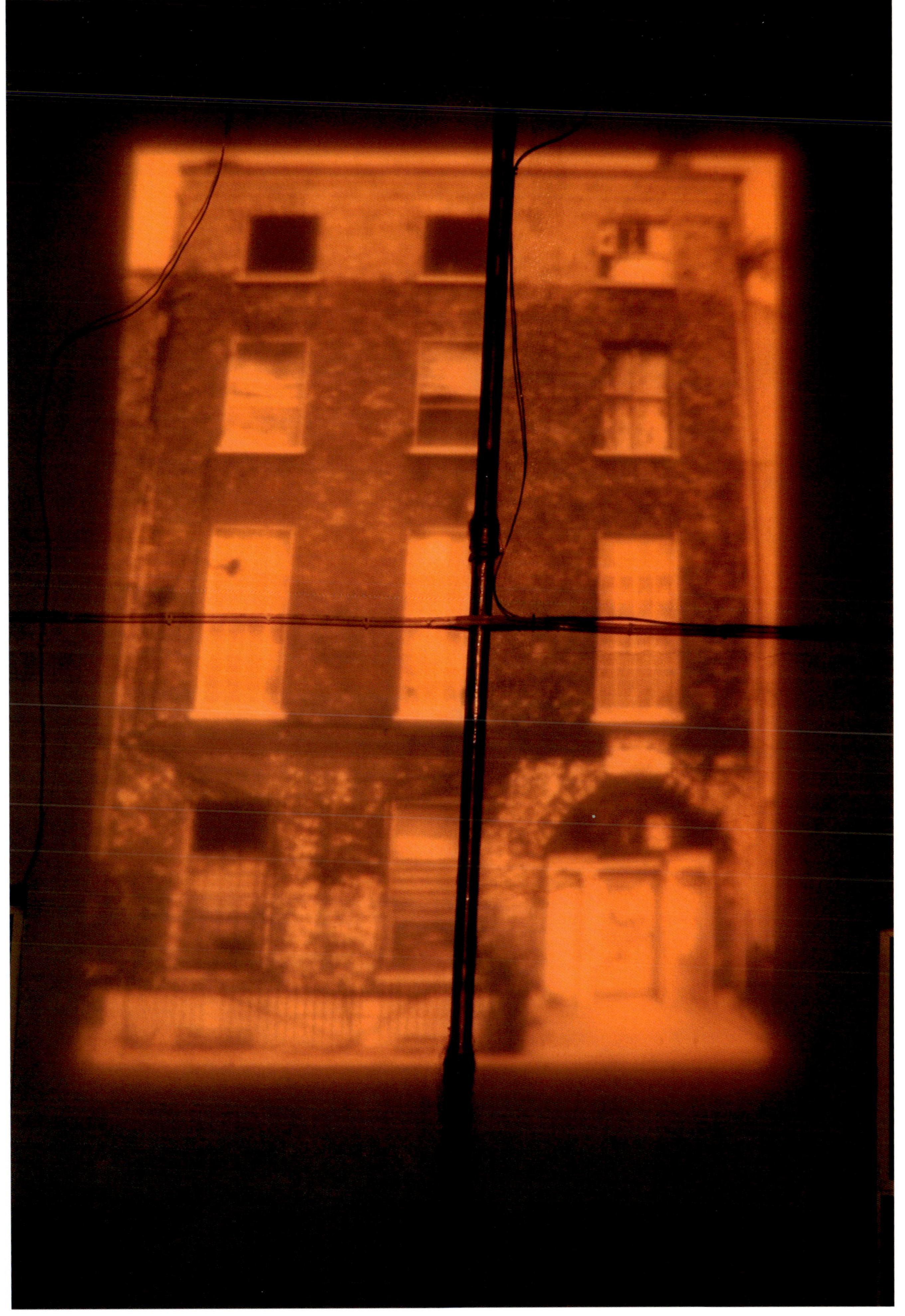

MenschenDinge—The Human Aspect of Objects, 2004–2006

Installation; 5 color videos, sound, 22 min., 14 min., 23 min., 14 min., and 12 min. respectively; 25 color photographs laminated on aluminum, Diasec mounted, 40 × 100 cm each

Invited to create a project for the Buchenwald Concentration Camp Memorial, Esther Shalev-Gerz chose to ask museum professionals to talk—the director, a historian, an archaeologist, a female restorer, and a female photographer: people who are in daily contact with the objects found in the grounds of the camp. They talk about their encounters—professional, personal, and imaginary—with these objects created or diverted by the prisoners, which attest to their ability to resist the inhuman conditions that were inflicted on them.

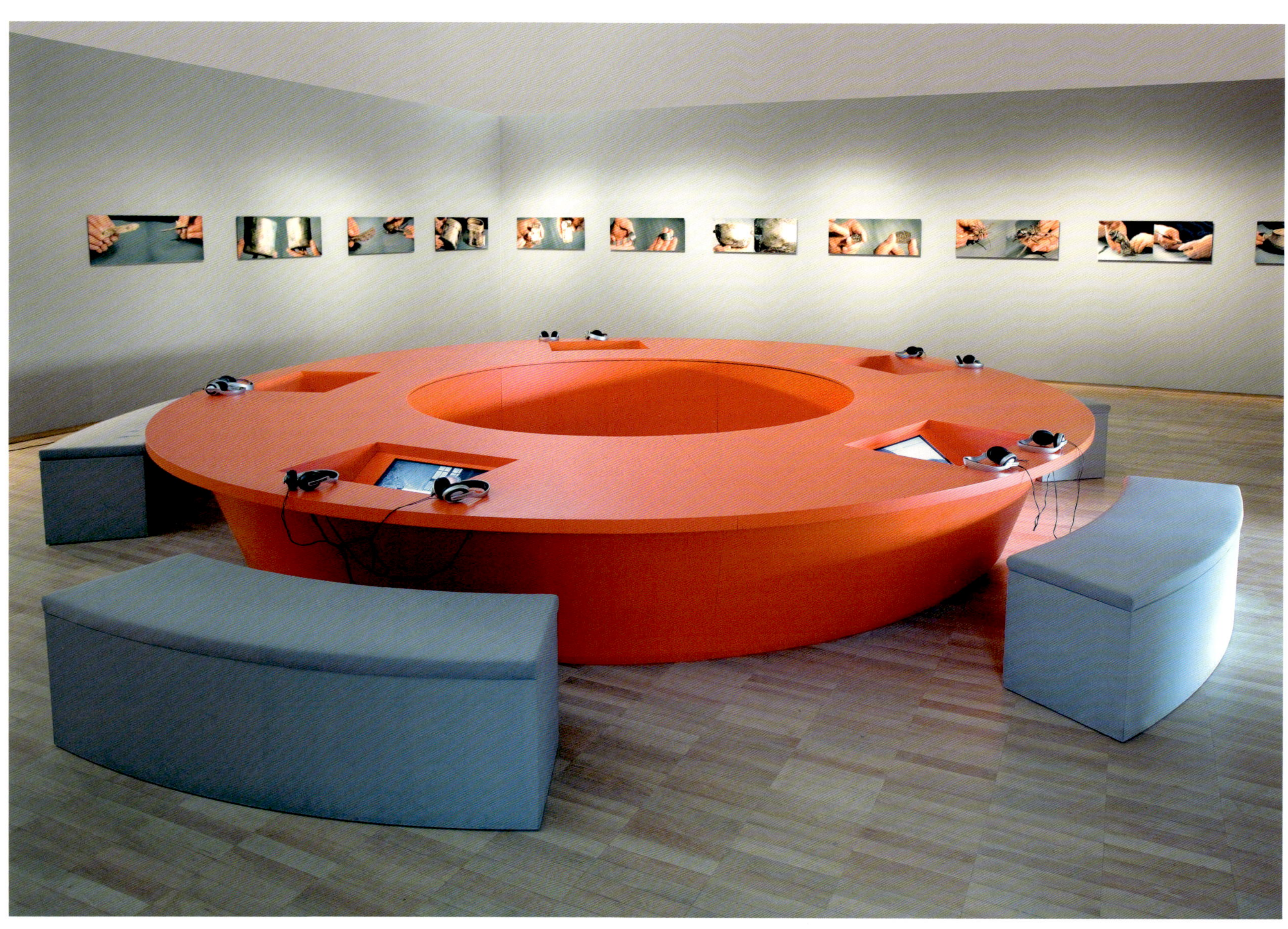

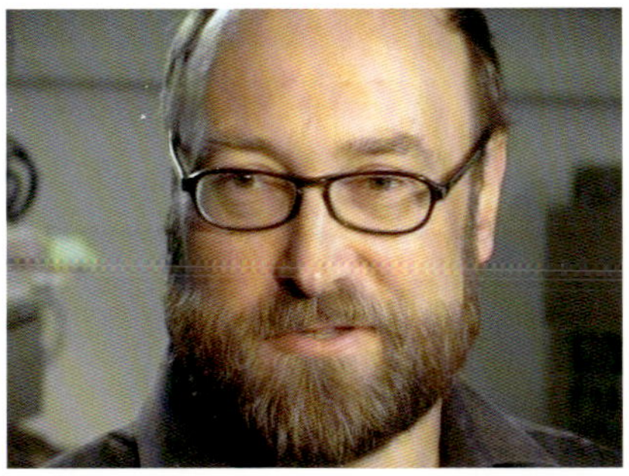

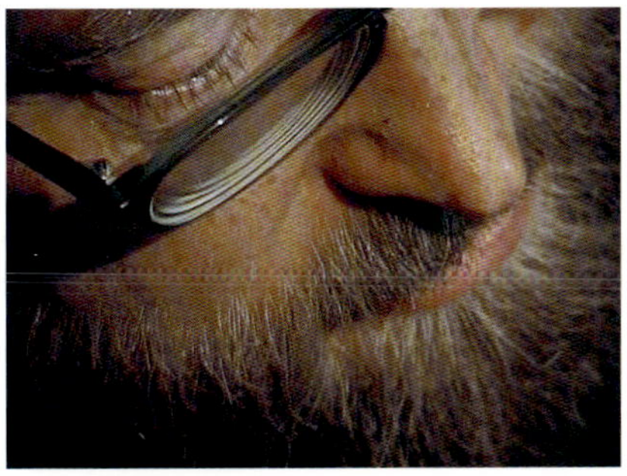

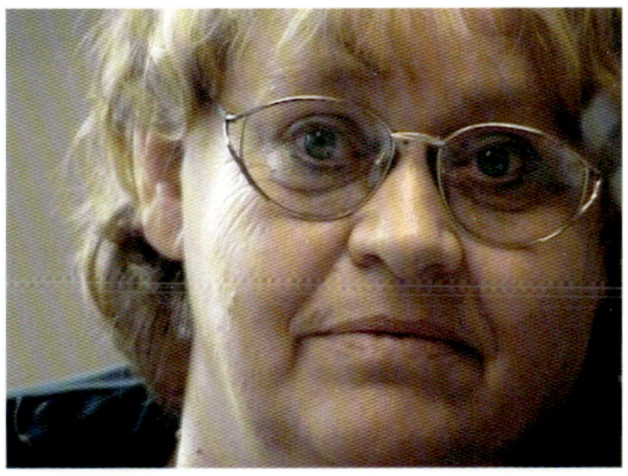

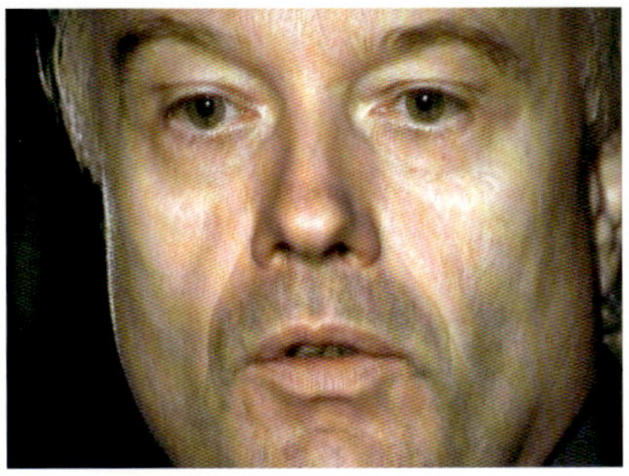

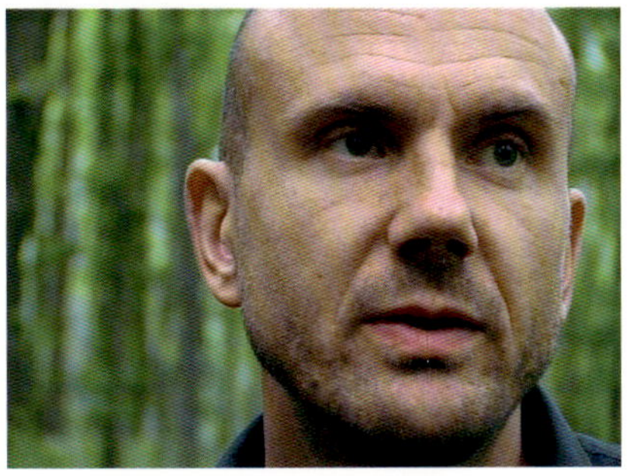

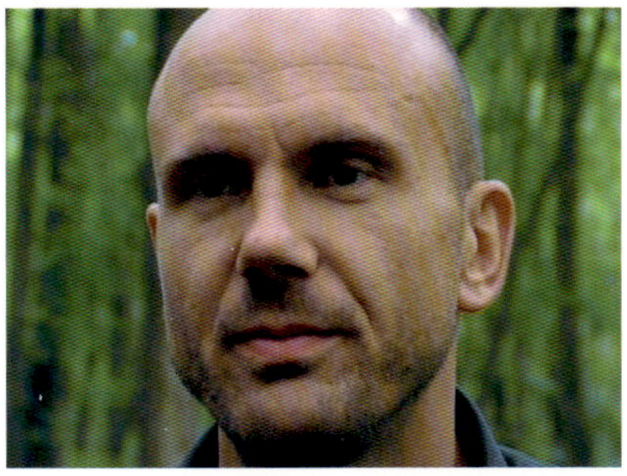

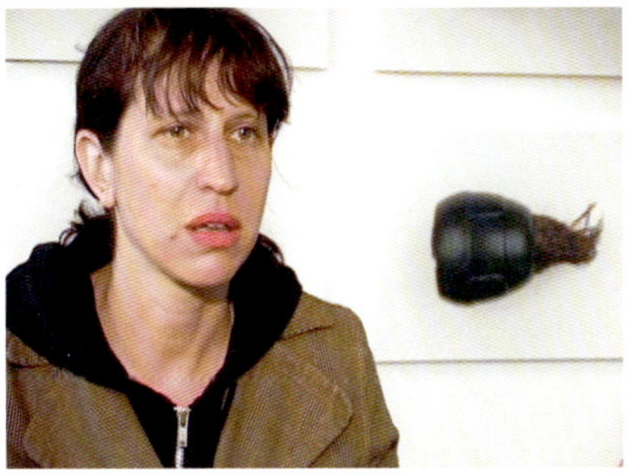

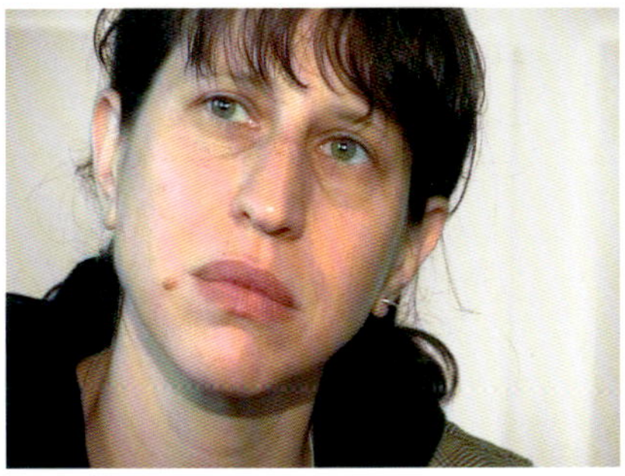

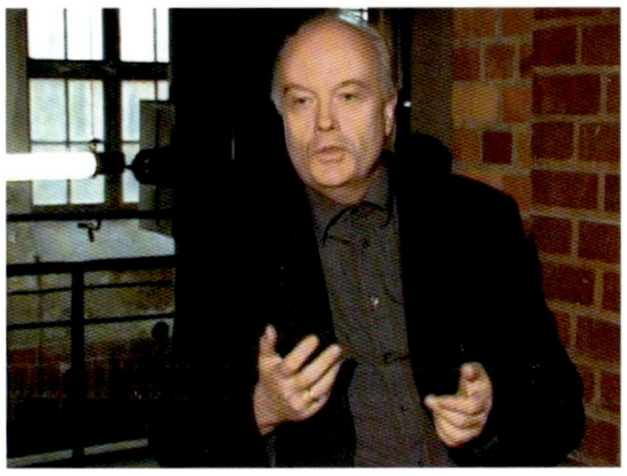

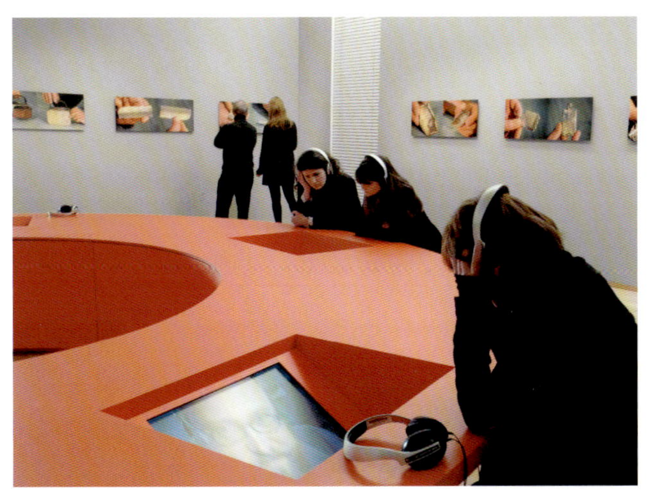

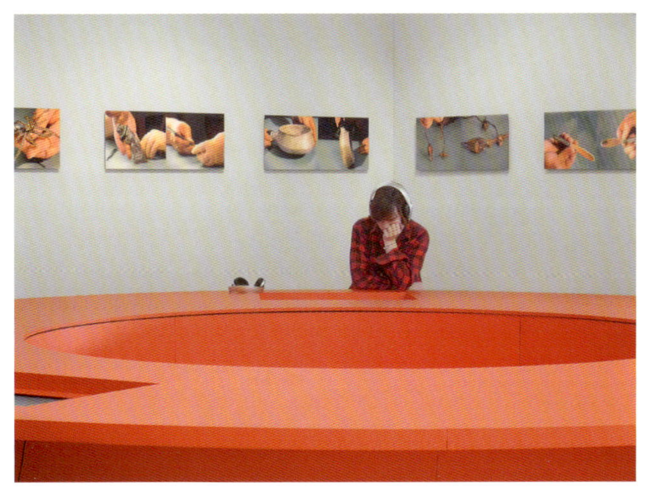

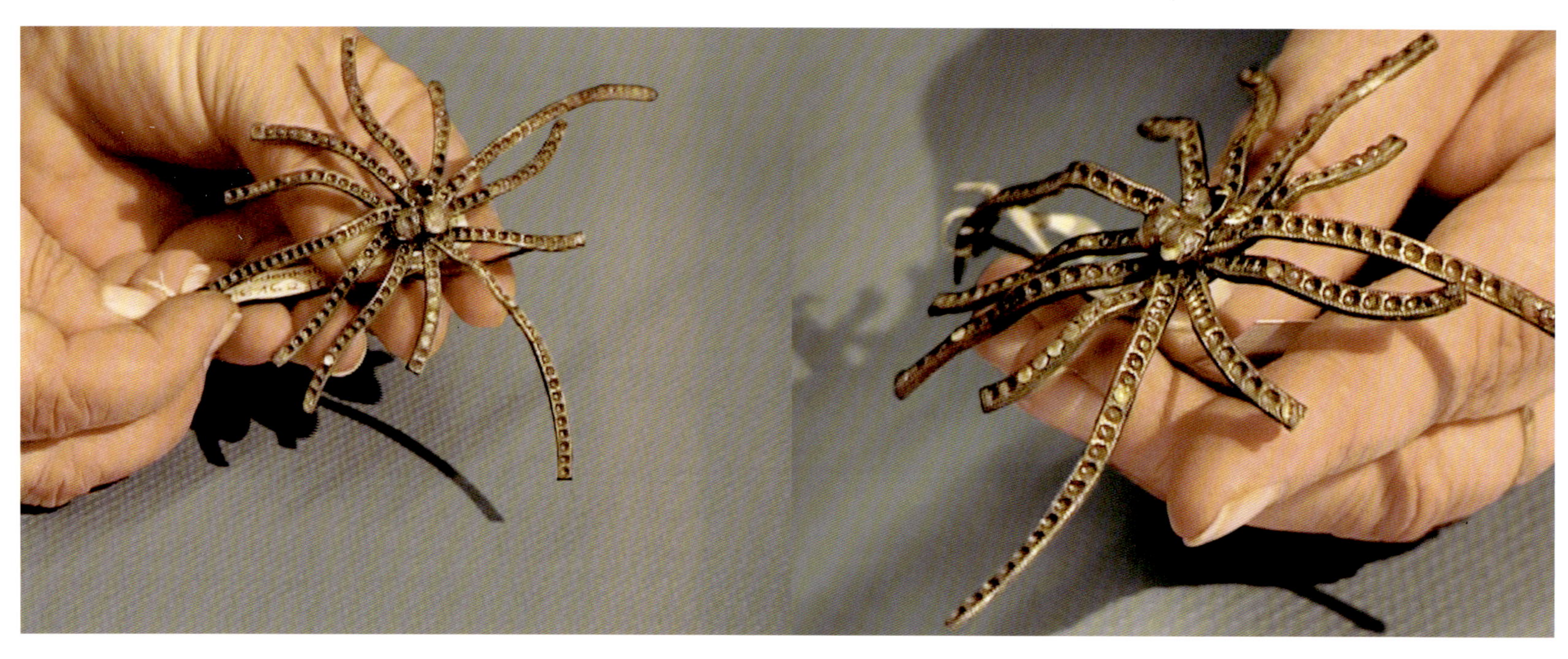

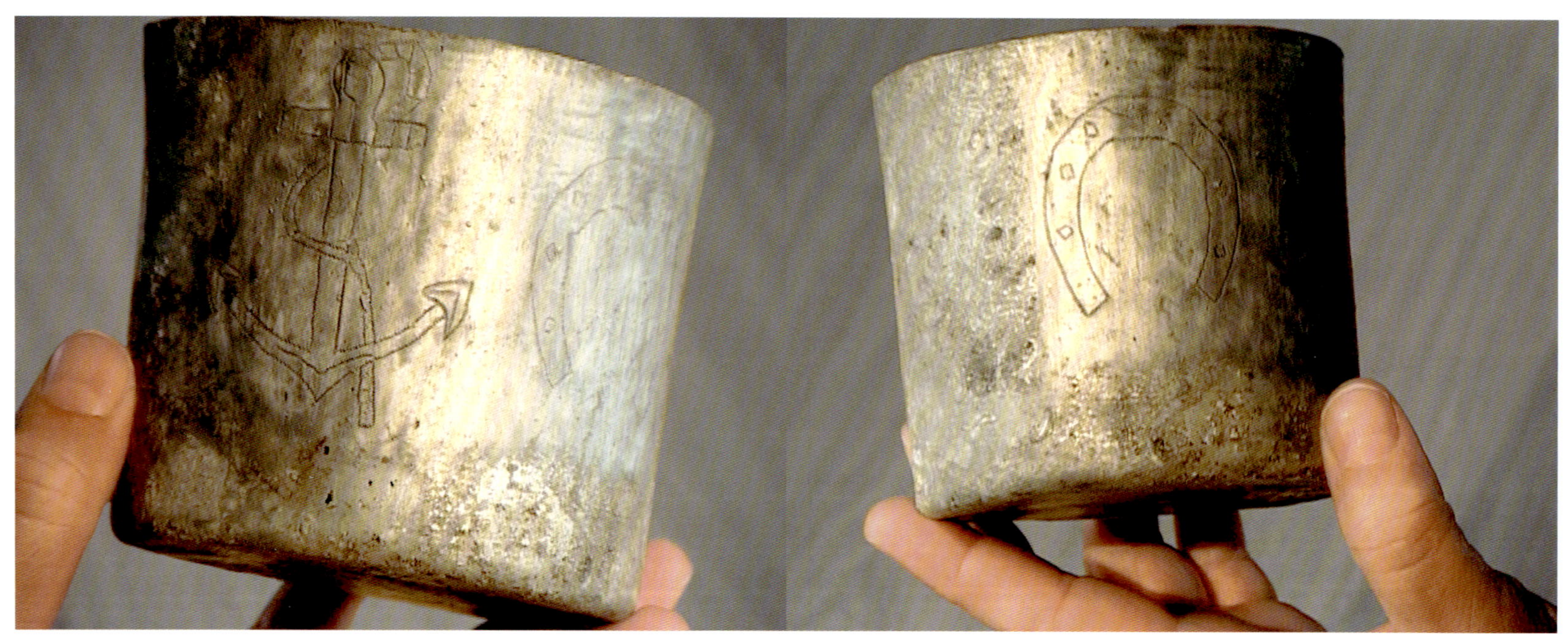

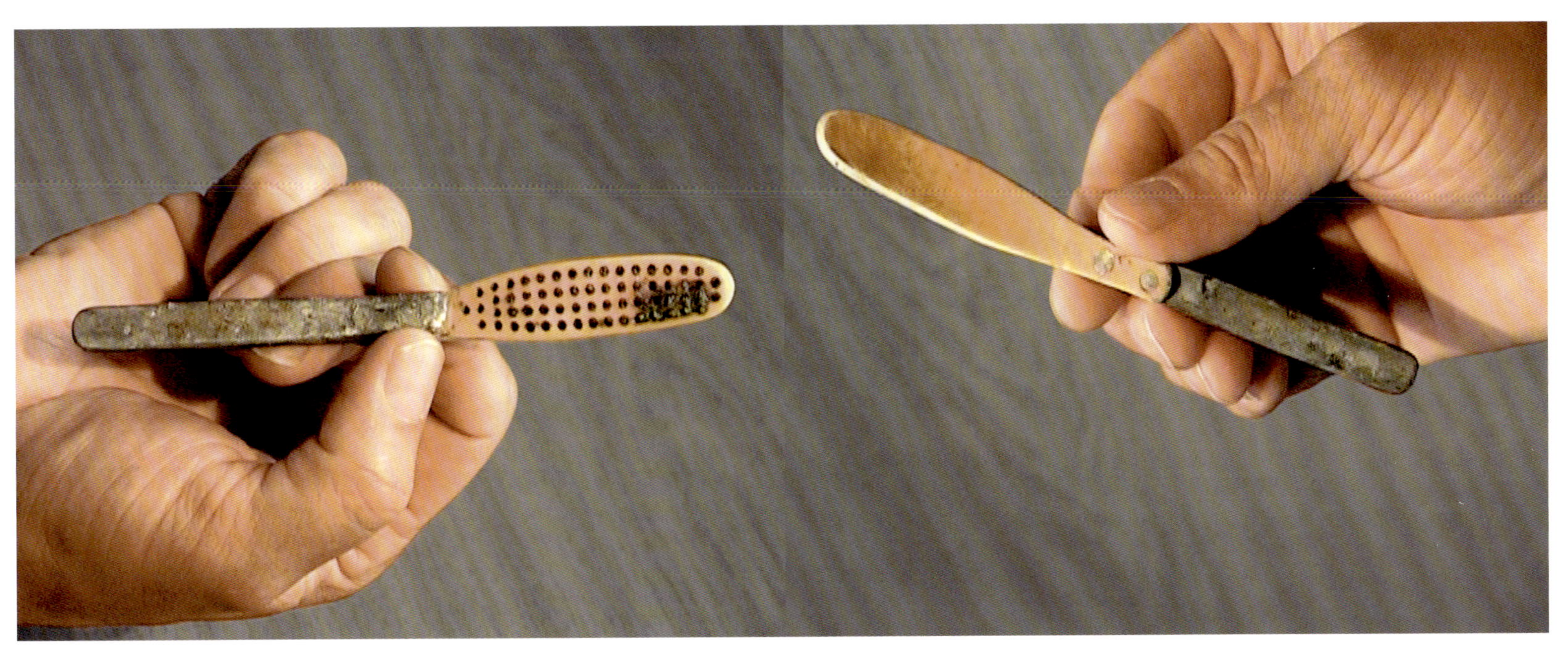

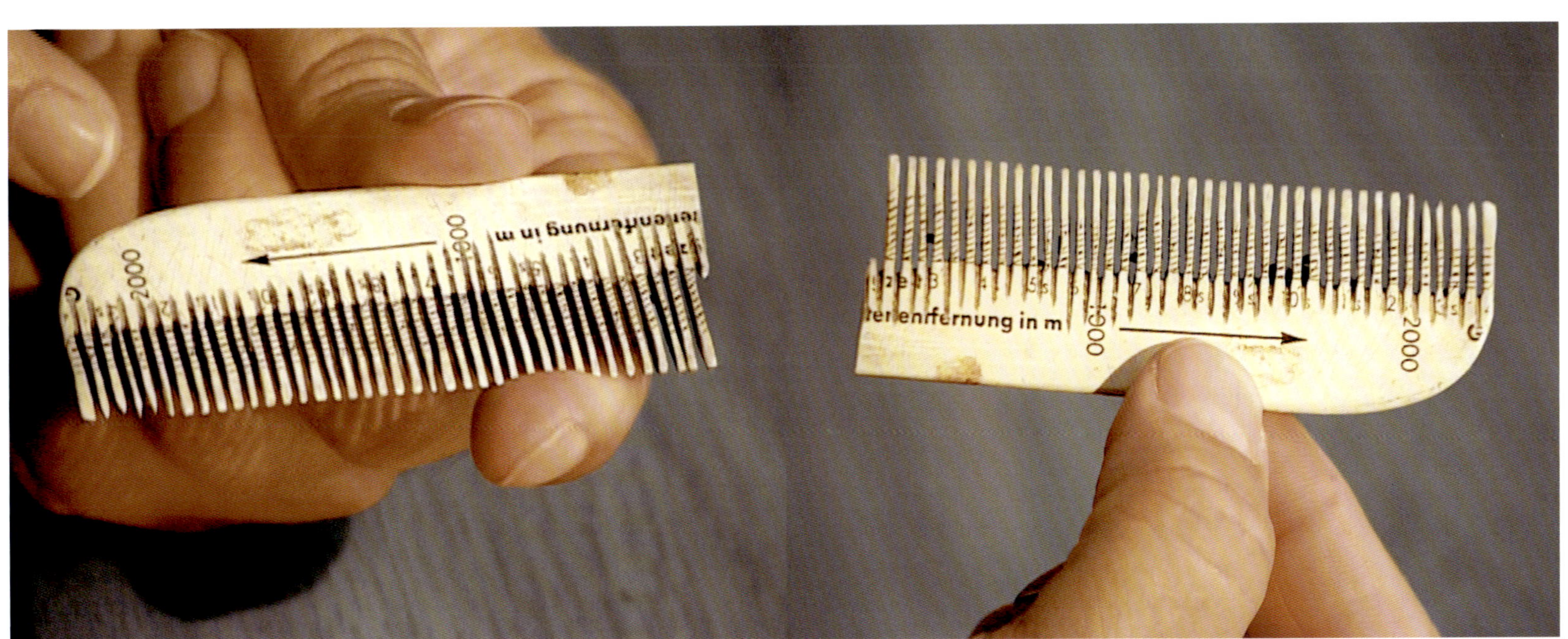

Between Listening and Telling: Last Witnesses, Auschwitz 1945–2005, 2005

Installation; 3 synchronized video projections, color, silent, 40 min.

In 2005, to commemorate the 60th anniversary of the liberation of Auschwitz-Birkenau concentration camp, Esther Shalev-Gerz collected the testimony of survivors living in Paris. Initially presented at the Hôtel de Ville in Paris, the work consists of 60 filmed interviews (which can today be consulted at the Mémorial de la Shoah, in Paris), and a three-screen video projection. The faces of the survivors, filmed in close-up, are captured in the silences that occur between a question and the articulation of the answer to it.

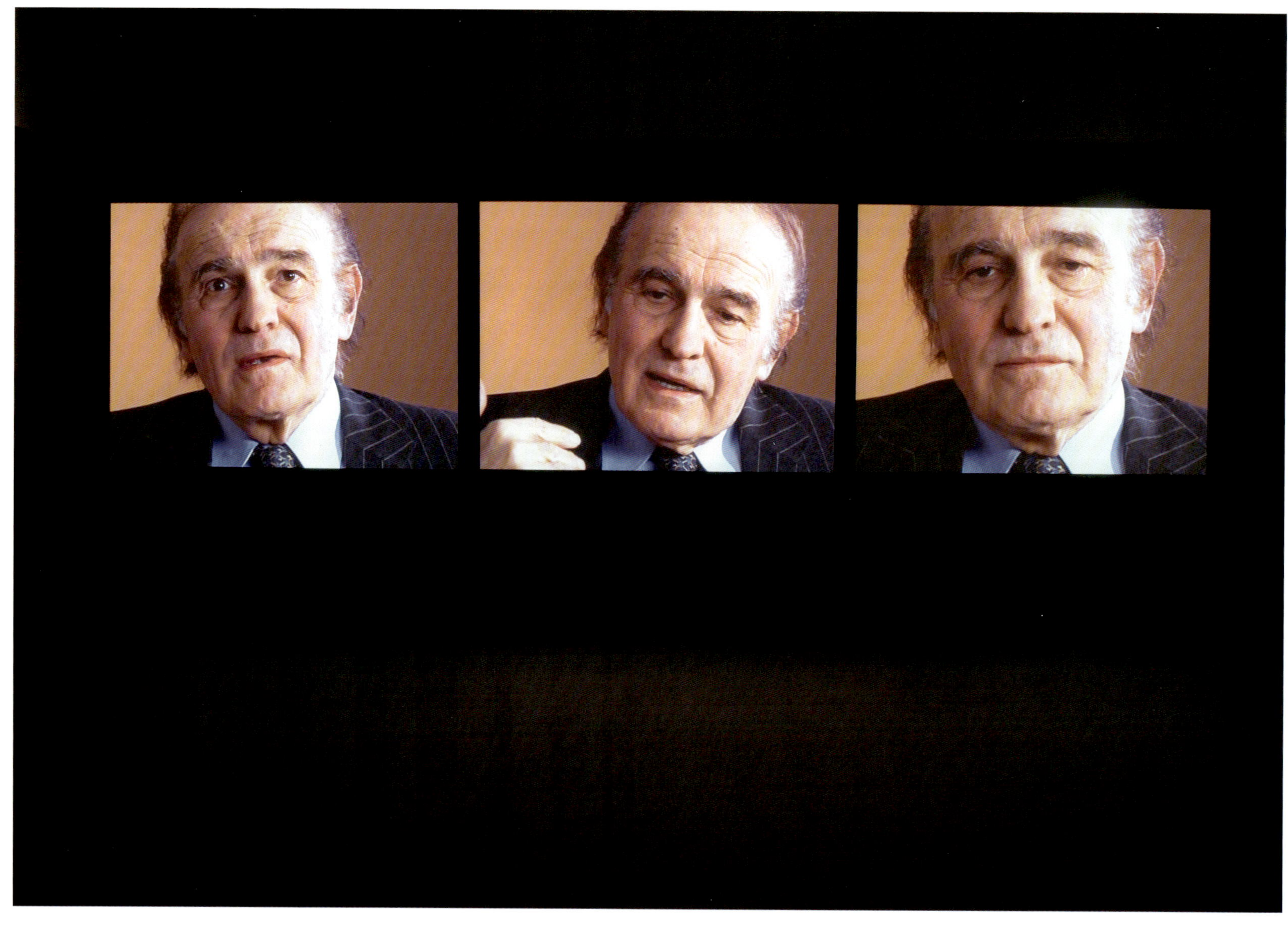

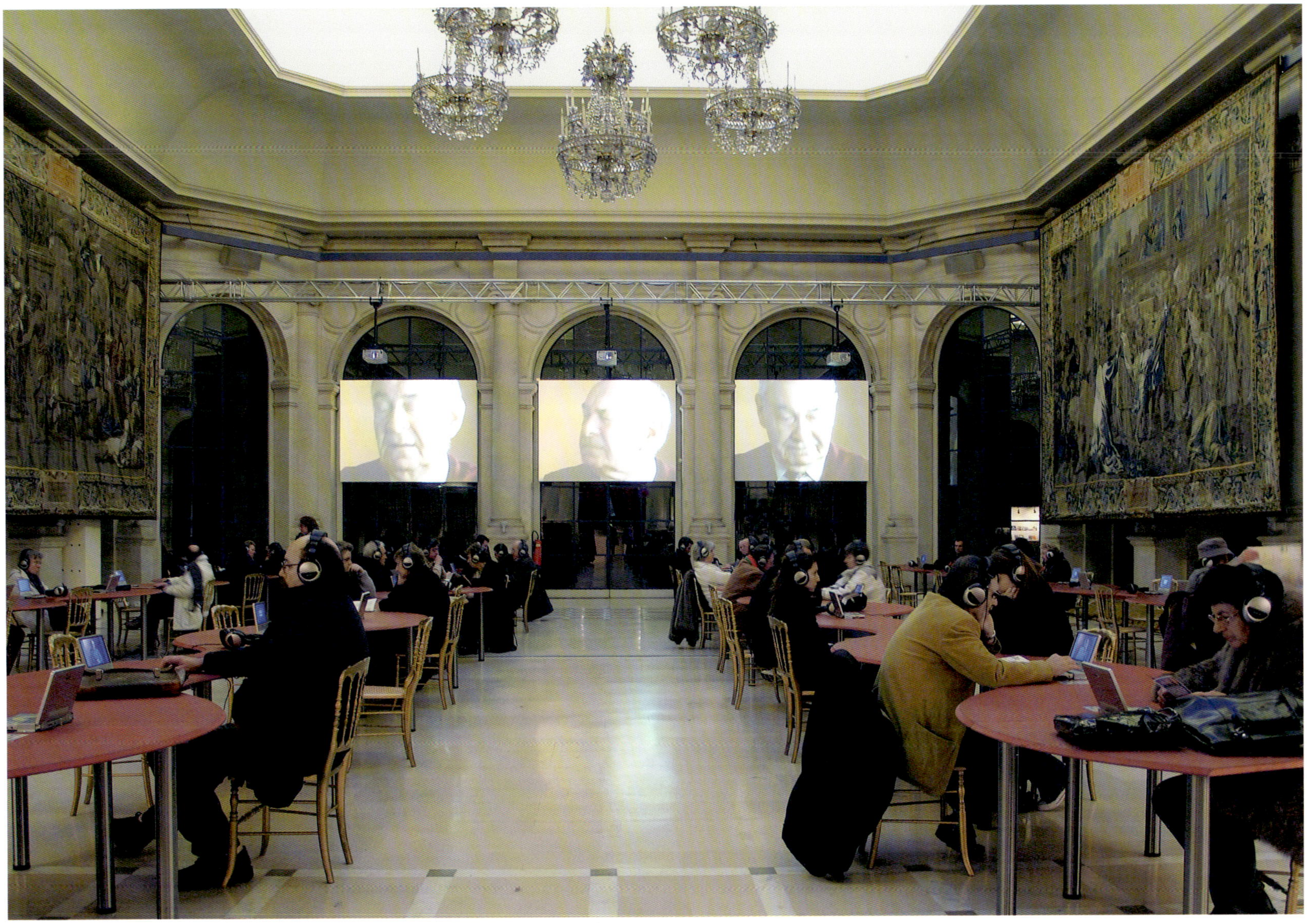

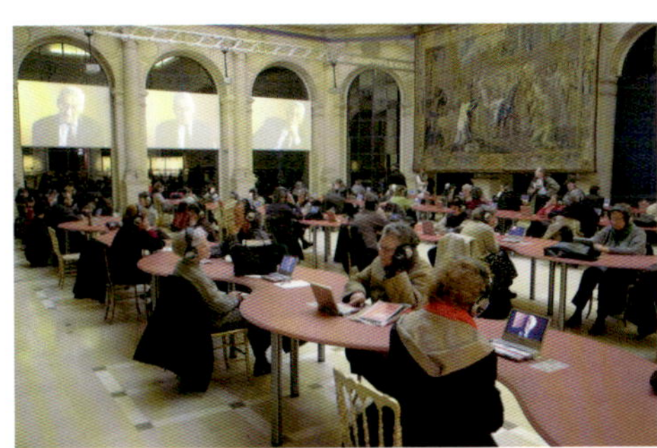

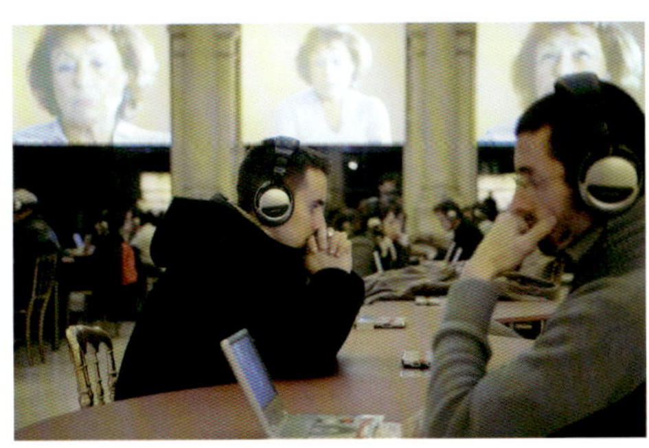

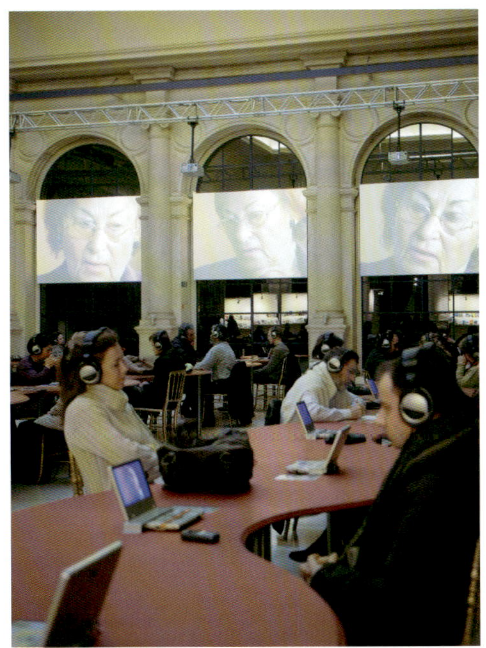

Vis-à-vis, 2006 *

Berlin

Invited to take part in the competition for a monument to homosexuals who had been victims of the Nazi regime, Esther Shalev-Gerz proposed *Vis-à-vis*, a sculpture in the form of a triple spiral. Serving both as a bench to sit on and a support for engraved texts recounting historical events and personal stories, as well as literary excerpts, the labyrinthine structure would be integrated into the Tiergarten park opposite the Holocaust Memorial as an element of repose and reflection.

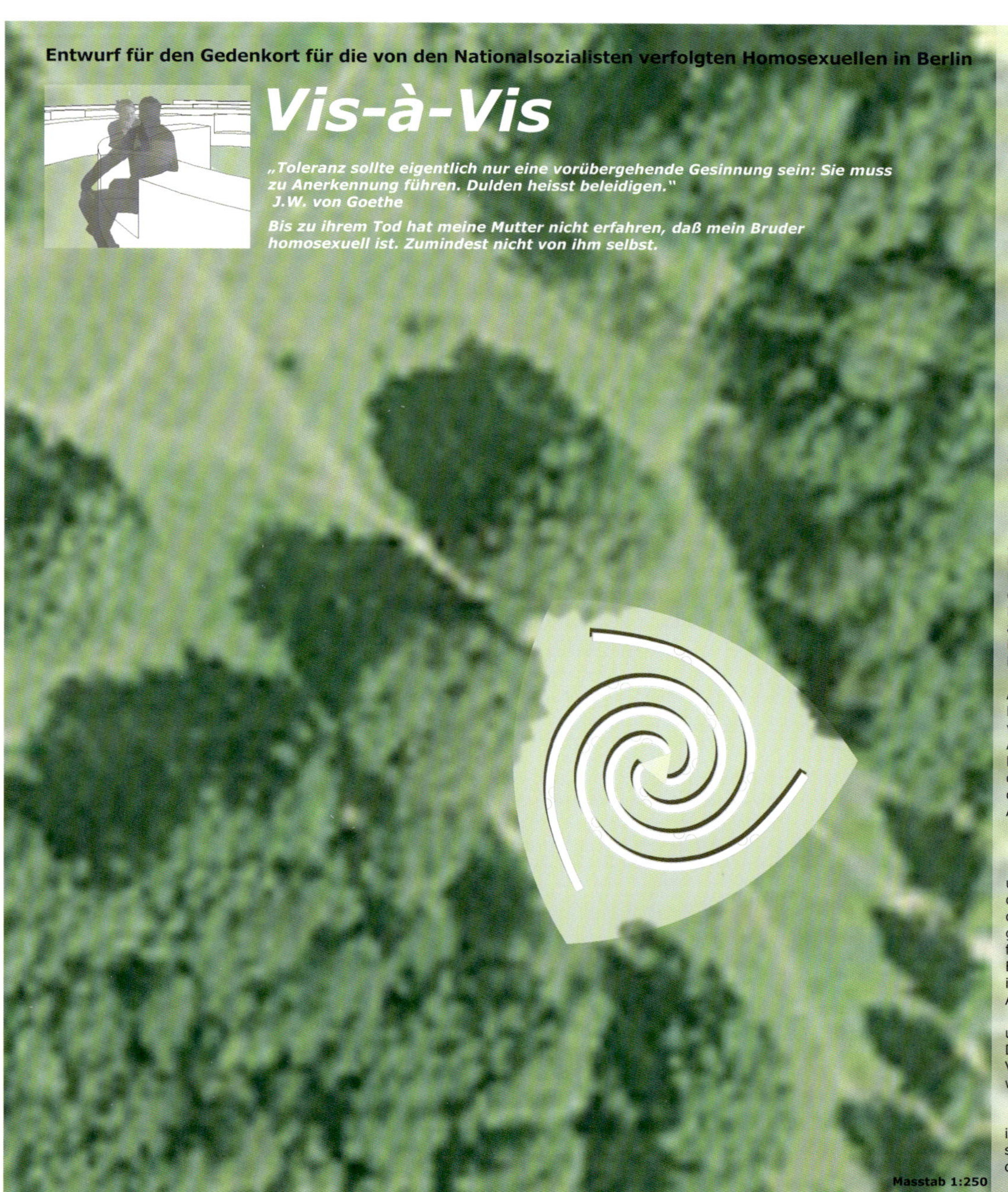

Still/Film, 2009

Installation; 1 black and white photograph, 60 × 80 cm; 7 black and white photographs, 40 × 60 cm each; 3 color photographs, 40 × 60 cm each; 1 black and white text, 60 × 80 cm; 1 color video, silent, 1 min.

With *Still/Film*, Esther Shalev-Gerz returns to the haunts of her childhood, as well as to those of her mother. One series of photographs shows the house at Vilnius where she lived until the age of eight, while another series shows the site of the house from which her mother was obliged to flee at the age of nine, which the artist rediscovered by chance in Alytus. Shalev-Gerz also photographs the forest and landscapes on the journey between these two towns.

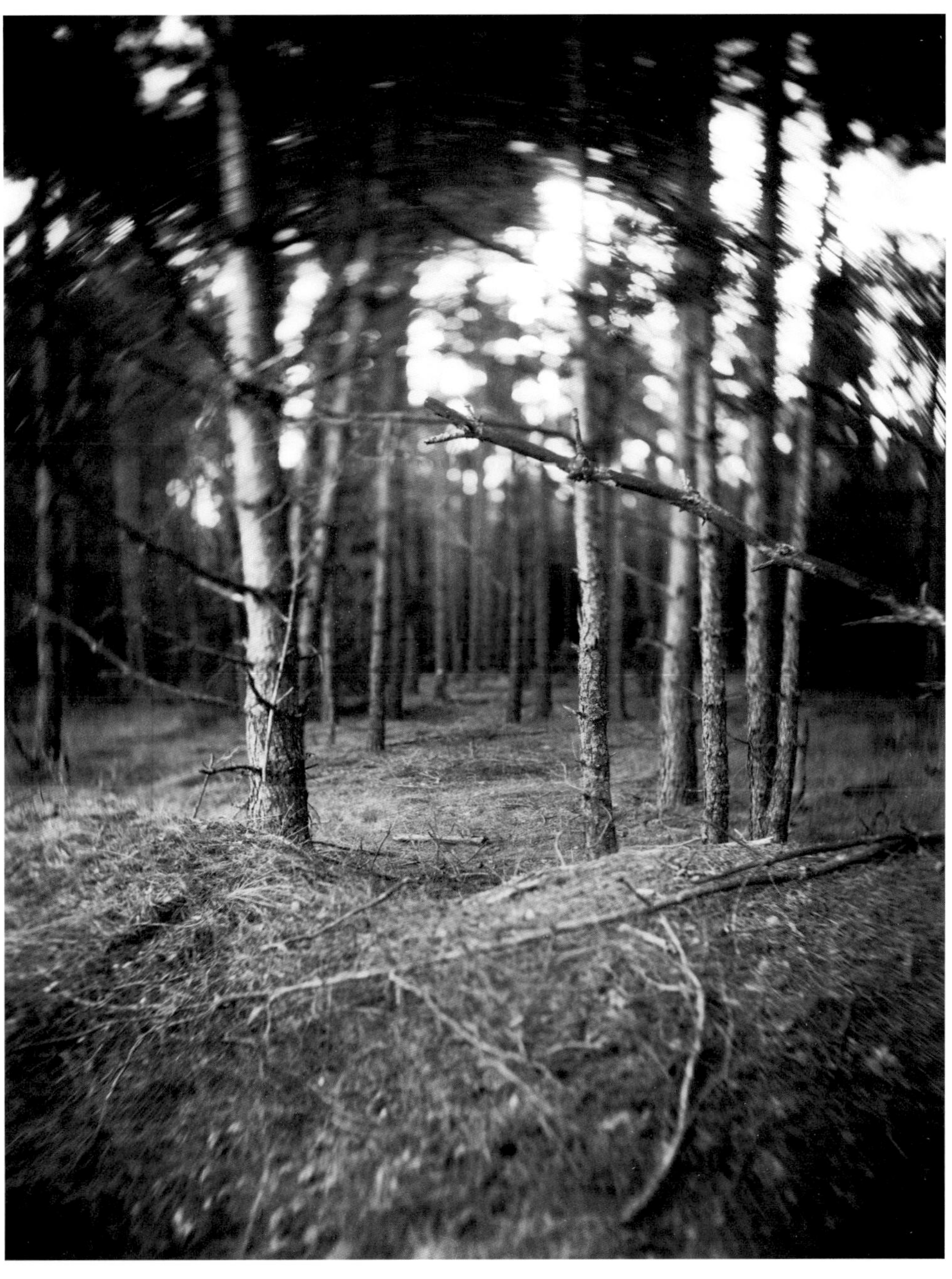

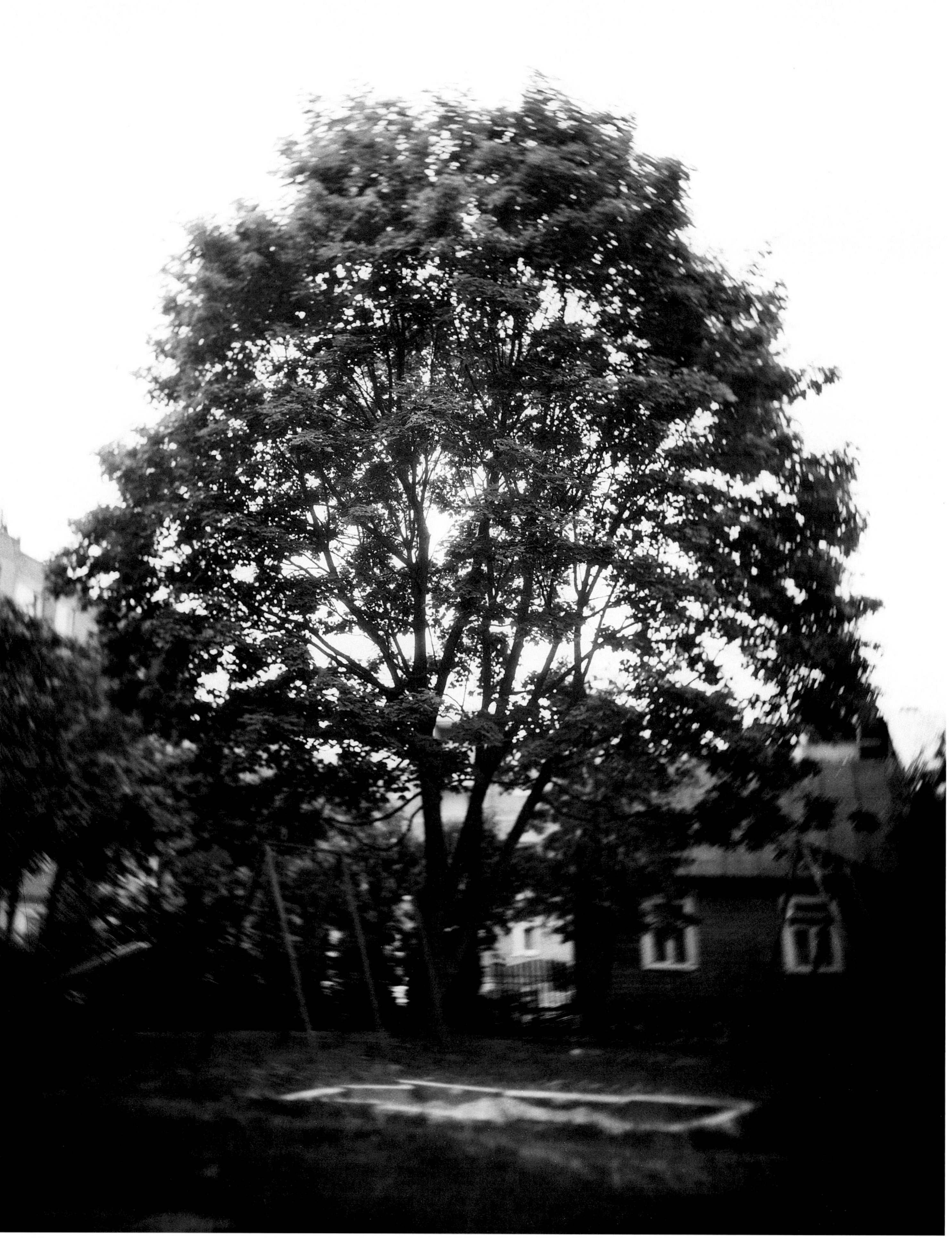

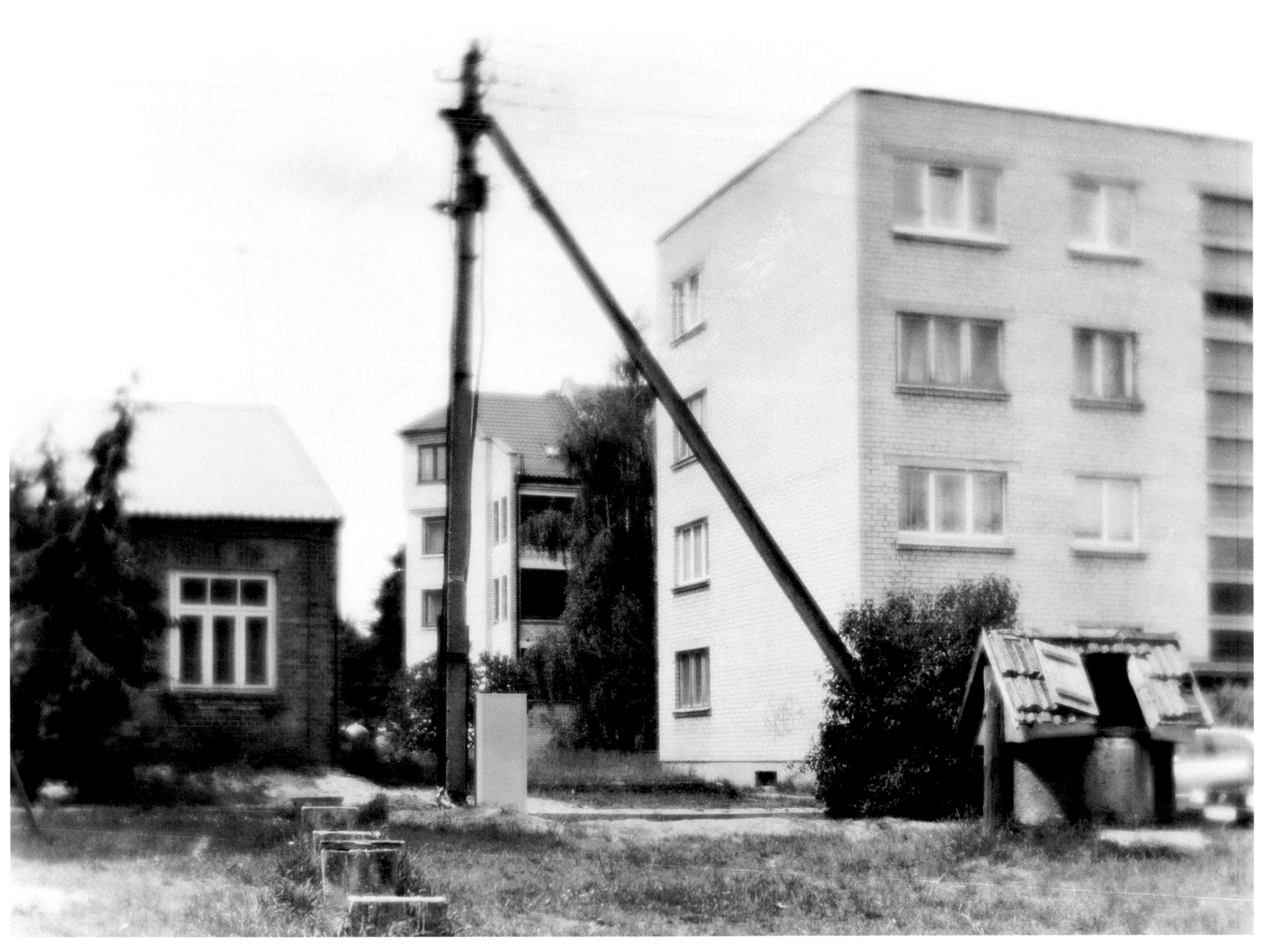

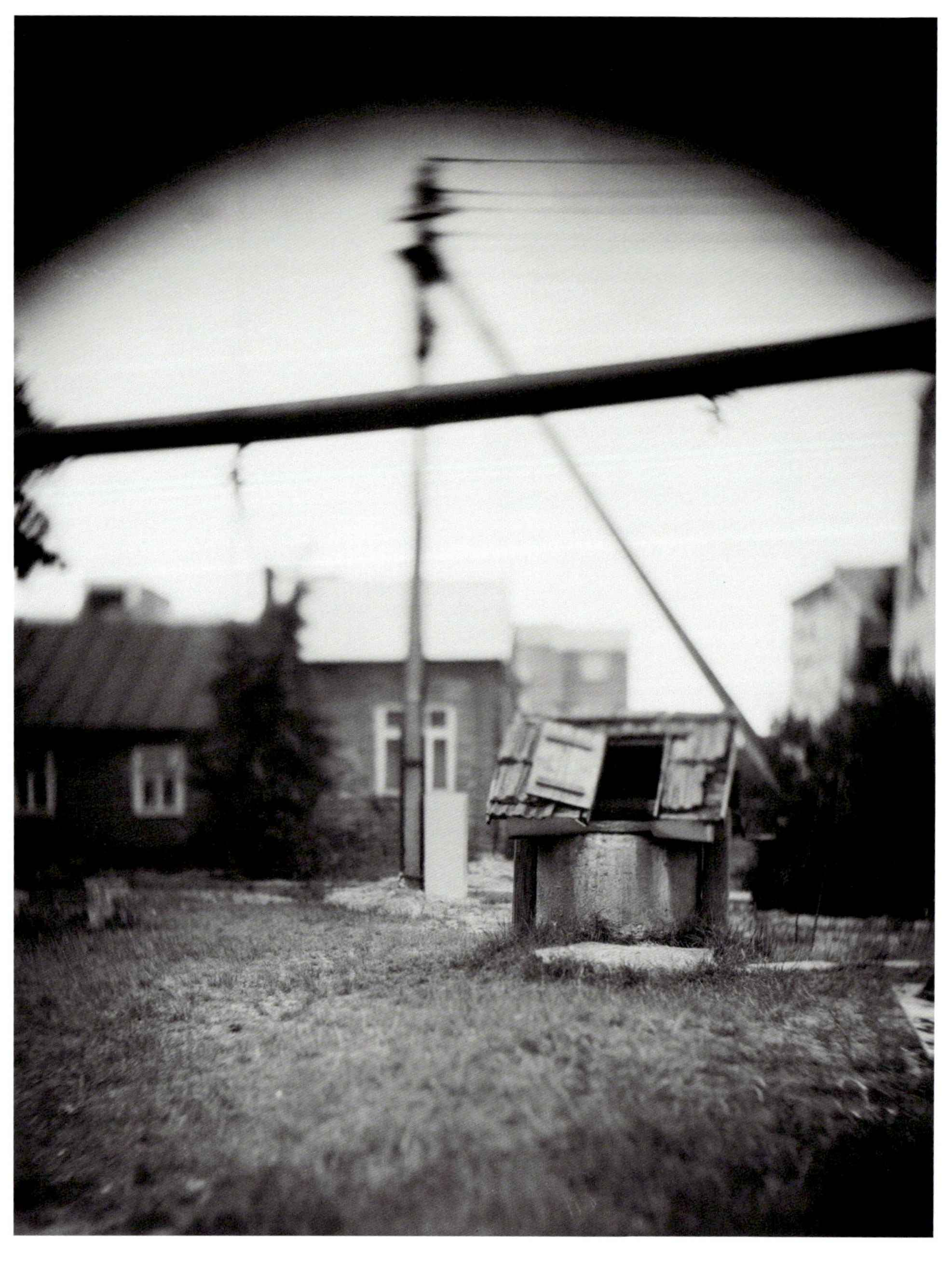

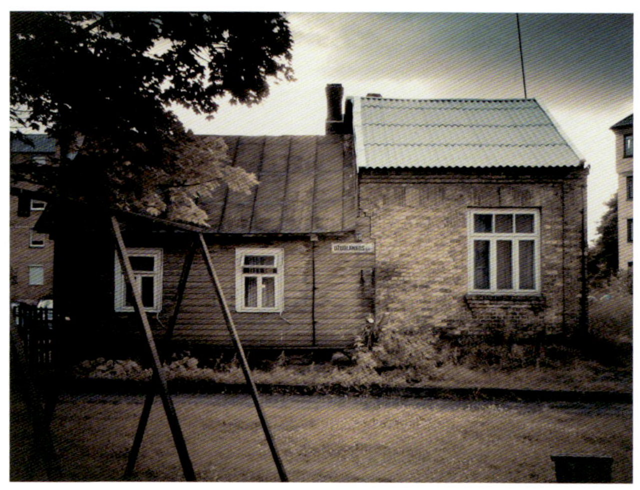

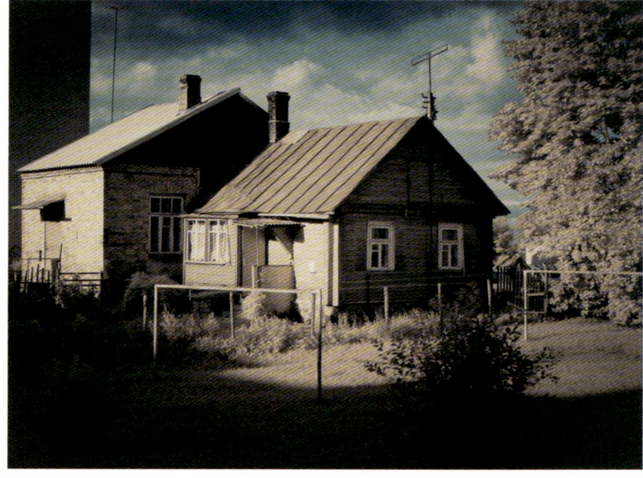

Mano namas yra Vilniuje, jos – Alytuje. Policijos
My house is in Vilnius, hers in Alytus. In the police
archyvuose randu jos adresą. Jos tėvas, kaltinamas
archive I find her address. On charges of
vairavimu išgėrus, nesileidžia suimamas. Jis meta savo
drunk-driving her father resists arrest. He throws
batus policininkui į veidą ir sumoka didžiulę baudą.
two shoes at the police officer's face and he pays an
Alytuje gyvena jo močiutė, visai netoli jos gatvės. Ši
expensive fine. In Alytus his grandmother lives next
vis dar tik žvyrkelis. Abiejose pusėse, naujų
to her street. It's still just a dirt road. On both sides,
daugiabučių įrėminti, stovi labai seni, dažyti mediniai
adjoined by new apartment blocks are very old
namai. Nors ieškome jau tris valandas, niekaip
painted wooden houses. After three hours of
negalime rasti 25 numerio. Aš nusprendžiu, kad
searching, we cannot find number 25. I decide to
gretimas sklypas, pažymėtas ant elektros stulpo
consider the adjoining lot to number 23, written on
užrašytu skaičiumi 23, yra labiausiai tikėtina vieta.
an electric pole, as the most probable location. There
Matyti, kad čia kadaise buvo žaidimų aikštelė, tačiau
are traces of a former playground but the swings
nei sūpynių, nei suolų nebėra. Vienintelis
and benches are missing. The only intact structure is
nesugadintas įrenginys tai – senas šulinys su stogeliu
an old well with a little roof and a small door.
ir mažomis durelėmis. Jį atidaręs išvysti grandinę,
Opened, it reveals a chain, a bucket, and below, water.
kibirą, o apačioje – vandenį. Aš noriu nufotografuoti
I want to photograph the other house from the
tą namą pro priešais esančio namo langą ir
window facing it, and vice versa. As number 25 cannot
atvirkščiai. Kadangi 25 numerio negalime rasti,
be found the photograph shows the empty space next
fotografijoje matyti tuščia erdvė greta šulinio. Kitoje
to the well. Across the street opposite is an old red,
gatvės pusėje, priešais, yra raudonas, pusiau mūrinis,
half brick half wood house bearing the number 30.
pusiau medinis namas, pažymėtas 30 numeriu. Jis
We photograph it with the well in the shot. After
patenka į kadrą su šuliniu. Tris valandas fotografavę
three hours of photographing we begin the drive
sėdame į automobilį ir važiuojame atgal į Vilnių. Jam
back to Vilnius. He receives a phone call informing us
paskambina ir pasako, kad 25 namas vis dėlto
that number 25 does indeed exist. By evening, it is
egzistuoja. Iki vakaro paaiškėja, kur jis yra. 25-asis,
found. Number 25 is in fact the red house, number 30
pasirodo, yra tas raudonas, fotografijose užfiksuotas
that appears in the photographs. Her room is on the
namas, pažymėtas 30 numeriu. Jos kambarys kairėje,
left, facing the well.
priešais šulinį.

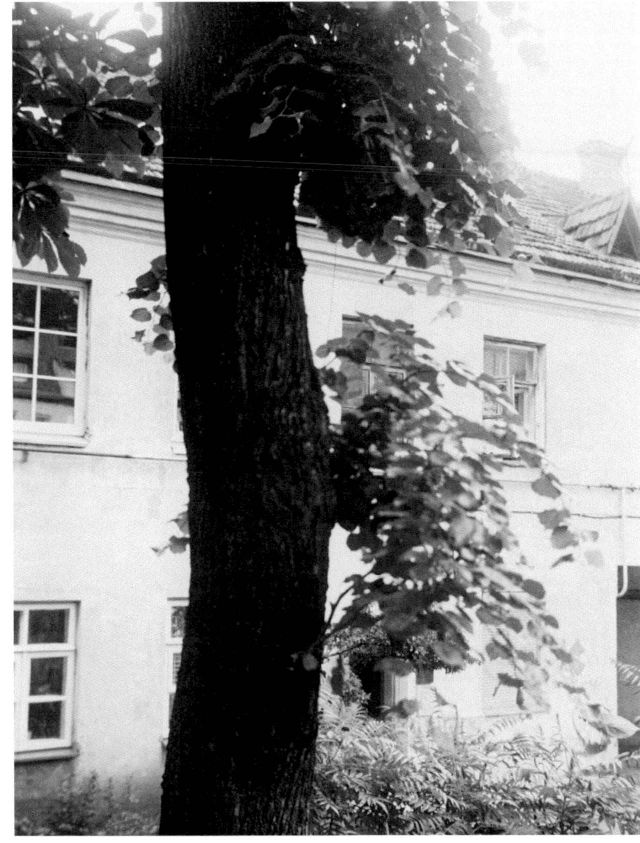

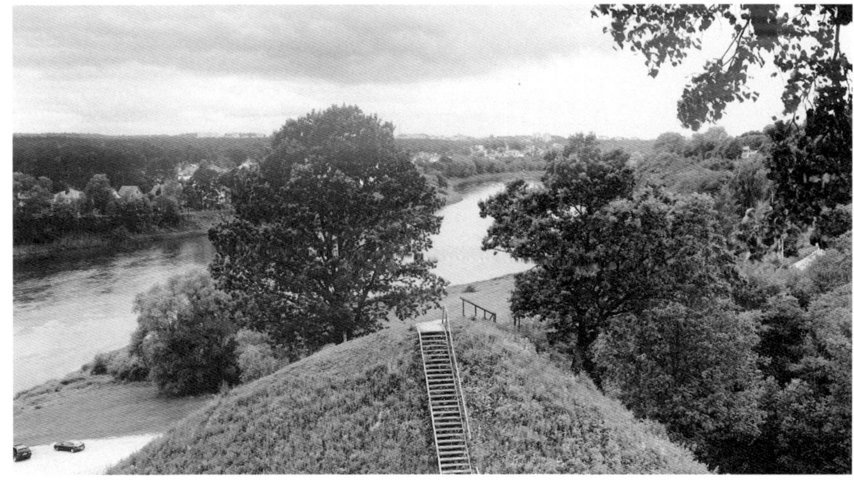

On Two, 2009

Installation; 2 synchronized HD video projections, color, sound, 30 min. each; 6 audiotapes, 10 min.; 12 black and white photographs, 40 × 60 cm each

On Two takes a look at two people Esther Shalev-Gerz met in Paris, and two landscapes: the île Seguin in Paris and Cortes Island in Canada. Rola Younes speaks of her passion for languages (Yiddish, Hebrew, Persian, Arabic …) which allow her to assimilate different stories, and Jacques Rancière reads a passage from his text, *The Emancipated Spectator*, in which he describes a formative moment in his thinking, which led him to "reformulate the established relationships between seeing, doing, and speaking," and comments on the function of contemporary art.

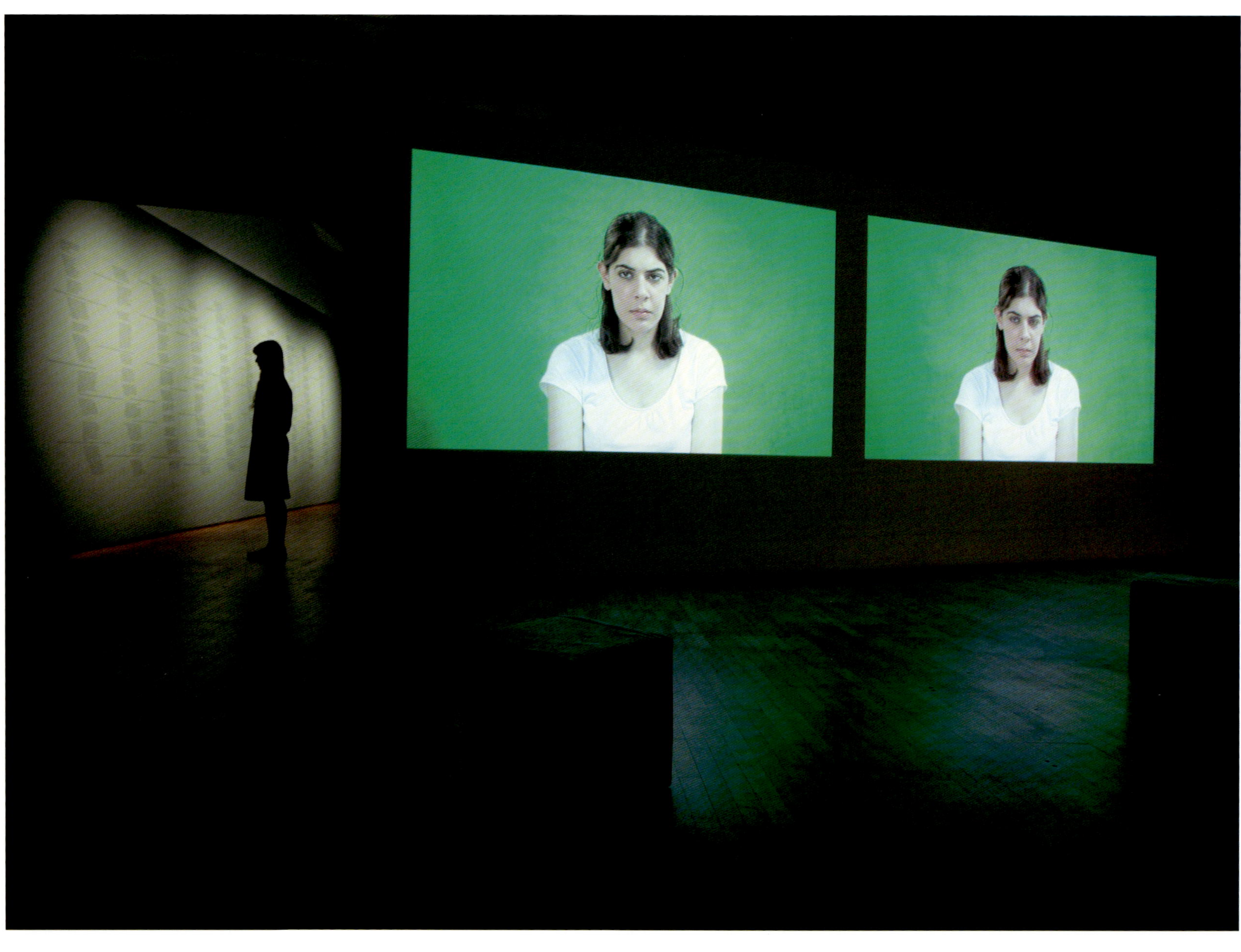

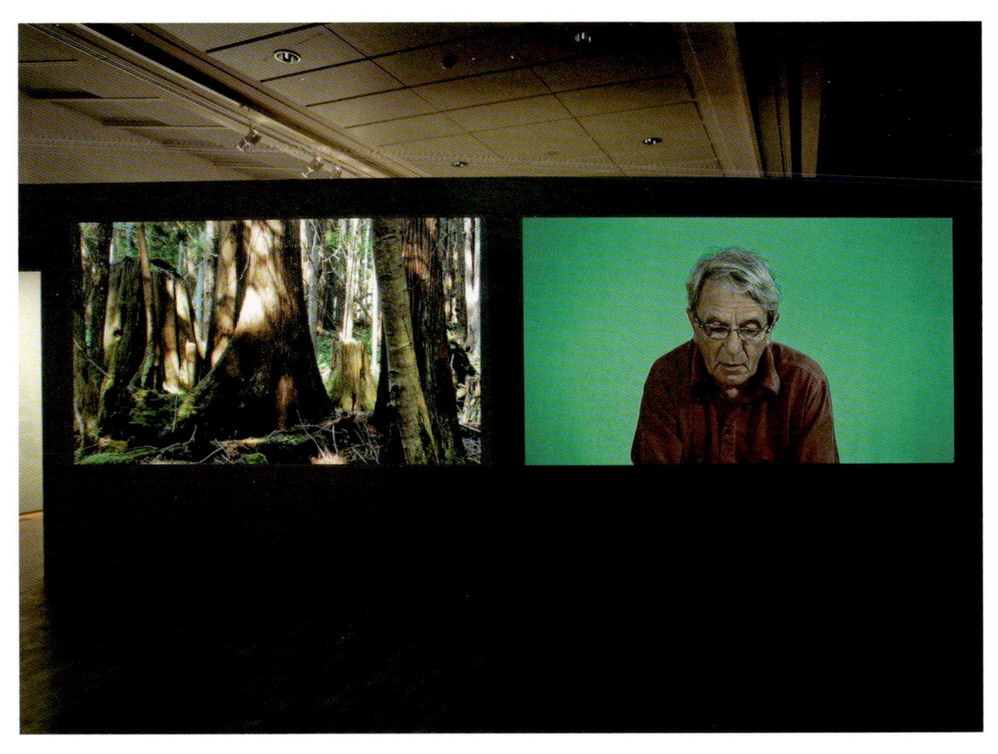

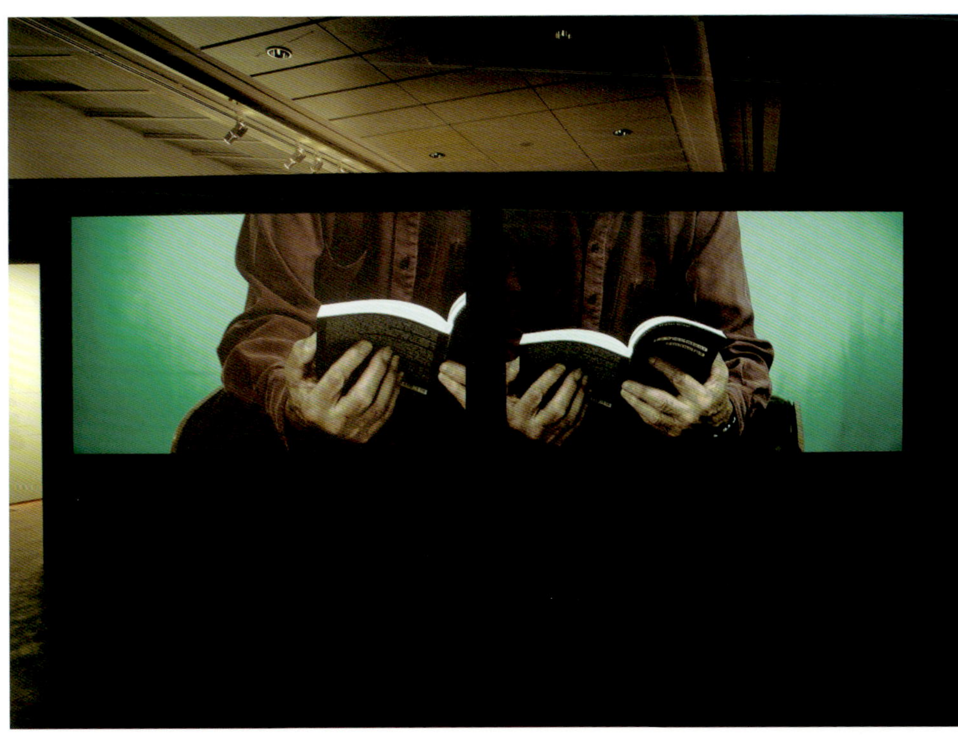

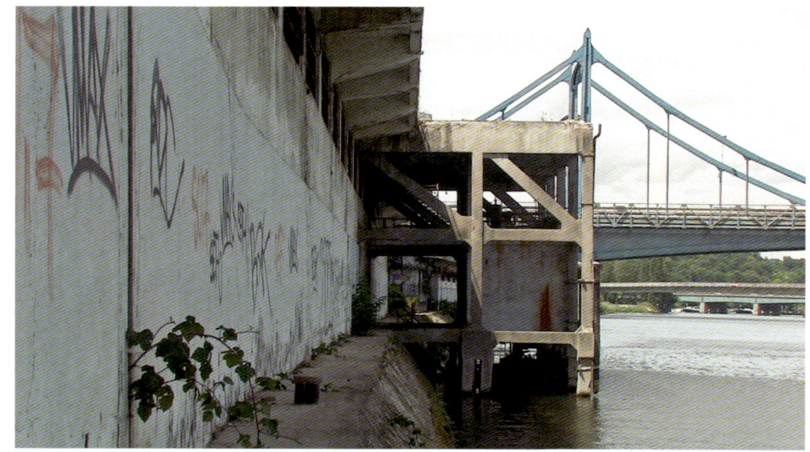
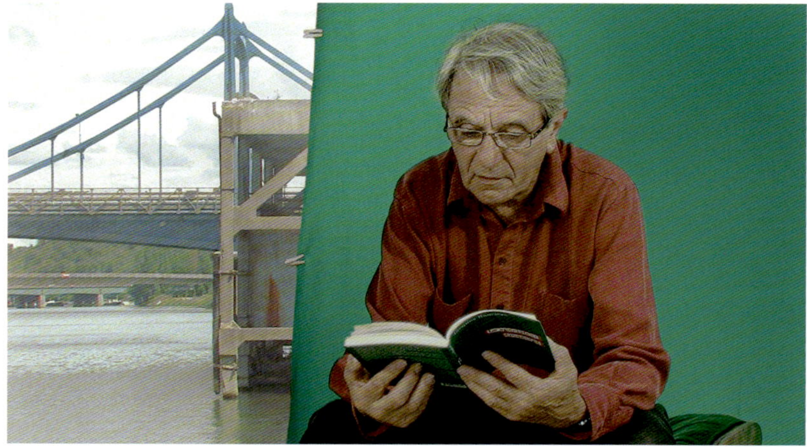
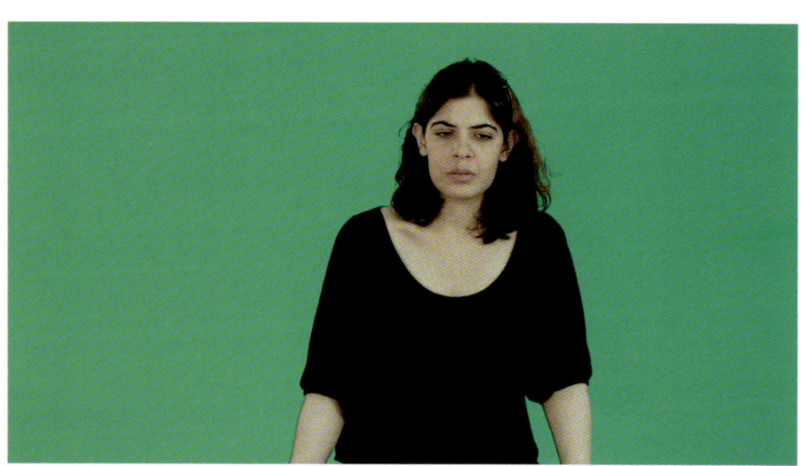
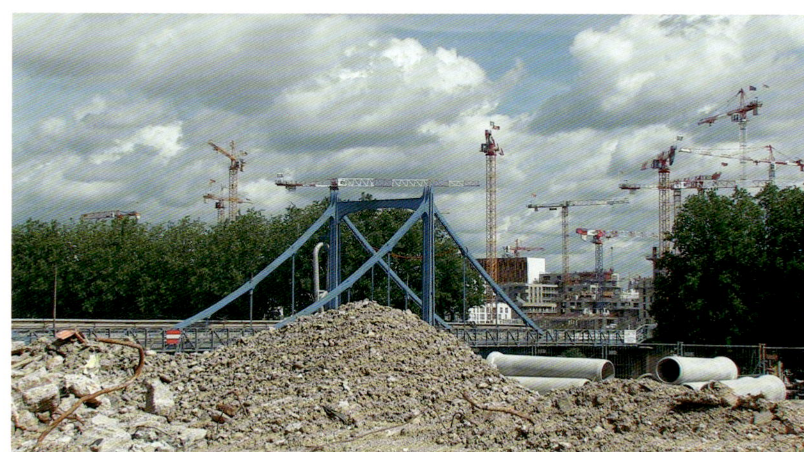
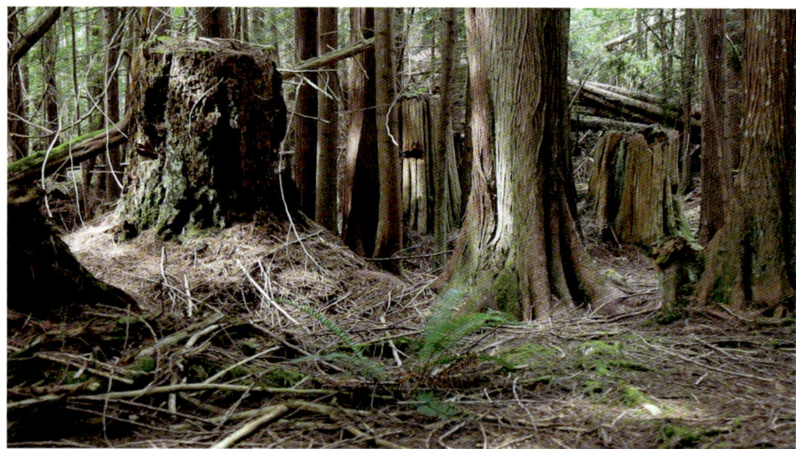
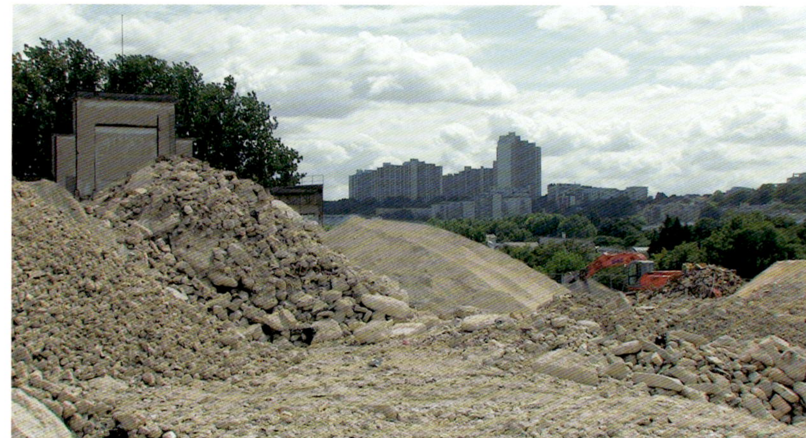

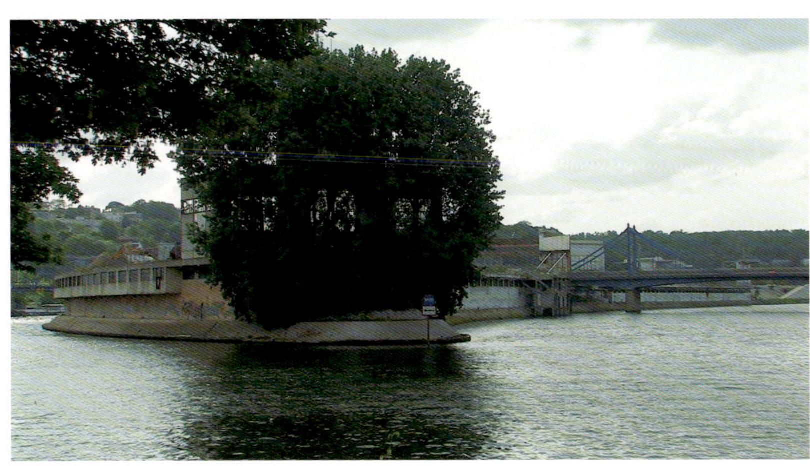
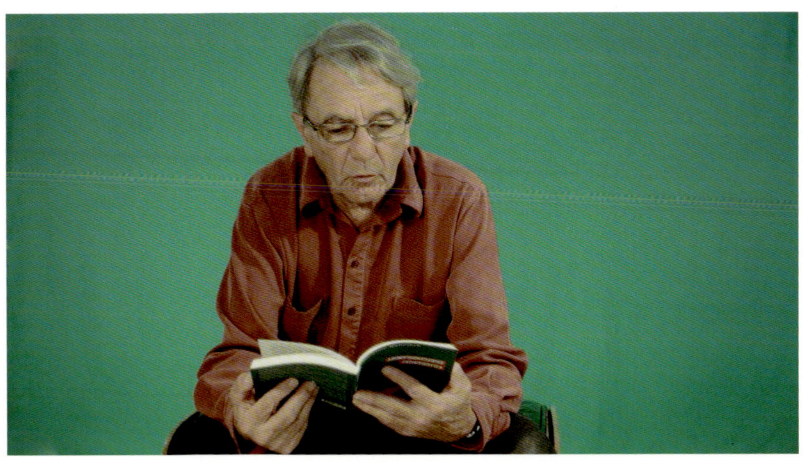
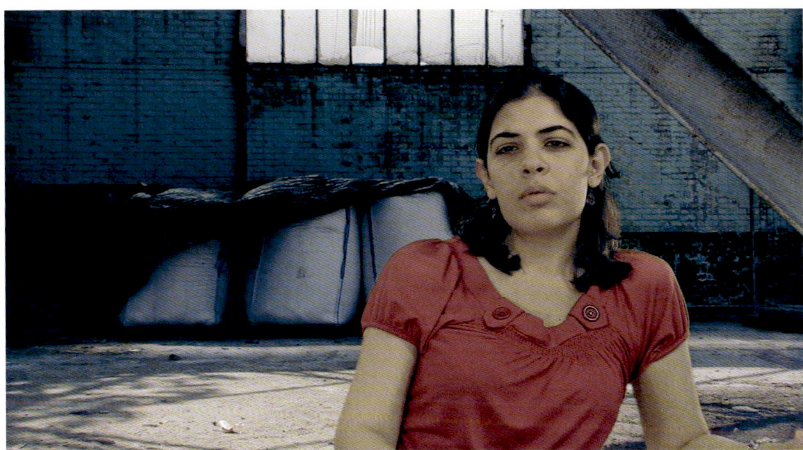
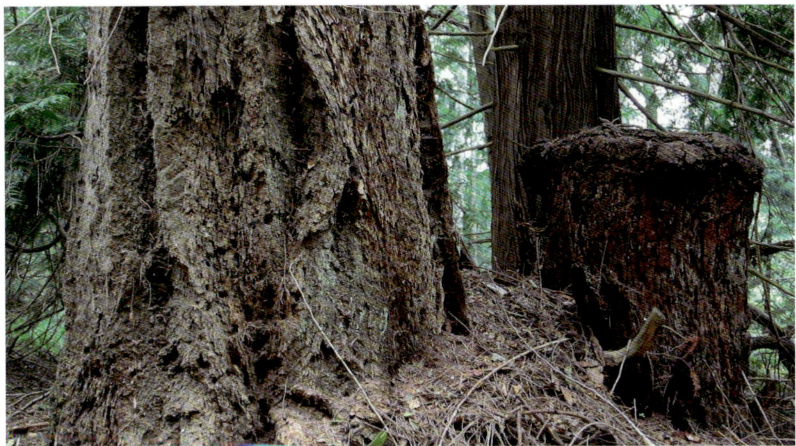
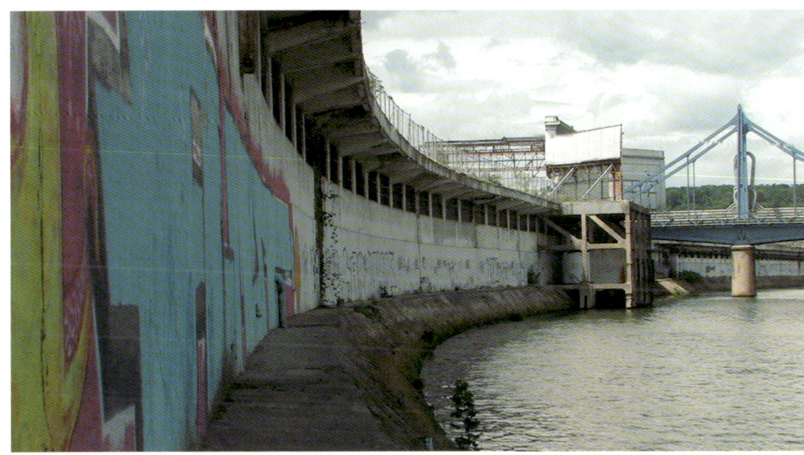
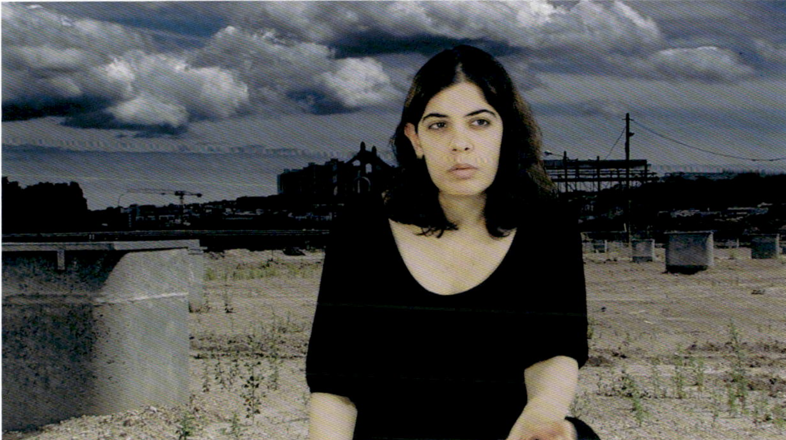

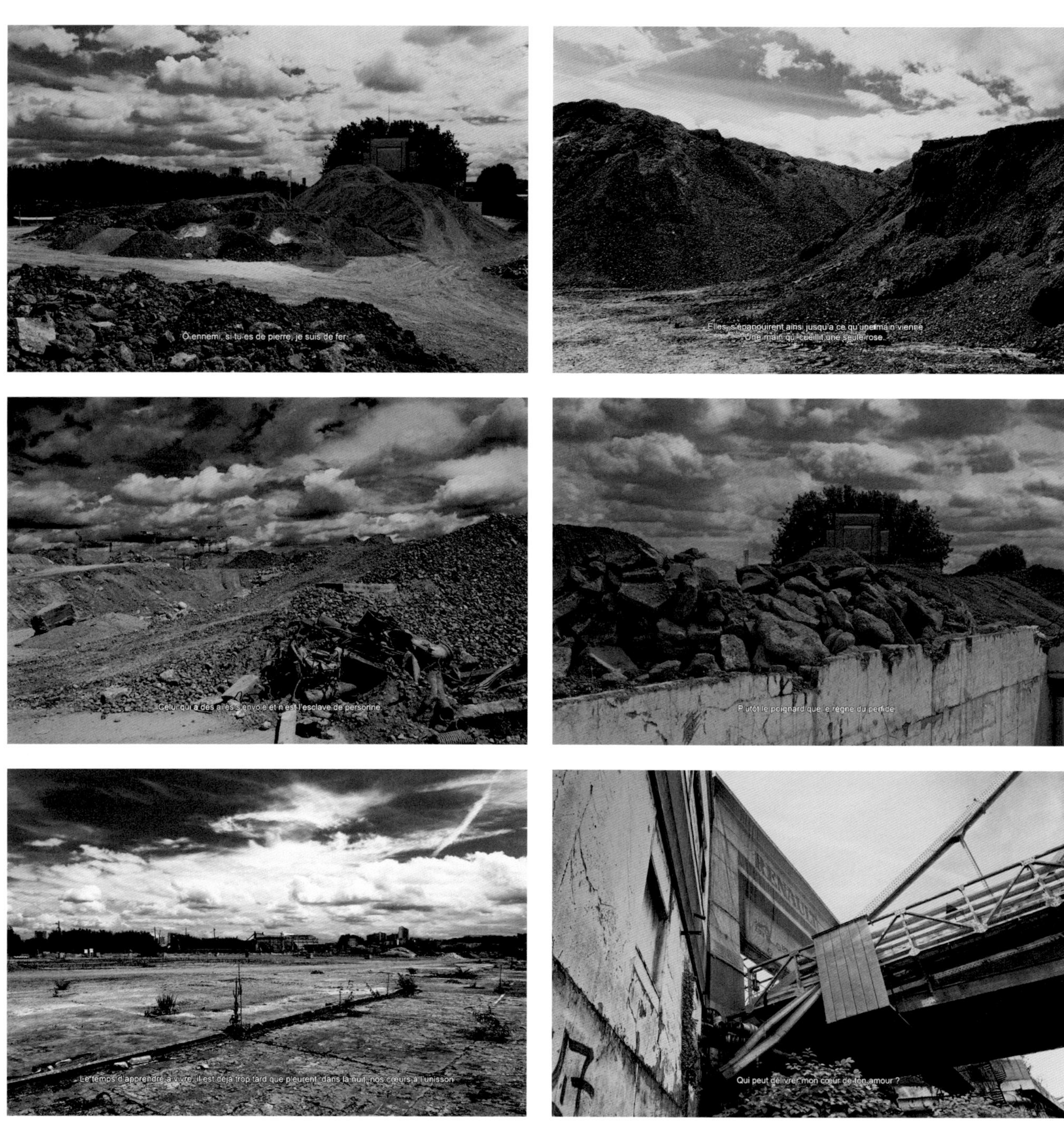
Ô ennemi, si tu es de pierre, je suis de fer.
Elles s'épanouirent ainsi jusqu'à ce qu'une main vienne
Une main qui cueillit une seule rose.
Celui qui a des ailes s'envole et n'est l'esclave de personne.
Plutôt le poignard que le règne du perfide.
Le temps d'apprendre à vivre, il est déjà trop tard que pleurent, dans la nuit, nos cœurs à l'unisson
Qui peut délivrer mon cœur de ton amour ?

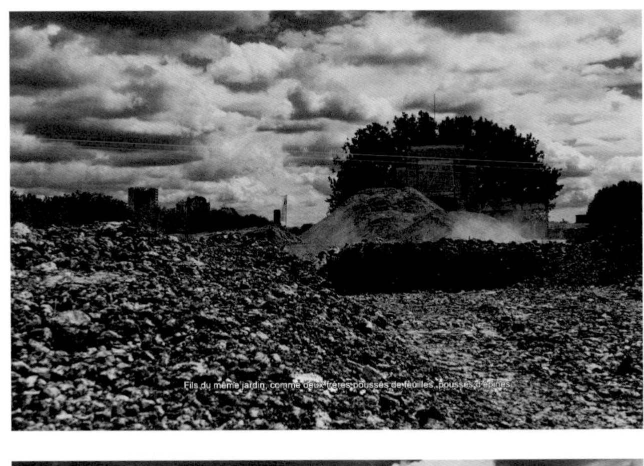
Fils du même jardin, comme deux frères poussés de feuilles, poussés d'épines

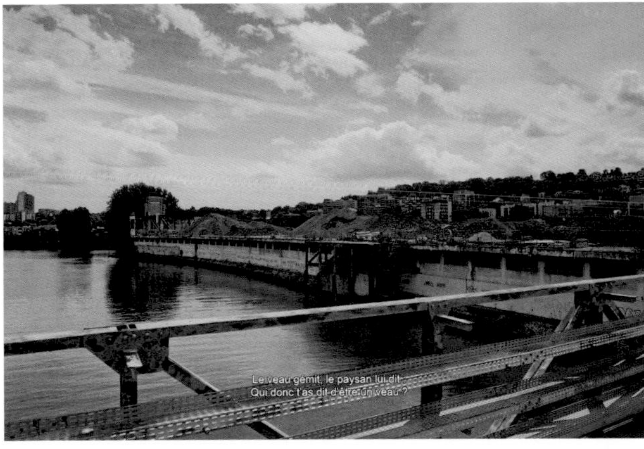
Le veau gémit, le paysan lui dit :
Qui donc t'as dit d'être un veau ?

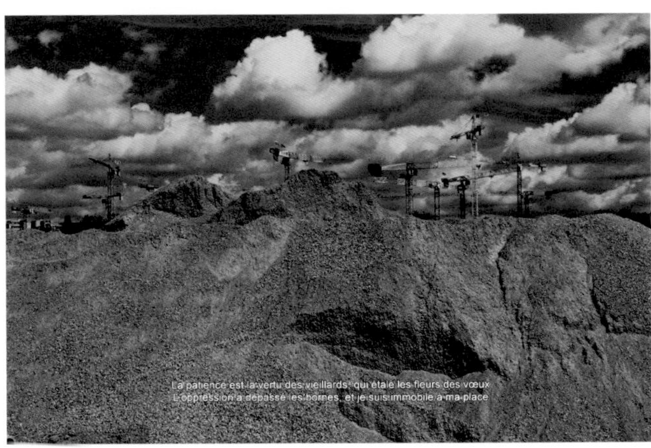
La patience est la vertu des vieillards, qui étale les fleurs des vœux
L'oppression a dépassé les bornes, et je suis immobile à ma place

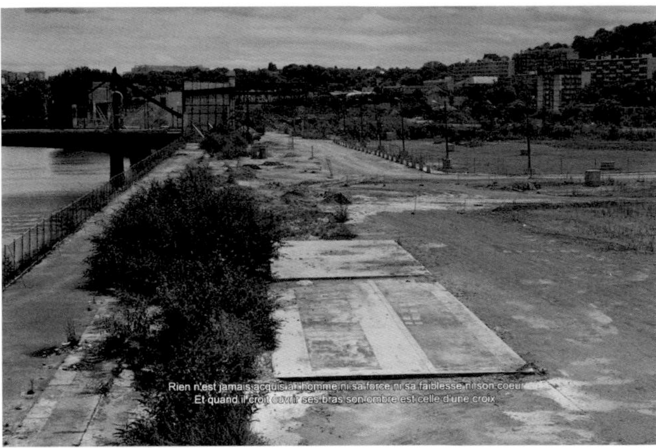
Rien n'est jamais acquis à l'homme ni sa force ni sa faiblesse ni son coeur
Et quand il croit ouvrir ses bras son ombre est celle d'une croix

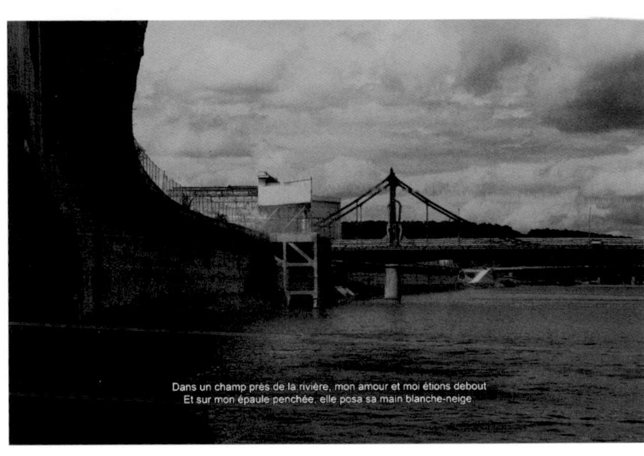
Dans un champ près de la rivière, mon amour et moi étions debout
Et sur mon épaule penchée, elle posa sa main blanche-neige.

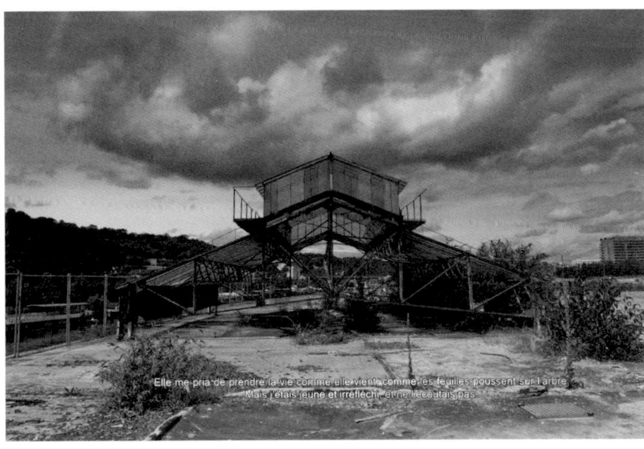
Elle me pria de prendre la vie comme elle vient, comme les feuilles poussent sur l'arbre.
Mais j'étais jeune et irréfléchi, et ne l'écoutais pas.

The Open Page, 2009

15 color photographs, dimensions variable

Commissioned for the Municipal Library of Vancouver, *The Open Page* consists of a series of photographs of rare books that can be consulted only with special permission, among them a 15th-century illustrated breviary, a 17th-century English botanical guide, and an early illustrated copy of *Peter Pan*. Each book is photographed with a very large-format camera which reveals these works in their minutest facets, as well as the hands of the librarians who are holding the book of their choice and drawing attention to details in it.

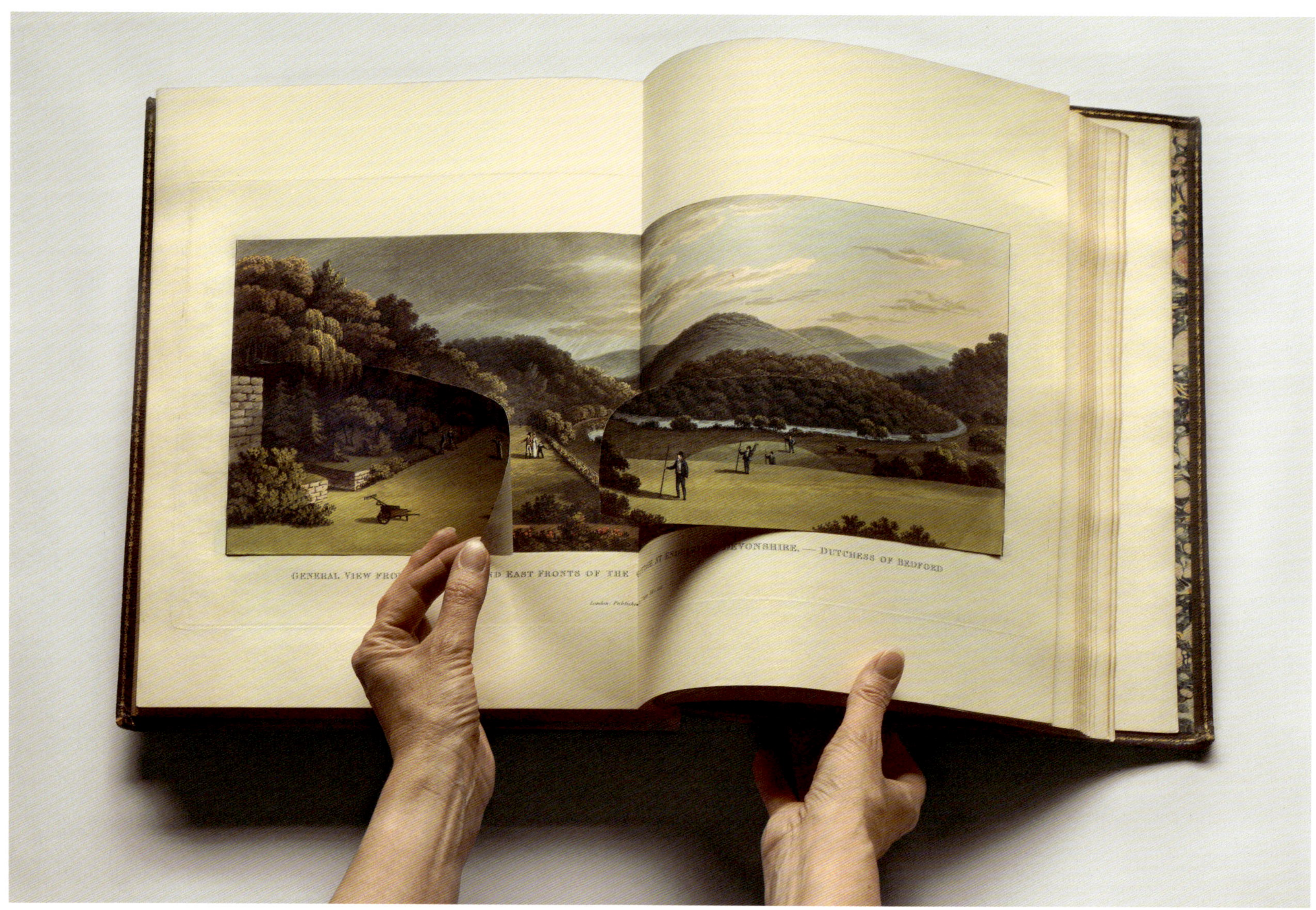

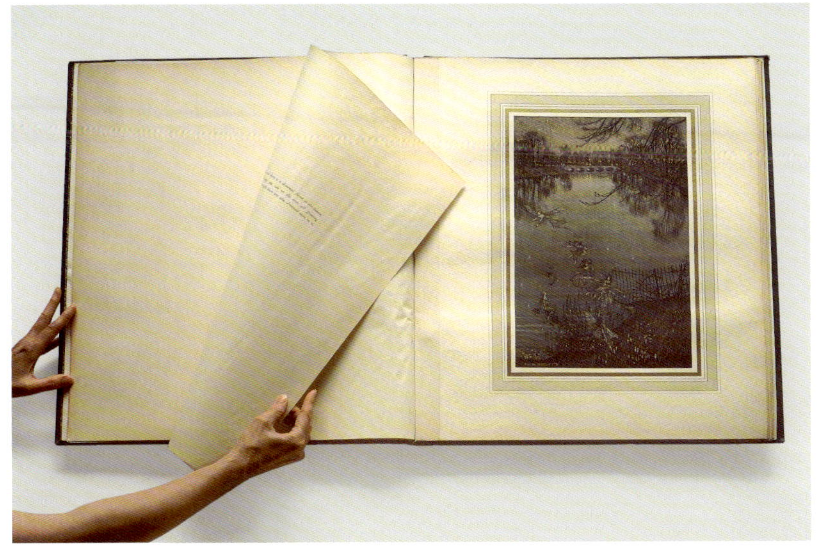

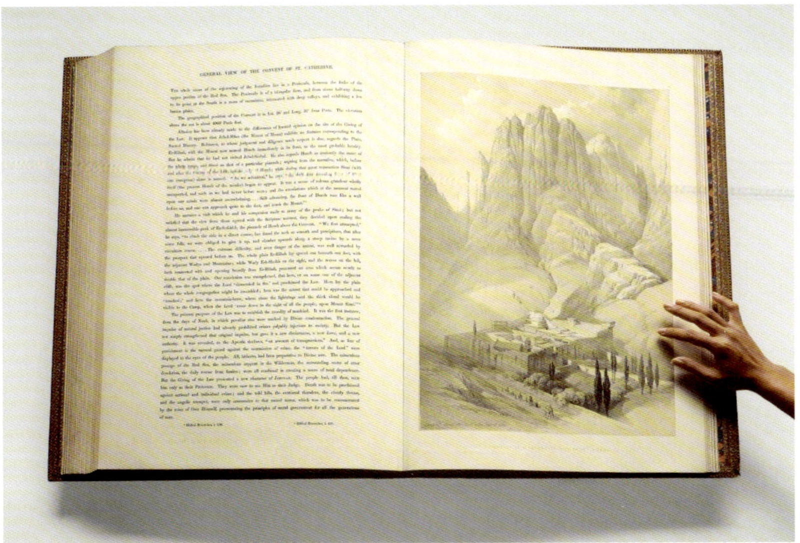

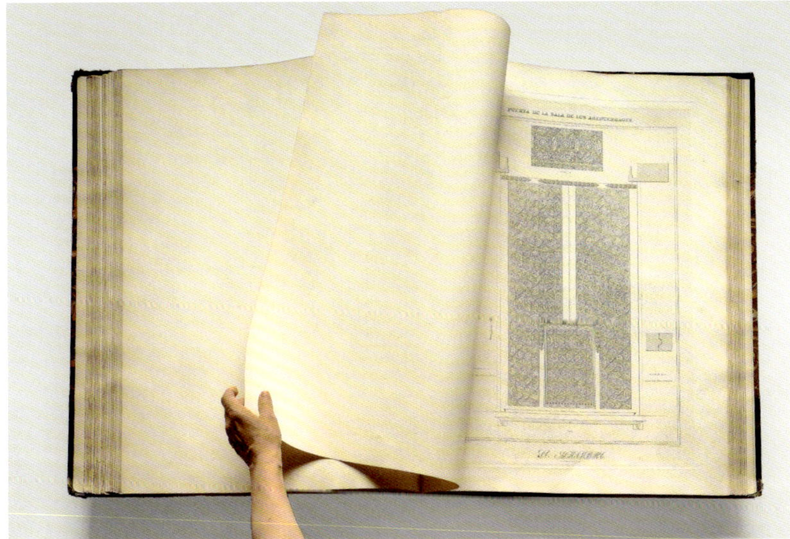

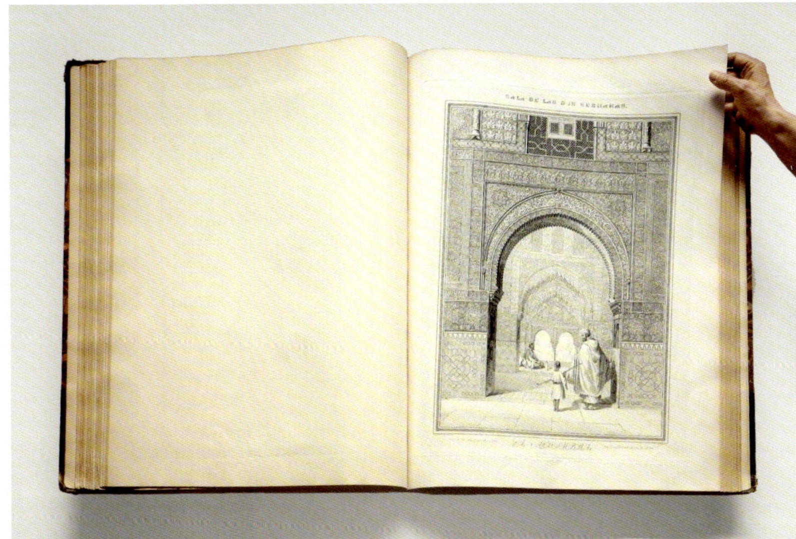

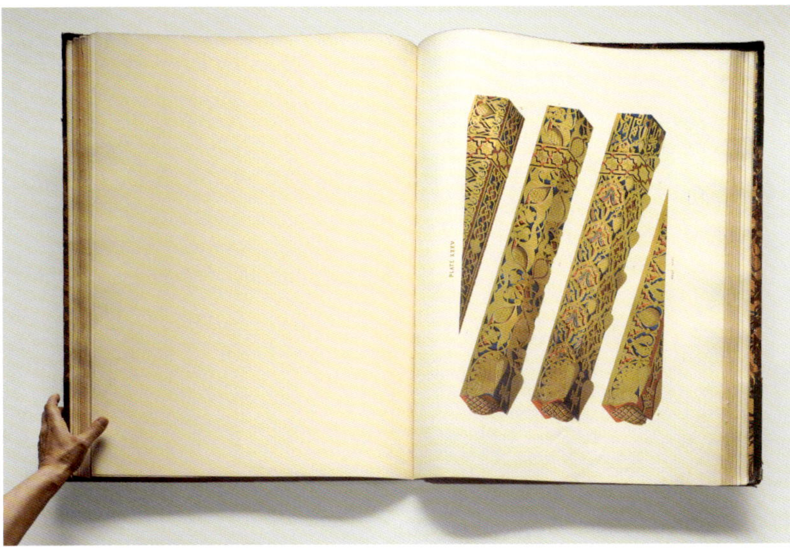

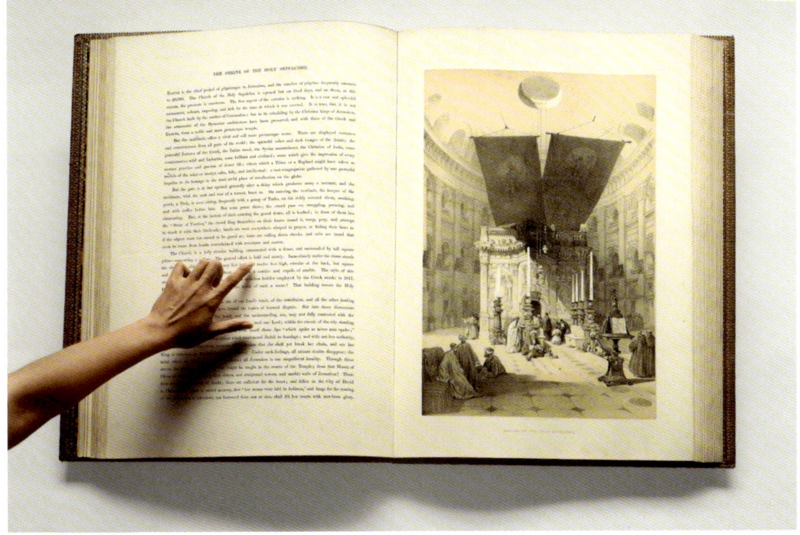

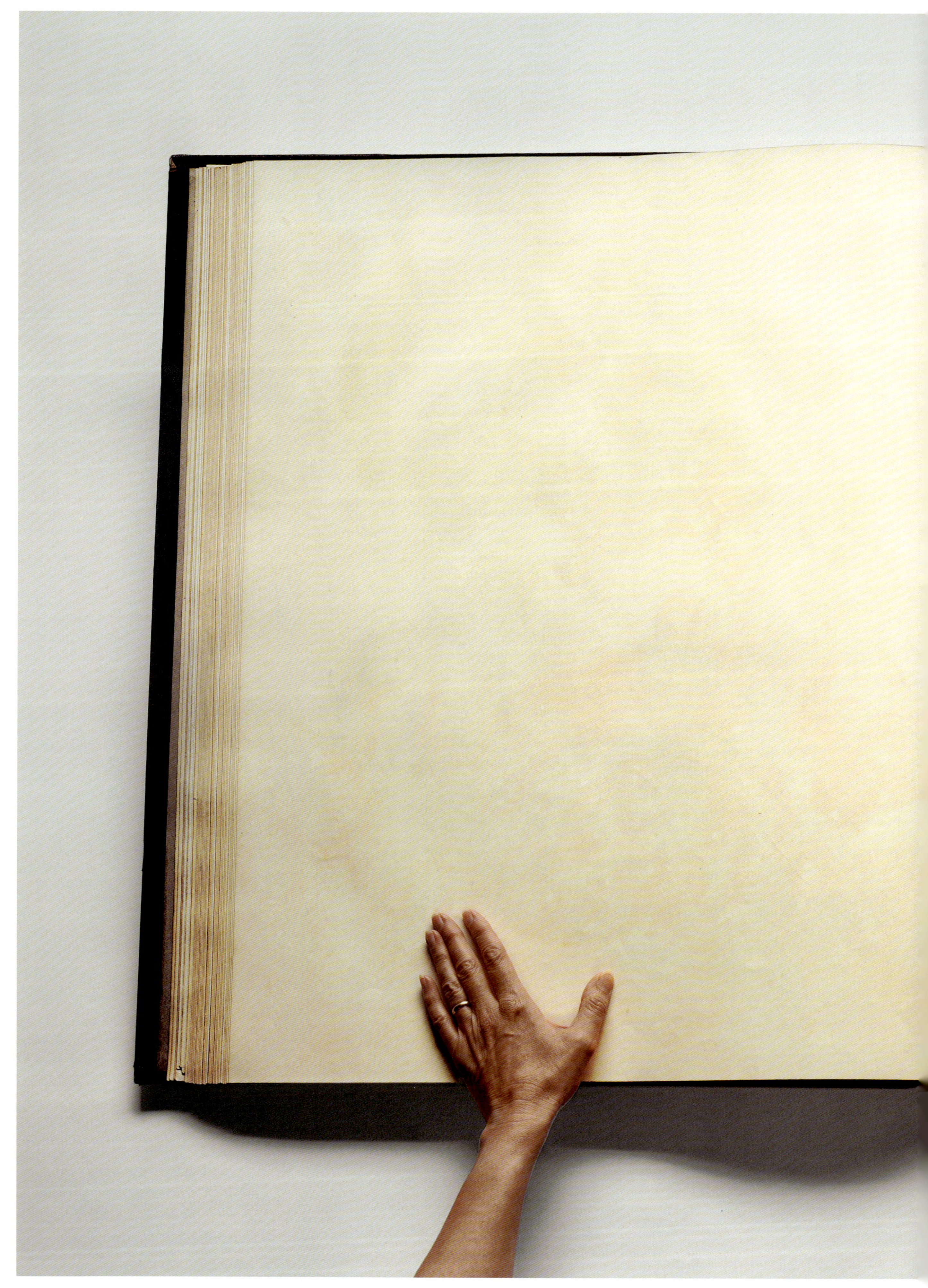

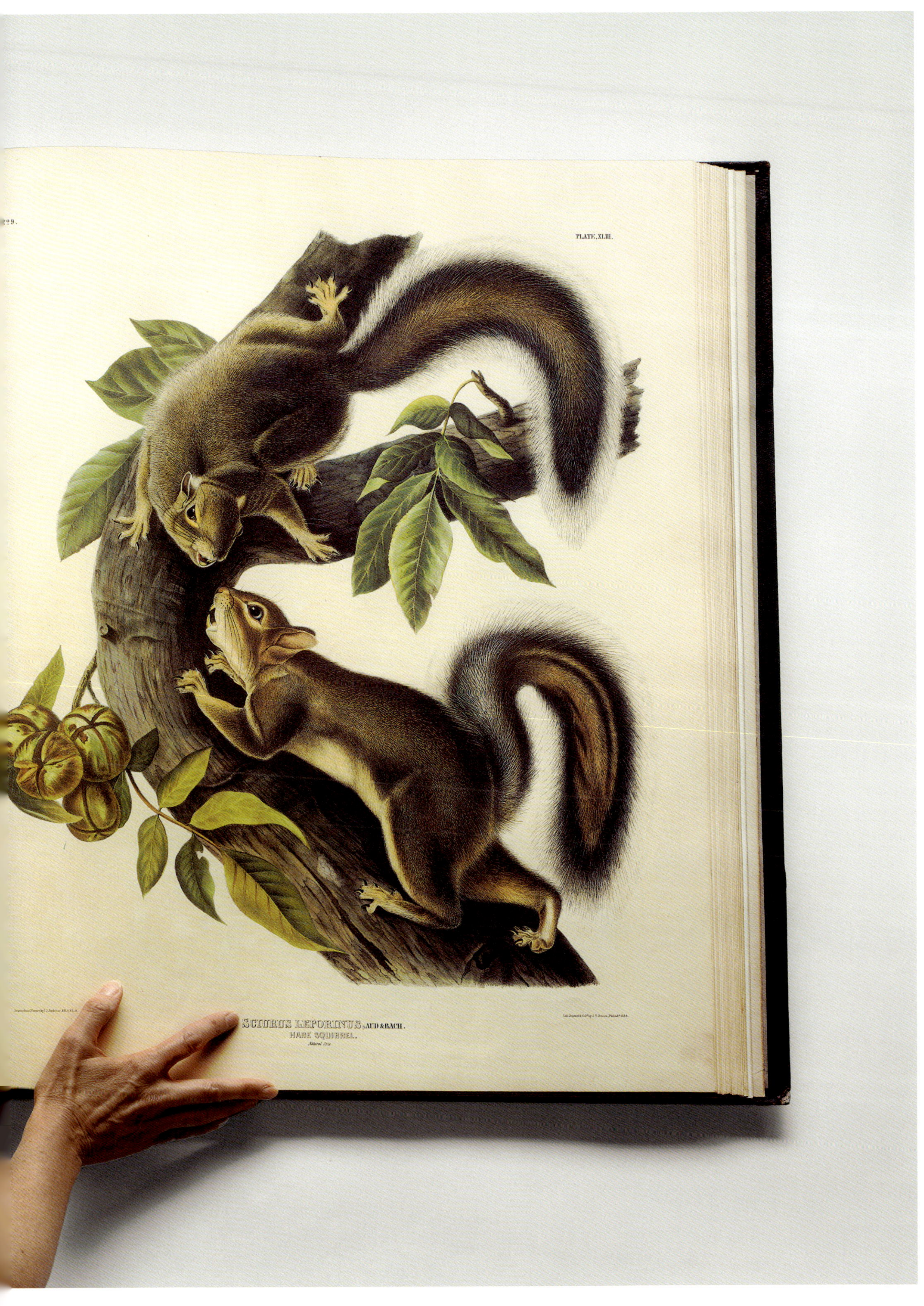
PLATE XLIII.
SCIURUS LEPORINUS, AUD & BACH.
HARE SQUIRREL.

A Monument to the Armenian Genocide, 2010 *

Geneva

Invited by the city of Geneva to take part in a competition to create a memorial to the Armenian genocide, Esther Shalev-Gerz proposed a monument carved out of a single block of white stone. The sculpture would represent the interior of a room in a house whose walls had been knocked down. On either side of the wall, the same room would be reflected symmetrically. Should the genocide be acknowledged by Turkey, that date would be engraved on the monument.

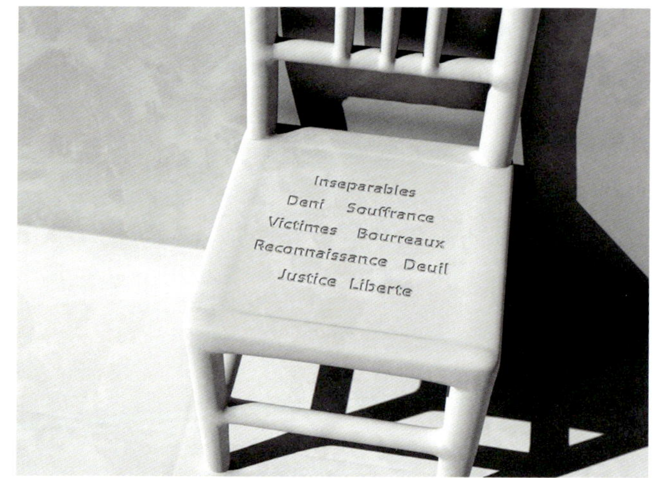

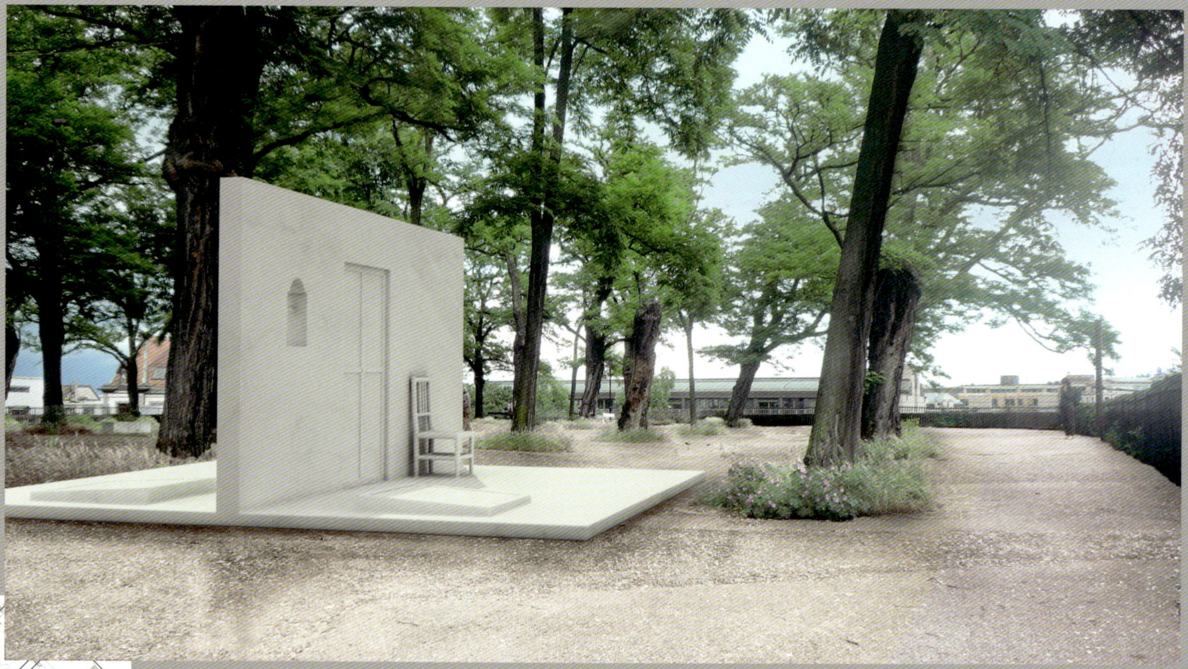

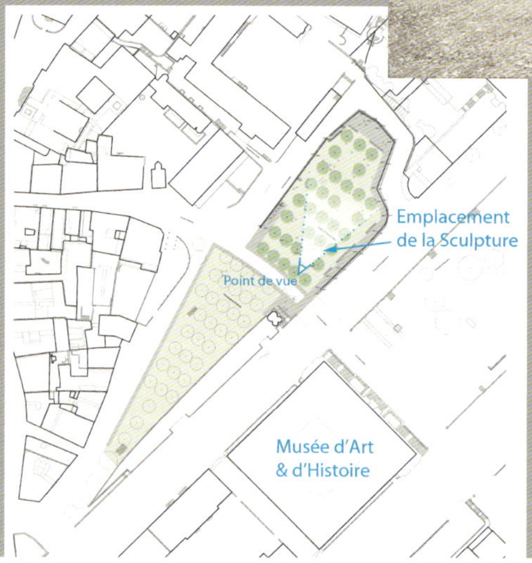

Emplacement de la Sculpture

Point de vue

Musée d'Art & d'Histoire

[..] Je souhaite présenter une sculpture de pierre qui montre l'intérieur d'une pièce dans une maison dont on aurait fait tomber les murs. [...]

[..] En effet, de part et d'autre du mur et de la porte, la même pièce se reflète symétriquement, miroir inversé qui trahit sa fonction normale, les deux parties demeurent aveugles l'une à l'autre. Seul le monde extérieur -vous, moi, les gens- peut observer leur dédoublement. [...]

extrait du texte de présentation.

Proposition pour un mémorial du génocide arménien – Esther Shalev-Gerz – Page 3

The Last Click, 2010

Installation; 70 color photographs, dimensions variable; 1 photo album with 13 black and white photographs, 21 × 21 cm; 1 video projection, color, sound, 26 min.

Invited to Braunschweig by the Museum of Photography, Esther Shalev-Gerz became interested in the Rollei company, which had its headquarters in that town, and is famous in particular for its Rolleiflex series of cameras. *The Last Click* explores the changes brought about by the journey leading from analog to digital technology, and their implications in terms of the construction of memory and the depiction of time. A photographic series shows the Rollei factories devoid of any human presence. A video shows people telling the stories that link them to the cameras they no longer want.

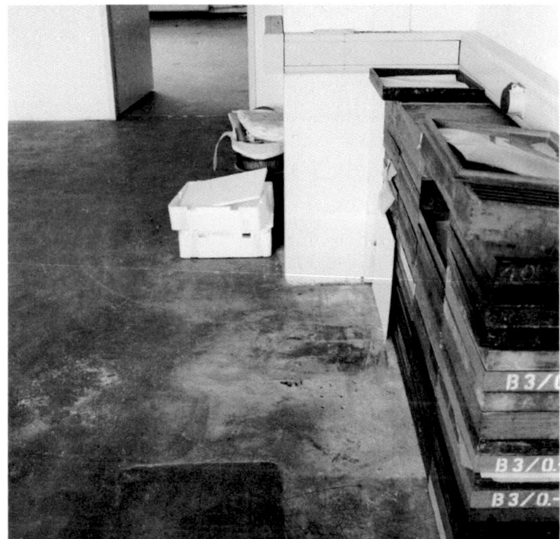

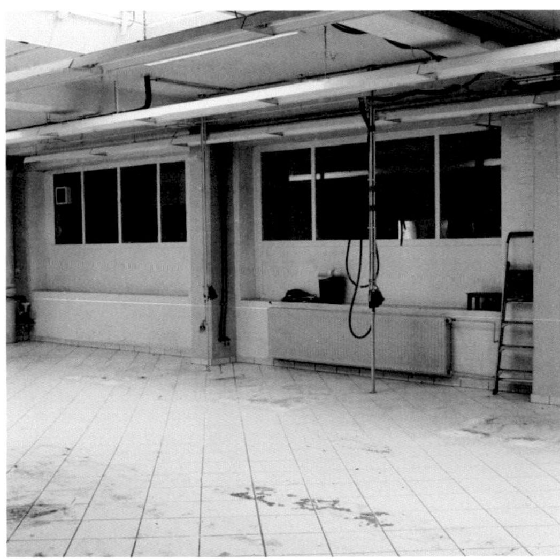

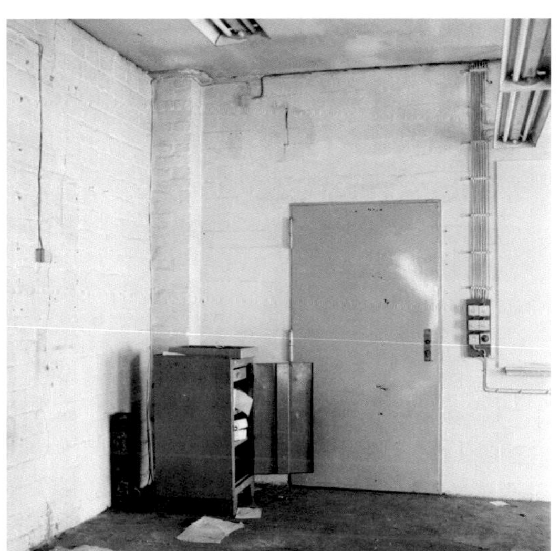

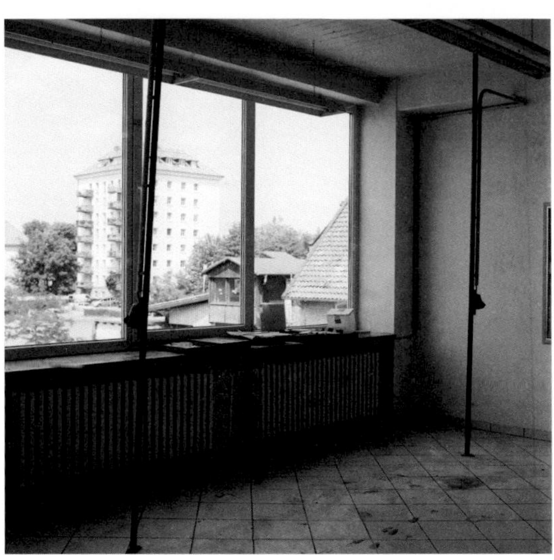

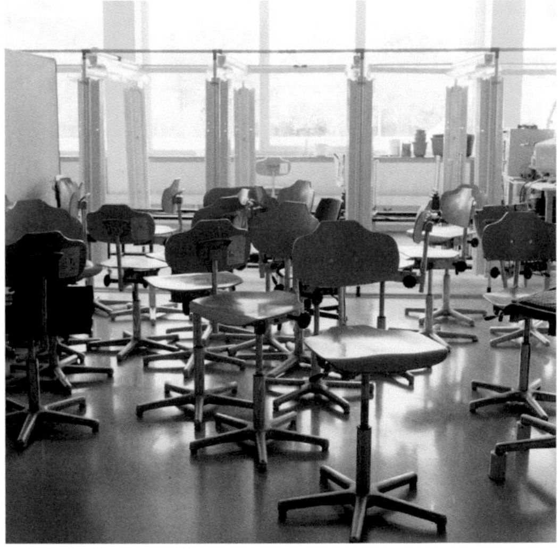

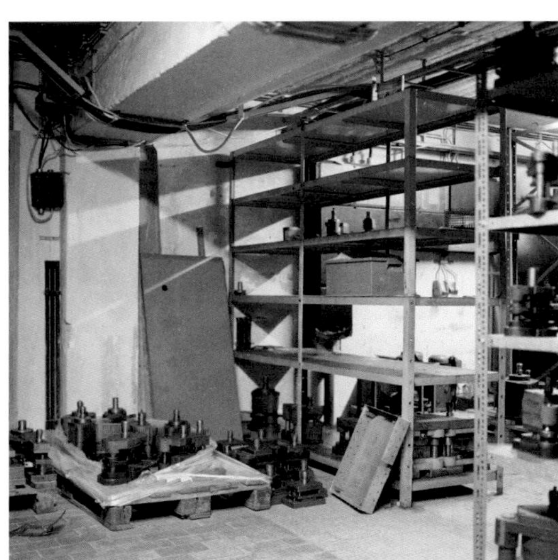

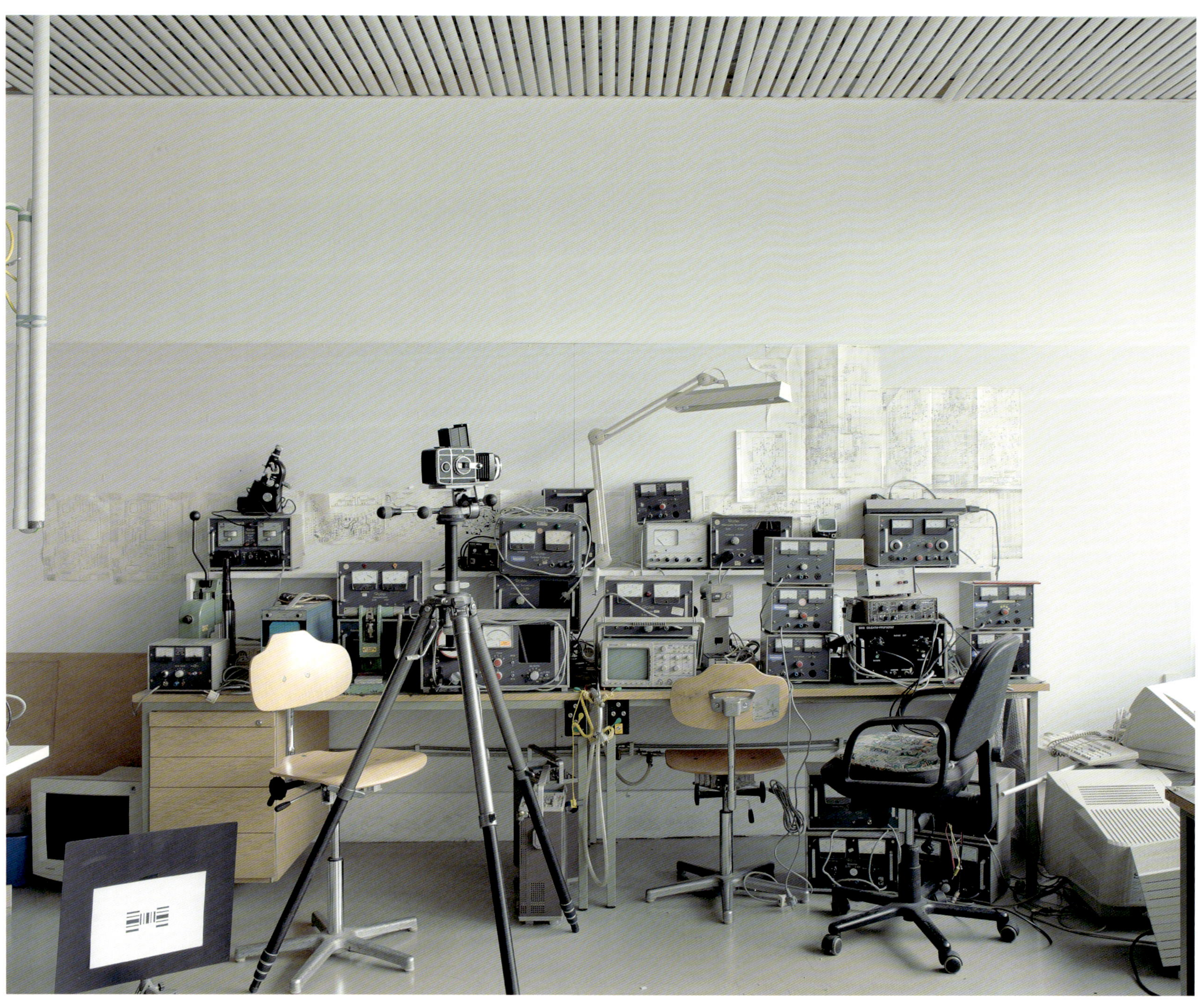

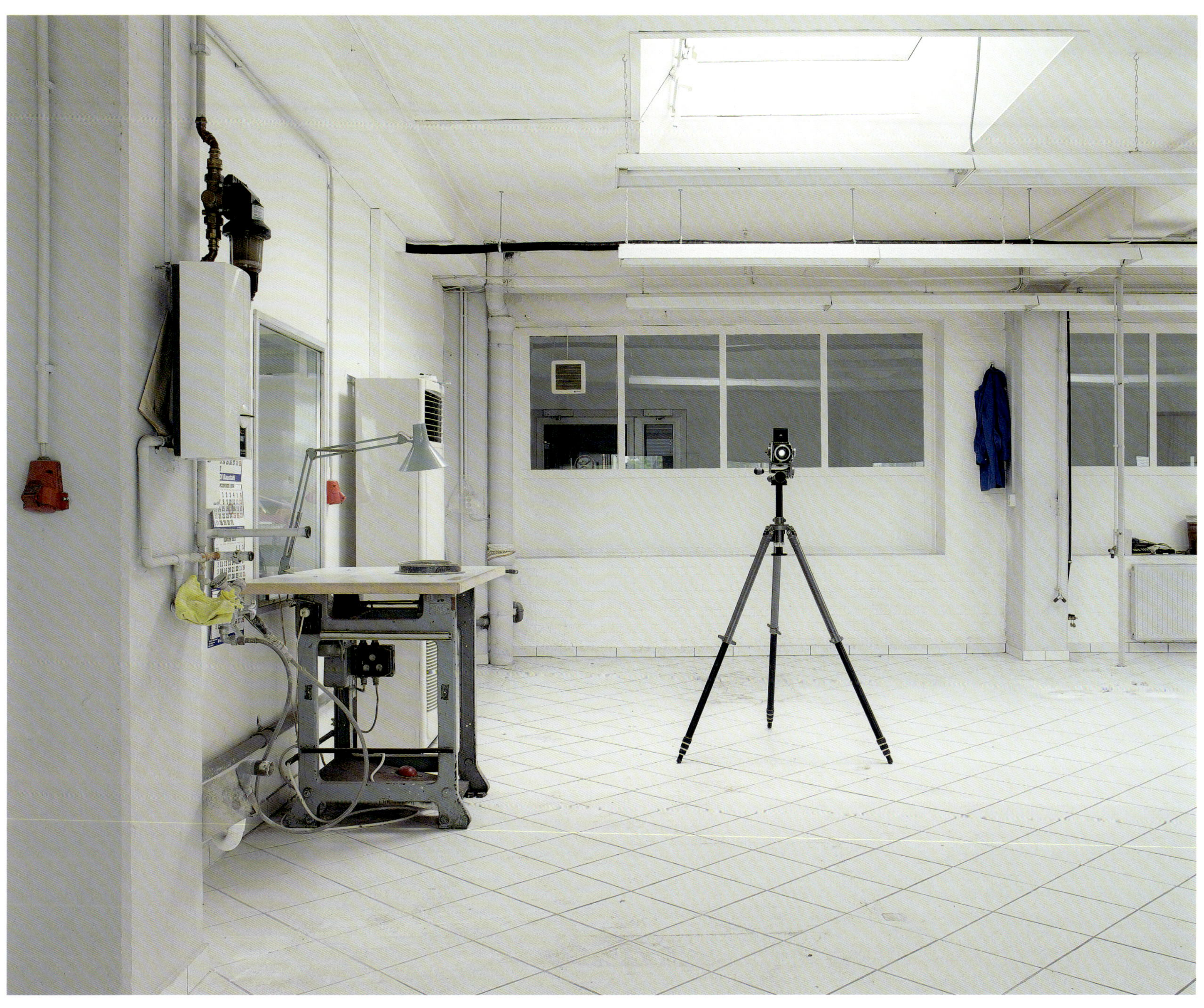

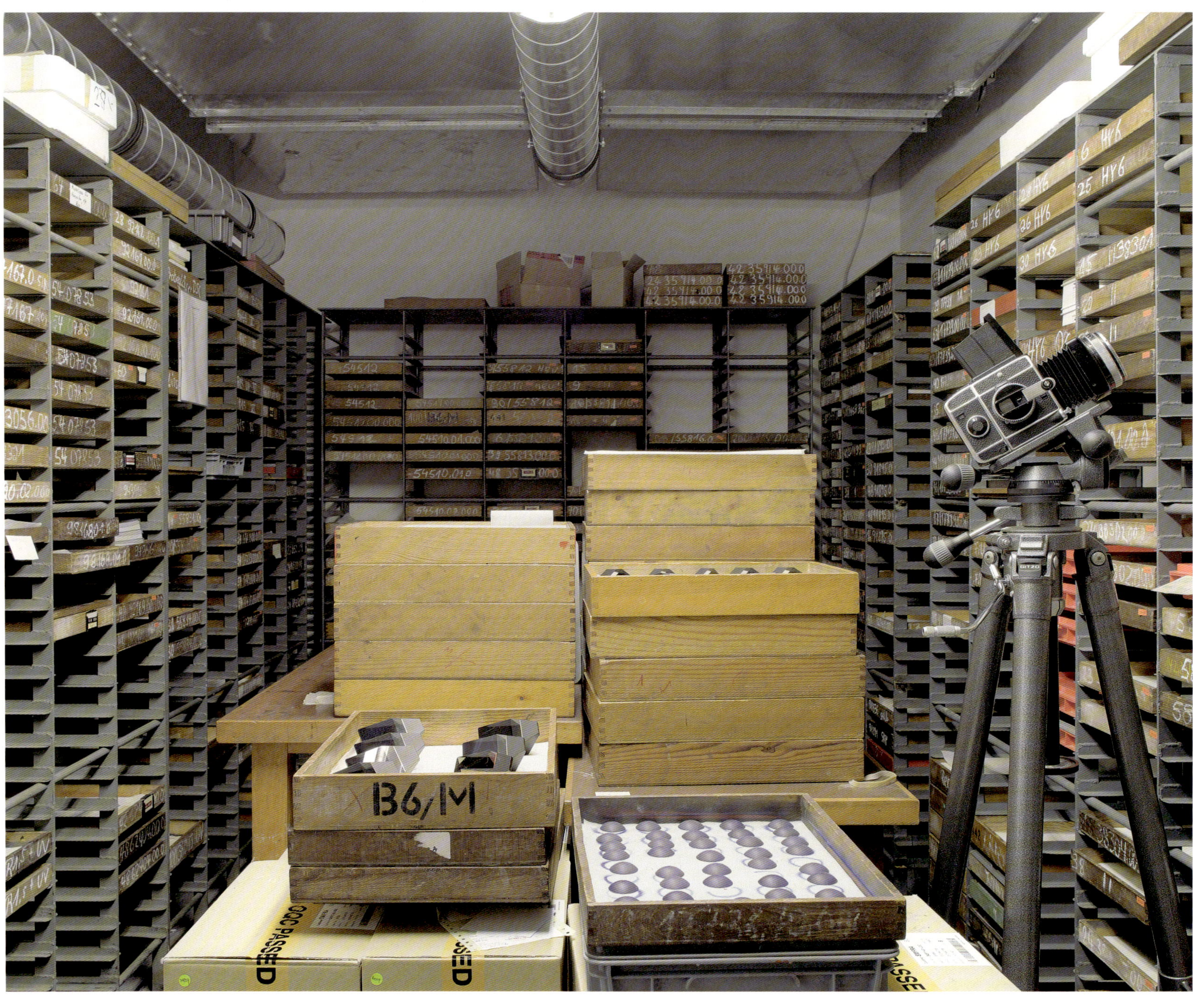
B6/M

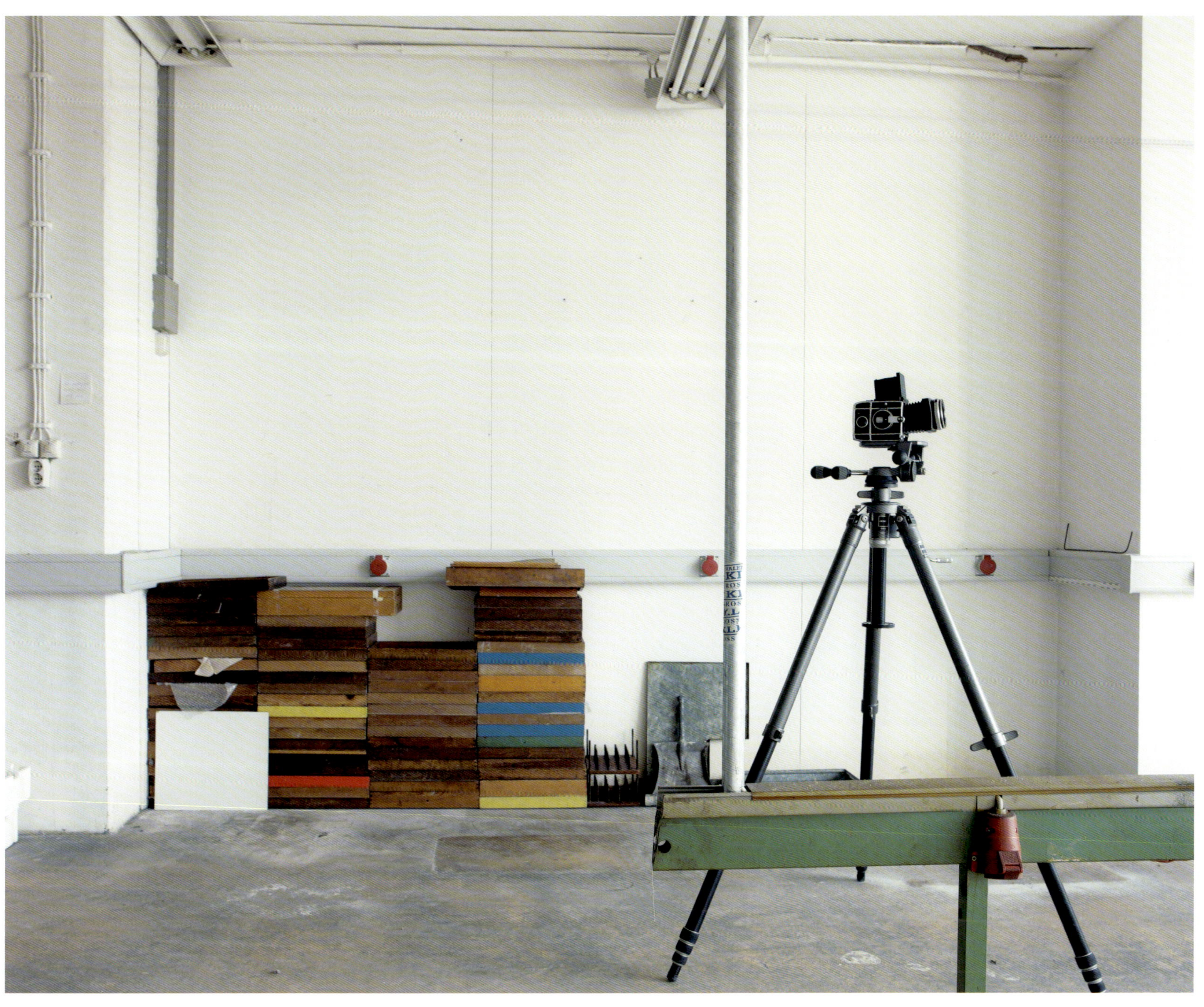

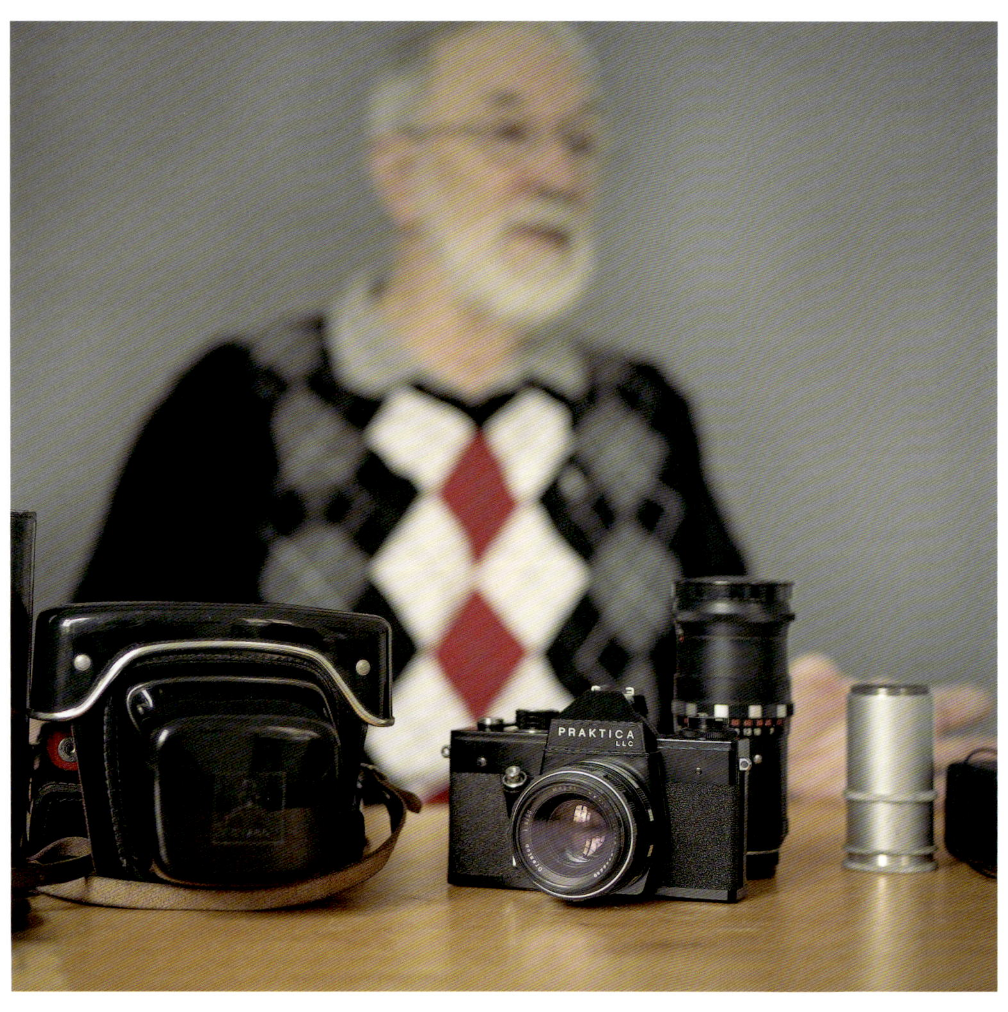
PRAKTICA
LLC

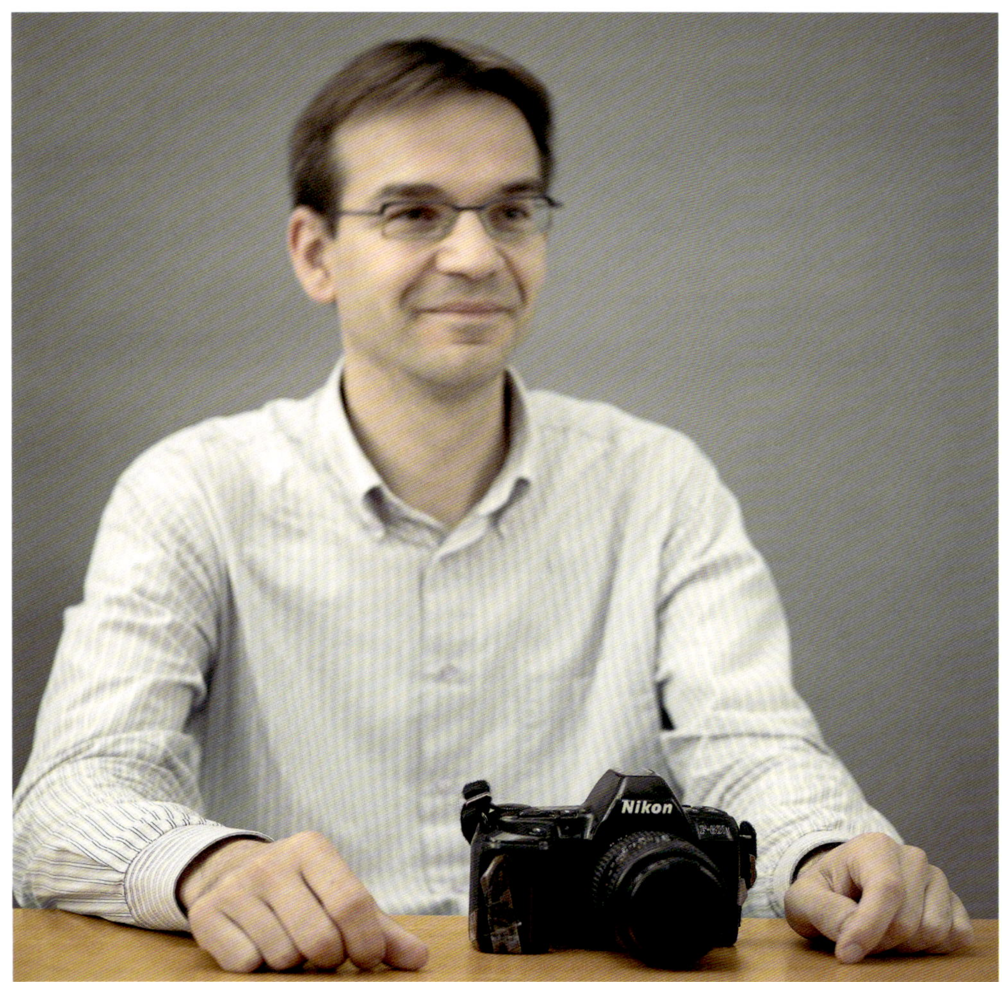
Nikon

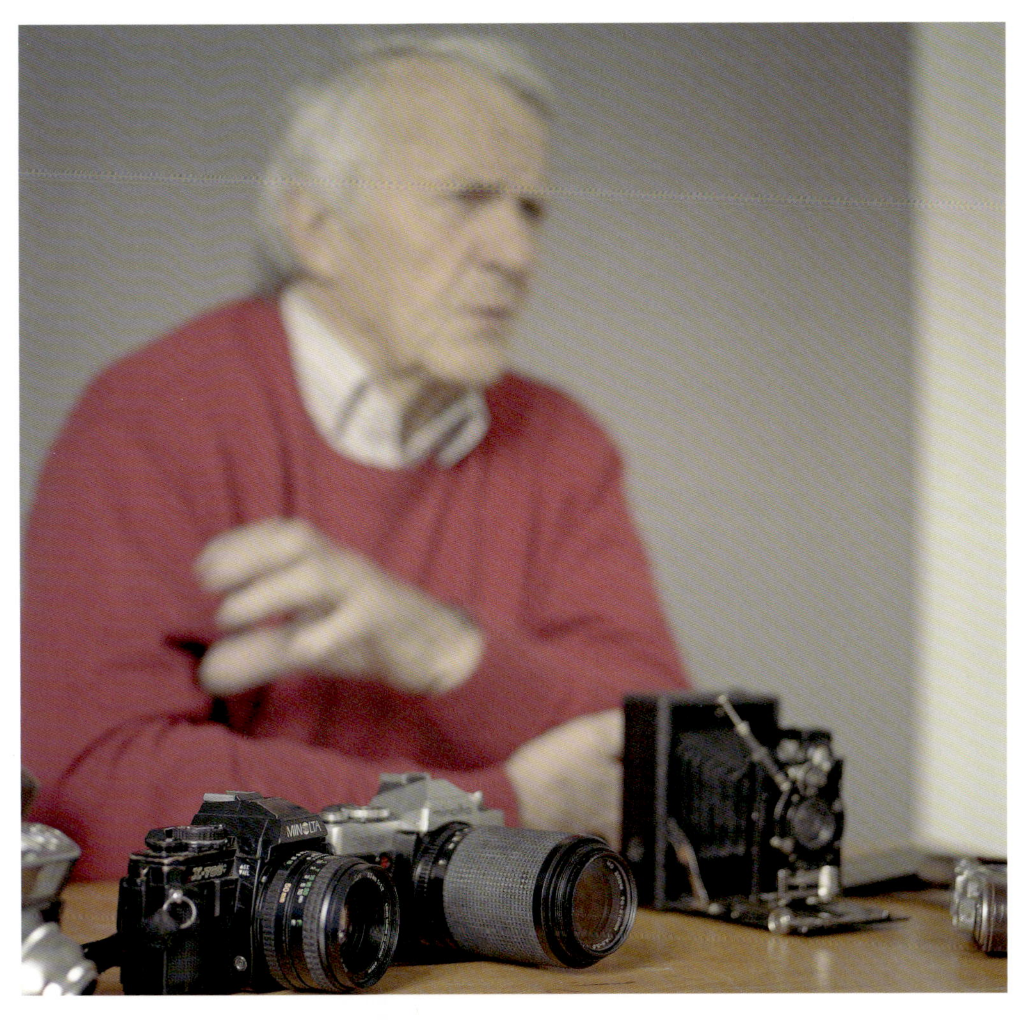
MINOLTA

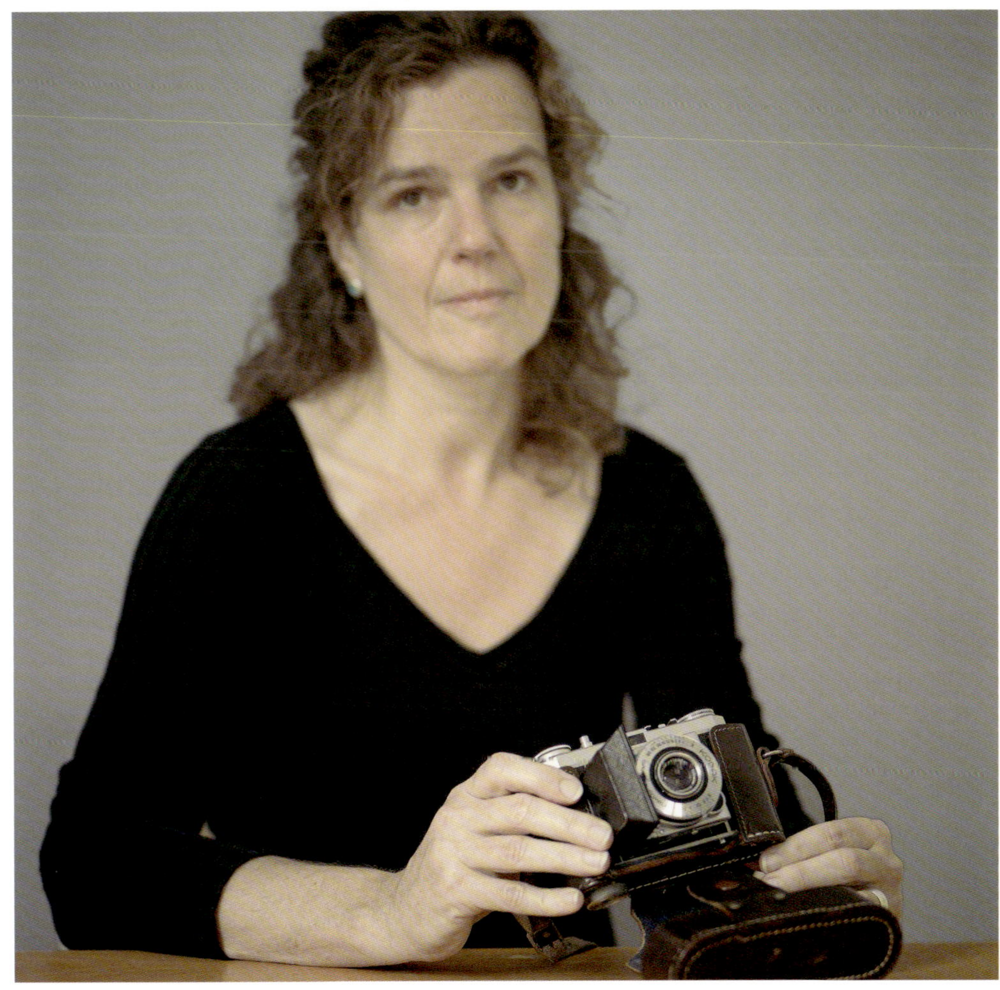

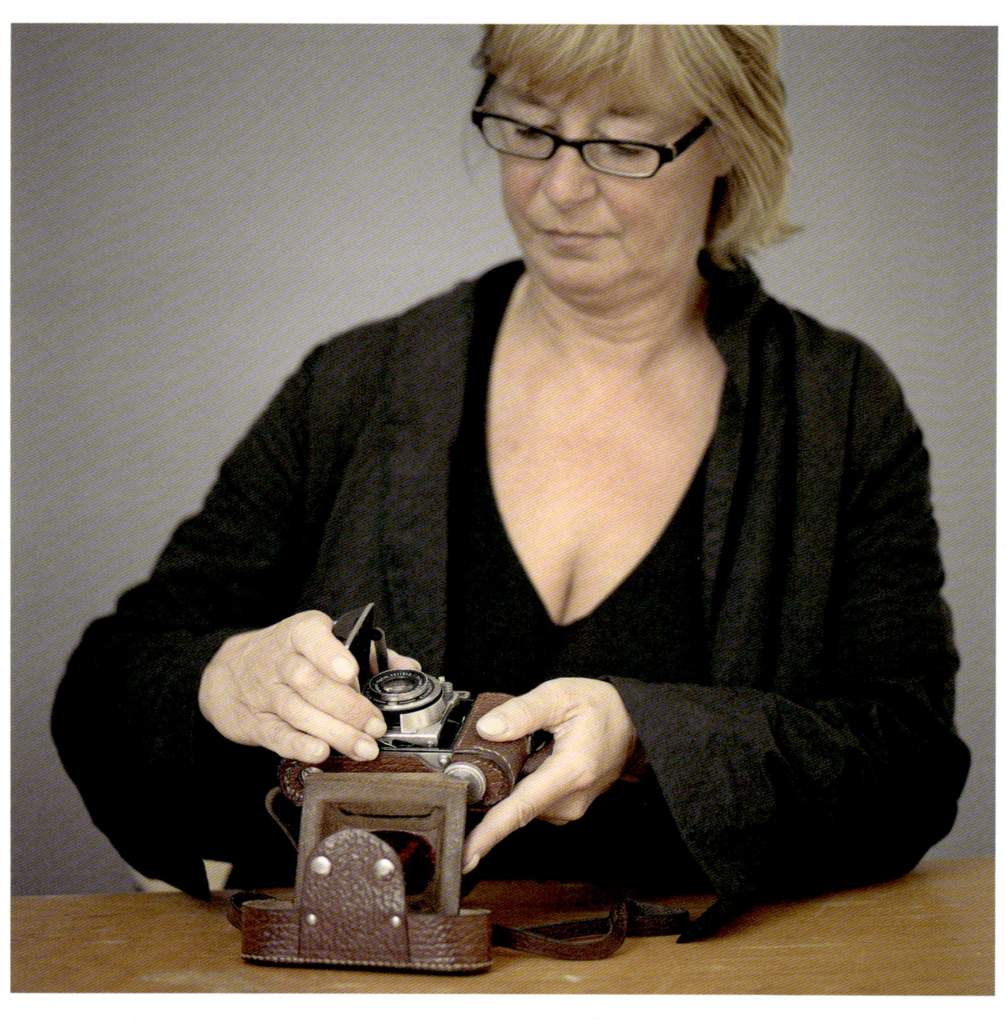

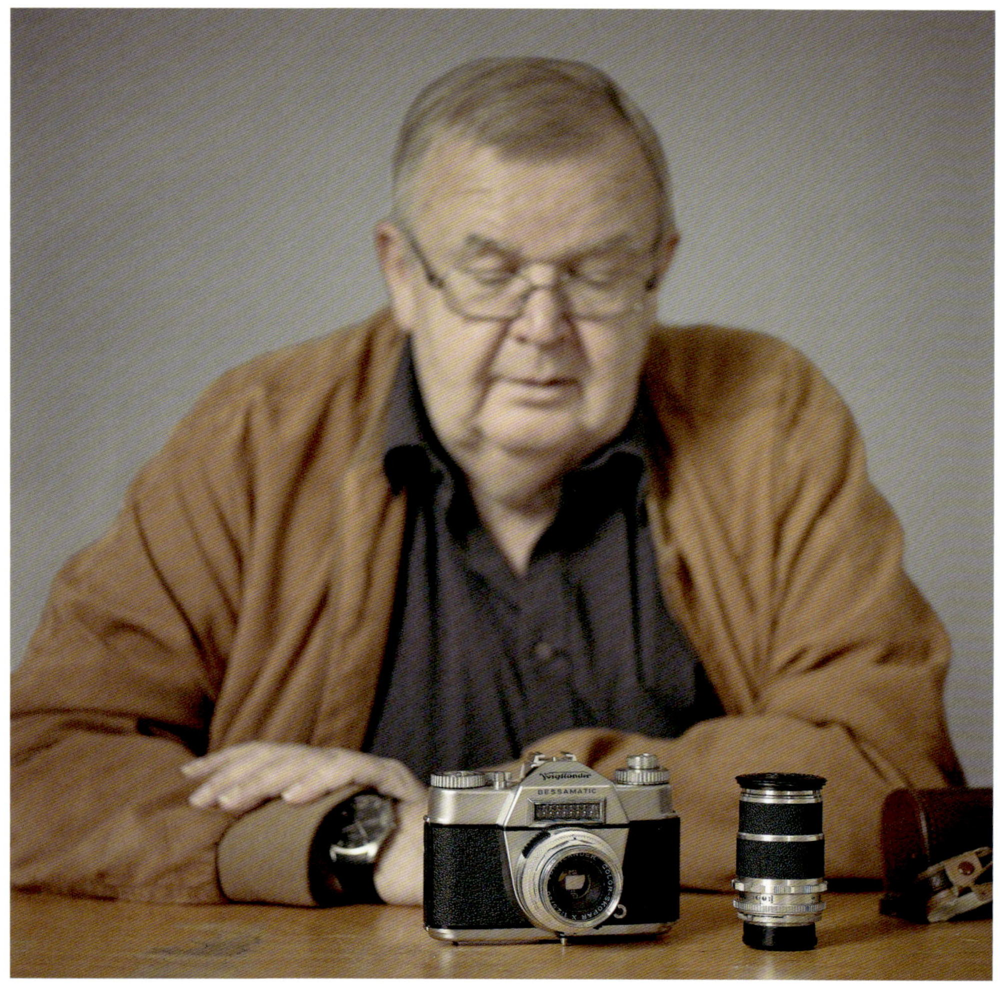
Voigtländer
BESSAMATIC

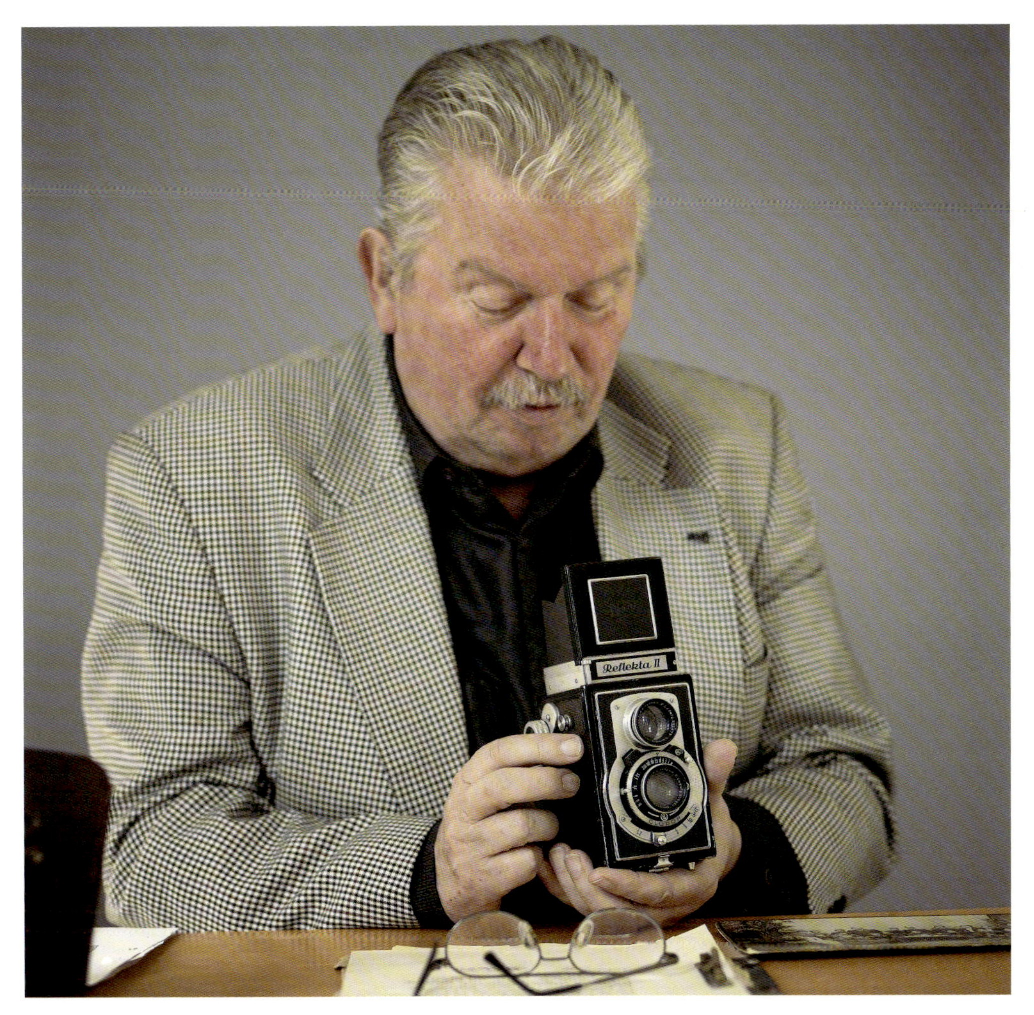
Reflekta II

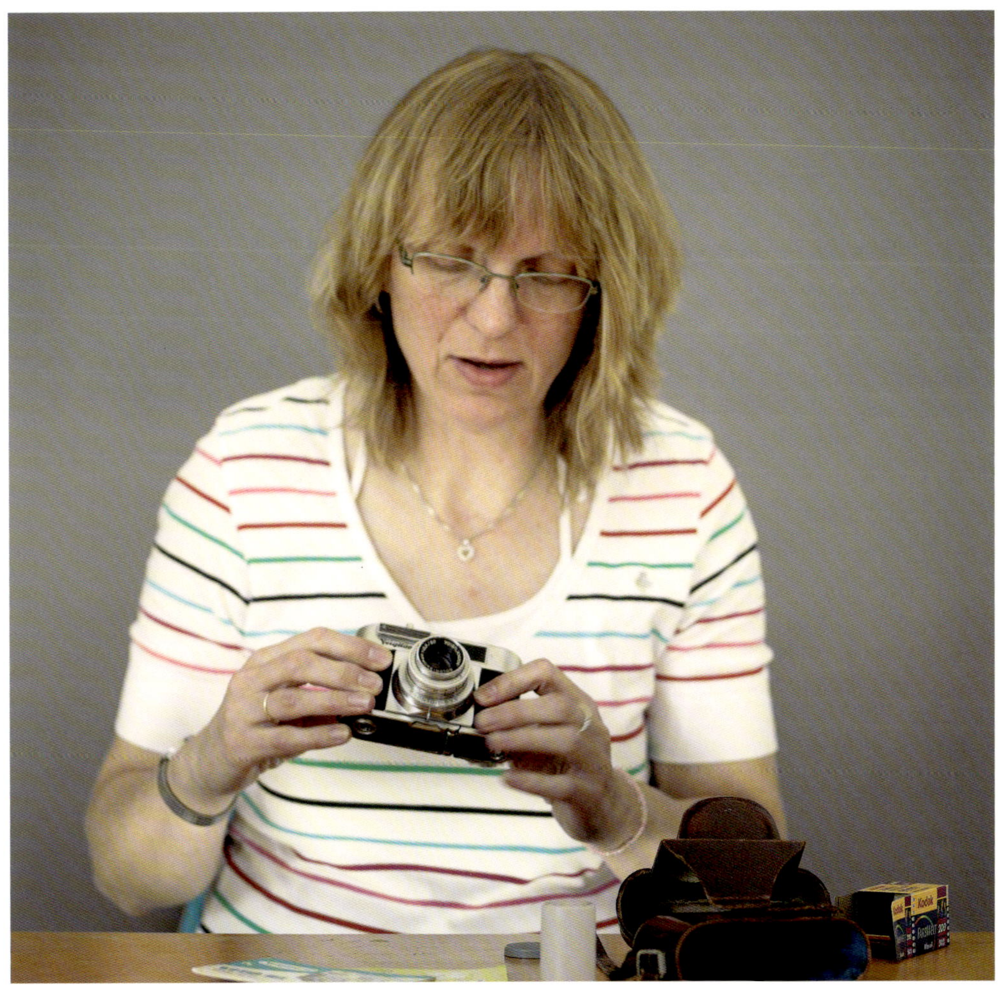

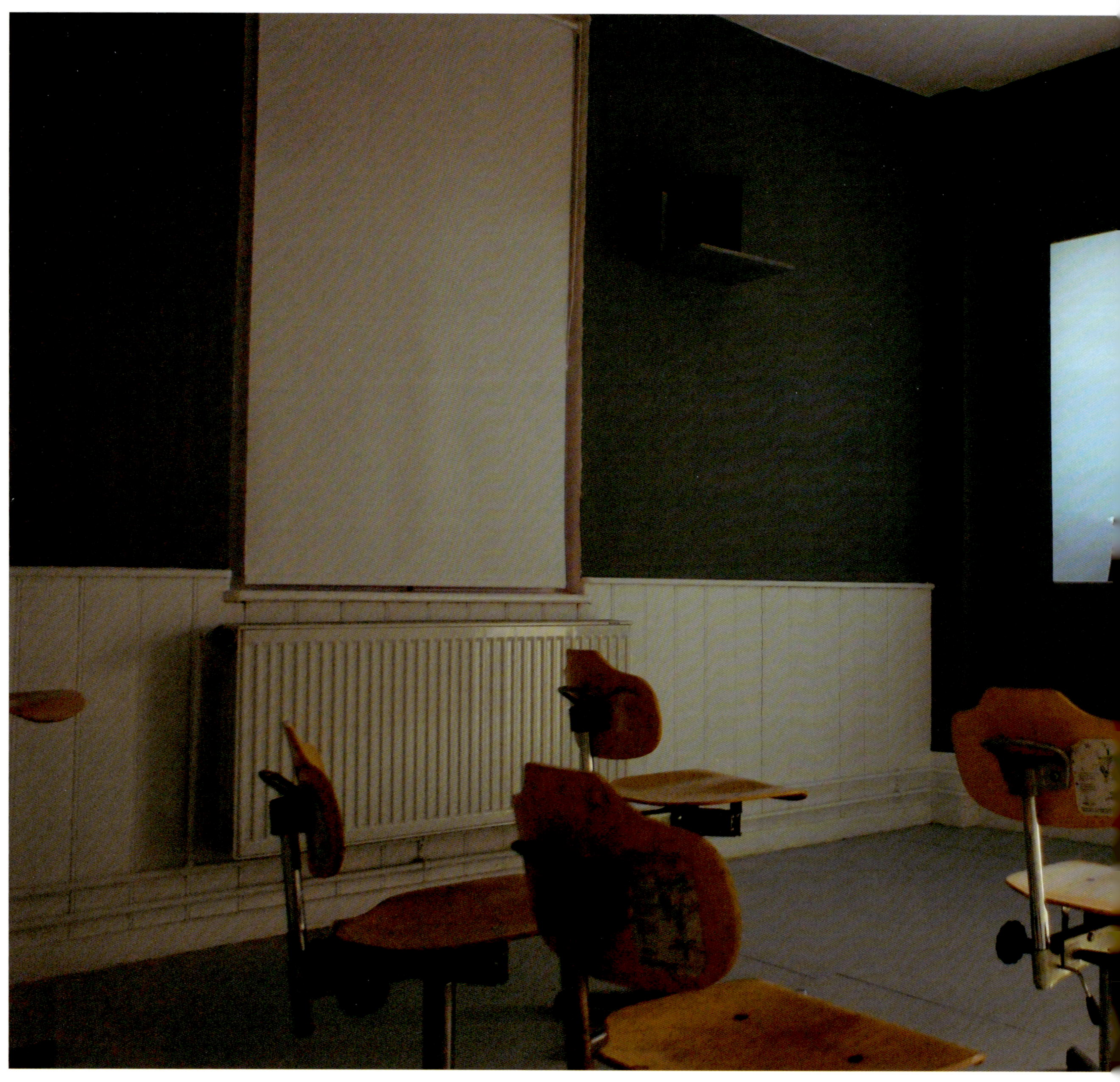

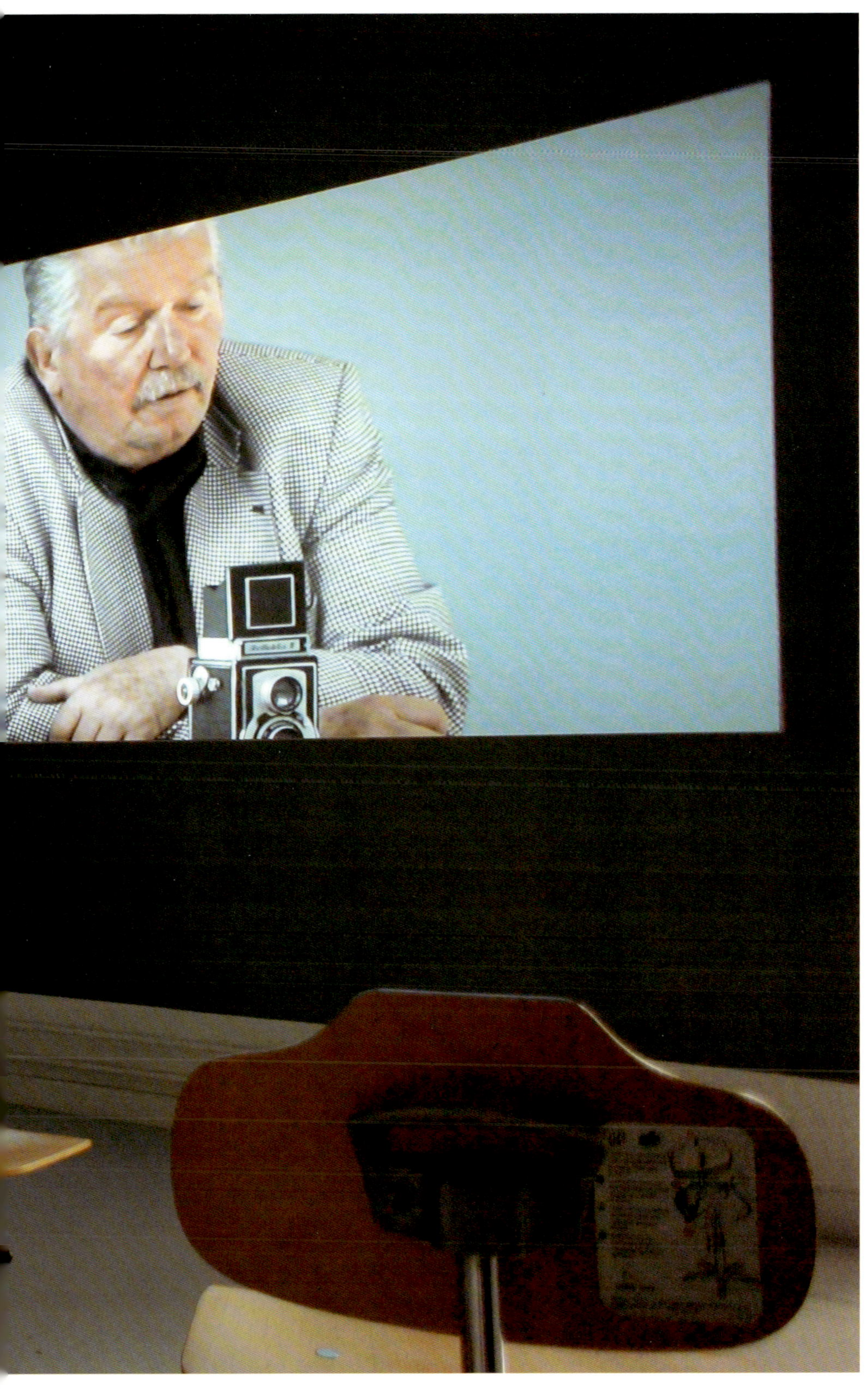

Describing Labor, 2011–2012

Video installation, sound and photographs, various objects; commissioned by the Wolfsonian-Florida, International University, Miami Beach, Florida, 2012

During a residency at the Wolfsonian Museum in Miami in 2011, Shalev-Gerz explored the museum's huge collection, looking for documents illustrating labor and workers. The figure of the worker, formerly a heroic image of class consciousness and the ideal of one nation—very much present during the Great Depression, the Soviet Revolution, and the two World Wars—has since almost disappeared from contemporary representations. Using video, photography, sound, and text, the installation gives a voice back to this figure who shapes our everyday realities. Just as the Wolfsonian's collection offers an image of labor at its heroic moment in history, *Describing Labor* rearticulates that image for our time.

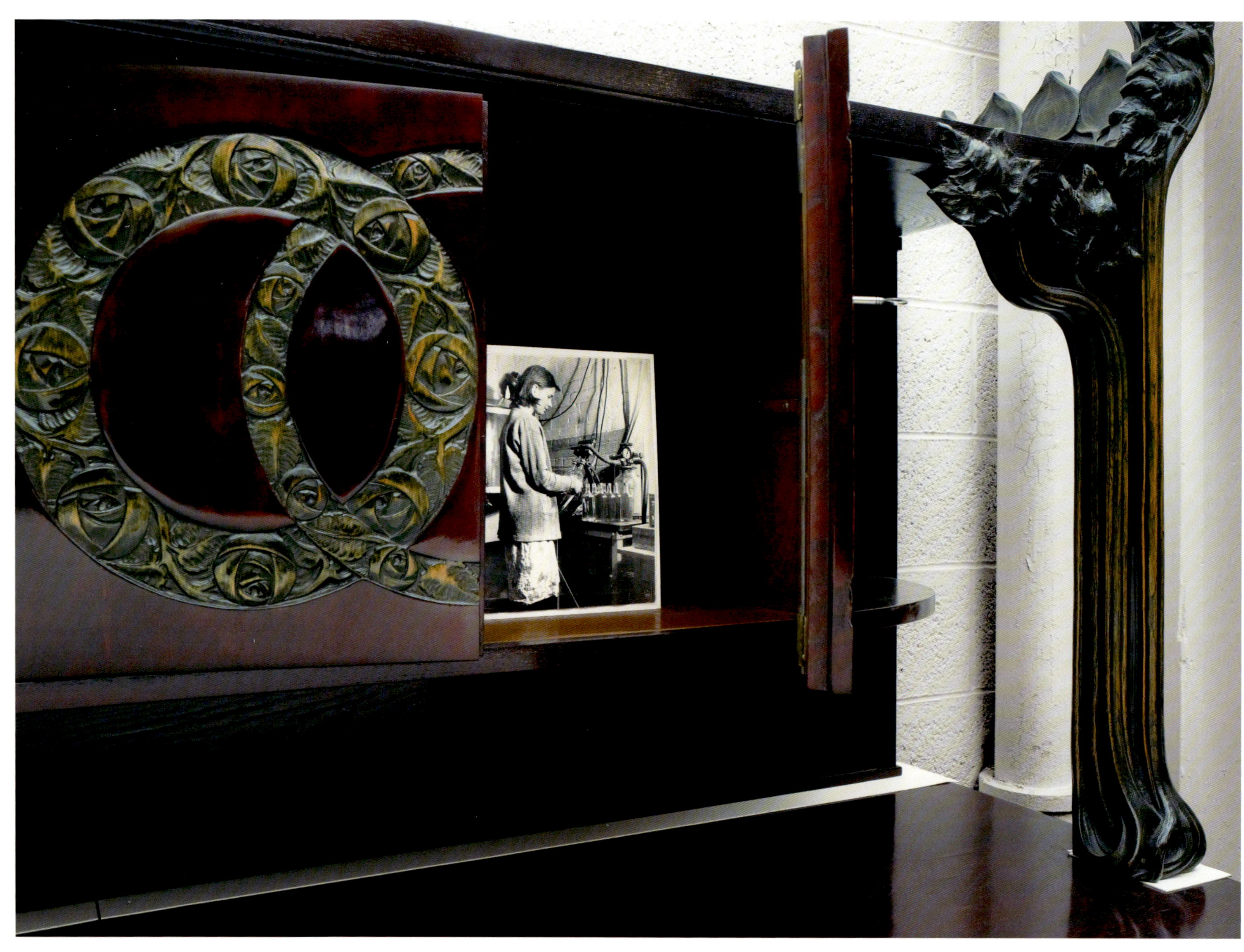

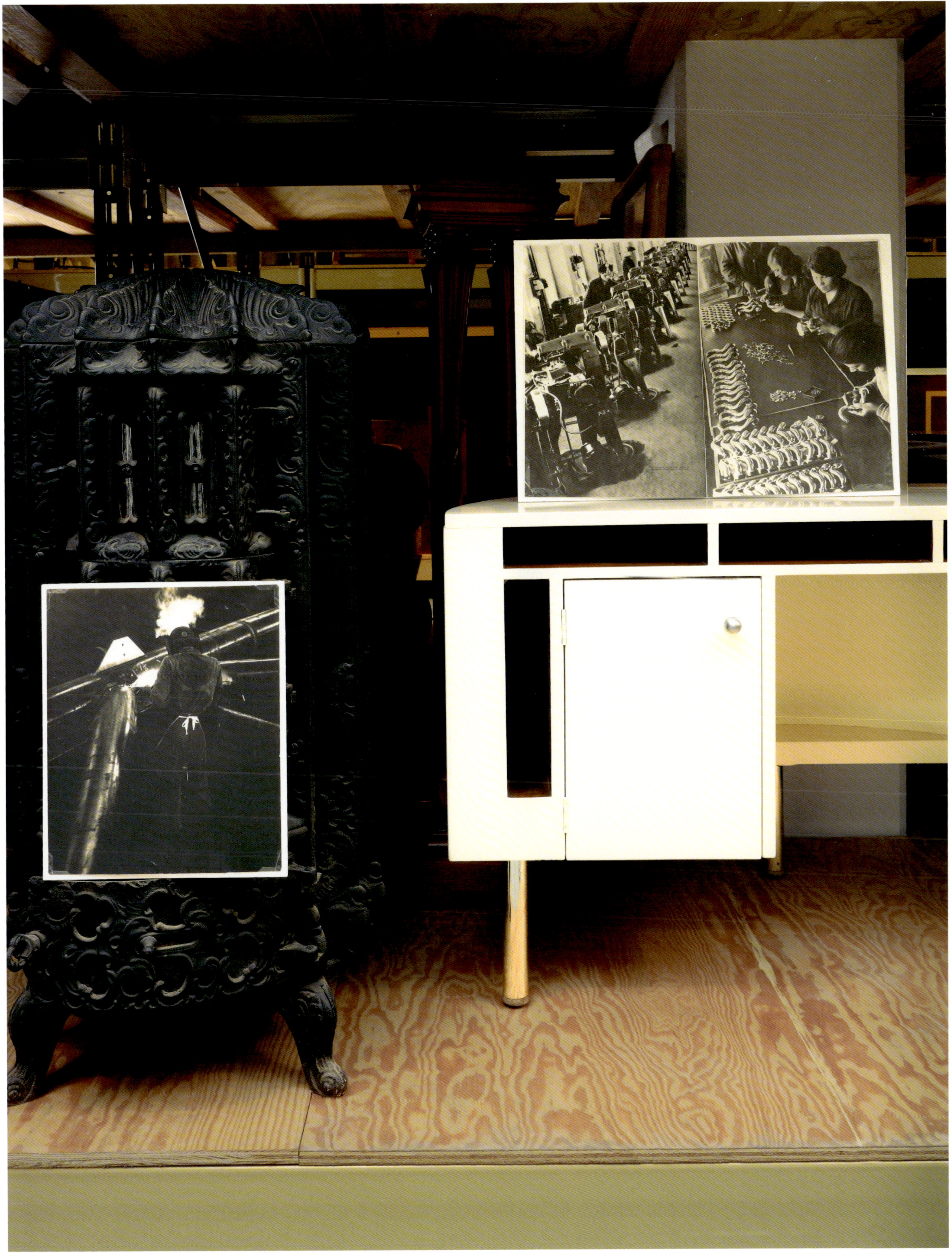

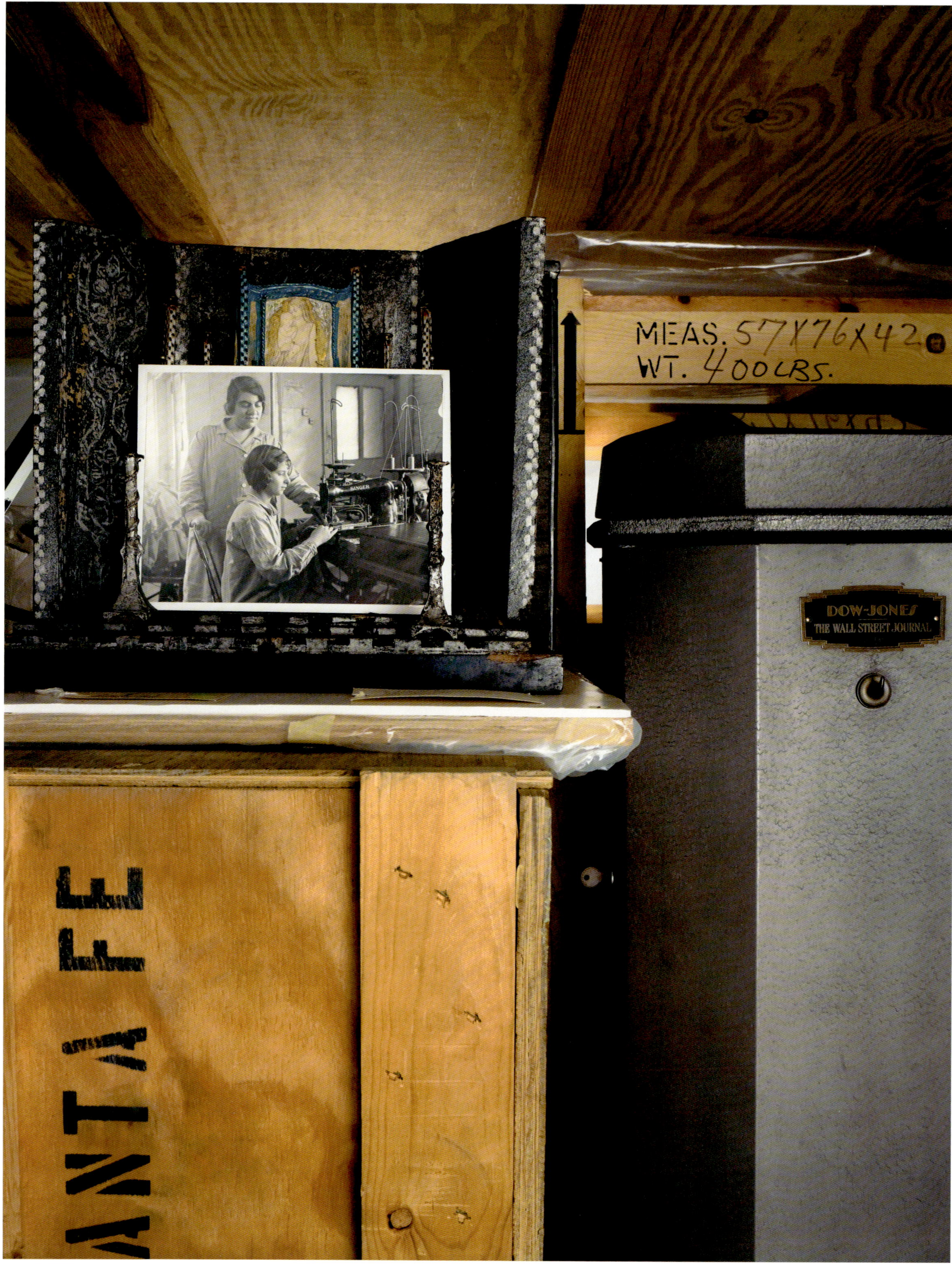
MEAS. 57X76X42
WT. 400LBS.
DOW-JONES
THE WALL STREET JOURNAL
ANTA FE

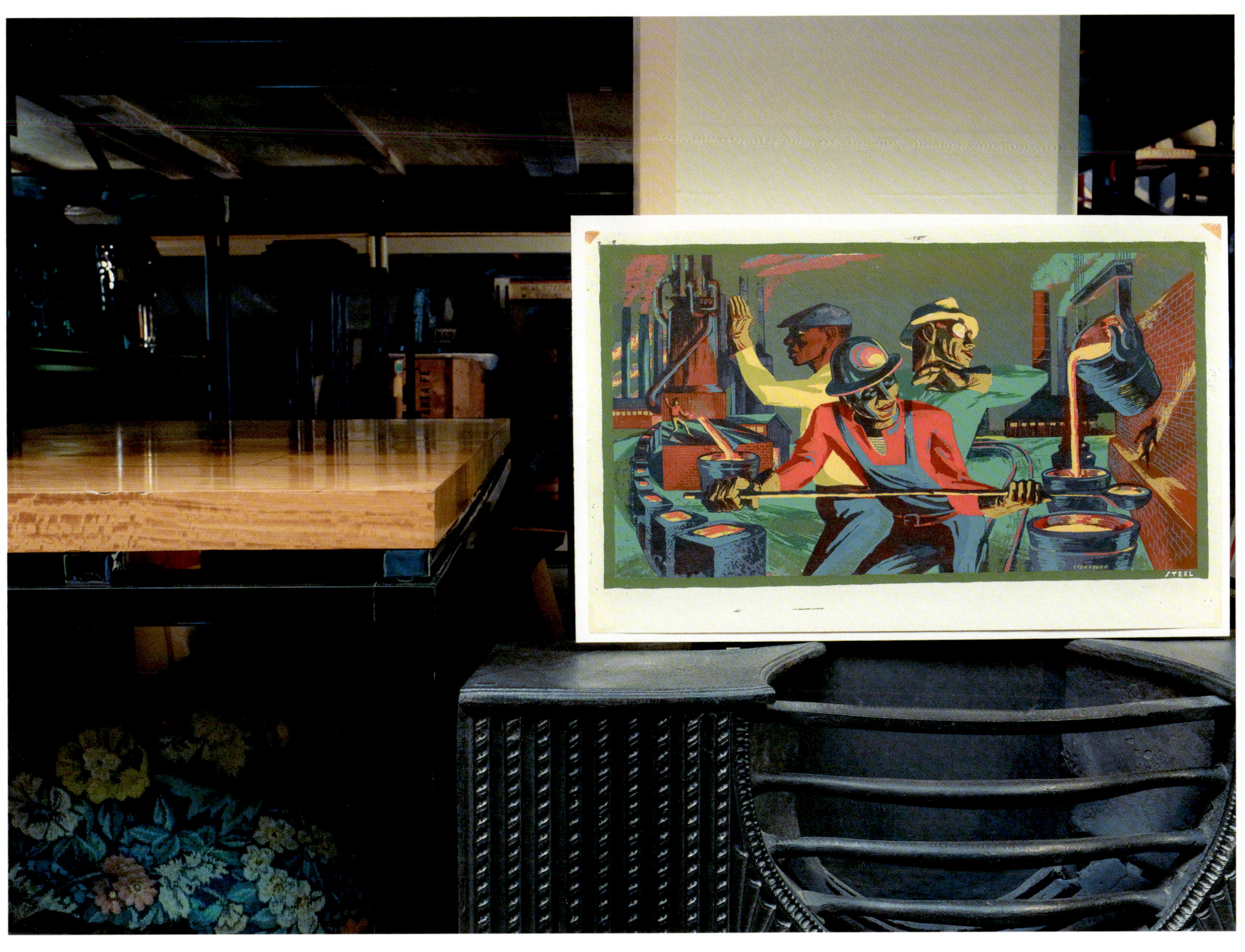
STEEL

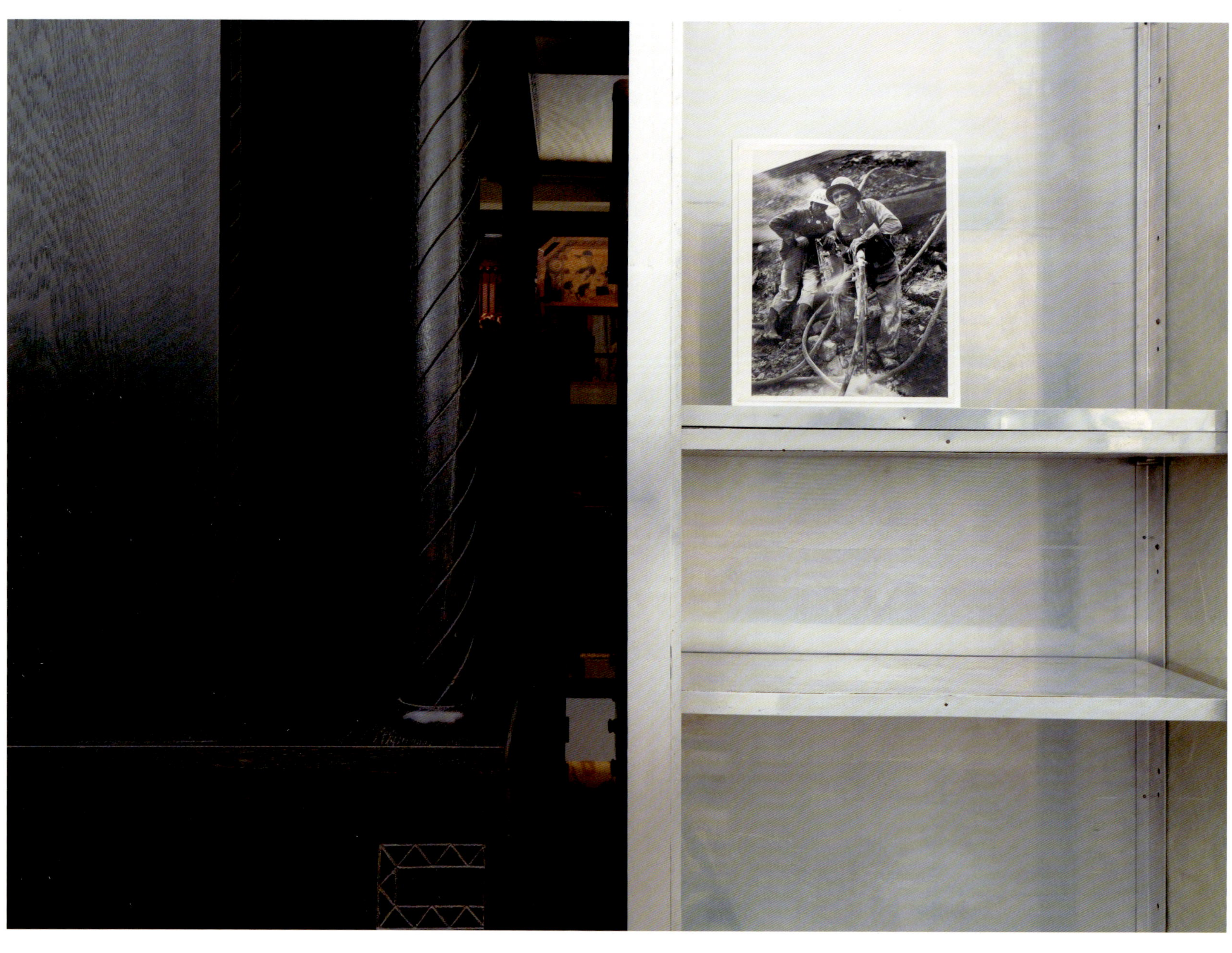

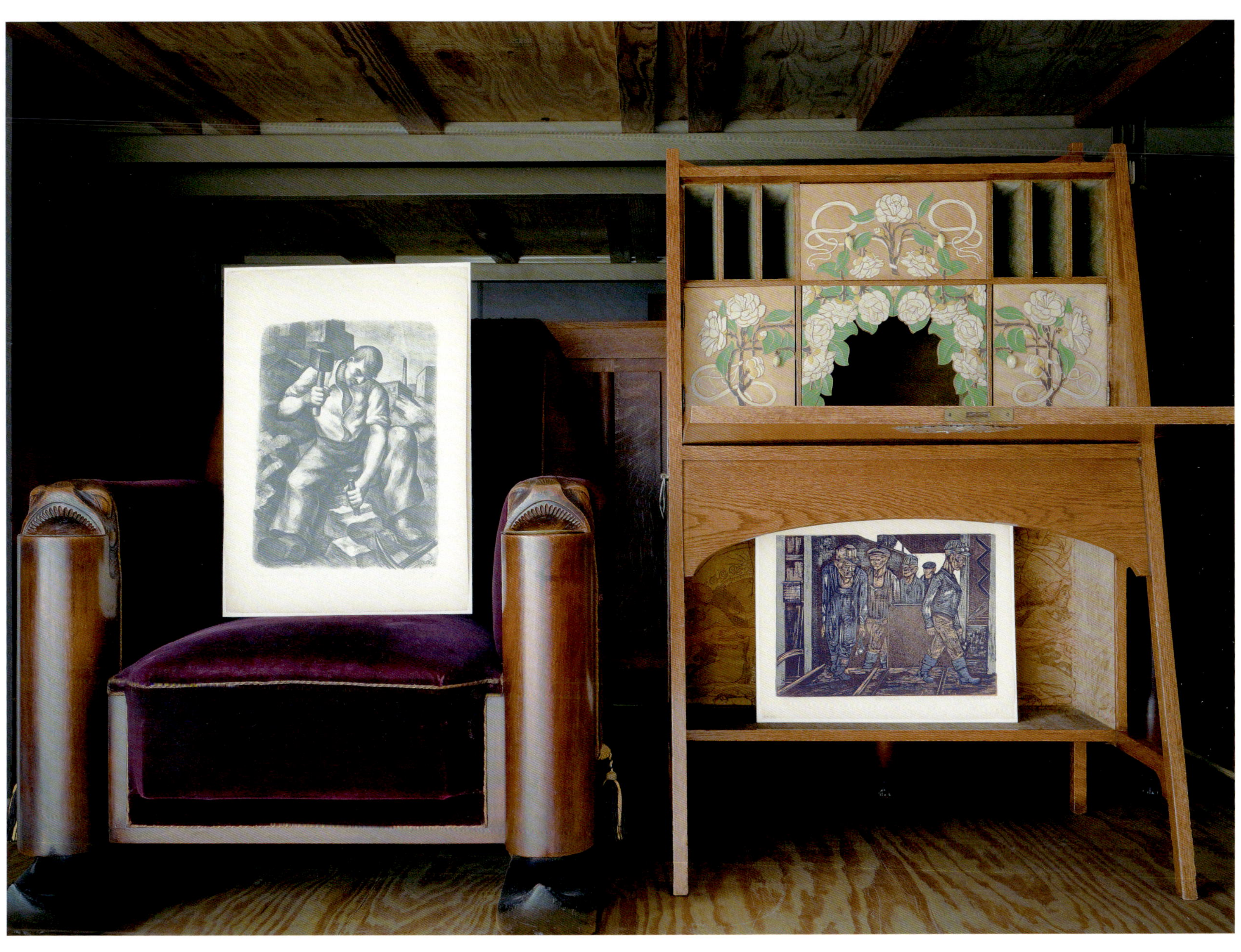

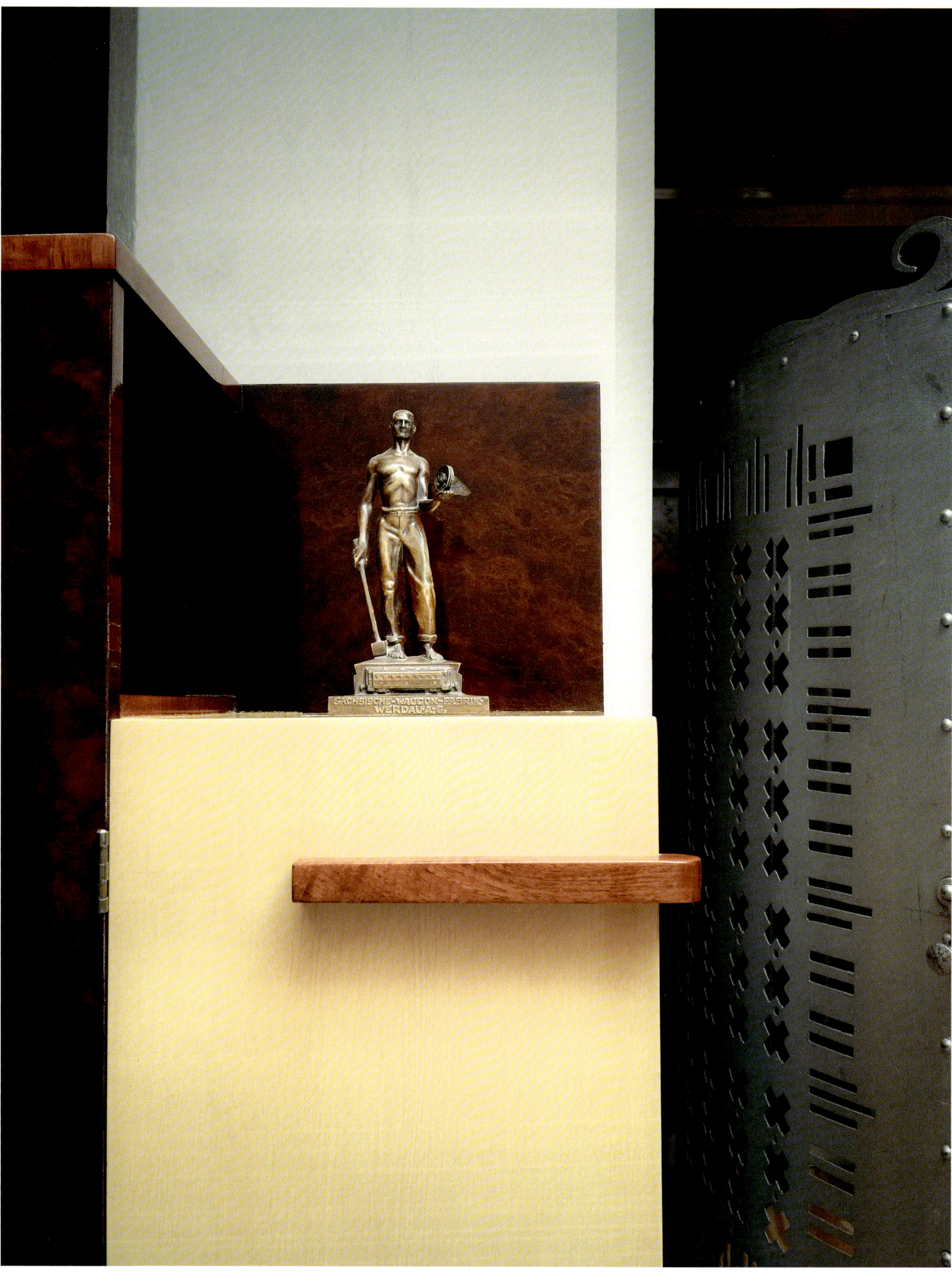
SÄCHSISCHE-WAGGON-FABRIK
WERDAU-A.-G.

SAMPLING THE PAST: AN AURAL HISTORY
NORA M. ALTER

What is at play in listening, what resonates in it, what is the tone of listening or its timbre? Is even listening sonorous?
—Jean-Luc Nancy[1]

An inquiry into the auditory is also an inquiry into the invisible. Listening makes the invisible present in a way similar to the presence of the mute in vision.
—Don Ihde[2]

The angel, I still hear him
Yet he no longer has a face other than
Yours, which I do not know
—Heiner Müller, *Glückloser-Engel 2*[3]

Writing in 1939, Brazilian filmmaker Alberto Cavalcanti observed, "Pictures speak to the intelligence. Noise seems to by-pass the intelligence and speaks to something very deep and inborn ... The picture lends itself to clear statement, while sound lends itself to suggestions."[4] Images, and the visual more generally, are often easier to identify than the ephemeral domain of sound. While an image may be stable and defined, sound is fleeting and unbounded. That which is visible is spatially fixed, whereas sound surrounds (even when emitting from one source such as a speaker, as soon as it enters the atmosphere it quickly disperses). Sound is intimately connected to the unconscious, unwittingly affecting the psyche. In response to Walter Benjamin's theory of an optical unconscious that reveals itself through the medium of photography and film, Siegfried Kracauer developed a theory of an "acoustic unconscious." Like those optical signs that emerge and signal concomitantly to the past, present, and even future, unconscious sonic chords flow through history and its representations. Sounds may serve as aural madeleines that uncontrollably trigger memories. Benjamin, in his recollection of his childhood in Berlin, reflects that more than images, sounds lead back to the past: "All these pictures I have preserved. But none would bring back New Lake and a few hours of my childhood so vividly as to hear once more the bars of music."[5]

History, traditionally, is represented through the visible and linguistic in the form of documents, written records, memoirs, photographs, paintings, illustrations, and the like. Vast archives—increasingly electronic—contain the traces of civilization. Perhaps with digitalization and its audiovisual capacities, the archive has become less silent. Oral histories are increasingly recorded and some theorists have looked to music to produce alternative histories.[6] But, for the most part, these exist with their linguistic counterpart; archives comprised only of sound documents are more rare. An early exception was the anthropologist Moses Asch, who sought to produce an encyclopedic catalogue of the "entire world of sounds." Like a Foley artist, Asch assembled an incredible array of music and sounds, "both those commercially produced, as well as those found in nature."[7] And yet, Asch's sounds are all classified under the rubric of music. What about those sounds that erupt unconsciously and that are barely detectable or often pass unnoticed? How does one salvage, recuperate, and store vocal intonations, pauses in speech, silences, and those sonic by-products or detritus that is sometimes referred to as "noise?" How to restore, preserve, and remember those aspects of language produced by the voice but composed of non-linguistic sounds such as laughing, crying, hiccupping, coughing, and sighing?[8]

Taking up such a challenge is Esther Shalev-Gerz. In her investigations on the recuperation of memory and the production of a history of events such as the Holocaust, diasporic migrations, and transformations of post-industrial societies, she attends not only to the visible traces but also concomitantly to the aural echoes. Through her use of video she produces audiovisual *gestus* of those events.

Among multiple sounds, the human voice stands out. Accompanying the timbre, pitch, and cadence of the voice is the manner in which words are spoken; rendering the grain of each person's voice as unique as a fingerprint. Voices lead to recognition even though an individual voice may sound differently depending on the context. Thus, there are differences in tone between a performance speech delivered on stage for an audience, versus an intimate tone of a conversation. In the former, the voice is consciously projected so that it may be heard and understood by those both close and faraway; in the latter it may be directed only to one other person in close proximity. There are also character traits and patterns that manifest in a voice of which the speaker may not be aware, such as those pauses, sighs, grunts, and "hmms." In addition to the aural component, when we speak, myriad expressions are registered on the face. Unless the body of the speaker is obscured, when a voice is perceived, it is registered both as an acoustic and a visual phenomenon. Speech is made for an audience, and the counterpart to speaking is listening. But listening not just to what is said, but also to what is unsaid and to the silences in-between words is what is significant. As noted by phenomenologist Don Ihde, "In conversation, when the other is silent there is also a 'speaking': we see the face which 'speaks' in its silence ... There is an adherence of speech to the silence of the other."[9] There are different modes of listening; for example, in a daily conversation we rapidly switch back and forth from speaker to listener actively decoding and producing a complex set of words, delivery, and expressions. In other contexts, such as that of a performance or a lecture, attention is devoted to focused listening to the enunciating subject. Our inner voice may engage in a dialogue or critique, but these thoughts are kept silent and we do not "look" for a response from the other person. Listening is an

1
Jean-Luc Nancy, *Listening*, Fordham University Press, New York 2007, p. 5.

2
Don Ihde, *Listening and Voice: Phenomenologies of Sound*, State University of New York Press, Albany New York 2007, p. 51.

3
Quoted by Esther Shalev-Gerz in *Inseparable Angels: An Imaginary House for Walter Benjamin*, 2000.

4
Alberto Cavalcanti, "Sound in Films," John Belton, Elisabeth Weis (ed.), *Film Sound: Theory and Practice*, Columbia University Press, New York 1985, p. 98–111, here p. 109.

5
Walter Benjamin, "A Berlin Chronicle," Peter Demetz (ed.), *Reflections*, Schocken Books, New York 1986, p. 7.

6
An important example of such a counter history would be Greil Marcus' *Lipstick Traces: A Secret History of the Twentieth Century*, Harvard University Press, Cambridge, Massachusetts 1989.

7
Asch assembled his vast archive of sounds on the record label *Folkways*, which was active from 1948 to 1986 and produced more than 2,000 sound recordings ranging from traditional ethnic music, spoken word, and folk music to scientific and documentary field recordings with titles like "Ionosphere (High Altitude Sounds)," or "Sounds of North American Frogs." Folkways also featured jazz, classical, and spoken-word recordings, sound effects, Comanche Flute Music, and Festival of Japanese Music in Hawai'i. The label's aim, according to Asch, was never to allow a recording to go out of print; he saw Folkways as a library of sound.

active process and consists of a constant oscillation in subject position. As Jean-Luc Nancy has observed, "to be listening is to be *at the same time* outside and inside, to be open *from* without and *from* within, hence from one to the other and from one in the other."[10]

The complicated act of listening both as an aural and as a visual process is tackled by Shalev-Gerz in her video practice. In *Inseparable Angels: An Imaginary House for Walter Benjamin* (2000) Shalev-Gerz intersplices a taxi driver's commentary with quotations referring to angels from Walter Benjamin, Franz Kafka, Paul Klee, Heiner Müller, and Gershom Sholem. The images taken from the seat next to the taxi driver record a drive from Weimar to Buchenwald and back. The driver's speech is informational, as he remarks on the environment, historical events, and local politics; in contrast, the philosophical musings of Benjamin, the literary reflections of Sholem, or the poetry of Müller are part of poetic speech. The speaker of those texts is never revealed and the disembodied words float through time and space. The spectator is positioned as if looking through a window, listening to words coming from the front seat that are occasionally interrupted and even intruded upon by these poetic fragments emanating from the inner voice of the passenger. Whereas the driver's words connect and comment directly on what is seen outside the window, the imaginary reflections are unmoored, flights of fantasy corresponding to a different plane of consciousness. The participation of these literary ghosts that haunt the here-and-now of the audiovisual text is registered visually by a stuttering, slowing down, and inchoateness of the images that alludes to the multiple layers of speech: informational as well as the philosophical. In this instance, Shalev-Gerz's imaginary spectator listens and processes a dual soundtrack composed of multiple sounds and thoughts. Responses to the changes in authorship manifest visually on the landscape as different voices take over, for we do not see the face or expressions of the passenger. We are the listener, inside that body, and therefore cannot see ourselves as auditor.

The multifaceted role of listening is further amplified in *Does Your Image Reflect Me* (2002), and *White Out—Between Telling and Listening* (2002). In the former, Shalev-Gerz videotaped—and here it is important to stress that the artist works almost exclusively in video—Isabelle Choko, a Polish Jew from Lodz who spent the war in the Auschwitz and Bergen-Belsen concentration camps, and Charlotte Fuchs, a successful German actress who passed the same time in the nearby city of Hannover. Each woman recounted to Shalev-Gerz her experiences before, during, and after the war. Shalev-Gerz then played each interview to the other woman through the medium of their televisions and recorded them listening to the other's account. Two subjects of the same gender and approximate age each had occupied the same geographical space and time in history, and yet had radically different experiences as each had been racially constructed as "other." Choko was on the path toward eradication and Fuchs toward recognition. Shalev-Gerz's camera records their faces close up as they listen to each other's histories; they encounter the other through both seeing and hearing their recorded memories. Each voice is distinct, and as it speaks, it both confirms what is seen—the female identity of the interviewees—but also reveals what is not visually apparent: a native versus non-native German speaker as revealed by their distinct accents. Their act of listening involves not only more than what is being said, but how it is being said. The encounter, although mediated through the public medium of television, is nonetheless an intimate and personal experience of a specific, tragically marked historical event of the 20th century. As Choko and Fuchs listen to each other's narrative they fill in the blanks, listen below the surface, register contradictions and ambiguities, counter silently with their own versions. Through representing each woman listening to the other, Shalev-Gerz underscores all that is not said, that which exists in the interstices and between language, not only for the two subjects, but for the potential spectator as well, who brings her own knowledge and history into the conversation.

Sometimes the other that one encounters is oneself. We all know the uncanny experience of hearing our voice recorded for the first time and the usual disavowal that it does not sound like "us." There is a momentary destabilization of our identity produced by an aural misrecognition. We become briefly estranged from ourselves through this acoustic displacement. In *White Out—Between Telling and Listening* (2002), Shalev-Gerz probes deeply into this confusion. For this project she interviewed a Sami woman, Åsa Simma, raised in the traditional Lapp minority community of Sweden who, when grown, assimilated into the dominant Swedish society. For the first part of the project, *Åsa Simma Tells*, Shalev-Gerz gathered numerous quotations from a variety of sources, both Swedish and Sami, which describe the two peoples and their interactions.[11] The artist then had Simma respond to these *bon mots* by reading them out loud while Simma repllied with her own stories and memories. Simma produces a complex audiotext interwoven with many different voices—Sami and Swedish, contemporary and historical. Shalev-Gerz films her in a medium-close shot against the backdrop of the interior of her modern apartment, as she animatedly narrates. For the second part of the project, Shalev-Gerz then transports Simma to her birthplace in Karesuando, Lapland, and has her listen to her previously recorded self-narration. This image is composed of a static close-up on her face as she concentrates on what her other self says. Her face registers a fascinated but puzzled expression as she concentrates on her other's words. We are reminded of Nancy's seminal question in his treatise on listening: "What does it mean for a being to be immersed entirely in listening, formed by listening or in listening, listening with all his being?"[12]

8
Mladen Dolar refers to such utterances as "Non-Voices." He explains, "from coughing and hiccups to babbling, screaming, laughing, and singing, are not linguistic voices; they are not phonemes, yet they are not simply outside the linguistic structure: it is as if by their very absence of articulation (or surplus—articulation in the case of singing), they were particularly apt to embody the structure as such, the structure at its minimal; or meaning as such, beyond the discernible meaning." Mladen Dolar, *A Voice and Nothing More*, MIT Press, Cambridge, Massachusetts 2006, p.32.

9
Ihde, *Listening and Voice*, p. 111.

10
Nancy, *Listening*, p. 14.

11
"The text's dialogic form embodies two peoples that have coexisted for centuries in the same place, on the same land. The text component of the project draws from numerous sources; from historical, archival, fictional, and travel literatures, and from both Sami and Swedish sources most of them voices, from speeches." Interview with Shalev-Gerz, Paris, 2011.

12
Nancy, *Listening*, p. 4.

The contrast between the two selves is striking—the animated cosmopolitan woman whose arms and hands expressively gesticulate while she shares her story, versus the reserved quiet face of the listener. The work divides the self between enunciator and receiver and between two lifestyles. Unlike the more recent *On Two* (2009) that contrasts two very different Parisian denizens who occupy the same space and time—one, the renowned elderly French philosopher, Jacques Rancière and the other Rola Younes, a young Lebanese philosopher—the divide in *White Out* between the two inhabited worlds exists in the same person. In this instance, the "between" is the space navigated continuously between the two contemporaneous identities, the constant oscillations of moving from one position of outside to another. In both contexts, however, the subject is always on the periphery. The silence accompanying listening is that other side, the audial corollary to the effect of visual shadowing.[13]

Between Listening and Telling: Last Witnesses, Auschwitz 1945–2005 (2005) takes us one step further into the complex realm of silence. Here Shalev-Gerz has edited out the silences, the pauses in-between the words that are spoken. Out of hours of interviews with Holocaust survivors, she sutures together those moments that exceed verbal articulation. On enlarged projections of facial close-ups, expressions rapidly change the faces as we "see" the effect of thoughts and reflections that move across the face, much as we witness the effect of wind rippling waves across water. Shalev-Gerz' editing summons forth visually the inaudible moments that occur before and after speech. The absence of words, the silences, become equally significant to what is said. Silence is also what a person withdraws into when they refuse to speak—silence is resistance. "Between" here refers to those silences, thought pauses, non-voiced or articulated memories, that most intimate private inner space. In both projects of *Between Listening and Telling,* the silence registered either through listening or through complex editing emphasizes the peripheral status or marginality of the subject. The subject being at one and the same time the individual as survivor or as ethnic minority resulting in the aesthetic phenomenological subject of the inaudible. Listening attentively to the "between" results in finer hearing and greater understanding.

It is not just the *human* voice that captivates, sometimes it may be the "voice" of objects. The unique sound that they produce can be as individual to that material as a voice is to a person. We may recall Jean-Luc Godard's famous formulation that tennis is the only televised sport that demands sound, for in order to follow the game the spectator needs to hear the precise thunk of the ball as it is hit with the racket.[14] In two remarkable and interrelated pieces, *Sound Machine* (2008) and *Last Click* (2010), Schalev-Gerz recalls the soon-to-be forgotten sounds of obsolescent machines. In *Sound Machine,* she researches the sonic legacy of a now defunct textile factory in the former industrial district of Norrköping, Sweden. The factories have been evacuated of their former contents and converted into modern spaces. Little remains of their former life, the machines no longer exist except as blue prints and drawings. An entire history of industrial production and the impact it had on the way of life for a large swathe of the local population has vanished. Not only has the visual imprint of the factory disappeared, but its acoustic component as well. The constant noise that was produced by the machines has been silenced. In *Sound Machine*, Shalev-Gerz restores that soon to be forgotten history. She virtually recreates images of the factory and the machines that then form the stage in which her contemporary subjects play. But it is not just the image of the factory that she seeks to fabricate. Equally important is her meticulous reconstruction of the sounds articulated by the workings of the factory. This reconstructed soundtrack (like the virtually reconstructed machines) filled with clickings, whirrings, and other noise was then played to five mother/daughter pairs; the mothers had been pregnant with their daughters while working in the factory. The pairs listen intently to the familiar sounds that evoke memories of a former life. In the silent video, we see them listening to the voice of the machine. Across their faces, a variety of expressions play as they concentrate on what the noise makes them remember. As in her earlier work, the silent act of *listening* plays a key role. However, in this instance it is not words or another's speech, but non-linguistic industrial sounds that speak to them. Shalev-Gerz broadcast this soundtrack at several sites in Norrköpping. The sonic recording of clickings and whirrings registered below the conscious surface of the spectator to reanimate and restore to memory that by-gone factory from the industrial era, a mode of production that has now been exported. Sound, for Shalev-Gerz, is the trace of that migration.

Similarly in *Last Click*, it is the clearly identifiable (for those of us of a certain age) "click" of a camera. Click Pavlovian effect—we need the click just as we need to hear the tennis ball. The click becomes an acoustic fetish. The click symbolizes the taking of a snapshot—an action. Sound identifies action just as with the factory it means production. The "shape-sound" of the camera is evoked. "We hear shapes."[15] The "click" also signals that the lens of the camera has opened and shut and that an image has been imprinted on the strip of celluloid. With the advent of digital image making, the click is no longer an integral by-product of the process; however, the click is now artificially produced precisely because it has been so embedded in our consciousness. Like the testimonies of witnesses, or Rancière reading from the accounts of workers, the click of the camera is a voice from a past machine, its audible presence today, a gesture to a vanishing technique of image production. To cite from a different work by Rancière, "aesthetics can be understood … as the system of a priori

13
As Ihde notes, "just as the visual is copresented as a face in profile and an intended absent depth, so in listening there is a sound which shades off into the copresenting 'emptiness' of silence. Silence is the 'other side' of sound." Ihde, *Listening and Voice,* p. 110.

14
Some tennis coaches claim they can follow a game with their eyes closed and recognize different shots such as slices, lobs etc., and even identify who is hitting the ball precisely by the sound.

15
See Ihde, *Listening and Voice,* p. 61.

forms determining what presents itself to sense experience. It is a delimitation of spaces and times, of the visible and the invisible, of speech and noise, which simultaneously determines the place and the stakes as a form of experience. Politics revolves around what is seen and what can be said about it, around who has the ability to see and the talent to speak, around the properties of spaces and the possibilities of time."[16]

Shalev-Gerz' practice tunes in to the audial world; she literally gives voice to myriad histories that would remain silent. As an audio archivist she gathers an array of acoustic samples, consisting of quotations, testimonies, readings, noises, and arranges them.[17] These narratives are offered to a public to listen to and through the act of listening to that which is not shown, what is not visible is brought forth. But it is not just the past that is evoked, for the movement of sound is temporal as well as spatial. Sound is a movement connecting past to present to future, but it also surrounds, encompasses, and unites subjects that exist in separate spaces at the same time.[18] To that extent sound is contemporaneous. Sound connects the temporal to the spatial; to that extent it becomes the mode for representing migration or diasporic movement of subjects.[19] Listening then for Shalev-Gerz is an ordering trope, a way of understanding the world—one that extends beyond the boundaries and horizons of the visible world to include blurriness, lack of distinction, and where silence is as important as what is said.

16
Jacques Rancière, *The Politics of Aesthetics: The Distribution of the Sensible,* Contiuum, London 2004, p.13.

17
To that extent, Shalev-Gerz is an archival artist, who, as Hal Foster notes, is "concerned less with absolute origins than with obscure traces (perhaps 'an archival impulse' is the more appropriate phrase), these artists are often drawn to unfulfilled beginnings or incomplete projects—in art and in history alike—that might offer points of departure again." In "An Archival Impulse," *October,* no. 110 (Fall 2004), p. 5.

18
"Whereas visible or tactile presence occurs in a motionless 'at the same time,' sonorous presence is essentially mobile 'at the same time,' vibrating from the come-and-go between the source and the ear, through open space, the presence of presence rather than pure presence. One might say: there is a *simultaneity* of the visible and a *contemporaneity* of the audible." Nancy, *Listening,* p. 16.

19
As Shalev-Gerz explains with reference to *White Out*: "I intentionally present such materials from disparate times and locations as if these things can exist synchronically across time, and ahistorically, outside of time—as a hypersystem, with interchangeable links, always in the present, even though history seems absent in the present." *Esther Shalev-Gerz. Two installations. White Out—Between Telling and Listening. Inseparable Angels: The Imaginary House of Walter Benjamin*, Historiska Museet, Stockholm 2002, p. 58.

PASSÉ SAMPLÉ : UNE HISTOIRE À L'OREILLE
NORA M. ALTER

« Qu'est-ce qui [se] joue [dans l'écoute], qu'est-ce qui y résonne, quel est le ton de l'écoute ou son timbre ? L'écoute serait-elle elle-même sonore ? »
– Jean-Luc Nancy[1]

« L'exploration de l'auditif est aussi une exploration de l'invisible. L'écoute rend l'invisible *présent* d'une manière similaire à cette présence mutique qui accompagne la vision. »
– Don Ihde[2]

« L'ange, je l'entends encore
Mais il n'a plus d'autre visage que
Le tien, que je ne connais pas. »
– Heiner Müller, *Glückloser-Engel 2*[3]

Dans un texte de 1939, le cinéaste brésilien Alberto Cavalcanti fait la remarque suivante : « L'image s'adresse à l'intelligence. Le bruit paraît quant à lui contourner l'intelligence et s'adresser à quelque chose de très profond et de très enfoui… L'image se prête à des énoncés clairs alors que le son se prête davantage à la suggestion. »[4] Les images, et plus généralement tout ce qui fait le domaine du visible, sont souvent plus faciles à identifier que le domaine éphémère du son. Alors qu'une image est stable et déterminée, le son flotte ; il est libre. Ce qui est visible est fixe dans l'espace alors que le son englobe – même lorsqu'il provient d'une source localisable comme un haut-parleur ; dès qu'il pénètre l'air, il se disperse rapidement. Le son est intimement lié à l'inconscient, il affecte involontairement le psychisme. En écho à la théorie de Walter Benjamin sur l'inconscient optique lié à des médiums comme la photographie et le cinéma, Siegfried Kracauer a développé une théorie de « l'inconscient acoustique ». De même que ces signes optiques qui surgissent et signalent simultanément le passé, le présent, voire le futur, les cordes de l'inconscient acoustique parcourent elles-mêmes l'histoire et ses représentations. Les sons peuvent jouer le rôle de *madeleines** auditives qui déclenchent librement les souvenirs. Dans les souvenirs de son enfance berlinoise, Walter Benjamin se dit que, plus encore que les images, ce sont les sons qui renvoient au passé : « Toutes ces images, je les ai conservées. Mais aucune ne pourra recréer le Nouveau Lac et ces quelques heures de mon enfance avec autant de vivacité que le seul fait d'entendre à nouveau quelques mesures de musique. »[5]

On représente traditionnellement l'histoire par l'intermédiaire du visible et du langagier sous la forme de documents, de comptes-rendus écrits, mémoires, photographies, peintures, illustrations et autres. De vastes archives – de plus en plus souvent numérisées – contiennent les traces de la civilisation. Peut-être la numérisation et ses capacités audiovisuelles ont-elles contribué à rendre l'archive moins silencieuse. Les histoires orales sont de plus en plus souvent enregistrées et certains théoriciens ont même vu dans la musique la capacité à produire des histoires alternatives[6]. Pour la plupart, toutefois, ces dernières existent avec leur contrepartie langagière ; les archives uniquement composées de sons sont plus rares. L'anthropologue Moses Asch y a cependant tôt fait exception en produisant un catalogue encyclopédique du « monde entier des sons ». Comme l'aurait fait un artiste bruiteur, il a assemblé un phénoménal éventail de musique et de sons, « qu'ils aient été produits commercialement ou trouvés dans la nature »[7]. Reste que tous les sons de Asch ont été rangés dans la rubrique de la musique. Mais qu'en est-il de ceux d'entre eux qui font irruption dans l'inconscient et qu'on ne détecte qu'à peine quand ils ne passent pas complètement inaperçus (ce qui arrive le plus souvent) ? Comment sauver, récupérer et stocker des intonations de la voix, des pauses dans le discours, des silences et ces à-côtés ou rebuts sonores qu'on met parfois sous le vocable « bruit » ? Comment restaurer, préserver et se rappeler ces aspects du langage qui proviennent de la voix mais qui sont composés de sons qui ne relèvent pas du langage, comme le rire, les sanglots, le hoquet, la toux ou le soupir[8] ?

Esther Shalev-Gerz se propose de relever pareil défi. Dans ses recherches sur la récupération de la mémoire et la réalisation de l'histoire d'événements comme l'Holocauste, les migrations de la Diaspora et les transformations des sociétés postindustrielles, elle s'en remet non seulement à leurs traces visibles mais aussi simultanément à leurs manifestations orales. À travers son utilisation de la vidéo, elle propose des *gestus* audiovisuels de ces événements.

Parmi la multiplicité des sons, la voix humaine fait exception. En plus du timbre, de la hauteur et de la cadence de la voix, il y a la manière avec laquelle les mots sont prononcés ; c'est ce qui rend le grain de la voix de chaque personne aussi unique qu'une empreinte digitale. On peut reconnaître quelqu'un à sa voix alors même qu'elle varie en fonction des contextes. Ainsi, il y a une différence de ton entre un discours donné sur scène pour un public et une conversation privée. Dans le premier, la voix est sciemment projetée de manière à être entendue et comprise tant par ceux qui sont proches que par ceux qui sont les plus éloignés, et dans le second, elle peut ne s'adresser qu'à une seule autre personne à proximité. Il y a aussi des traits de caractère et des motifs qui se manifestent dans une voix et que son propriétaire peut ne pas percevoir lui-même, comme les pauses, les soupirs, les grommellements et les « euh ». En plus de la composante orale, lorsque quelqu'un parle, son visage est parcouru de myriades d'expressions. À moins que le corps de celui qui parle ne soit dissimulé, à l'instant où la voix est perçue, il est identifié comme un phénomène visuel et acoustique à la fois. La parole

1
Jean-Luc Nancy, *À l'écoute*, Galilée, Paris 2002, p. 17.

2
Don Ihde, *Listening and Voice : Phenomenologies of Sound*, State University of New York Press, Albany New York 2007, p. 51.

3
Cité dans Esther Shalev-Gerz in *Anges inséparables : la maison éphémère pour Walter Benjamin*, 2000 (traduit à partir de la version anglaise, NdT).

4
Alberto Cavalcanti, « Sound in Films », in John Belton et Elisabeth Weis (éds.), *Film Sound : Theory and Practice*, Columbia University Press, New York 1985, p. 98-111, ici p. 109.

*
En français dans le texte original

5
Walter Benjamin, « A Berlin Chronicle », Peter Demetz (éd.), *Reflections*, Schocken Books, New York 1986, p. 7.

6
Le *Lipstick traces (une histoire secrète du XXe siècle)* de Greil Marcus (éditions Allia, Paris 1998) est un exemple majeur d'une telle contre-histoire.

7
Moses Asch a compilé son énorme archive sonore sur le label Folkways entre 1948 et 1986. Il a produit plus de 2000 enregistrements sonores parmi lesquels de la musique ethnique traditionnelle, des conversations et de la musique folk, mais aussi des enregistrements documentaires et scientifiques avec des titres comme « Ionosphère (sons de haute altitude) » ou « Sons des grenouilles d'Amérique du Nord ». Folkways éditait également du jazz, de la musique classique et des enregistrements parlés, des effets sonores, de la flûte comanche et le Festival de musique japonaise de Hawaï. Le but du label, selon Asch, était de toujours préserver la disponibilité des enregistrements ; il envisageait Folkways comme une bibliothèque de sons.

est destinée à un public et la contrepartie de la parole est l'écoute. Ce n'est pas seulement l'écoute de ce qui est dit qui est importante mais aussi celle de ce qui n'est pas dit et des silences entre les mots. Comme le phénoménologue Don Ihde l'a fait remarquer : « Dans la conversation, lorsque l'autre est silencieux, il y a encore une "parole" : nous observons un visage qui "parle" dans son mutisme… La parole adhère au silence de l'autre. »[9] Il y a différents modes d'écoute, par exemple, dans une conversation du quotidien : nous passons rapidement de celui qui parle à celui qui écoute, tout en décodant activement et en produisant un ensemble complexe de mots, de réponses et d'expressions. Dans d'autres contextes, comme celui de l'interprétation ou de la conférence, l'attention est vouée à se concentrer sur l'écoute du sujet énonciateur. Notre voix intérieure peut entamer un dialogue ou une critique mais de telles pensées restent silencieuses et nous n'allons pas « chercher » de réponse chez l'autre personne. L'écoute est un processus actif et consiste en une oscillation constante de la position subjective. Comme l'a fait observer Jean-Luc Nancy : « Être à l'écoute, c'est être *en même temps* au dehors et au dedans, être ouvert *du* dehors et *du* dedans, de l'un à l'autre donc et de l'un en l'autre. »[10]

C'est cet acte compliqué de l'écoute comme processus à la fois auditif et visuel qui est interrogé dans la pratique vidéo de Shalev-Gerz. Dans *Anges inséparables : la maison éphémère pour Walter Benjamin* (2000), elle entrecoupe le commentaire d'un chauffeur de taxi de citations de Walter Benjamin, Franz Kafka, Paul Klee, Heiner Müller et Gershom Sholem à propos des anges. Les images prises depuis le fauteuil passager enregistrent un trajet aller-retour entre Weimar et Buchenwald. La parole du chauffeur est informative, il fait des remarques sur l'environnement, les événements historiques et la politique locale ; de leur côté, les rêveries philosophiques de Benjamin, les réflexions littéraires de Sholem ou la poésie de Müller participent d'une parole poétique. Celui qui dit ces textes n'est jamais montré et les mots désincarnés flottent dans le temps et dans l'espace. La position du spectateur est celle de quelqu'un qui regarderait par la vitre, écoutant les paroles qui viennent du siège avant, interrompues voire assaillies de temps à autre par ces fragments poétiques qui émanent du for intérieur du passager. Alors que les paroles du chauffeur sont en lien et commentent directement ce que l'on voit à l'extérieur de la vitre, les réflexions imaginaires sont sans attaches, des envolées de l'imagination correspondant à un autre niveau de conscience. L'irruption de ces fantômes littéraires venus hanter l'ici-et-maintenant du texte audiovisuel est visuellement rendue par des images incomplètes qui bégaient, ralentissent et renvoient ainsi aux couches multiples du discours : informatives aussi bien que philosophiques. Dans ce cas précis, le spectateur imaginaire d'Esther Shalev-Gerz écoute et analyse une double bande son composée de pensées et de sons divers. Des réponses à l'évolution du statut de l'auteur se manifestent visuellement dans le paysage au gré de l'arrivée des voix, car on ne voit jamais le visage du passager et ses expressions. Nous sommes à l'écoute, à l'intérieur de ce corps, et nous ne pouvons nous voir nous-mêmes comme auditeurs.

Le rôle multiple de l'écoute allait encore s'amplifier dans *Est-ce que ton image me regarde ?* (2002) et *White Out – Entre l'écoute et la parole* (2002). Dans la première, Esther Shalev-Gerz a enregistré en vidéo – et il faut insister ici sur le fait que les œuvres de l'artistes sont presque exclusivement réalisées en vidéo – Isabelle Choko, juive polonaise de Lodz qui a passé la guerre dans les camps d'extermination de Auschwitz et Bergen-Belsen, ainsi que Charlotte Fuchs, actrice allemande à succès qui a passé la même période dans la ville voisine de Hanovre. Chaque femme lui raconte son expérience avant, pendant et après la guerre. Esther Shalev-Gerz a par la suite présenté les entretiens de l'une à l'autre sur leurs postes de télévision et les a filmées pendant qu'elles écoutaient. Deux personnes de même sexe et approximativement du même âge ont chacune occupé une position géographique similaire à la même période de l'histoire, cependant elles en ont fait des expériences radicalement différentes, chacune ayant été racialement fabriquée en tant qu'« Autre ». Isabelle Choko était sur le chemin de l'extermination, Charlotte Fuchs avançait vers la reconnaissance. La caméra capte leurs visages en gros plan pendant qu'elles écoutent les récits l'une de l'autre, qu'elles font la rencontre l'une de l'autre en voyant et en entendant leurs souvenirs enregistrés. Chaque voix est différente et, au fur et à mesure qu'elle s'exprime, elle confirme ce que l'on voit – l'identité féminine des interviewées – mais dévoile aussi quelque chose qui ne se donne pas à voir : une allemande d'origine et une immigrée, ainsi que le révèlent leurs accents bien distincts. Leur écoute implique non seulement plus que ce qui est dit, mais aussi la manière dont cela est dit. La rencontre, bien qu'elle se fasse par l'intermédiaire du médium public qu'est la télévision, n'en reste pas moins l'expérience intime et personnelle d'un événement historique tragique du XXe siècle. Alors qu'Isabelle Choko et Charlotte Fuchs écoutent le récit l'une de l'autre, elles remplissent les blancs, lisent entre les lignes, repèrent les contradictions et les ambiguïtés, réfutent intérieurement selon leurs propres versions des faits. À travers la représentation de chaque femme écoutant l'autre, l'artiste souligne tout ce qui n'est pas dit, ce qui existe dans les interstices et sous le langage, non seulement chez ces deux sujets mais aussi chez le spectateur potentiel qui apporte son propre savoir et sa propre histoire dans cette conversation.

Parfois, c'est soi-même que l'on rencontre comme autre. Nous avons tous fait l'expérience étrange d'entendre notre voix enregistrée pour la première fois et de réagir par le désaveu habituel selon lequel elle n'est pas « nous ». Cette déstabilisation momentanée de notre identité provient d'une reconnaissance orale déformée. Nous devenons brièvement

8
Mladen Dolar appelle de tels énoncés des « non-voix ». Il explique : « De la toux et du hoquet au babil, du hurlement au rire et au chant, on n'est pas en présence de voix langagières ; aucun phonème, et pour autant ni les uns ni les autres ne sont simplement hors de toute structure langagière : c'est un peu comme si de par leur absence même d'articulation (ou de par leur supplément d'articulation comme dans le cas du chant), ils étaient tout à fait aptes à incarner la structure en tant que telle, la structure à son minimum ; ou le sens comme tel, par-delà de toute signification identifiable. », in Mladen Dolar, *A Voice and Nothing More*, MIT Press, Cambridge Mass. 2006, p. 32.

9
Don Ihde, *Listening and Voice*, p. 111.

10
Jean-Luc Nancy, *À l'écoute*, p. 33.

étrangers à nous-mêmes lors de ce déplacement acoustique. Dans *White Out – Entre l'écoute et la parole*, Esther Shalev-Gerz creuse davantage cette confusion. À l'occasion de ce projet, elle est allée interviewer une Saami, Åsa Simma, élevée au sein de la communauté traditionnelle de la minorité laponne suédoise et qui, une fois qu'elle eut grandi, intégra la société suédoise. Dans la première partie du projet, *Åsa Simma raconte*, Esther Shalev-Gerz a rassemblé un ensemble de citations issues de sources diverses, à la fois suédoises et saamies, qui décrivent les deux peuples en question et leurs interactions[11]. L'artiste a ensuite envisagé une réponse à ces *bons-mots** en les lisant elle-même à voix haute, Åsa Simma répondant avec ses propres histoires et ses propres souvenirs. Elle a ainsi contribué à un texte audio complexe où s'entremêlent quantité de voix différentes – saamies, suédoises, contemporaines et historiques. Elle la filme en plan moyen dans son intérieur moderne pendant qu'elle raconte son histoire avec animation. Dans la deuxième partie du projet, elle transporte Åsa Simma jusqu'à sa ville natale de Karesuando, en Laponie, où elle lui fait écouter l'enregistrement de son précédent récit. L'image consiste en des plans fixes sur son visage alors qu'elle se concentre sur ce que son autre moi raconte. Son visage a une expression à la fois fascinée et interloquée. On se rappelle alors la riche question de Jean-Luc Nancy dans son essai sur l'écoute : « Qu'est-ce qu'un être adonné à l'écoute, formé par elle ou en elle, écoutant de tout son être ? »[12]

Le contraste entre les deux moi est frappant : d'un côté, la métropolitaine animée dont les mains et les bras s'agitent de façon expressive pendant qu'elle partage son histoire ; de l'autre, le visage calme et réservé de celle qui écoute. L'œuvre divise le moi entre le sujet de l'énoncé et le sujet récepteur mais aussi entre deux styles de vie. Contrairement au plus récent *D'Eux* (2009) qui joue sur le contraste entre deux habitants de Paris qui occupent pourtant le même espace et le même temps – l'un, Jacques Rancière, philosophe français de renom ; l'autre, Rola Younes, jeune philosophe libanaise –, le clivage dans *White Out* entre les deux mondes habités réside dans la même personne. En l'occurrence, l'« entre-deux » est l'espace continûment traversé de l'une à l'autre de deux identités contemporaines, l'oscillation permanente d'une position extérieure à l'autre. Dans les deux contextes, cela dit, le sujet se trouve systématiquement à la périphérie. Le silence qui accompagne l'écoute est cet autre bord, corollaire auditif de l'effet d'obscurcissement visuel[13].

Entre l'écoute et la parole : derniers témoins, Auschwitz 1945-2005 (2005) nous entraîne un peu plus loin dans la complexité du silence. Là, Esther Shalev-Gerz a monté les silences, les pauses entre les phrases prononcées. À partir de nombreuses heures d'entretiens avec des survivants de l'Holocauste, elle suture ensemble ces moments au-delà de toute articulation verbale. Sur des projections en très grandes dimensions de gros plans de visages, nous « voyons » les expressions changer au gré des pensées et des réflexions qui traversent les esprits, un peu comme l'on observe l'effet du vent dans les ridules à la surface de l'eau. Le montage de Shalev-Gerz s'en remet visuellement aux moments inaudibles qui interviennent juste avant et juste après la parole. L'absence de paroles, les silences, prennent la même importance que ce qui est dit. Le silence, c'est aussi ce qu'une personne prolonge lorsqu'elle ne veut pas parler – le silence comme résistance. L'« entre-deux » se réfère ici à ces pauses de réflexion, ces souvenirs non verbalisés, non articulés, à cet espace intérieur le plus intime. Dans les deux projets intitulés *Entre l'écoute et la parole*, le silence manifesté à la fois par le biais de l'écoute et par la complexité du montage souligne le statut marginal et périphérique du sujet. Ce dernier incarne simultanément l'individu en tant que survivant et en tant que minorité ethnique pour finir comme sujet phénoménologico-esthétique de l'inaudible. L'écoute attentive de l'« entre-deux » ouvre sur une appréhension plus fine et une meilleure compréhension.

Il n'y a pas seulement la voix *humaine* qui captive, mais aussi parfois la « voix » des objets. Le son unique qu'ils produisent peut être aussi caractéristique d'un matériau que la voix d'une personne. On peut se rappeler ici la célèbre phrase de Jean-Luc Godard selon laquelle le tennis est le seul sport télévisé qui requiert le son car, pour suivre le jeu, le spectateur a besoin d'entendre le « plop » exact de la balle au moment où elle est frappée par la raquette[14]. Dans deux œuvres remarquables et liées entre elles, *Sound Machine* (2008) et *Le dernier déclic* (2010), Esther Shalev-Gerz nous rappelle les sons périmés de machines obsolètes. Dans *Sound Machine*, elle se met en quête de l'héritage sonore d'une usine textile abandonnée dans le district autrefois industrialisé de Norrköping en Suède. Les usines ont été vidées de leur contenu et converties en espaces modernes. Il ne reste que peu de choses de leur vie passée, les machines ont disparu et ne subsistent que sous la forme de dessins et d'imprimés. C'est toute une histoire de la production industrielle et de son impact sur le mode de vie d'une bonne partie de la population locale qui n'est plus là. C'est non seulement l'emprise visuelle de l'usine mais aussi sa composante sonore qui ont disparu. Le bruit continuel que produisaient les machines a été réduit au silence. Dans *Sound Machine*, Esther Shalev-Gerz restaure cette histoire en passe d'être oubliée. Elle recrée virtuellement les images de l'usine et des machines qui constituent la scène sur laquelle ses sujets contemporains vont jouer. Mais ce n'est pas seulement l'image de l'usine qu'elle cherche à recréer. Sa reconstitution méticuleuse des sons de l'usine prend une importance tout aussi grande. Tout comme les machines virtuellement remontées, cette bande son reconstruite pleine de clics, de ronronnements et d'autres bruits a été jouée à cinq couples de mères et filles : des mères enceintes de leurs filles au moment où elles travaillaient dans l'usine. Chacune écoute

11
« La forme dialogique du texte incarne les deux peuples tels qu'ils ont cohabité pendant plusieurs siècle en un même lieu, dans un même pays. La composante textuelle du projet est tirée de nombreuses sources ; de la littérature historique, de voyage, de fiction et des archives, à des sources tant saamies que suédoises, la plupart orales et provenant de discours », entretien avec Esther Shalev-Gerz, Paris, 2011.

12
Jean-Luc Nancy, *À l'écoute*, p. 16.

13
Comme le signale Don Ihde : « De la même manière que le visuel s'accompagne d'un visage de profil et d'une absence volontaire de profondeur, il y a dans l'écoute un son qui s'estompe dans la coprésence "vide" du silence. Le silence est "l'autre côté" du son. », in *Listening and Voice*, p. 110.

14
Certains entraîneurs de tennis prétendent qu'ils peuvent même suivre un match les yeux fermés et reconnaître à leur bruit les différents coups comme les liftés, les lobes, etc., voire qu'ils peuvent identifier grâce au son qui frappe la balle.

intensément ces sons familiers qui évoquaient les souvenirs d'une vie antérieure. Dans la vidéo muette, nous les regardons écouter la voix de la machine. Sur leurs visages, les expressions se succèdent alors qu'elles se concentrent sur ce que le bruit leur rappelle. Comme dans son œuvre précédente, l'action silencieuse de *l'écoute* joue un rôle essentiel. Quoi qu'il en soit, ce ne sont pas le discours ou les mots d'un autre qui parlent à leur place, mais des sons industriels non langagiers. L'artiste a fait entendre cette bande son sur plusieurs sites de Norrköping. L'enregistrement des clics et des vrombissements demeurait en deçà de la surface de la conscience du spectateur pour réanimer et restaurer cette usine disparue de l'ère industrielle, un mode de production désormais délocalisé. Pour l'artiste, le son est la trace de cette migration.

De la même façon, dans *Le dernier déclic*, c'est le « clic » clairement identifiable – pour ceux d'entre nous qui en ont l'âge – d'un appareil photo. Un clic à l'effet pavlovien – il nous faut le clic de la même façon qu'il nous faut entendre la balle de tennis. Le clic devient un fétiche acoustique. Il symbolise la prise de vue – une action. Ce son identifie l'action tout comme il en va de la production dans une usine. Il y a évocation de la « forme-son » de l'appareil photo. « Nous entendons des formes. »[15] Il signale également que l'objectif de l'appareil s'est ouvert et refermé et qu'une image a été imprimée sur la bande de celluloïd. Avec l'avancée de l'image numérique, le clic ne fait plus partie des à-côtés du processus, et si on l'a artificiellement reproduit, c'est précisément parce qu'il s'est imprimé dans nos consciences. Comme dans le témoignage, ou lorsque Jacques Rancière lit des récits de travailleurs, le clic de l'appareil est la voix d'une machine du passé, sa présence audible aujourd'hui, un geste vers une technique de production de l'image en voie d'extinction. Pour citer un autre essai de Jacques Rancière : « [l'esthétique peut s'appréhender comme] le système des formes *a priori* déterminant ce qui se donne à ressentir. C'est un découpage des temps et des espaces, du visible et de l'invisible, de la parole et du bruit qui définit à la fois le lieu et l'enjeu de la politique comme forme d'expérience. La politique porte sur ce qu'on voit et ce qu'on peut en dire, sur qui a la compétence pour voir et la qualité pour dire, sur les propriétés des espaces et les possibles du temps. »[16]

La pratique de Shalev-Gerz se met au diapason du monde de l'audition ; elle donne littéralement voix à une myriade d'histoires qui seraient autrement demeurées silencieuses. Archiviste sonore, elle rassemble un ensemble d'échantillons acoustiques, composés de citations, de témoignages, de lectures, de bruits pour les mettre en forme[17]. Ces récits sont offerts à l'écoute du public et, à travers elle, ce qui n'est pas montré, ce qui n'est pas visible finit par venir au premier plan. Ce n'est pas seulement le passé qu'elle évoque, car le mouvement du son est temporel aussi bien que spatial. Le son est un mouvement qui relie le passé au présent et au futur, mais il environne, englobe et unit également les sujets qui sont, en même temps, dans des espaces séparés[18]. À ce titre, le son est contemporain, il lie le temporel au spatial. À ce titre, il se fait le mode de représentation d'une migration, d'un mouvement diasporique des sujets[19]. L'écoute d'Esther Shalev-Gerz est donc une manière d'ordonnancement, une façon de comprendre le monde – à travers le dépassement des frontières et des horizons du monde visible pour atteindre au flou, à l'indistinct, ce lieu où le silence vaut tout autant que ce qui est dit.

15
Don Ihde, *Listening and Voice*, p. 61.

16
Jacques Rancière, *Le Partage du sensible, esthétique et politique*, La Fabrique, Paris 2000, p. 13-14.

17
De ce point de vue, Esther Shalev-Gerz est une artiste archiviste qui, comme Hal Foster l'a fait remarquer, « se préoccupe moins des origines absolues que des traces occultes ("un élan archiviste" est une expression qui conviendrait sans doute mieux), ces artistes sont souvent contraints à des commencements inachevés, des projets incomplets dans l'art comme dans l'histoire qui sont autant de points de recommencements. », in « An Archival Impulse » [« Un élan archiviste »], *October*, n°110 (hiver 2004), p. 5.

18
« Là où la présence visible ou tactile se tient dans un "en même temps" immobile, la présence sonore est un "en même temps" essentiellement mobile, vibrant de l'aller-retour entre la source et l'oreille, à travers l'espace ouvert, présence de présence plutôt que pure présence. On pourrait proposer de dire : il y a le *simultané* du visible et le *contemporain* de l'audible. », in Jean-Luc Nancy, *À l'écoute*, p. 36.

19
Comme l'explique l'artiste à propos de *White Out* : « Je présente volontairement ce genre de matériel issu de lieux et d'époques différents comme si toutes ces choses pouvaient exister de façon synchrone à un moment donné, mais aussi anhistoriquement, en dehors du temps – comme un hypersystème avec des liens interchangeables, toujours actualisé, même si l'histoire paraît ne pas faire partie du présent. », in *Esther Shalev-Gerz. Two installations*, Historiska Museet, Stockholm 2002, p. 58.

ON TWO, 2009
SCRIPT OF THE VIDEO INSTALLATION
JACQUES RANCIÈRE & ROLA YOUNES[1]

Jacques Rancière

[I]n a theater, in front of a performance, just as in a museum, school, or street, there are only ever individuals plotting their own paths in the forest of things, acts, and signs that confront or surround them. The collective power shared by spectators does not stem from the fact that they are members of a collective body, or from some specific form of interactivity. It is the power each of them has to translate what she perceives in her own way, to link it to the unique intellectual adventure that makes her similar to all the rest in as much as this adventure is not like any other. This shared power of the equality of intelligence links individuals, makes them exchange their intellectual adventures, in so far as it keeps them separate from one another, equally capable of using the power everyone has to plot their own path. What our performances verify—be they teaching or playing, speaking, writing, making art or looking at it—is not our participation in a power embodied in the community. It is the capacity of anonymous people, the capacity that makes everyone equal to everyone else. This capacity is exercised through irreducible distances; it is exercised by an unpredictable interplay of associations and dissociations.

It is in this power of associating and dissociating that the emancipation of the spectator consists—that is to say, the emancipation of each of us as spectator. Being a spectator is not some passive condition that we should transform into activity. It is our normal situation. We learn and teach, act and know, as spectators who all the time link what we see to what we have seen and said, done and dreamed. There is no more a privileged form than there is a privileged starting point. Everywhere there are starting points, intersections, and junctions that enable us to learn something new if we refuse, firstly, radical distance, secondly, the distribution of roles, and thirdly the boundaries between territories. We do not have to transform spectators into actors, and ignoramuses into scholars. We have to recognize the knowledge at work in the ignoramus and the activity peculiar to the spectator. Every spectator is already an actor in her story; every actor, every man of action, is the spectator of the same story.

I shall readily illustrate this point at the cost of a little detour via my own political and intellectual experience. I belong to a generation that found itself pulled between two opposite requirements. According to the first, those who possessed an understanding of the social system had to teach it to those who suffered because of that system so as to arm them for struggle. According to the second, supposed scholars were in fact ignoramuses who knew nothing about what exploitation and rebellion meant, and had to educate themselves among the workers whom they treated as ignoramuses. To respond to this dual requirement, I first of all wanted to discover the truth of Marxism, so as to arm a new revolutionary movement, and then to learn the meaning of exploitation and rebellion from those who worked and struggled in factories. For me, as for my generation, neither of these endeavors was wholly convincing. This state of affairs led me to search in the history of the working-class movement for the reasons for the ambiguous or failed encounters between workers and the intellectuals who had come to visit them to educate them or be educated by them. I thus had the opportunity to understand that the affair was not something played out between ignorance and knowledge, any more than it was between activity and passivity, individuality and community. One day in May when I consulted the correspondence of two workers in the 1830s, in order to find information on the condition and forms of consciousness of workers at that time, I was surprised to encounter something quite different: the adventures of two other visitors on different May days, 145 years earlier. One of the two workers had just joined the Saint-Simonian community in Ménilmontant and gave his friend the timetable of his days in utopia: work and exercise during the day, games, choirs, and tales in the evening. In return, his correspondent recounted the day in the countryside he had just spent with two friends enjoying a springtime Sunday. But what he recounted was nothing like the day of rest of a worker replenishing his physical and mental strength for the working week to come. It was an incursion into quite a different kind of leisure: the leisure of aesthetes who enjoy the landscape's forms and light and shade, of philosophers who settle into a country inn to develop metaphysical hypotheses there, of apostles who apply themselves to communicating their faith to all the chance companions encountered on their path or in the inn.

These workers, who should have supplied me with information on working conditions and forms of class-consciousness, provided me with something altogether different: a sense of similarity, a demonstration of equality. They too were spectators and visitors within their own class. Their activity as propagandists could not be separated from their idleness as strollers and contemplators. The simple chronicle of their leisure dictated a reformulation of the established relations between *seeing, doing*, and *speaking*. By making themselves spectators and visitors, they disrupted the distribution of the sensible which would have it that those who work do not have time to let their steps and gazes roam at random; and that the members of a collective body do not have time to spend on the forms and insignia of individuality. That is what the word "emancipation" means: the blurring of the boundary between those who act and those who look; between individuals and members of a collective body. What these days brought the two correspondents and their fellows was not knowledge of their condition and energy for the following day's work and the coming struggle. It was a reconfiguration in the here and now of the distribution of space and time, work and leisure.

Understanding this break made at the very heart of time was to develop the implications of a similarity and an equality, as opposed to ensuring its mastery in the endless

1
In the video installation, *On Two* the two texts are spoken in alternation. They are transcribed here as continuous texts to make them easier to read. The scripts of Esther Shalev-Gerz's other videos are almost all reproduced in other catalogues. Please refer to the bibliography. The text by Jacques Rancière is excerpted from *The Emancipated Spectator*, trans. Gregory Elliott, Verso, London 2009, p. 16–23.

task of reducing the irreducible distance. These two workers were themselves intellectuals, as is anyone and everyone. They were visitors and spectators, like the researcher who a century and a half later read their letters in a library, like the visitors of Marxist theory or the distributors of leaflets at factory gates. There was no gap to be filled between intellectuals and workers, any more than there was between actors and spectators. There followed various conclusions as to the discourse that could account for this experience. Recounting the story of their days and nights made it necessary to blur other boundaries. This story, which told of time, its loss, and re-appropriation, only assumed meaning and significance by being related to a similar story, told elsewhere, in another time and a quite different genre of writing—in Book 2 of the *Republic* where Plato, before assailing the mendacious shadows of theater, explains that in a well-ordered community everyone has to do one thing and that artisans do not have the time to be anywhere other than their workplace and to do anything other than the work appropriate to the (in)capacities allocated them by nature.

To understand the story of these two visitors, it was therefore necessary to blur the boundaries between empirical history and pure philosophy; the boundaries between disciplines and the hierarchies between levels of discourse. There was not on the one hand the factual narrative and on the other the philosophical or scientific explanation ascertaining the reason of history or the truth concealed underneath. It was not a case of the facts and their interpretation. There were two different ways of telling a story. And what it came down to me to do was a work of translation, showing how these tales of springtime Sundays and the philosopher's dialogues translated into one another. It was necessary to invent the idiom appropriate to this translation and counter-translation, even if it meant this idiom remaining unintelligible to all those who requested the meaning of this story, the reality that explained it, and the lesson it contained for action. In fact, this idiom could only be read by those who would translate it on the basis of their own intellectual adventure.

This biographical detour returns me to my central point. These stories of boundaries to cross, and of a distribution of roles to be blurred, in fact coincide with the reality of contemporary art, in which all specific artistic skills tend to leave their particular domain and swap places and powers. Today, we have theater without speech, and spoken dance; installations and performances by way of plastic work; video projections transformed into series of frescos; photographs treated as *tableaux vivants* or history paintings; sculpture metamorphosed into multimedia shows; and other combinations. Now, there are three ways of understanding and practicing this mélange of genres. There is that which relaunches the form of the total artwork. It was supposed to be the apotheosis of art become life. Today, it instead tends to be that of a few outsize artistic egos or a form of consumerist hyper-activism, if not both at once. Next, there is the idea of a hybridization of artistic means appropriate to the postmodern reality of a constant exchange of roles and identities, the real and the virtual, the organic and mechanical and information-technology prostheses. This second idea hardly differs from the first in its consequences. It often leads to a different form of stultification, which uses the blurring of boundaries and the confusion of roles to enhance the effect of performance without questioning its principles.

There is a third way that aims not to amplify effects, but to problematize the cause-effect relationship itself and the set of presuppositions that sustain the logic of stultification. Faced with the hyper-theater that wants to transform representation into presence and passivity into activity, it proposes instead to revoke the privilege of vitality and communitarian power accorded the theatrical stage, so as to restore it to an equal footing with the telling of a story, the reading of a book, or the gaze focused on an image. In sum, it proposes to conceive it as a new scene of equality where heterogeneous performances are translated into one another. For in all these performances what is involved is linking what one knows with what one does not know; being at once a performer deploying her skills and a spectator observing what these skills might produce in a new context among other spectators. Like researchers, artists construct the stages where the manifestation and effect of their skills are exhibited, rendered uncertain in the terms of the new idiom that conveys a new intellectual adventure. The effect of the idiom cannot be anticipated. It requires spectators who play the role of active interpreters, who develop their own translation in order to appropriate the "story" and make it their own story. An emancipated community is a community of narrators and translators.

I am aware that of all this it might be said: words, yet more words, and nothing but words. I shall not take it as an insult. We have heard so many orators passing off their words as more than words, as formulas for embarking on a new existence; we have seen so many theatrical representations claiming to be not spectacles but community ceremonies; and even today, despite all the "postmodern" skepticism about the desire to change existence, we see so many installations and spectacles transformed into religious mysteries that it is not necessarily scandalous to hear it said that words are merely words. To dismiss the fantasies of the word made flesh and the spectator rendered active, to know that words are merely words and spectacles merely spectacles, can help us arrive at a better understanding of how words and images, stories and performances, can change something of the worlds we live in.

Rola Younes

I was born on May 2, 1984, in Beirut. I am the only child in my family to have been born in Beirut; my brother was born in Paris and my sister in Nicosia, Cyprus. When I was born my parents lived in the western part of the city, the area known as *the Muslim part*. According to my mother, at the sound of blasts and shells, I would jump in her womb. It seems quite plausible and I do feel I have retained a memory of this period—feelings of insecurity and a way of being permanently on edge and on the alert. My parents lived in the western part of Beirut, but I was born in the eastern part, at Geitawi Hospital. During my birth the hospital was bombed, but the maternity ward was in the basement and wasn't hit.

When my mother left hospital and wanted to go home, she couldn't, as the crossing between the two parts of the town had been blocked and it was too dangerous to go from one part to the other. So she went to her mother-in-law's home. My grandmother wasn't renowned for her tact, or her kindness, or her hospitality. My mother stayed ten days at my grandmother's, ten days during which she suffered a lot because my grandmother made unpleasant remarks such as: "In my time, we would give birth and then get up right away and do the laundry, without resting like you do." My mother had had enough of it, so she took my brother and me—I was ten days old—and went home through the bombing, saying, "I don't care, I'm going home."

Once she got home she broke down, and fell into a depression that lasted for a month. A childhood friend of my father's came and helped her. All this occurred under the shelling, and then there was my mother's depression too. Starting in 1990 there was the sound of Beirut's reconstruction. I had spent two years in Cyprus and I came back to Lebanon in 1991, and Beirut was an enormous building site. There was noise and hammering the whole day long. I think that I have kept some kind of memory of that noise, the noise of shells, the noise of explosions, in my relations with my mother.

To me, being part of a minority is far more important than the identity of that minority. What is determining, for me, is not whether my parents are Maronite Christians, Druzes, Shia Muslims, or Jews, but that I come from a minority. Above all it's a *minority consciousness*. Bearing a different memory and a different history, and feeling marginal to the Sunni mainstream is what gives me this open-mindedness and ease of communication with anybody. Well, as it happens, there are only minorities in Lebanon. Even the Sunnis are a minority. There are more Muslims than Christians in Lebanon, but Muslims are so divided that I don't feel they are a majority, and even less do I see them as oppressive. The great divide in Lebanon isn't between Christians and Muslims but between Shias and Sunnis; and Christians themselves are divided between these two camps. In a sense, coming from a minority makes it easy for me to communicate and bond with all the other minorities—Copts, Jews...

There is no consensual history in Lebanon of what happened after November 22, 1943, when Lebanon gained independence. Official history, the history we read in schoolbooks, stops at 1943. When it comes to what happened after independence up to the present, every community or political tendency has its own story, its own account of the facts, and its own viewpoint, whereas in Iran, there is a continuous history that goes back several thousand years. How can I put it, it's a lot more—it's a history that is massively present and can be stifling—but it is consistently there. In Iran there can be different histories remembered by minorities, but in Lebanon there are only minorities. There is no official history that could be remembered by a mainstream majority; only small minorities each with a divergent point of view and an alternative history. There are only mutually contradictory narratives, or sometimes narratives that contradict themselves. And so far I feel it is still too soon to start to examine all these narratives in order to make a synthesis out of them, because at the end of the war there was an amnesty law for crimes perpetrated during the civil war. Since the end of that civil war the obsession has been with forgetting; people try to forget, and even when they are talking about a political leader, they try not to talk about his criminal activities during the civil war. It reminds me of an Athenian law that forbade all mention of crimes committed during war, during the wars the Greek region experienced in the 5th century BC. So in Lebanon we all did our best to forget. In a sense, this is inevitable to start with, in order to make peace. And I think that today, 20 years after the end of the war, the subject is still too sensitive to be put on to the agenda.

I think that every language has a particular usage or, to be more precise, a particular tone. Yiddish, for instance, is really a language I find very tormented and that I use when I'm very distressed, when I feel as if I'm being torn apart. It's a language for times of crisis, a language I use to console myself. When I cry, for example, I sing a Yiddish song to myself called, "Yingele nit veyn" which means "Don't Cry Little Boy," but when I sing it to myself I change some of the lyrics. I don't tell myself "Yingele nit veyn" but "Meydele nit veyn" (don't cry little girl) or "Kindele nit veyn" (don't cry little child).

To me, Persian is much more peaceful and confident, much less tormented. There's this foundation in Persian, a deep-rootedness in an age-old culture that gives a kind of tranquil power.

Hebrew is a language I find very, very muddy. It's very, very laryngeal, I don't know how to put it, it's in the throat, it's a language of the throat, "safa gronit" as they say in Hebrew. It's a language in which I very quickly feel hemmed in, and very quickly suffocate, even if the narrowness of the language creates a kind of intimacy. But personally I very quickly feel confined in this language, then very quickly feel the need to switch to Yiddish. Yiddish is much more airy, and there's more space, even when it comes to the language itself—to the syntax, the order of the words in a sentence. Hebrew is a very logical language whereas Yiddish sentences are not linear and are more like a bouquet, with interjections, with words that can belong to several different grammatical categories. For instance, the song "Yingele nit veyn" has a verse saying, "mir zol zayn far dayn lib Hersetele umshuldik un reyn." How can "mir zol zayn" be translated? "Leave for me your heart"? You can't say that in English, or in French, but you can say it in Arabic: "khallili 'albak" (خليلي قلبك).

Actually I wanted to translate Primo Levi's book called *If This Is a Man* into English. I could have considered working from the French translation, but I wanted to learn Italian in order to translate the original text. I wanted to, but it's already been done. A few months ago it was translated by a Palestinian poet called Salem Jibran who lives in Nazareth. Now I'd like to translate Levi's last work *The Drowned and the Saved*,[2] which is the book that affected me most.

Initially I wanted to translate *If This Is a Man* so that the text would be available to Arabic speakers, so that it would be a translation made by a Lebanese woman, an Arab, and not an Israeli translation that could be instrumentalized in the interests of Israeli propaganda. Because when I did a search on the Internet to see if it had already been translated, I found an excerpt in Arabic on the website of Israel's Ministry of Defense, so there was a clawback that was quite clear and worrying.

Italian isn't a language I'm especially drawn to, but as I already have a good grasp of French, I thought I could learn it easily. Another reason why I wanted to translate that particular text was to explore a bit more deeply the closeness I feel I have with that author, with Primo Levi, and also to force myself to study Auschwitz, and the Shoah, systematically, and the Second World War in general, to emerge a bit from this phantasm, because we have a tendency, and I have a tendency, to turn Auschwitz into a symbol.

In fact I'm very fond of the languages of the diaspora. Yiddish isn't the official language of any country, not even of Israel. In Israel, Arabic is an official language, but not Yiddish. Someone told me that Yiddish has the status of a minority language in Sweden, I don't know if that's true. I have an affection for the languages of the diaspora and I think I may end up learning Romany. I also like Esperanto a lot, but I've learnt and forgotten Esperanto ten times now, because it's very easy and I don't practice it. Esperanto is an ideological language, like Yiddish in a sense, an ideological language of the diaspora; it's the mother tongue of lots of people now, even if it's a language they say is artificial, and it's not linked to a territory. Yiddish is a dialect, but in a sense it's also an artificial language like Esperanto because at one time it was standardized, according to what I've read, according to Baumgarten's book, to try and pin Yiddish down and give it rules so that it would be possible to translate revolutionary texts, to pass knowledge and the great political texts on to the people, so that they could read them.

So to sum up the story of my languages, I was born with three languages: English, Arabic, and French. And then living in Paris enabled me to learn Hebrew, then Yiddish, and then Persian, and now I hope to learn Sinhalese and Guarani. As a Lebanese woman and as an Arab, the figure of the Other is the Jew, and the Iranian. For me, taking an interest in Iranian culture and the Iranian language meant continuing along this path of discovering the Other, and incorporating it, eating it, digesting it is an accomplishment. For me it's an achievement, it's something important I've accomplished in my life. And especially where Yiddish and Hebrew are concerned, what was important for me was to do what we call in Arabic "at-ta'arof al ahli" (التعارف الأهلي), literally meaning people knowing one another, and for me it was very important to know the Hebrew world and the Yiddish world from inside. That has to do with my personal experience: my mother is Druze and my father is Maronite, and I have links with both communities, and I think it's a very good vaccine against any form of fanaticism.

2
Editor's note: Primo Levi's *If This Is a Man* and *The Drowned and the Saved* were published in their original Italian versions in 1946 and 1986 respectively.

D'EUX, 2009
SCRIPT DE L'INSTALLATION VIDÉO JACQUES RANCIÈRE & ROLA YOUNES[1]

Jacques Rancière

[D]ans un théâtre, devant une performance, tout comme dans un musée, une école ou une rue, il n'y a jamais que des individus qui tracent leur propre chemin dans la forêt des choses, des actes et des signes qui leur font face et les entourent. Le pouvoir commun aux spectateurs ne tient pas à leur qualité de membres d'un corps collectif ou à quelque forme spécifique d'interactivité. C'est le pouvoir qu'a chacun ou chacune de traduire à sa manière ce qu'il ou elle perçoit, de le lier à l'aventure intellectuelle singulière qui les rend semblables à tout autre pour autant que cette aventure ne ressemble à aucune autre. Ce pouvoir commun de l'égalité des intelligences lie des individus, leur fait échanger leurs aventures intellectuelles, pour autant qu'il les tient séparés les uns des autres, également capables d'utiliser le pouvoir de tous pour tracer leur chemin propre. Ce que nos performances vérifient – qu'il s'agisse d'enseigner ou de jouer, de parler, d'écrire, de faire de l'art ou de le regarder – n'est pas notre participation à un pouvoir incarné dans la communauté. C'est la capacité des anonymes, la capacité qui fait chacun(e) égal(e) à tout(e) autre. Cette capacité s'exerce à travers des distances irréductibles, elle s'exerce par un jeu imprévisible d'associations et de dissociations.

C'est dans ce pouvoir d'associer et de dissocier que réside l'émancipation du spectateur, c'est-à-dire l'émancipation de chacun de nous comme spectateur. Être spectateur n'est pas la condition passive qu'il nous faudrait changer en activité. C'est notre situation normale. Nous apprenons et nous enseignons, nous agissons et nous connaissons aussi en spectateurs qui lient à tout instant ce qu'ils voient à ce qu'ils ont vu et dit, fait ou rêvé. Il n'y a pas plus de forme privilégiée que de point de départ privilégié. Il y a partout des points de départ, des croisements et des nœuds qui nous permettent d'apprendre quelque chose de neuf si nous récusons premièrement la distance radicale, deuxièmement la distribution des rôles, troisièmement les frontières entre les territoires. Nous n'avons pas à transformer les spectateurs en acteurs et les ignorants en savants. Nous avons à reconnaître le savoir à l'œuvre dans l'ignorant et l'activité propre au spectateur. Tout spectateur est déjà acteur de son histoire, tout acteur, tout homme d'action spectateur de la même histoire.

J'illustrerai volontiers ce point au prix d'un petit détour par ma propre expérience politique et intellectuelle. J'appartiens à une génération qui se trouva tiraillée entre deux exigences opposées. Selon l'une, ceux qui possédaient l'intelligence du système social devaient l'enseigner à ceux qui souffraient de ce système afin de les armer pour la lutte ; selon l'autre, les supposés savants étaient en fait des ignorants qui ne savaient rien de ce qu'exploitation et rébellion signifiaient et devaient s'en instruire auprès de ces travailleurs qu'ils traitaient en ignorants. Pour répondre à cette double exigence, j'ai d'abord voulu retrouver la vérité du marxisme pour armer un nouveau mouvement révolutionnaire, puis apprendre de ceux qui travaillaient et luttaient dans les usines le sens de l'exploitation et la rébellion. Pour moi, comme pour ma génération, aucune de ces deux tentatives ne fut pleinement convaincante. Cet état de fait me porta à rechercher dans l'histoire du mouvement ouvrier la raison des rencontres ambiguës ou manquées entre les ouvriers et ces intellectuels qui étaient venus leur rendre visite pour les instruire ou être instruits par eux. Il me fut ainsi donné de comprendre que l'affaire ne se jouait pas entre ignorance et savoir, pas plus qu'entre activité et passivité, individualité et communauté. Un jour de mai où je consultais la correspondance de deux ouvriers dans les années 1830 pour y retrouver des informations sur la condition et les formes de conscience des travailleurs en ce temps, j'eus la surprise de rencontrer tout autre chose : les aventures de deux autres visiteurs en d'autres jours de mai, cent quarante-cinq ans plus tôt. L'un des deux ouvriers venait d'entrer dans la communauté saint-simonienne à Ménilmontant et donnait à son ami l'emploi du temps de ses journées en utopie : travaux et exercices du jour, jeux, chœurs et récits de la soirée. Son correspondant lui racontait en retour la partie de campagne qu'il venait de faire avec deux compagnons pour profiter d'un dimanche de printemps. Mais ce qu'il lui racontait ne ressemblait en rien au jour de repos du travailleur restaurant ses forces physiques et mentales pour le travail de la semaine à venir. C'était une intrusion dans une toute autre sorte de loisir : le loisir des esthètes qui jouissent des formes, des lumières et des ombres du paysage, des philosophes qui s'installent dans une auberge de campagne pour y développer des hypothèses métaphysiques et des apôtres qui s'emploient à communiquer leur foi à tous les compagnons rencontrés au hasard du chemin ou de l'auberge.

Ces travailleurs qui auraient dû me fournir des informations sur les conditions du travail et les formes de la conscience de classe m'offraient tout autre chose : le sentiment d'une ressemblance, une démonstration de l'égalité. Eux aussi étaient des spectateurs et des visiteurs au sein de leur propre classe. Leur activité de propagandistes ne pouvait se séparer de leur oisiveté de promeneurs et de contemplateurs. La simple chronique de leurs loisirs contraignait à reformuler les rapports établis entre *voir*, *faire* et *parler*. En se faisant spectateurs et visiteurs, ils bouleversaient le partage du sensible qui veut que ceux qui travaillent n'aient pas le temps de laisser traîner au hasard leurs pas et leurs regards et que les membres d'un corps collectif n'aient pas de temps à consacrer aux formes et insignes de l'individualité. C'est ce que signifie le mot d'émancipation : le brouillage de la frontière entre ceux qui agissent et ceux qui regardent, entre individus et membres d'un corps collectif. Ce que ces journées apportaient aux deux correspondants et à leurs semblables n'était pas le savoir de leur condition et l'énergie pour le travail du lendemain et la lutte à venir. C'était la reconfiguration ici et maintenant du partage de l'espace et du temps, du travail et du loisir.

1
Dans l'installation vidéo *D'Eux*, les deux textes ne se suivent pas mais sont dits en alternance. Ils sont restitués ici comme des textes à part entière afin d'en faciliter la lecture. Les autres scripts des vidéos d'Esther Shalev-Gerz sont presque tous reproduits dans d'autres catalogues. Se référer à l'annexe bibliographique. Le texte dit par Jacques Rancière est extrait de son ouvrage *Le Spectateur émancipé*, La Fabrique, Paris 2008, p. 22-29.

Comprendre cette rupture opérée au cœur même du temps, c'était développer les implications d'une similitude et d'une égalité, au lieu d'assurer sa maîtrise dans la tâche interminable de réduire l'écart irréductible. Ces deux travailleurs étaient des intellectuels eux aussi, comme l'est n'importe qui. Ils étaient des visiteurs et des spectateurs, comme le chercheur qui, un siècle et demi plus tard, lisait leurs lettres dans une bibliothèque, comme les visiteurs de la théorie marxiste ou les diffuseurs de tracts aux portes des usines. Il n'y avait nul écart à combler entre intellectuels et ouvriers, non plus qu'entre acteurs et spectateurs. Il s'en tirait quelques conséquences pour le discours propre à rendre compte de cette expérience. Raconter l'histoire de leurs jours et de leurs nuits obligeait à brouiller d'autres frontières. Cette histoire qui parlait du temps, de sa perte et de sa réappropriation ne prenait son sens et sa portée qu'à être mise en relation avec une histoire similaire, énoncée ailleurs, en un autre temps et dans un tout autre genre d'écrit, au livre II de la *République* où Platon, avant de s'en prendre aux ombres menteuses du théâtre, avait expliqué qu'en une communauté bien ordonnée, chacun devait faire une seule chose et que les artisans n'avaient pas le temps d'être ailleurs que sur leur lieu de travail et de faire autre chose que le travail convenant aux (in)capacités que leur avait octroyées la nature.

Pour entendre l'histoire de ces deux visiteurs, il fallait donc brouiller les frontières entre l'histoire empirique et la philosophie pure, les frontières entre les disciplines et les hiérarchies entre les niveaux de discours. Il n'y avait pas d'un côté le récit des faits, de l'autre l'explication philosophique ou scientifique découvrant la raison de l'histoire ou la vérité cachée derrière. Il n'y avait pas les faits et leur interprétation. Il y avait deux manières de raconter une histoire. Et ce qu'il me revenait de faire était une œuvre de traduction, montrant comment ces récits de dimanches printaniers et les dialogues du philosophe se traduisaient mutuellement. Il fallait inventer l'idiome propre à cette traduction et à cette contre-traduction, quitte à ce que cet idiome demeure inintelligible à tous ceux qui demanderaient le sens de cette histoire, la réalité qui l'expliquait et la leçon qu'elle donnait pour l'action. Cet idiome, de fait, ne pouvait être lu que par ceux qui le traduiraient à partir de leur propre aventure intellectuelle.

Ce détour biographique me ramène au centre de mon propos. Ces histoires de frontières à traverser et de distribution des rôles à brouiller rencontrent en effet l'actualité de l'art contemporain où toutes les compétences artistiques spécifiques tendent à sortir de leur domaine propre et à échanger leur place et leurs pouvoirs. Nous avons aujourd'hui du théâtre sans parole et de la danse parlée ; des installations et des performances en guise d'œuvres plastiques ; des projections vidéos transformées en cycles de fresques ; des photographies traitées en tableaux vivants ou peintures d'histoire ; de la sculpture métamorphosée en show multimédia, et autres combinaisons. Or il y a trois manières de comprendre et de pratiquer ce mélange des genres. Il y a celle qui réactualise la forme de l'œuvre d'art totale. Celle-ci était supposée être l'apothéose de l'art devenu vie. Elle tend plutôt à être aujourd'hui celle de quelques égos artistiques surdimensionnés ou d'une forme d'hyper-activisme consumériste, sinon les deux à la fois. Il y a ensuite l'idée d'une hybridation des moyens de l'art propre à la réalité postmoderne de l'échange incessant des rôles et des identités, du réel et du virtuel, de l'organique et des prothèses mécaniques et informatiques. Cette seconde idée ne se distingue guère de la première dans ses conséquences. Elle conduit souvent à une autre forme d'abrutissement, qui utilise le brouillage des frontières et la confusion des rôles pour accroître l'effet de la performance sans questionner ses principes.

Reste une troisième manière qui ne vise plus l'amplification des effets mais la remise en cause du rapport cause-effet lui-même et du jeu des présuppositions qui soutient la logique de l'abrutissement. Face à l'hyper-théâtre qui veut transformer la représentation en présence et la passivité en activité, elle propose à l'inverse de révoquer le privilège de vitalité et de puissance communautaire accordé à la scène théâtrale pour la remettre sur un pied d'égalité avec la narration d'une histoire, la lecture d'un livre ou le regard posé sur une image. Elle propose en somme de la concevoir comme une nouvelle scène de l'égalité où des performances hétérogènes se traduisent les unes dans les autres. Car dans toutes ces performances il s'agit de lier ce que l'on sait avec ce que l'on ignore, d'être à la fois des performers déployant leurs compétences et des spectateurs observant ce que ces compétences peuvent produire dans un contexte nouveau, auprès d'autres spectateurs. Les artistes, comme les chercheurs, construisent la scène où la manifestation et l'effet de leurs compétences sont exposés, rendus incertains dans les termes de l'idiome nouveau qui traduit une nouvelle aventure intellectuelle. L'effet de l'idiome ne peut être anticipé. Il demande des spectateurs qui jouent le rôle d'interprètes actifs, qui élaborent leur propre traduction pour s'approprier l'« histoire » et en faire leur propre histoire. Une communauté émancipée est une communauté de conteurs et de traducteurs.

Je suis conscient que de tout ceci il est possible de dire : des mots, encore et seulement des mots. Je ne l'entendrai pas comme une insulte. Nous avons entendu tant d'orateurs faisant passer leurs mots pour plus que des mots, pour la formule de l'entrée dans une vie nouvelle ; nous avons vu tant de représentations théâtrales prétendant être non plus des spectacles mais des cérémonies communautaires ; et même aujourd'hui, en dépit de tout le scepticisme « postmoderne » à l'égard du désir de changer la vie, nous voyons tant d'installations et de spectacles transformés en mystères religieux qu'il n'est pas nécessairement scandaleux d'entendre dire que des mots sont seulement des mots. Congédier les fantasmes du verbe fait chair et du spectateur rendu actif, savoir que les mots sont seulement des mots et les spectacles seulement des spectacles peut nous aider à mieux comprendre comment les mots et les images, les histoires et les performances peuvent changer quelque chose au monde où nous vivons.

Rola Younes

Je suis née le 2 mai 1984, à Beyrouth, et je suis la seule parmi mes frères et sœurs à être née à Beyrouth. Mon grand frère est né à Paris et ma petite sœur est née à Nicosie, à Chypre. Quand je suis née, mes parents habitaient en zone Ouest, la zone qu'on disait être la zone musulmane. Alors que j'étais encore dans le ventre de ma mère, d'après ce que me racontait ma mère, je sursautais au bruit des explosions, au bruit des obus. Moi, ça me semble assez vraisemblable, et j'ai l'impression d'avoir gardé un souvenir de cette période-là, avec une espèce de sentiment d'insécurité et une manière d'être tout le temps sur le qui-vive. Donc mes parents habitaient à l'Ouest de Beyrouth. Moi je suis née dans la partie Est, à l'hôpital Geitawi. Pendant l'accouchement, l'hôpital a été bombardé, la maternité se trouvait au sous-sol et n'a pas été atteinte. Et donc au moment où ma mère est sortie de l'hôpital, elle voulait rentrer chez elle mais elle ne le pouvait plus parce que le passage avait entre temps été coupé. Elle ne pouvait plus passer d'une zone à l'autre, c'était trop dangereux. Donc elle est allée chez sa belle-mère, ma grand-mère, qui n'est réputée ni pour sa diplomatie, ni pour sa gentillesse, ni pour son hospitalité. Elle a passé dix jours chez ma grand-mère où elle a beaucoup souffert, d'après ce qu'elle m'a dit, parce que ma grand-mère avait fait des remarques désobligeantes du type : « À mon époque, on accouchait et on se levait pour aller faire le linge, tout de suite, sans se reposer comme ça. » Donc, ma mère en a eu marre, et elle m'a prise – j'avais dix jours –, elle a pris mon frère, et elle est rentrée chez elle sous les bombes. Elle a dit : « Je m'en fiche, je rentre chez moi. » Et en arrivant à la maison, elle s'est effondrée, elle a fait une dépression qui a duré un mois, et donc une amie, une ancienne amie d'enfance de mon père est venue l'aider. Et tout cela se passe sous les bombardements, et il y a aussi la dépression de ma mère. Et voilà. Il y a aussi le bruit de la reconstruction de Beyrouth. La ville a commencé à être reconstruite au début des années 1990. Moi, j'avais passé deux ans à Chypre, donc je suis rentrée au Liban en 1991, et Beyrouth, c'était un énorme chantier. C'étaient des bruits, du matraquage toute la journée, donc il y avait aussi ce bruit là. Et je pense avoir gardé une espèce de mémoire de ce bruit-là, du bruit des obus, du bruit des explosions, dans mon rapport avec ma mère.

Et, pour moi, faire partie d'une minorité est beaucoup plus important que l'identité de cette minorité. Ce qui a été marquant dans ma vie, ce n'est pas d'avoir eu des parents maronites, druzes, ou chiites ou juifs, mais d'être issue d'une minorité. C'est surtout la conscience minoritaire. Être porteur d'une autre mémoire, et être porteur d'une autre histoire, et se sentir un peu à la marge du *mainstream* sunnite. Et donc voilà ce qui fait une espèce de facilité de communication et d'ouverture sur le monde. Bon, il se trouve qu'au Liban, il n'y a que des minorités ; même les sunnites sont une minorité. Il se trouve qu'au Liban il y a plus de musulmans que de chrétiens, mais les musulmans sont tellement divisés, que moi je ne sens pas cette majorité-là et je la ressens encore moins comme oppressive, parce qu'actuellement la grande fracture au Liban n'est pas du tout entre musulmans et chrétiens mais entre sunnites et chiites ; les chrétiens sont eux-mêmes divisés entre ces deux camps. Être issue d'une minorité, en un sens, ça donne une facilité de contact et de lien avec toutes les autres minorités. Les Coptes, les Juifs...

Au Liban, il n'y a pas d'histoire consensuelle de ce qui s'est passé après 1943, après le 22 novembre 1943 – date de l'indépendance du pays. L'histoire officielle, l'histoire telle qu'on l'étudie dans les manuels scolaires, s'arrête en 1943. Et concernant la période post-indépendance, jusqu'à nos jours, chaque communauté ou chaque sensibilité politique a son propre récit, et sa propre narration des faits, son propre point de vue, alors qu'en Iran il y a une histoire continue qui remonte assez loin, à plusieurs millénaires en arrière. Et c'est beaucoup plus, comment dire… C'est une histoire qui est très présente, qui est massive, qui peut être étouffante mais qui est là. Et il peut y avoir des histoires différentes portées par des minorités qui existent en Iran, mais au Liban, il n'y a que des minorités. Il n'y a pas une histoire officielle qui pourrait être portée par un *mainstream*, par une majorité qui formerait le *mainstream*, avec des petites minorités qui auraient un point de vue divergent, ou une histoire alternative. Il n'y a que des récits contradictoires entre eux, ou parfois qui se contredisent eux-mêmes. Et jusqu'à maintenant, j'ai l'impression qu'il est encore trop tôt pour commencer à examiner tous ces récits, pour essayer d'en tirer la synthèse, parce qu'au lendemain de la guerre civile, il y a eu une loi d'amnistie qui a amnistié tous les crimes perpétrés pendant la guerre civile. Et depuis la fin de la guerre civile, l'attitude, ou plutôt l'obsession, est à l'oubli. On essaie d'oublier, on essaie de ne pas évoquer... Même en parlant d'un leader politique, de ne pas parler de ses activités criminelles pendant la guerre. Et ça me rappelle une loi athénienne qui interdisait de faire mention de crimes commis pendant la guerre, pendant les guerres que l'Attique a pu connaître au Ve siècle. Donc, au Liban, tout le monde s'est efforcé d'oublier. Ce qui, en un sens, est inévitable, dans un premier temps pour faire la paix. Et je pense qu'aujourd'hui, on arrive presque vingt ans après la fin de la guerre, c'est encore trop sensible, le sujet est encore trop sensible pour être remis à l'ordre du jour.

Je pense que chaque langue a un usage particulier ou, pour être plus précis, chaque langue a une tonalité particulière. Le yiddish est vraiment une langue que je trouve très tourmentée, ou une langue que j'utilise quand je suis très tourmentée, quand je suis angoissée, quand je suis déchirée, c'est une langue de crise pour moi. Et c'est une langue que j'utilise pour me consoler. Quand je pleure par exemple, je me chante une chanson qui s'appelle en yiddish *Yingele nit veyn*, c'est-à-dire «Petit garçon, ne pleure pas.» Mais je la chante en en changeant un peu les paroles. Je ne me dis pas «yingele nit veyn» mais «meydele nit veyn» ou «kindele nit veyn», à savoir «petite fille, ne pleure pas» ou «petit enfant, ne pleure pas».

Pour moi, le persan est beaucoup plus paisible, c'est beaucoup plus confiant, c'est beaucoup moins tourmenté. Dans le persan, il y a cette espèce d'assise, d'enracinement dans la culture, une culture vieille de millénaires, une espèce de force tranquille.

L'hébreu est une langue que je trouve très, très boueuse, et très très laryngale, je ne sais pas comment dire, c'est dans la gorge, c'est une langue de la gorge, «safa gronit». L'hébreu est une langue dans laquelle je me sens très vite à l'étroit, dans laquelle j'étouffe très vite, même si du fait que c'est étroit, cela crée une certaine intimité. Mais personnellement, je me sens très vite à l'étroit dans cette langue, alors j'ai très vite besoin de passer au yiddish. Le yiddish est beaucoup plus aéré, il y a beaucoup plus d'espace, et même au niveau de la langue elle-même, de la syntaxe par exemple, de l'ordre des mots dans une phrase. L'hébreu est une langue qui est très logique alors que la phrase yiddish n'est pas linéaire, c'est un bouquet, avec des interjections, des mots qui peuvent appartenir à plusieurs catégories grammaticales différentes. Par exemple, dans la chanson *Yingele nit veyn*, il y a un vers «mir zol zayn far dayn lib hertsele umshuldik un reyn». «Mir zol zayn», comment traduire cela? «Laisse pour moi ton cœur»? Ça ne se dit pas en français, alors qu'en arabe ça se dit «khallili 'albak» (خليلي قلبك).

Effectivement, je voulais traduire l'ouvrage de Primo Levi dont le titre français est *Si c'est un homme* [1947]. J'aurais pu envisager de le traduire du français mais je voulais apprendre l'italien pour pouvoir le traduire. J'ai voulu; maintenant c'est déjà fait, cela a été traduit il y a quelques mois par un poète palestinien qui s'appelle Salem Jibran et qui habite à Nazareth. Ce que j'aimerais aujourd'hui traduire est plutôt son dernier ouvrage *Les Naufragés et les rescapés. Quarante ans après Auschwitz* [1986], qui est l'ouvrage qui m'a le plus touché.

Au départ, je voulais traduire *Si c'est un homme* pour mettre ce texte à disposition des arabophones, pour que ce soit une traduction faite par une Libanaise, une Arabe, et non pas une traduction israélienne, qui puisse être instrumentalisée dans le sens de la propagande israélienne. Parce que, quand j'ai fait une recherche sur Internet pour voir si ce texte avait déjà été traduit, j'ai trouvé un extrait en arabe sur le site du Ministère de la Défense d'Israël, donc il y avait une récupération qui était assez claire et inquiétante.

L'italien n'est pas une langue qui m'attire particulièrement mais comme je maîtrise déjà le français, j'ai pensé pouvoir l'apprendre facilement. Je voulais aussi traduire ce texte-là pour creuser un peu l'intimité que j'estime avoir avec cet auteur, avec Primo Levi, et aussi pour me forcer à étudier de manière systématique Auschwitz, et la Shoah, et la Seconde Guerre mondiale de manière générale, pour sortir un peu du fantasme, parce qu'on a tendance, et j'ai tendance, à faire d'Auschwitz un symbole.

En fait, j'aime beaucoup les langues diasporiques. Le yiddish n'est la langue officielle d'aucun pays, pas même d'Israël. En Israël, l'arabe est langue officielle mais pas le yiddish. Quelqu'un m'a dit que le yiddish avait le statut de langue minoritaire en Suède, je ne sais pas si c'est vrai. J'aime beaucoup les langues diasporiques et je pense que je vais peut-être finir par apprendre le rom. J'aime aussi beaucoup l'espéranto, mais l'espéranto cela fait dix fois que je l'apprends et que je l'oublie, parce qu'il est très facile et que je n'ai pas de pratique. L'espéranto est une langue idéologique, comme en un sens le yiddish, une langue idéologique et diasporique; c'est la langue maternelle de beaucoup de gens maintenant même si c'est une langue qu'on dit artificielle, et elle n'est pas liée à un territoire. Le yiddish est un dialecte, mais c'est aussi en un sens une langue artificielle comme l'espéranto parce qu'à un moment, elle a été normatisée, pour d'après ce que j'ai lu, d'après le livre de Baumgarten, essayer de fixer le yiddish et de lui donner des règles pour pouvoir traduire les textes révolutionnaires, pour faire parvenir le savoir et les grands textes politiques au peuple, pour que le peuple puisse les lire.

Alors, pour l'histoire de mes langues, je suis née avec trois langues: l'anglais, l'arabe, le français. Et puis vivre à Paris m'a permis d'apprendre l'hébreu, puis le yiddish, et puis le persan, et puis maintenant j'espère apprendre le singhalais et le guarani. En tant que libanaise, et en tant qu'arabe, la figure de l'autre, c'est le Juif, et c'est l'Iranien. Pour moi, m'intéresser à la culture iranienne et à la langue, c'était continuer dans cette voie de découvrir l'autre et l'incorporer, et le manger, et le digérer, c'est un accomplissement. Pour moi, c'est un *achievement*, c'est quelque chose d'important que j'ai accompli dans ma vie. Et surtout pour le yiddish et l'hébreu, ce qui était important pour moi était de faire ce qu'on appelle en arabe «at-ta'arof al ahli», (التعارف الأهلي), c'est-à-dire littéralement que les gens se connaissent et, pour moi, c'était très important de connaître de l'intérieur le monde hébraïque et le monde yiddish. Cela a à voir avec mon expérience personnelle: ma mère est druze et mon père est maronite, et j'ai des liens avec les deux communautés, et je trouve que c'est un très bon vaccin contre toute forme de fanatisme.

LÉGENDES ET DESCRIPTIFS DES ŒUVRES REPRODUITES

L'astérisque signale les projets pour l'espace public non réalisés.

p. 9
Huile sur Pierre, Tel Hai, 1983
Installation permanente ;
sculpture en pierre de Jérusalem, 2,50 × 1,20 × 1,70 m

En 1983, pendant la guerre du Liban, Esther Shalev-Gerz installe la sculpture *Huile sur pierre* sur le flanc d'une montagne de Galilée, sur le site historique de Tel Hai (« La colline de la vie » en hébreu). Taillée à partir d'un bloc de pierre blanche de Jérusalem, la sculpture consiste en un mur de briques coupé en deux en diagonale. Suivant le point de vue, une silhouette humaine indiquant le nord s'y découpe. Vu d'ailleurs, on ne voit qu'un mur en ruines.

p. 12
Irréparable, 1986-2000
Photographies noir & blanc et couleur, dimensions variables

Dans la série *Irréparable*, Esther Shalev-Gerz interroge la possibilité de capter la réalité au moyen de la photographie. Travaillant avec des photographies noir et blanc ou couleur, elle découpe des rectangles dans ces images puis les repositionne – en les insérant de façon décalée dans l'image originale ou en y insérant des rectangles noir ou blanc. En déplaçant ainsi les composantes de la photographie, en introduisant une rupture dans sa lisibilité, elle déstabilise la concordance entre le réel et sa représentation.

p. 18
Monument contre le fascisme,
Hambourg-Harbourg, 1986-1993
En collaboration avec Jochen Gerz
Installation permanente ; colonne en aluminium recouverte de feuilles de plomb, 12 × 1 × 1 m, 7 tonnes, panneau avec un texte traduit en sept langues

Commandé par la ville de Hambourg, le *Monument contre le fascisme* est érigé en 1986 sur une place très fréquentée de la ville. Il consiste en une colonne de douze mètres revêtue de plomb, sur laquelle les habitants sont invités par un texte reproduit en sept langues à inscrire leur nom. Dès qu'une partie accessible est entièrement recouverte d'inscriptions, elle est abaissée dans le sol. Depuis 1993, après sept étapes d'enfouissement, seuls demeurent visibles le sommet de la colonne et un texte se terminant par ces mots : « Car à la longue, nul ne s'élèvera à notre place contre l'injustice. »

p. 22
Juste un ciel, 1987-1989
Projection de diapositives, neuf images couleur, dimensions variables

Esther Shalev-Gerz crée la série *Juste un ciel* en écho à des affiches anonymes qui couvrent alors les murs de Jérusalem. Elle photographie sous différents angles la ville qu'elle a quittée en 1984 puis superpose ces images, juxtaposant ainsi des espaces disjoints dans la réalité. La projection des diapositives permet l'introduction d'un rythme, d'un mouvement d'une image à l'autre, travail précurseur de l'œuvre vidéo à venir.

p. 26
Erase the Past, 1990-1991
Projection de diapositives, 24 images noir et blanc, dimensions variables

Erase the Past est constitué de deux séries d'images et fonctionne comme un « flip book ». Dans les deux séries, un pan de pièce avec un portrait au mur. En faisant défiler rapidement ces images, un seul élément demeure figé à la même échelle : d'une part, le portrait officiel d'Erich Honecker, leader communiste de la RDA jusqu'en 1989, de l'autre, celui de Bertolt Brecht.

p. 28
La Dispersion des semences, la récolte des cendres, Genève, 1995
En collaboration avec Jochen Gerz
Installation permanente ; 2 colonnes en acier, 18 m × 20 cm, 3 plateformes en acier, 40 × 40 cm chaque

À l'occasion du 50ᵉ anniversaire de l'ONU, le gouvernement allemand commande une œuvre à Esther Shalev-Gerz et Jochen Gerz pour le Parc des Nations Unies de Genève. Deux mâts presque identiques sont érigés l'un à côté de l'autre. L'un est surmonté d'une plate-forme simple, l'autre d'une plate-forme double, symbolisant d'un côté la possibilité de nouveaux départs, de l'autre la nécessité de rassembler les histoires. En 1996, un pendant de cette sculpture est inauguré à Marl, en Allemagne.

p. 29*
Les Oies de Feliferhof, Graz, 1996
En collaboration avec Jochen Gerz

En 1996, Esther Shalev-Gerz et Jochen Gerz remportent le concours lancé par le gouvernement autrichien pour rendre hommage aux opposants au régime nazi. Ils proposent d'installer quatre drapeaux blancs munis d'inscriptions (« Le courage est puni de mort », « La fiancée du soldat, c'est la barbarie », etc.) sur le site de Feliferhof où de nombreux résistants furent fusillés entre 1941 et 1945. Refusé par l'armée autrichienne, le projet ne verra pas le jour. La polémique a été largement reprise par la presse qui l'a relancée plusieurs années de suite.

p. 30
Regards pour l'Algérie – Ne regarder qu'à travers tes yeux, 1997
Projet sur Internet et photographies, dimensions variables

Regard pour l'Algérie propose un défi à Internet en tant qu'espace de conscience collective. Le monde a pu voir des images de l'Algérie dans les médias à un moment tourmenté de son histoire, alors que ses propres habitants ignoraient qu'elles étaient diffusées. Au moyen de webcams rudimentaires, des participants de Rome, Paris, Skopje, Sofia, Istanbul et Bucarest furent invités à envoyer leurs regards vers l'Algérie pendant soixante secondes. Chaque regard individuel fut alors projeté simultanément sur des écrans dans chacun des pays.

p. 31
Passage des Juifs, Berlin, 1997-2000
Installation ; projection vidéo, couleur, son, 132', projection vidéo, couleur, muet, 5', 43 photographies, dimensions variables

Le *Passage des Juifs* (*Judengang*) est le nom d'un passage condamné longeant un ancien cimetière juif du XIXᵉ dans le quartier du Prenzlauerberg de Berlin. On raconte que les Juifs n'avaient pas le droit d'accéder au cimetière par son entrée principale parce que la vue de leurs processions funéraires dérangeait le voisinage. Le *Judengang*, devenu depuis un no man's land, est utilisé par les résidents comme débarras. Dans l'une des vidéos, Esther Shalev-Gerz les invite à imaginer un nouvel usage pour ce lieu.

p. 32*
Tour (sans murailles), Jérusalem, 1998

En 1998, Esther Shalev-Gerz propose l'intervention *Tour (sans murailles)* à la ville de Jérusalem. Le projet consiste à imaginer Jérusalem sans murailles, en projetant sur l'extérieur du mur d'enceinte l'image des rues qui se trouvent de l'autre côté, en souvenir des prises de possession de territoires par les Juifs en Palestine dans les années 1930 sous forme de villages constitués de tours ceintes de murailles (*Homa u-Migdal*).

p. 33
L'Instruction berlinoise, Berlin, 1998
En collaboration avec Jochen Gerz
Cinq représentations théâtrales au Hebbel Theatre Berlin, Berliner Ensemble et Volksbühne am Rosa Luxemburg Platz, en collaboration avec *Der Tagesspiegel*, ZDF, Deutschland-radio et SFB-Hörfunk

En 1998, Esther Shalev-Gerz et Jochen Gerz invitent le public de trois théâtres berlinois à rejouer la pièce de Peter Weiss *Die Ermittlung (L'Instruction)* écrite en 1965 d'après les témoignages recueillis lors des procès d'Auschwitz entre 1963 et 1965. Le déroulement de chaque représentation dépendait de la participation de tous, ébranlant les distinctions conventionnelles entre spectateurs/témoins et acteurs. Des fragments du projet étaient diffusés en parallèle à la télévision, à la radio et dans les journaux.

p. 36
Irréparable 85, Berlin, 1998
Intervention dans l'espace public ; sérigraphie, 119 × 175 cm avec une boîte lumineuse

Irréparable 85 propose un lien entre le passé et le présent. Un panneau lumineux est installé en hommage à l'artiste engagée Käthe Kollwitz (1867-1945) à l'emplacement de son ancienne maison, détruite pendant la Seconde Guerre mondiale. Le négatif d'une photographie ancienne de la maison y est inséré. Sur ce négatif se trouve l'image du panneau lumineux, rempli d'une couleur bleue reprenant la couleur de la façade du bâtiment actuel. La nuit, seule l'image en négatif de la maison illuminée est visible. Ce travail propose un aller-retour impossible dans le temps.

p. 37
Livres aspirés par le ciel, 1998
Projection vidéo, couleur, son, 14'

Livres aspirés par le ciel est tourné dans la Rotonde du Musée de Louviers, lequel contient une collection significative mais peu consultée d'ouvrages historiques ou religieux confisqués aux abbayes des alentours pendant la Révolution. Les dos des livres sont filmés de très près, à un rythme de plus en plus rapide. La vidéo se termine sur le plan d'un homme jetant des livres vers le ciel – d'où ils ne retombent jamais. Cette vidéo participe de la réflexion d'Esther Shalev-Gerz sur le rôle des archives et la relation iconologique entre texte et image.

p. 40
Anges inséparables : la maison éphémère pour Walter Benjamin, 2000
Installation ; 3 photographies noir et blanc, 70 × 90 cm chaque
Ange 10, 2000-2010 : horloge électrique double face, 120 cm
Ange 11 : chaise double, 82 cm × 65 cm × 43 cm *Ange 12* : vidéo, couleur, son, 15'

Pensée comme une maison éphémère pour Walter Benjamin, l'installation *Anges inséparables* porte ce titre en référence au tableau de Paul Klee *Angelus Novus* (1920). Elle consiste en une vidéo retraçant le trajet entre Weimar et le camp de concentration de Buchenwald filmé par la fenêtre d'un taxi. Le chauffeur raconte les histoires des lieux qu'il traverse. Par moment, l'image vacille, ralentit ou se dédouble. La voix off dit des textes de Franz Kafka, Heiner Müller, Gershom Sholem, Klee et Benjamin, évoquant tous des anges. Une horloge à deux cadrans dont les aiguilles tournent en sens opposés et une chaise double sans dossier ainsi que trois photographies accompagnent la vidéo.

p. 44
Les Inséparables, Wanas, 2000-2008
Installation permanente ; horloge à double cadran, 183 × 296 × 35 cm

À l'occasion de l'exposition collective *Loss* organisée par la Fondation Wanas à Wanas en Suède, Esther Shalev-Gerz crée une nouvelle version de la double horloge de *Anges inséparables : la maison éphémère pour Walter Benjamin*. À la suite de l'exposition, celle-ci fut définitivement installée sur la façade de la Kunsthalle de la Fondation, qui rassemble sur son site quarante-neuf œuvres permanentes conçues pour l'espace public.

p. 45*
Le Jugement – Une promenade philosophique, Berlin, 2001

Proposé dans le cadre d'un concours pour un monument aux victimes des tribunaux militaires nazis, le monument consiste en un parcours de drapeaux lumineux en plexiglas installés le long du chemin menant jusqu'à l'ancien lieu d'exécution des condamnés à mort. L'une des deux faces des drapeaux est consacrée à l'histoire du condamné, l'autre à celle du juge, afin de souligner le lien irréductible entre les deux parties.

p. 46
White Out – Entre l'écoute et la parole, 2002
Installation ; 2 projections vidéo synchronisées, couleur, son, 40' chacune, 7 photographies couleur montées sous diasec, 80 × 120 cm chacune, 6 textes contrecollés sur aluminium, 80 × 120 cm chacun

White Out – qui signifie la perte du sens de l'orientation dans une tempête de neige – est une installation vidéo consacrée à Åsa Simma, une femme d'origine saami vivant à Stockholm. Deux plans fixes de Åsa sont projetés face à face, l'un filmé à Stockholm, l'autre dans son paysage natal en Laponie. Dans le premier, elle réagit à des citations évoquant les cultures suédoise et laponne. Dans l'autre, elle écoute ses propres paroles. Une série de photographies du dépôt du Musée historique de Stockholm, ainsi que des textes, complètent l'installation.

p. 50
Est-ce que ton image me regarde ?, 2002
Installation ; 4 projections vidéo synchronisées, couleur, deux avec son, deux muettes, 38' chacune; 11 photographies couleur montées sous Diasec, dont 8 : 40 x 90 cm et 3 : 100 × 150 cm; 1 sérigraphie, 74 × 100 cm

Poursuivant sa recherche sur l'intervalle entre l'écoute et la parole, Esther Shalev-Gerz réalise un double portrait, celui d'une femme juive polonaise rescapée du camp de concentration de Bergen-Belsen, situé non loin de Hanovre, et celui d'une femme allemande ayant passé les années de guerre dans cette ville. Elles racontent chacune leur histoire et s'écoutent chacune, par image interposée, dans leur poste de télévision. Du même temps, leurs histoires sont de lieux différents. Le dispositif de l'installation place le spectateur à l'intersection de ces paroles.

p. 54
Un fil, Glasgow, 2003-2006
Installation permanente ; 10 abris en acier surmontés de bâches, 300 × 200 × 200 cm chaque

Un fil est une installation permanente réalisée en collaboration avec des habitants récemment relogés du quartier de Castlemilk, au sud de Glasgow. Les participants étaient invités à choisir leur vue préférée dans l'ancien parc d'un château adjacent à leur nouveau logement. À chaque point de vue, un banc circulaire recouvert d'un dais réalisé par les résidents est installé, traçant ainsi une ligne imaginaire à travers le parc.

p. 89
Daedal(us), 2003
Intervention dans l'espace public et installation ; 15 photographies couleur, montées sous diasec, 108 × 80 cm, 15 photographies couleur, 65 × 53 cm

Développé avec la participation des habitants d'un quartier déshérité du nord-est de Dublin, *Daedal(us)* existe d'abord comme intervention éphémère dans l'espace public, avant de se décliner en installation photographique. Des photographies de douze façades sont projetées sur douze bâtiments situés à proximité. Produisant simultanément un effet de déplacement et de reconnaissance, ce labyrinthe invite à découvrir d'autres lieux du quartier et à se réapproprier l'espace de la ville.

p. 94
First Generation, Botkyrka, 2004
Installation permanente ; rétroprojection couleur, muet, 40', bande son, 60' en boucle

Trente-quatre personnes issues de la première génération d'immigrés vivant à Botkyrka, dans la banlieue de Stockholm, ont contribué au projet *First Generation* en acceptant d'être filmées alors qu'elles écoutaient les réponses qu'elles avaient individuellement données à quatre questions identiques : *Qu'avez-vous perdu ? Qu'avez-vous trouvé ? Qu'avez-vous reçu ? Qu'avez-vous donné ?*
Projeté en continu sur la façade en verre du Centre multiculturel de la ville, le film se détache de nuit, tandis que la bande son n'est audible qu'à l'intérieur du bâtiment.

p. 95*
Point blanc – Point de rencontre, Oslo, 2004

Invitée à participer au concours pour une œuvre destinée au nouveau Centre de l'Holocauste d'Oslo installé à la Villa Grande, ancienne résidence du politicien pronazi Vidkun Quisling, Esther Shalev-Gerz propose d'enduire d'une couche de peinture domestique blanche tout le pourtour du bâtiment. Au dehors, les traces du passage des futurs visiteurs s'accumuleraient sur cette surface vulnérable. La couleur blanche s'estompant graduellement, des écoliers de la région seraient chaque année invités à la rafraîchir, afin d'engager un dialogue entre passé et présent.

p. 96
MenschenDinge – L'aspect humain des choses, 2004-2006
Installation ; 5 vidéos, couleur, son, 22', 14', 23', 14' et 12', 25 photographies couleur contrecollées sur aluminium, montées sous diasec, 40 × 100 cm chaque

Invitée à créer un projet pour le Mémorial du camp de concentration de Buchenwald, Esther Shalev-Gerz choisit de faire parler les professionnels du musée – le directeur, un historien, un archéologue, une restauratrice, une photographe – qui sont en contact quotidien avec les objets trouvés sur le terrain du camp. Ils racontent leur rencontre à la fois professionnelle, personnelle et imaginaire avec ces objets créés ou détournés par les prisonniers, objets qui témoignent de la capacité de ces derniers à résister aux conditions inhumaines qui leur ont été infligées.

p. 100
Entre l'écoute et la parole : derniers témoins, Auschwitz 1945-2005, 2005
Installation ; 3 projections vidéo synchronisées, couleur, muet, 40'

En 2005, pour commémorer le 60e anniversaire de la libération du camp de concentration d'Auschwitz-Birkenau, Esther Shalev-Gerz recueille le témoignage de survivants résidant à Paris. Initialement présentée à l'Hôtel de Ville de Paris, l'œuvre consiste en soixante entretiens filmés (consultable aujourd'hui au Mémorial de la Shoah, Paris) et en une projection vidéo sur trois écrans. Les visages des survivants, filmés en gros plan, sont captés dans le silence qui s'installe entre une question et l'articulation de sa réponse.

p. 102*
Vis-à-vis, Berlin, 2006

Invitée à participer au concours pour un monument aux homosexuel-le-s victimes du régime nazi, Esther Shalev-Gerz propose *Vis-à-vis*, une sculpture en forme de triple spirale. À la fois banc où s'asseoir et support de textes gravés reprenant faits historiques, histoires personnelles et extraits littéraires, la structure labyrinthique s'intègre dans le parc du Tiergarten, face au Mémorial de l'Holocauste, comme un élément de repos et de réflexion.

p. 103
Still/Film, 2009
Installation ; photographie noir et blanc, 60 × 80 cm, 7 photographies noir et blanc, 40 × 60 cm chaque, 3 photographies couleur, 40 × 60 cm chaque, texte noir et blanc, 60 × 80 cm, vidéo, couleur, muet, 1'

Avec *Still/Film*, Esther Shalev-Gerz revient sur les lieux de son enfance et de l'enfance de sa mère. Une série de photographies montre la maison où elle vécut à Vilnius jusqu'à l'âge de huit ans, l'autre série l'emplacement de la maison que sa mère dut fuir à l'âge de neuf ans et que l'artiste a retrouvée par hasard à Alytus. Elle photographie également la forêt et des paysages situés sur le trajet entre les deux villes.

p. 108
D'Eux, 2009
Installation ; 2 projections vidéo HD synchronisées, couleur, son, 30' chacune, 6 bandes son, 10', 12 photographies noir et blanc, 40 × 60 cm chaque

D'Eux propose un regard sur deux personnes, qu'Esther Shalev-Gerz a rencontrées à Paris, et deux paysages : l'île Seguin à Paris et l'île Cortes au Canada. Rola Younes parle de sa passion pour les langues (le yiddish, l'hébreu, le perse, l'arabe, etc.) pour pouvoir incorporer différentes histoires, et Jacques Rancière lit un passage de son texte, *Le Spectateur émancipé*, dans lequel il commente la fonction de l'art contemporain et décrit un moment constitutif de sa pensée l'ayant amené à « reformuler les rapports établis entre voir, faire et parler ».

p. 114
The Open Page, 2009
15 photographies couleur, dimensions variables

Commandité pour la Bibliothèque municipale de Vancouver, *The Open Page* consiste en une série de photographies de livres rares, consultables uniquement sur autorisation, parmi lesquels un bréviaire illustré du XVe siècle, un guide botanique anglais du XVIIe siècle ou encore une ancienne copie illustrée de *Peter Pan*. Chaque livre est photographié avec une caméra très grand format révélant ces ouvrages dans leur moindre détail ainsi que les mains de bibliothécaires tenant l'exemplaire de leur choix ou en pointant des détails.

p. 118*
Monument à la mémoire du génocide arménien, Genève, 2010

Invitée par la Ville de Genève à participer à un concours pour la création d'un mémorial pour le génocide arménien, Esther Shalev-Gerz propose un monument taillé dans un seul bloc de pierre blanche. Cette sculpture représente l'intérieur d'une maison dont les murs extérieurs seraient tombés. De part et d'autre du mur intérieur, une pièce identique se reflète symétriquement. En cas de reconnaissance du génocide par la Turquie, la date de cette reconnaissance serait gravée sur le monument.

p. 119
Le dernier déclic, 2010
Installation ; 70 photographies couleur, dimensions variables ; album photo avec 13 photographies noir et blanc, 21 × 21 cm chaque, projection vidéo, couleur, son, 26'

Invitée par le Musée de la Photographie de Brunswick, Esther Shalev-Gerz s'intéresse à la firme Rollei, célèbre notamment pour ses appareils photographiques Rolleiflex, dont le siège se situe à Brunswick. *Le dernier déclic* explore les changements induits par le passage de l'argentique au numérique, et son implication en terme de construction de la mémoire et de représentation du temps. Une série photographique montre les usines Rollei vidées de toute présence humaine. Dans la vidéo, des personnes souhaitant se débarrasser de leur appareil argentique reviennent sur les histoires les liant à cet objet.

p. 130
Describing Labor, 2011-2012
Installation vidéo, son et photographies, divers objets
Commande de la Wolfsonian-Florida International University, Miami Beach, Floride, 2012

Au cours d'une résidence au Wolfsonian Museum de Miami en 2011, Esther Shalev-Gerz a exploré sa vaste collection à la recherche de documents illustrant le travail et les travailleurs.
Jadis image héroïque de la conscience de classe et de l'idéal d'une nation – largement présente durant la Grande Dépression, la révolution soviétique et les deux guerres mondiales –, la figure du travailleur a depuis disparu des représentations contemporaines.
Au moyen de la vidéo, de la photographie, du son et du texte, l'installation redonne la parole à cette figure qui façonne nos réalités quotidiennes.
De même que la collection du Wolfsonian offre une image du travail dans son moment historique héroïque, *Describing Labor* réarticule cette image pour notre temps.

LIST OF EXHIBITED WORKS[1]

Irreparable, 1986–2000
Irréparable
Black and white and color photographs, variable dimensions

Just One Sky, 1987–1989
Juste un ciel
Slide show (9 color images), variable dimensions

Erase the Past, 1990–1991
Slide show (24 black and white images), variable dimensions

Books Inhaled by the Sky, 1998
Livres aspirés par le ciel
Video projection, color, sound, 14 min.

Inseparable Angels: An Imaginary House for Walter Benjamin, 2000
Anges inséparables: la maison éphémère pour Walter Benjamin
Installation
3 black and white photographs, 70 × 90 cm; *Angel 10*, 2000–2010: a two-faced electric clock, 120 cm; *Angel 11*: 1 double chair, 82 cm × 65 cm × 43 cm; *Angel 12*:1 video projection, color, sound, 15 min.

White Out—Between Telling and Listening, 2002
White Out – Entre l'écoute et la parole
Installation
2 synchronized video projections, color, sound, 40 min. each; 7 color photographs, Diasec mounted, 80 × 120 cm each; 6 texts laminated on aluminum, 80 × 120 cm each

Does Your Image Reflect Me?, 2002
Est-ce que ton image me regarde?
Installation
4 synchronized video projections, color, 2 with sound, 2 silent, 38 min. each
Courtesy Sprengel Museum, Hannover

Daedal(us), 2003
Intervention in public space and installation
9 color photographs, Diasec mounted, variable dimensions

MenschenDinge—The Human Aspect of Objects, 2004–2006
MenschenDinge – L'aspect humain des choses
Installation
5 color videos, sound, 22 min., 14 min., 23min., 14 min. and 12 min. respectively; 25 color photographs laminated on aluminum, Diasec mounted, 40 × 100 cm
Collection Stiftung Gedenkstätten Buchenwald und Mittelbau-Dora

Between Listening and Telling: Last Witnesses, Auschwitz 1945–2005, 2005
Entre l'écoute et la parole : derniers témoins, Auschwitz 1945–2005
Installation
3 synchronized video projections, color, silent, 40 min.

Still/Film, 2009
Installation
1 black and white photograph, 60 × 80 cm; 7 black and white photographs, 40 × 60 cm; 3 color photographs, 40 × 60 cm; 1 black and white text, 60 × 80 cm; 1 video projection, color, silent, 1 min.

On Two, 2009
D'Eux
Installation
2 synchronized HD video projections, color, sound, 30 min. each, 6 audiotapes, 10 min; 12 black and white photographs, 40 x 60 cm each

The Open Page, 2009
11 color photographs, variable dimensions

The Last Click, 2010
Le dernier déclic
Installation
10 color photographs, variable dimensions
1 photo album with 13 black and white photographs, 21 × 21 cm;
1 video projection, color, sound, 26 min.

Documentation of Permanent Works in Public Spaces and Unrealized Works (the latter are marked with an asterisk *)/ Documentation des installations permanentes dans l'espace public et projets non réalisés (ces derniers sont signalés par une astérisque *)

Oil on Stone, 1983
Huile sur Pierre
Tel Hai
Permanent installation
Sculpture in Jerusalem stone, 2.5 × 1.2 × 1.7 m

Monument against Fascism, 1986–1993
Monument contre le fascisme
with Jochen Gerz
Hamburg-Harburg
Permanent installation
1 aluminum column covered with sheets of lead, 12 × 1 × 1 m, 7 metric tons; 1 panel with a text translated into seven languages

The Geese of Feliferhof
*Les Oies de Feliferhof**
with Jochen Gerz
1996
Graz

The Berlin Inquiry
L'instruction berlinoise
with Jochen Gerz
1998
Berlin
5 theater performances
Hebbel Theater Berlin, Berliner Ensemble, Volksbühne am Rosa Luxemburg Platz, in collaboration with Der Tagesspiegel, ZDF, Deutschland-radio, and SFB-Hörfunk

Tower (Without Walls)
*Tour (sans murailles)**
1998
Jerusalem

The Judgement. A Philosophical Walk
*Le Jugement – une promenade philosophique**
2001
Berlin

A Thread
Un fil
2003–2006
Glasgow
Permanent installation
10 steel shelters with canopies, 300 × 200 × 200 cm

First Generation
Première Génération
2004
Botkyrka, Sweden
Permanent installation
1 back projection, color, silent, 40 min.;
1 audiotape in a loop, 60 min.

1
Unless otherwise indicated, the works are courtesy of the artist/Sauf mention contraire, les œuvres sont courtoisie de l'artiste

BIOGRAPHIES & BIBLIOGRAPHY

Artist's Biography

Esther Shalev-Gerz (née Gilinsky) was born in 1948 in Vilnius, Lithuania. Her family moved to Jerusalem in 1957. She graduated with a BFA from Bezalel Academy of Art and Design, Jerusalem, in 1979. She lived in New York from 1980 to 1981, then moved to Paris in 1984, where she has been living and working ever since. She has been teaching at Valand School of Fine Arts, University of Gothenburg, Sweden, since 2003.

Selected Solo Exhibitions

2012
Describing Labor, Wolfsonian Museum, Miami; *Entre l'écoute et la parole*, Musée cantonal des Beaux-Arts, Lausanne; *White Out: Between Telling and Listening*, Kamloops Art Gallery, Kamloops

2010
Ton image me regarde ?, Jeu de Paume, Paris; *Der letzte Klick/The Last Click*, Museum für Photographie, Braunschweig; *Still/Film*, Vilnius Art Academy Museum, Vilnius

2009
Still/Film, Galerija Akademija, Vilnius; *The Open Page*, Vancouver Public Library, Vancouver

2008
Konstens plats/The Place of Art, Art Monitor, Göteborg; Maritime Museum, Greenwich, London

2006
MenschenDinge—The Human Aspect of Objects, Stiftung Gedenkstätten Buchenwald und Mittelbau-Dora, Weimar

2005
Entre l'écoute et la parole, Hôtel de Ville, Paris; *Daedal(us)*, Fire Station Artists' Studios, Dublin

2004
First Generation, Multicultural Centre Botkyrka, Fittja

2002
Geht dein Bild mich an?, Sprengel Museum, Hannover; *Two Installations–White-Out/The Imaginary House of Walter Benjamin*, Historiska Museet, Stockholm

1999
Les Portraits des histoires. Aubervilliers, Les Laboratoires d'Aubervilliers, Aubervillers

1996
Irréparable, Musée municipal de La Roche-sur-Yon, La Roche-sur-Yon

1991
Erase The Past, DAAD, Berlin

1990
COPAN, Galerie Giovanna Minelli, Paris

Selected Grants and Residencies

DAAD Grant, Berlin, Residency, 1990; IASPIS Grant, Stockholm, 2002: The Wolfsonian Museum, Florida International University, Miami, Residency, 2011; Swedish Council Research Grant, 2011–2013

For more information, please consult www.shalev-gerz.net

Bibliography (Selected Monographs)

COPAN, Galerie Giovanna Minelli, Paris 1990

Esther Shalev-Gerz. Erase The Past, DAAD, Berlin 1991

Jochen Gerz & Esther Shalev-Gerz: das Harburger Mahnmal gegen Faschismus/The Harburg Monument Against Fascism, Hatje, Ostfildern 1994

Esther Shalev-Gerz. Irréparable, Musée municipal de La Roche-sur-Yon, La Roche-sur-Yon 1996

Esther & Jochen Gerz. Das 20. Jahrhundert. Wenn das 20. Jahrhundert noch einmal stattfände, was würden Sie ändern?, Klartext Verlag, Essen 1996

Esther & Jochen Gerz. Raisons de sourire. Le fragment d'Arles, Actes Sud, Arles 1997

Esther Shalev-Gerz, *Für Paul Klee*, Stiftung Weimarer Klassik, Weimar 2000

Esther Shalev-Gerz. Les portraits des histoires. Aubervilliers, École nationale supérieure des Beaux-Arts/Les Laboratoires d'Aubervilliers, Aubervillers 2000

Esther Shalev-Gerz. Les portraits des histoires. Belsunce, Marseille, Images en manœuvres, Marseille 2000. [Contains the video scripts of *The Portraits of Stories*, 1998]

Esther Shalev-Gerz. Två installationer/Two installations, Historiska Museet, Stockholm 2002 [Contains the video scripts of *Inseparable Angels: An Imaginary House for Walter Benjamin*, 2000, and *White Out—Between Telling and Listening*, 2002]

Esther Shalev-Gerz. Geht Dein Bild mich an?, Sprengel Museum, Hannover 2002 [Contains the video scripts of *Does Your Image Reflect Me?/Est-ce que ton image me regarde ?*, 2002]

Esther Shalev-Gerz. Entre l'écoute et la parole: derniers témoins, Auschwitz, 1945–2005, Mairie de Paris, Direction générale de l'information et de la documentation, Paris 2005

Esther Shalev-Gerz. Daedal(us), Fire Station Artists' Studios, Dublin 2005

Theater als öffentlicher Raum: die Berliner Ermittlung von Jochen Gerz und Esther Shalev-Gerz, Christel Weiler (ed.), Theater der Zeit, Berlin 2005

Esther Shalev-Gerz. MenschenDinge–The Human Aspect of Objects, Stiftung Gedenkstätten Buchenwald und Mittelbau-Dora, Weimar 2006 [Contains the video scripts of *MenschenDinge—The Human Aspect of Objects*, 2004–2006]

Esther Shalev-Gerz. First Generation, Multicultural Centre Botkyrka, Fittja 2006

Esther Shalev-Gerz. Konstens plats/The Place of Art, Art Monitor, Göteborg 2008

Esther Shalev-Gerz. A Thread, Aye-Aye Books, in association with CCA, Glasgow 2008

Esther Shalev-Gerz. Still/Film, Vilnius Art Academy Museum, Vilnius 2010

Esther Shalev-Gerz, Fage Éditions/Éditions du Jeu de Paume, Lyon/Paris 2010

Esther Shalev-Gerz. Der letzte Klick, Museum für Photographie, Bulletin no. 17, Braunschweig 2010

Esther Shalev-Gerz, Kamloops Art Gallery, Kamloops 2012

Esther Shalev-Gerz. Describing Labor, The Wolfsonian, FIU, Miami Beach 2012 (forthcoming)

Biographies of the Authors

Nora M. Alter is Chair of Film and Media Arts at Temple University, Philadelphia. She is the author of *Vietnam Protest Theatre: The Television War on Stage* (Indiana University Press, 1996), *Projecting History: Non-Fiction German Film* (University of Michigan Press, 2002), *Chris Marker* (University of Illinois Press, 2006), and the co-editor with Lutz Koepnick of *Sound Matters: Essays on the Acoustics of Modern German Culture* (Berghahn Books, 2004).

Georges Didi-Huberman is an art historian and philosopher, Associate Professor at the École des hautes études en sciences sociales (EHESS), Paris. He is the author of (among many others) *Devant l'image. Question posée aux fins d'une histoire de l'art* (1990), *Ce que nous voyons, ce qui nous regarde* (Éditions de Minuit, 1992), *L'Image survivante. Histoire de l'art et temps des fantômes selon Aby Warburg* (Éditions de Minuit, 2002), *Images malgré tout* (Éditions de Minuit, 2004), *Quand les images prennent position. L'Œil de l'histoire, vol. 1* (Éditions de Minuit, 2009), *Survivance des lucioles* (Éditions de Minuit, 2009), *Remontages du temps subi. L'Œil de l'histoire, vol. 2* (Éditions de Minuit, 2010), *Atlas ou le gai savoir inquiet. L'Œil de l'histoire, vol. 3* (Minuit, 2011), and *Écorces* (Éditions de Minuit, 2011).

Annika Wik is a Professor in the Department of Cinema Studies, Stockholm University, Sweden. She is the author of *Förebild film. Panoreringar över den samtida konstscenen/Framing Films. On the Contemporary Art Scene* (Aura förlag, 2001), and co-editor with Magdalena Malm Lund of *Rörlig Konstproduktion/Mobile Art Production* (Propexus, 2010).

James E. Young is Distinguished University Professor & Director at the Institute for Holocaust, Genocide, and Memory Studies, University of Massachusetts Amherst. He is the author of *Writing and Rewriting the Holocaust* (Indiana University Press, 1988), *The Texture of Memory* (Yale University Press, 1993), *At Memory's Edge: After-images of the Holocaust in Contemporary Art and Architecture* (Yale University Press, 2000), *The Stages of Memory at Ground Zero: A Juror's Report on the World Trade Center Memorial Process* (forthcoming), and editor of *The Art of Memory* (Prestel Verlag, 1994).

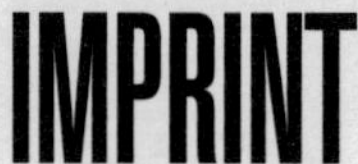

This book is published on the occasion of the exhibition *Esther Shalev-Gerz. Between Telling and Listening – Entre l'écoute et la parole*, Musée cantonal des Beaux-Arts de Lausanne, on view from September 22, 2012, through January 6, 2013.

Exhibition

Head of Exhibitions
Bernard Fibicher (Museum Director)

Exhibition Curator
Nicole Schweizer (Curator)

With the collaboration of
Loïse Cuendet
(Press and Public Relations)
Françoise Delavy (Conservator)
Sébastien Dizerens (Registrar)
Danielle Ducotterd-Waeber (Librarian)
Catherine Lepdor
(Curator, Keeper of the Collections)
Camille Lévêque-Claudet (Curator)
Yvan Mamin (Administration)
Anne Moix (Secretary)
Sandrine Moeschler (Education)
Nora Rupp (Photographer)

Technical Crew
Francis Devaud (Head of Installation)
Édouard Besson, Jean-Jacques Bussard, Julien Simond

Reception
Claudine Bergdolt
Anne-Françoise Clerc
Eric Mohler

Artist's Assistant
Julia Bastard

Film Editing & Calibration
Yannig Willman

Musée cantonal des Beaux-Arts
Palais de Rumine, C.P.
Place de la Riponne 6
CH–1014 Lausanne
T 41 21 316 34 45
F 41 21 316 34 46
E info.beaux-arts@vd.ch
www.mcba.ch

mcb-a
MUSÉE CANTONAL DES BEAUX-ARTS LAUSANNE

Acknowledgments

The Musée cantonal des Beaux-Arts wishes to thank all those who made the exhibition and publication possible: Esther Shalev-Gerz; Luc Bergeron; Lionel Bovier, Clément Dirié, and Nicolas Eigenheer (JRP|Ringier); Cinémathèque Suisse, Lausanne; André Décosterd (www.codact.ch); Gilles Gavillet (Gavillet & Rust, Geneva); Elise Girardot; Volkhard Knigge (Stiftung Gedenkstätten Buchenwald und Mittelbau-Dora); Ulrich Krempel (Sprengel Museum, Hanover); Naël Lafer; Filip dos Santos (Musée d'art de Pully, Lausanne), Videocompany (www.videocompany.ch), as well as the authors of the catalogue.

The artist wishes to thank Nicole Schweizer, Georges Didi-Huberman, James E. Young, Annika Wik, Nora M. Alter, Christopher Fleischner, Marta Gili, Jason Bowman, Stefanie Bauman, Jill Silverman, Gary Wasserman, François Laborie, Florian Ebner, Petras Saulenas, Rola Younes, Jacques Rancière, Johan Oberg, Patrick Latour, the team of the Musée cantonal des Beaux-Arts de Lausanne, Valand Fine Art School of Gothenburg University, and all the participants in the projects.

Publication

Editor
Nicole Schweizer

Editorial Coordination and French Editing
Clément Dirié

English Editing and Proofreading
Clare Manchester

Translations
Judith Hayward (French to English), Gauthier Herrmann (English to French), Rachel Willson-Broyles (Swedish to English), Yves Gauthier (Swedish to French)

The excerpt from Jacques Rancière's *The Emancipated Spectator* (*Le Spectateur émancipé*) is published with kind permission from the author and Verso for its English version, and La Fabrique for its original French version.

Design
Gavillet & Rust, Geneva/
Nicolas Eigenheer, Zurich

Typeface
Theinhardt (www.optimo.ch)

Cover
Esther Sahlev-Gerz, *The Last Click*, 2010 (detail)

Photo Credits
André Lützen (p.18, 19, 20, 21); Christina Damasceno (p.34); Christer Ahling (p.42, 43, 47); Anders Norrsell (p.44); Scott Massey (p.46); Maik Schuck (p.50); Alan Dimmick (p.55); Andrzej Markiewicz (p.94); Sadie Wiarda, Justine Olausson, Manav Menon, Edward McShane (p.96, 108); Yannig Willman (p.97), graphic design (p. 102, 118); Arno Gisinger (p.100, 109); P. Simon (p.101); Petras Saulenas (p.128, 129); Esther Shalev-Gerz (p. 9, 10, 11, 18, 19, 20, 21, 28, 30, 31, 33, 34, 36, 45, 95)

Color Separation & Print
Musumeci S.p.A., Quart (Aosta)

Printed in Europe

Published by
JRP|Ringier
Letzigraben 134
CH–8047 Zurich
T + 41 (0) 43 311 27 50
F + 41 (0) 43 311 27 51
www.jrp-ringier.com
info@jrp-ringier.com

with the Musée cantonal des Beaux-Arts de Lausanne

ISBN 978-3-03764-276-4

JRP|Ringier books are available internationally at selected bookstores and from the following distribution partners:

Switzerland
AVA Verlagsauslieferung AG
Centralweg 16
CH–8910 Affoltern a.A.
verlagservice@ava.ch, www.ava.ch

France
Les Presses du réel
35 rue Colson
F–21000 Dijon
info@lespressesdureel.com, www.lespressesdureel.com

Germany and Austria
Vice Versa Vertrieb
Immanuelkirchstrasse 12
D–10405 Berlin
info@vice-versa-vertrieb.de, www.vice-versa-vertrieb.de

UK and other European countries
Cornerhouse Publications
70 Oxford Street
UK–Manchester M1 5NH
publications@cornerhouse.org, www.cornerhouse.org/books

USA, Canada, Asia, and Australia
D.A.P./Distributed Art Publishers
155 Sixth Avenue, 2nd Floor
USA–New York, NY 10013
dap@dapinc.com, www.artbook.com

For a list of our partner bookshops or for any general questions, please contact JRP|Ringier directly at info@jrp-ringier.com, or visit our homepage www.jrp-ringier.com for further information about our program.